Music and Medicine

Other books by Anton Neumayr

Music & Medicine, Volume 1
Haydn, Mozart, Beethoven, Schubert
Notes on Their Lives, Works, and Medical Histories

Music & Medicine, Volume 2
Hummel, Weber, Mendelssohn, Schumann, Brahms, Bruckner
Notes on Their Lives, Works, and Medical Histories

Dictators
In the Mirror of Medicine
Napoleon, Hitler, Stalin

Anton Neumayr

Music and Medicine

Chopin
Smetana
Tchaikovsky
Mahler

Notes on Their Lives, Works, and Medical Histories

Translated by David J. Parent

Library of Congress Cataloging-in-Publication Data:
Neumayr, Anton.
    [Musik und Medizin. English]
    Music and medicine / Anton Neumayr.
    v. cm.
    Translation of: Musik und Medizin.
    Includes bibliographical references and index.
    Contents: [3] Chopin, Smetana, Tchaikovsky, Mahler: notes on their
lives, works, and medical histories.
    ISBN 0-936741-08-2 (v. 3)
    1. Composers—Medical care. 2. Composers--Health and hygiene.
3. Music--18th/19th century--History and criticism. I. Title.
ML390.N38513 1994
780'.92'2--dc20   94-21413
                                                  CIP
                                                  MN

Medi-Ed Press
Constitution Place, Suite A
716 East Empire Street
Bloomington, Illinois 61701
1-800-500-8205

Contents

Preface to Volume 3

The third volume of *Music & Medicine* examines, from a medical standpoint, the composers Frédéric Chopin, Bedrich Smetana, and Peter Ilyich Tchaikovsky, three representatives of 19th century Slavic music, and Gustav Mahler, whose rich intellectual world anticipates the 20th century. Drawing once again on all discoverable biographical and medical sources, a reconstruction is made of the diseases and causes of death of these great composers, free of speculation and romantically or politically motivated embellishments, and a diagnosis is reached that can be regarded as certain in the light of current medical science. Such a diagnosis has sometimes made it necessary to revise or discard completely some ideas on the subject handed down even in the most recent literature. Some traditional stereotypes have thus undergone an astonishing transformation.

In the medical analysis of specific traits of personality and character of each composer, the historical and socio-political backgrounds of their surrounding world had to be studied, as well as their most deeply personal intimate life. This provided knowledge about their psyche and the factors that shaped it, and it made many psychological reactions and their transformation into music more understandable for the reader. Finally, aspects of medical history had to be woven in; otherwise, many diagnostic and therapeutic procedures of doctors in the past, seemingly incomprehensible to us today, would be judged unfairly. In this volume, too, I could not resist the temptation to trace down and exhibit connections between creativity and diseases, insofar as they could be documented biographically, or at least inferred credibly from references to biographical facts. Problematic as such efforts may seem, they can show the reader some new, perhaps better, approaches to individual musical creations of these masters.

I am especially obligated to the Austrian National Library and the Institute for the History of Medicine at the University of Vienna for making available written primary sources and pictorial material. My gratitude also goes to Dr. Zielinski for obtaining documents from Mount Sinai Hospital in New York. Finally I owe thanks to Mrs. A. Orlova, an employee for many years at the Tchaikovsky Museum in Klin, for her assistance in gathering valuable information for this work.

Anton Neumayr
Vienna, Austria
May 1991

Preface to the English Edition

We are pleased to have the privilege of offering Volume 3 of the *Music & Medicine* series to English-speaking audiences with an interest in classical music and historical medical treatment of the 19th century. Originally published in Austria in the German language, the task of translating *Musik & Medizin* was indeed challenging. The German language with its complex, lengthy sentences, full of descriptive prepositional phrases, requires patience and skill. We believe that this series of volumes is worth that effort, since it conveys the results of more than twenty years of original research by the author. The final English version is possible only as a result of the individual efforts and subsequent teamwork of many. Our common goal was to portray the original text as accurately as possible. Our thanks to the author Anton Neumayr, the Austrian publisher Jugend & Volk, the translator David J. Parent, the medical editor Victoria J. Brockhouse, D.O., and many others.

Our thanks also to Dr. Harald F. Zehetgruber, Austria, who helped expedite this three-volume series in many ways and who was responsible for introducing Dr. Neumayr and Dr. Harold O. Conn, who was also instrumental in the process.

Frédéric Chopin

(1810–1849)

As a composer, Chopin falls in the category Schiller defined as "sentimental" artists. In contrast with Franz Liszt, in whom the close relations between literature and music are obvious, Chopin's music was but rarely inspired by a literary experience. Yet, with his music and its numerous literary interpretations within modern Chopin research, he occupies a solid place in the literary-musical culture of Romanticism.

Unfortunately, almost all works on music history and biographies of Chopin to date contain highly subjective portrayals. This is true particularly of the Romantic Age, which eagerly sought to idealize the artist's life and works. Chopin's image thus was frequently embellished with heart-moving legends, and a kind of "myth" was created around the composer that virtually made a prisoner of the historical Chopin and was the basis for many a misunderstanding of his works by posterity. The paragon of such an idealizing portrayal was Franz Liszt's monograph on Chopin published in 1851, comparing the artist in his delicate fragility with "wonderfully colored flowers swaying on ineffably delicate stems." Such descriptions suited the taste of contemporary society, but they also promoted the rise of crude distortions. Indeed, Countess Marie d'Agoult, Liszt's mistress, once dared—with stinging irony—to call Liszt's book an "over-sugared oyster." Such a superficial, shallow perspective does in fact completely overlook Chopin's other side, which could at times suddenly flare up with passionate excitement and wild rebellion and to some degree embodied the "creative antithesis" of his artistic soul.

In contrast with Weber or Schumann, Chopin unfortunately left no written documents explaining his artistic ideology. Certainly, he was one of the most consistent of the Romantic composers, although vocal music, Romanticism's favorite genre of creative production, remained quite in the background for him. The Romanticism of Chopin's music is unmistakably of German origin, as Heinrich Heine remarked in his *Parisian Letters on Art*: "Germany gave him his Romantic profundity." This does not, however, imply that his creativity had been schooled on any particular German master. Rather, Chopin's immediate creative impulse in his earliest period came from Polish folk music and the professional piano music cultivated in the first decades of the 19th century, which mostly adulated the *"style brillant"* so loved at that time. Young Chopin was at that time indeed impressed primarily by the technical piano-playing achievements of Hummel, Field, or Weber; but very soon he began to transform and develop their style creatively. While Field, who enriched cultured parlor music with the genre of the lyrical, dreamy nocturne, influenced Chopin mostly externally, Hummel was a greater influence with regard to passage technique. Most of the compositions produced in Chopin's first creative period display the unmistakable influence of Classicism. To a considerable extent, Hummel was certainly the one who communicated this taste to young Chopin, for during his Warsaw period Hummel's newest works always lay on Chopin's piano stand. This preference for classical forms also characterizes Chopin's Polish forerunners, such as Oginski, Lessel, or Kurpinski, and they too certainly exerted an influence that cannot be overlooked. But, without a doubt, Bach, Mozart, and Beethoven, whom he learned from his outstanding teacher Elsner, were his greatest models, outshining all others by far. For instance, the problem of logic was, in his mind, inseparably linked with Johann Sebastian Bach, who embodied for Chopin the absolute ideal of perfect form. Bach's *Well-Tempered Clavier* was his guide in the particular kind of cyclical form of his preludes. With such combining of miniatures into greater unities, Chopin was simultaneously paying tribute to contemporary Romantic ideology, whose stylistic change also found expression in cyclical series of works by other contemporary composers, such as

Schumann's *Carnaval* or his *Papillons*. On the contrary, in the treatment of counterpoint and polyphonic scoring, Chopin displays definite weaknesses; this becomes clear in his few chamber-music and orchestral works and in this he differs greatly from Bach, Beethoven, or Schumann.

Much as the achievements of Hummel, Field, and Weber in the field of piano technique may well represent the starting point for Chopin's piano compositions, his creative mind strove at a very early age to elevate the current craft for the purpose of achieving the highest musical expression and true art. This applied first of all to the ornamentation profusely employed by Field and Hummel, expressing an aesthetic need of nascent bourgeois culture in Europe and intended merely as an effective decoration for the melody. In Chopin's earliest works, where the influence of Hummel shows through in the preference for passages, this reverence for the "*style brillant*" is still clearly recognizable, but soon Chopin assigned completely new functions to the ornament to energize the course of the melody. Hummel's or Kalkbrenner's ornamentation, as well as that of contemporary Polish composers of the early 19th century, was limited exclusively to superficial brilliance. Chopin, however, gave a drastic reorientation to prior tradition by emancipating the ornamentations from being merely decorative adjuncts to the melody to being an essential component of the composition in the field of instrumental music.

This tradition reached back to the late 18th century, when composers were inclined to pay homage to the "familiar gurgle" of a prima donna, as Mozart so aptly stated in a letter of 26 September 1781 to his father. But with the dawn of the age of virtuosos in the 19th century, the allurements began to overflow all bounds not only for singers, but also for instrumentalists, until finally ornaments became more important than the sustaining melody. No wonder the representatives of German Romanticism, with their strict adherence to mostly undecorated forms, finally rebelled against such a development and E.T.A. Hoffmann resignedly stated: "What help is all splendor, all glitter, all glory, if it serves only to clothe a dead corpse." Chopin too must have had a similar feeling. In his second creative period, when his personality had reached full maturity, he developed his specific ornamentation with its inexhaustible wealth of figures and arabesques that achieved more and more coloristic significance and, as an essential component of the melody, helped create the artist's specific, absolutely distinctive musical language. In Schumann's opinion, even Chopin's ornamentation of the late, third creative period still remained merely adornment, although of "the more meaningful kind, behind which the nobility of the composition shines through all the more charmingly" and since he saw Chopin's ornamentations only as the expression of the virtuoso's bowing before a philistine, blasé Parisian public, he still felt compelled to deny any justification for their existence as the expression of an idea inherent in the work.

Chopin, however, saw essential impulses for his composition activity not only in the classical models. He was also extraordinarily receptive to the "*belcanto*" of the Italian opera of a Rossini or a Bellini, which can be recognized in the songlike melodiousness of his themes. Indeed, besides the ornamentation, what distinguishes the originality of Chopin's musical idiom is the type of instrumental music created from vocal music, with the character of a cantilena transposed to the piano.

The characteristic and real charm of his compositions, however, is due considerably to the influence of Polish folk music, which can be discerned again and again in harmonic tonal reminiscences. Originating from the Polish musical tradition, Chopin's music is the result of that Romantic movement which raised the national element in art and literature to one of its essential characteristics. Previously, compositions with elements of Polish folk music were rather primitive, in accord with the low cultural level of the Polish lower nobility of the 18th century, also labeled "Sarmatianism," but now Chopin lifted them to a previously unknown height. Striving to permeate the elementary national means with personal expression, he achieved a seamless fusion of the various elements of Polish folklore with his own individual style, so that today his music strikes us primarily as his own personal melodic idiom and only secondarily as Polish, similarly to the way we also feel Beethoven's music to be not typically German but his very own personally invented idiom. Although a glowing allegiance to his Polish homeland speaks out of the national elements of Chopin's music, his own individual personal style always prevails, in contrast with the nationally colored music of a Dvořák, Grieg or Albeniz. And in some areas he gave Polish folk music a completely new stamp—for instance, in the creation of his mazurkas. Indeed, Chopin's place in the history of music is essentially shaped by the fact that he managed to represent the music of a whole country by himself alone and "made Poland into a musical concept comparable to other musical countries."

It seems remarkable that Chopin's very first beginnings must be located in so-called "salon music." The elegant society of the Warsaw world in the 1820s was the audience before whom the highly talented youth improvised in the style of a refined salon music appealing to the prevalent taste. But increasing dilettantism, with its touch of trivial music, did not stop at the doors of the elite aristocratic and bourgeois salons of Paris, to which the virtuoso pianists Thalberg, Kalkbrenner, and Liszt paid homage, as did young Chopin. All his life, Chopin resisted the "empty cling-clang" of virtuosity as well as the superficial "Romantic addiction" of Parisian society under the July Monarchy. But from the very first what distinguished him from other virtuosos was his "highly intricate musical form of simultaneous refusal and adaptation" with which he moved socially and musically in the salons of Paris. The salon-motif can perhaps be understood as the visual expression of the complex social relationships within the Parisian society of the July Monarchy. Yet Chopin saw it as an opportunity to try out the possibilities of shaping the conventions inherent in the salon atmosphere with his waltzes, using the salon as a field of experimentation, so to speak. And actually his waltzes are so constituted as to make a merely superficial enjoyment impossible when one hears them, since they quite often omit every conventional waltz gesture.

As a composer, Chopin is the founder of a previously unknown genre, a completely new piano style, which Liszt adopted without really developing it any further. This new style is marked by bold innovations and an uncommonly rich use of the chromatic. It does not shrink from shrill dissonances or new ornamental means and a totally innovative harmonic accompaniment emphasizing, for instance, the expressive resources of the left hand; and the breadth and beauty of its melodic line is striking. In sum, Chopin created a completely new and original piano style in which national elements were permeated with his own personal expression. This style is also distinguished by a mixture of melancholy and demonic passion that can at times plunge into a sea of sound.

Chopin's style of piano composition can hardly be separated from his own way of playing, whose most essential qualities were its melodious delivery and its delicately modulated dynamism. His famous *tempo rubato* captivates the audience by its elegance and transparency and its incomparably sonorous sound—the famous "blue sound." But even on a purely technical level his unusual talent for this instrument progressed well and it became like a second self, notably in the perfect style of keyboard composition. This made possible an excellent "adaptation of the playing hand to the keyboard." Together with the production of tones of a chord in rapid succession and not simultaneously (*arpeggio*) and the use of the pedal, it produced a completely new piano culture in sound and technique. In the area of piano music, Chopin is recognized today as incontestably the greatest individual of the 19th century. Hardly any of the important composers of his time could escape his influence. By his style and his revolutionary piano technique he decisively influenced the further development of piano music from Paderewski and Szymanovski, via Scriabin and Rachmaninov, César Franck, Fauré, Debussy and Ravel, to Franz Liszt and Adolf Henselt, who could also be called "the German Chopin." It is therefore almost incomprehensible to posterity that among his contemporaries only Berlioz and Schumann really understood immediately how significant Chopin's music was for the future. When Chopin's Opus 2 with its variation for piano and orchestra on the theme "Give me your hand, my life," from Mozart's opera *Don Giovanni*, appeared in print in 1831, Robert Schumann wrote a long review in the Berlin *Allgemeine Musikalische Zeitung* introducing the young Pole to the world as a genius of high caliber and originality, with the prophetic words: "Hats off, gentlemen, a genius."

Chopin's classification in music history was long made difficult by the painstaking task of separating truth from fiction and dispersing the fog around his person. But in order to build a solid bridge between the artist and the man, it is necessary not only to critically examine all accessible data from his biography, but also to seek any clues linking the decisive events in his life with his physical ailments and psychological disturbances that may have influenced his artistic creativity.

Between France and Poland—Family Origins and Childhood

Romanticism, weaving a web of legends, led to idealized portrayals of Chopin as an artist, and it even influenced historical reflections on the true origin of the artist's family. This was further complicated by emotional factors based on history and deeply affecting Polish society. The Polish state, a great power in size until 1772, had been completely wiped off the map of Europe after the bloody suppression of the heroic and desperate national uprising against the Russian usurper and the subsequent Third, this time total, Partition of Poland. But the very statelessness imposed on the Polish nation made it continue to be a strong political and cultural factor in Europe, where a strong national consciousness remained the supreme ideological law. Such considerations made it understandable that, despite his father's definitely French origin, an eager search was made for Polish ancestors in Chopin's family. The largest, three-volume biography of Chopin by Ferdynand Hoesick, published in Poland in 1912, thus contains such an attempt to prove Frédéric Chopin's Polish ancestry, beginning with the words:

> There are traditions indicating that Polish blood flowed in the veins of this Lorraine Frenchman, that the first ancestor of the Chopin family in Lorraine was a Pole, Nikolai Szop, a courtier of the unfortunate King Stanislav Leszcynski, who as governor of Lorraine enjoyed great sympathies of the native population....It was customary then for Polish families who settled in Lorraine and had

> names hard to pronounce to change them to French
> names. The son of that Nikolai Szop-Chopin was
> Jean-Jacques Chopin....

The untenableness of this notion was meanwhile disproved beyond any doubt, although many questions on Chopin's genealogy at first remained unanswered. Only after World War II did meticulous detective work turn up documents slumbering in the archives of several towns out of which the paternal line could be traced back without a gap to the 17th century. A similar study of the genealogy of Frédéric's Polish mother unfortunately still does not exist.

The real paternal ancestor is Antoine Chapin, the great-grandfather of Frédéric's grandfather. He lived in the Dauphiné until about 1683. Then together with his seventeen-year-old son François, he left his family—possibly to engage in the profitable tobacco-smuggling trade. When François died in 1714, he left his wife with four sons, the youngest of whom, born in 1712, was baptized Nicolas. Nicolas lived in Ambacourt, married three times and had a total of twelve children; from the third marriage was born in 1738 François, who like his father before him no longer spelled his name Chapin, but rather Chopin. He was brought up by an uncle, a well-known instrument-maker, and by the Canon of Ambacourt, whose parsonage in Marainville was visited frequently by the young François. After his marriage with Marguerite Deflin, he moved to Marainville, where the two bought a small house. Five children were born of this marriage, the youngest of whom, Nicolas, born in 1771, was to become Frédéric's father.

The Marainville manor was responsible for Nicolas Chopin's further destiny, especially his later emigration to Poland. When François Chopin came to Marainville in 1769, this county had already been transferred to the Count de Rutand, chamberlain of Stanislaus I Leszcynski, the unfortunate, twice-deposed king of Poland and, since 1737, Duke of Lorraine. Since Rutand died in 1779 without a direct heir, it was decided to sell the castle of Marainville, and the only interested purchaser turned out to be a certain Jean Michel, Count Pac, who came from Poland.

This Count Pac was originally chamberlain to the Polish King Stanislaus II, August Poniatovski. (This king, a former lover of the Russian Empress Catherine II and successor of the Prince Elector of Saxony, August III, had been elected in 1764 to be the new King of Poland, due to the strong Russian influence in Poland.) In the course of the First Partition of Poland, Count Pac, as a general of the Latvian army, had led the dissolved Confederation of Bar and in the end had emigrated to France.

Count Pac's assumption of power in Marainville opened up decisive contacts for the Chopin family's future, indeed not merely with the Polish Count himself, who continued his zealous efforts to represent his fatherland's cause abroad, but especially also with the Polish nobleman Jan Adam Weydlich, the Count's deputy and manager, who administered the entire county. Through François Chopin's position in the community as trustee, responsible for making the yearly financial report, it was possible for him, with consent of the Count, the pastor, and the schoolteacher, as well as the manager and his wife, to have his little son Nicolas receive a high school education. By the age of ten, Nicolas, living with his family in poor circumstances, gained access to the manorial residence, where French, German, and Polish were spoken and song and music also had their place. The manager's wife gradually became a "second mother" to him, and the fourteen-year-old clung to her with respectful shyness and childlike love.

This lengthy description of the historical and social events comprising the childhood background of the boy Nicolas, born in 1771, only five years after the official annexation of Lorraine to France, serves to clear up simply and realistically the biographical speculations on the circumstances and reasons for Nicolas Chopin's emigration to Poland, speculations replete with fantastic and nationalistic tendencies. For when Count Pac had to give up Marainville Castle in 1785, he returned to Strasbourg, where he died two years later. Manager Weydlich and his wife, together with their two-year-old child, also moved away, and they took along Nicolas, who was fifteen years old by that time. Whether they followed Count Pac to Strasbourg is not known, since nothing is known of their fate during the time between 1785 and 1787. It is certain, however, that Nicolas emigrated to Poland with the former manager Weydlich and his wife, that "noble lady, toward whom he showed himself to be a genuine son until his death." They arrived in Warsaw at Christmas in 1787. Probably Nicolas' parents, whom he visited before departing, did not agree with this decision, as can be suspected from a letter of Nicolas Chopin to his parents, dated Warsaw, 15 July 1790, for this letter suggests that he went a full two years without any news from his parents. It also contains a clue that, besides his attachment for the Weydlich family and the career advantages anticipated through their influential mediation, a further reason for his emigration may have been significant. He informed his parents that he had gotten the news that, in Lorraine, men eighteen years and older would be drafted into the army.

In Warsaw, Nicolas worked from 1787 to 1790 as an accountant for a tobacco manufacturer and enthusiastically followed the work of the Great Imperial Congress (*Seym*). The only things he had taken with him from home were a volume of Voltaire's *Candide*, plus a violin and a flute. Although he was hardly interested in religious or philosophical subjects, he followed political events in Poland all the more eagerly. From 1788 to 1792, the so-called Great Imperial Congress, in part influenced by the French Revolution, skillfully exploited Russia's entanglement in wars against the Turks and the Swedes to implement an admirable work of reform. Probably the most important accomplishment of those days was the Polish constitution of May 1791, drawn up with the strong personal sympathy of King Stanislaus II Poniatovski. It replaced the hereditary monarchy with an elective monarchy; it abolished the "arbitrary veto" [*liberum veto*]; and it even designated the Chamber of Delegates as the seat of the "nation's supreme power." This constitution was at first guaranteed by Prussia and Austria, but by May 1791 Prussia and Austria by mutual consent moved their armies into Poland. After a bitter struggle, Poland was finally compelled to abolish this new constitution; and at the so-called "silent Imperial Congress" of Gradno in 1793 Poland had to cede vast territories to Russia and Prussia in the Second Partition of Poland. This national catastrophe, however, soon brought a resurgence of ardent patriotism, ready for any sacrifice. Under the leadership of an experienced general,

Tadeusz Kosciuszko, a heroic national revolt of the Polish people ensued, and its freedom fighters, struggling against a mighty Russian military superiority, at first succeeded in liberating wide portions of Poland from the Muscovites, although the peasants were in some instances fighting with lances and pitchforks against Russians equipped with rifles and cannons. This uprising was finally suppressed only by bloody massacres after additional Prussian troops marched in from the West.

Although Nicolas Chopin, in the letter to his parents in France, had shown little inclination for the military, apparently in the few years since his arrival in Warsaw he had become so involved in the life of Polish society that as half-Polish he felt deeply affected by the sufferings of his host country and refused to stand by and watch the precipitous flow of events. Carried away with national enthusiasm, he joined the Polish national guard and fought shoulder to shoulder with his friends against the Muscovite usurpers. No doubt he was given a decisive impetus for his decision by the outstanding personality of Kosciuszko. Tadeusz Kosciuszko had fought as a general in the American War of Independence and for the liberation of the slaves. He was a personal friend of Washington and Jefferson and had been declared an honorary citizen of France. At any rate, Nicolas Chopin supported the Polish cause with all his heart, as can be seen from Fryderyk Skarbek's portrayal of him in his later published diaries:

> Nicolas Chopin revered the Poles; he was grateful to the country and the people who gave him hospitality and a suitable livelihood....He lived in our country for many years, maintained friendly relations with Polish families; and moreover he married a Polish woman and was transformed into a genuine Pole through his marital and friendly relations.

After the revolt was put down, Poland ceased to exist. The Third Partition in 1795 left no national territory at all. Nicolas for a time toyed with the idea of returning to Lorraine. But he was prevented from carrying out this idea by an illness contracted shortly before his planned departure. Its precise nature is not known to us—supposedly it involved an "asthmatic" pulmonary disease. After his recovery, Nicolas, because Warsaw had been annexed to Prussia, saw no possibility of again working as a tutor for important families of the capital, as he had done in the years from 1790 to 1794. He therefore moved out to the country, accepting an offer from the young widow of his friend Laszynski, who had fallen at his side during the battle for freedom, to manage the estate and tutor her four children. The youngest of his pupils, Maria, born in 1786, later was to play a significant role in Napoleon's life. As Countess Walewska, this Polish woman not only astonished the Emperor with her knowledge of the French language and of French history and geography—which she had learned from Nicolas Chopin—as well as with her musical training, but she also enchanted him with her beauty—although she responded to his quickly ignited love only after Polish authorities had told her she could do her hard-pressed fatherland a great service by having a closer relationship with Napoleon.

One of Maria's playmates during the years that Nicolas Chopin spent on her mother's estate was, among others, Fryderyk Skarbek, the son of the divorced Countess Skarbek. The countess was the ruler of Zelazowa-Wola and soon esteemed this tutor so highly that she decided to entrust her children's education to him. In 1802 he therefore moved to the new domain, where he functioned not only as tutor but also carried out the duties of accountant, dance instructor, pharmacist, and infirmarian. The Countess had previously been assisted in the education of her children by a young widowed distant relative of hers, a housekeeper by the name of Tekla Justyna Krzyzanowska. She played cembalo and had a beautiful soprano voice; Nicolas played violin and flute; so they had the opportunity of playing music together during the long winter evenings. Her modest and equable manner and her charming personality, as the visible expression of her noble ancestry, so captivated him that he proposed marriage and they were wed on 2 June 1806 in the Church at Brochow.

The young couple moved into a simple home on the castle lands. There the Countess introduced Nicolas to the rector of the French high school in Warsaw—an event that would prove significant for him. In 1806, the same year the young people were married, Napoleon, after his victory near Austerlitz, led his armies into the Province of Warsaw, under Prussian occupation since the partition of Poland, and he was greeted as a liberator by the populace. He then transformed the province into the "Duchy of Warsaw." Nicolas was eager to return to such a Warsaw under French control, and so in 1810 he enthusiastically accepted the school director's invitation to come to the high school there as a French teacher.

But six months before he left the service of the Countess Skarbek, an event occurred in Zelazowa-Wola that would be memorable for posterity, namely, the birth of a second child to the Chopin family, a son who was baptized under the name Fryderyk Franciszek and who later would become the most important piano composer of his century.

The exact date of his birth was the subject of a long-lasting dispute, although both the birth certificate and the baptismal record clearly give 22 February 1810 as the date on which Frédéric Chopin saw the light of day at six o'clock in the evening. For allegedly Chopin later attested that he was born on 1 March under the sign of Pisces and that he knew this date from his parents, "who had made one mistake, but did not want to make a second one." But since the date of 22 February was certified in the birth register by the signatures both of the father and of the pastor and registrar and the same date was also attested on the baptismal certificate by the godparents who had been present, all participants would have signed falsely, which can hardly be assumed. Therefore this quarrel should be ended once and for all and the officially entered date of birth, namely, 22 February 1810, should be recognized as the correct one.

Soon after moving to Warsaw in October 1810, his father Nicolas was permitted by the directors of the Lyceum to establish a private boarding school for a small number of students from aristocratic or bourgeois families. A few of them would later count among Frédéric's closest friends: Titus Woyciechowski, Jan Matuszynski, Julian Fontana, Jan Bialoblocki, and the Wodzinski brothers. Nicolas' outstanding pedagogic abilities led to his receiving an appointment as Professor of French at the Warsaw Artillery and Engineering School, so that the family's economic situation was decisively improved by his dual incomes and his wife Justyna's earnings from the boarding school. And the family increased in size through the birth of their daughters Isabella and Emilia in 1811 and 1813. Frédéric thus had three sisters, counting Ludwika, the oldest, who was born in 1807. An unusually harmonious relationship prevailed among all the family members. The soul of the family was their mother, loved by all, a caring person, always with a modest demeanor. Frédéric honored her as "the best of all mothers" and, in George Sand's opinion, she also was his "only love."

Unfortunately, hardly anything is known of the first years of Frédéric's life. We know only that with the exception of Ludwika, the healthiest and strongest of the siblings, they all frequently suffered from colds and apparently went through the customary childhood diseases, and therefore the two family doctors, Dr. Malcz and Dr. Roemer, were often called upon by the ever-concerned mother. Frédéric was, according to contemporary descriptions, an extremely delicate, sickly child; but, apart from occasional toothaches and a temporary loss of appetite, no details were reported. We do know that the parents were very worried about the delicate constitution of their often ailing son and they noted with relief and joy every slightest sign of physical good health—for instance, the letter sent by their son from the school holidays with the news that he had developed an "unusual appetite." Otherwise sicknesses must have played a rather insignificant role in Chopin's childhood and early youth, since his letters almost always speak of youthful pranks, joyful holiday experiences, and musical performances. On the other hand, it is striking that by the age of fourteen he regularly took medications such as oak-essence and was ordered to avoid eating rye bread.

Frédéric's musical talent became evident very early on. As a child he could not hold back the tears when he heard piano music in the next room, and scarcely of school age he already could play on the piano all the melodies his mother used to play, or express his own feelings in the form of free improvisation. Besides their mother, his older sister Ludwika was mainly the one who accompanied his first fingering attempts on the piano; and so, herself hardly able to read and write yet, she became his first piano teacher.

When his parents noticed this precocious musical interest and "obvious talent" of their son, they decided to have him take piano lessons. No sooner had he turned seven years old, when he received his first piano lessons from the Czech music teacher Wojciech Zwyny. Although Zwyny, who had been trained in the tradition of Johann Sebastian Bach, was not given very satisfactory marks by most biographers because of his somewhat old-fashioned and pedantic teaching methods and probably also because of his unimpressive and somewhat crotchety external appearance, he nonetheless played a leading role in Chopin's musical education. By communicating the essential foundations of piano playing, he enabled the boy at an early age to develop further on his own, although he soon excelled his teacher in technique. Frédéric therefore held him in high esteem; and he never could forget him even in later years, when he himself was famous.

As early as the age of seven, his creative talent began to show, especially in the form of marches, waltzes, and polonaises. The *Warsaw Memories*, after the first publication of a polonaise by young Chopin, called attention to the young artist with the following enthusiastic words:

> A real musical genius, for he not only plays with admirable ease and great feeling the most difficult piano pieces, but he is, moreover, the composer of several dances and variations that instill great admiration in music-lovers.

In fact, this polonaise, which has meanwhile been discovered, is said to stand comparison very well with a polonaise by Oginski or Kurpinski, so that it is not surprising when Clementina Hofmanowa in her *Memorial of a Good Mother*, published in 1819, reported of a child not yet eight years old "who in the opinion of experts promises to become a second Mozart." Soon Chopin's name was known far and wide in Warsaw, and when on 24 February 1818 he performed brilliantly in a charity concert for the first time the Concerto in E Minor for piano by Adalbert Gyrowetz, who was modern at the time, from then on the salons of the princely families Czartoryski, Radziwill, or Potocki, as well as of many other prominent noble families, were open to him. Little Chopin even became a favorite of the Russian Grand Prince Konstantin Pavlovich, who as the son of Czar Paul I ruled the former Duchy of Warsaw as a Russian territory once again, after the Fourth Partition of Poland in 1815. In 1818, Frédéric dedicated to him a military march, which the Prince reportedly liked to hear played in military parades in an arrangement for wind instruments, and little Chopinek, as his diminutive term of endearment went at the time, was the only person who could soothe Konstantin's dreaded fits of rage by playing the piano. In Belvedere, the ruler's residence, he also met the daughter of the governor Count de Moriolles, whom he later called Moriolka and with whom he was linked in sincere friendship during his Warsaw period.

Until his twelfth year, Frédéric received home schooling from his father and only in 1823, after successfully passing the admission examination at the Warsaw Lyceum, did he receive a thorough and comprehensive education. Beyond that, the frequent invitations to various salons and palaces exercised a decisive influence on the development of his personality. Besides learning the French language from his father, he received instruction in Latin and Greek, as well as German, Italian, and English; he attended courses in extemporaneous public speaking and oral delivery and received a solid education in the natural sciences as well as in the history of literature and drawing. Like Mendelssohn, he had an extraordinary talent for drawing, and his extremely lively imagination contributed greatly to his verse-writing and his activity as an actor, in which his imitative talents stood in the foreground. All in all, hardly another musician can be said to have received so distinguished an education as did Chopin, and the frequently mentioned epithet, "the young prince," is surely accurate, insofar as from his youth he preferred aristocratic society to any other—less from a snobbish attitude than from a feeling of intellectual equality.

Studies in piano technique especially fascinated him. Under the guidance of his eccentric teacher Zwyny, he practiced on the instrument for hours every day, paying special attention to his hand-span. Again like Robert Schumann he tried to achieve the greatest possible effect with a special contraption using pieces of wood especially prepared for the purpose which he placed between his fingers during the night. When it became clear that he no longer had much to learn with Zwyny, his father in 1822 transferred the training of his highly gifted son, celebrated as a Wunderkind or "child prodigy," to his friend Josef Elsner, who had just become director of the Warsaw Conservatory. Elsner, a native of the German-Silesian Grothkau, was a many-talented musician, active as a violinist and conductor, but also as a productive composer able to communicate harmonics theory and counterpoint to his pupil from firsthand experience. He immediately recognized that the young pupil he was dealing with was a genius, and therefore he very soon gave him free rein according to his individual nature, but only under the watchful and, if necessary, guiding eyes of the experienced teacher. He answered critics of this procedure with the words:

> Let him alone. He is not going the ordinary way, because his talent is extraordinary. He does not hold strictly to the old customary method, it is true. Instead he has his own method and he will display an originality in his works like no one before.

But Chopin also benefited a great deal in piano playing from Wilhelm Würfel, himself an outstanding pianist who after leaving Warsaw in 1826 became Kapellmeister at the Kärntnertor Theater in Vienna. Above all, Würfel also introduced him to the organ.

Chopin's improvements in piano playing were astonishing. At the age of fourteen, he perfected the techniques of Hummel and Weber, on the one hand, by mastering with almost astonishing ease the entire keyboard of the piano and, on the other, by beginning to use ornamentation as an essential means of expression. The skill at the piano he had already attained can be estimated from contemporary press notices, reporting that he mastered without difficulty such technically demanding piano concerts as those of Hummel, Moscheles, or Kalkbrenner. In his Warsaw Lyceum period, he also wrote a good number of compositions, mainly polonaises and mazurkas. But whereas in his earlier polonaises he had mainly imitated contemporary Polish composers, now he rather took works of Wilhelm Friedemann Bach as a model to emulate. He also began composing mazurkas, the artistic dance form which can be called Chopin's most personal domain, because it never existed before in this form. His greatest success during his Lyceum period was, however, achieved with his Rondo in C Minor from 1825, which he considered worthy to open the series of his later compositions as Opus 1.

A decisive event in his life, from an artistic point of view, is the vacation he spent in 1825 in Szafarnia on the estate of his friend Dominik Dziewanowski, from where he was able to broaden his horizon considerably by excursions to Thorn and Danzig. His letters reporting of many new impressions, such as the visit to the house where Copernicus was born, also show clearly that even then he had a lively interest in Polish folk songs, for he described remarkable details about their instrumental and melodic performance.

> While we sat at dinner and had almost finished eating the meal we heard from far away a singing with a high treble, whether by women, warbling through their nose, or by girls a half tone too high, unmercifully screeched, accompanied by a violin with only three strings, which after each sung stanza repeated the melody in deep tones in the background.

Later those folk origins can be discovered again and again in his mazurkas.

Even during these school holidays in Szafarnia, Frédéric was ordered by his family doctors to eat plenty of oatmeal, drink an extract of burned acorns, and spend a lot of time outdoors, as well as to get enough sleep—the preferred prescriptions made in those days for a tendency to bronchial catarrhs. Actually, Chopin's letters in his youth show that he often suffered from sniffles, colds, and symptoms of inflammation of the upper airways. Supposedly his fragile state of health was the reason why he was not permitted to attend a public school and received schooling at home until he was thirteen years old. But young Chopin should by no means be pictured as a constantly ailing child; rather, all contemporary portrayals speak of a cheerful boy, well liked by all and full of bubbling high spirits, who did not lag behind his play-mates in stage-plays at the Chopin boarding school or during his stays in the country.

He first caught a more serious illness in 1826. After celebrat-ing several carnival days, he fell sick with a headache and swol-len glands in his throat, and, as he reported in a letter, he had to stay in bed. The family physician, Dr. Roemer, applied leeches to his throat, and Dr. Malcz prescribed an emetic as well as several dietetic measures, so that in his own words he was "being fed oatmeal like a horse." No doubt at that time his resistance was not at its best; and besides the nightly composing and the fre-quent invitations to various Polish salons, the strenuous studies for the approaching matriculation examination at the Lyceum must have contributed no little to his weakened state of health. His delicate bodily constitution really was always a cause of concern to his father, as can be gathered from his statement about this:

> He had so little resistance that he broke into tears on the slightest occasion.

On 12 February 1826, Frédéric wrote to his friend Jan Bialoblocki, who lay incurably ill from tuberculosis of the bones:

> Everyone is falling ill, and so am I. Maybe you think I've been writing everything I've scribbled down so far, sitting in an armchair; it is not true, I am writing on top of a blanket, my head wrapped in a nightcap because for four days I've had a headache, I know not why. They've applied leeches to my neck because my glands are swol-len, and our Doctor Roemer says it is a catarrhic inflammation.

However, his family doctor's orders seem to have had only mod-est success, since four months later the young patient still referred to himself as "ailing." After Frédéric had successfully passed the matriculation examination at the Lyceum and his sister Emilia had meanwhile fallen seriously ill, the decision was therefore made to send him, together with Emilia, under the care of his mother and his older sister Ludwika for treatment at Bad Reinerz in Lower Silesia. Emilia was at this time already seriously ill and must have presented signs of an open tuberculosis of the lungs in Bad Reinerz, and hence been dangerously infectious, whereas Frédéric had come along more as a companion and convalescent. The two concerts he presented as benefits for orphans should be judged in this sense and they brought him great recognition. On the other hand, the fact that his doctors forbade him to climb a nearby hill indicates that his health was not yet in the best shape. Whether at this point in time he himself was already ill with tuberculosis can today no longer be decided definitely; but it seems at least very probable in view of the close family contact with his sister Emilia and the described swollen lymph nodes in his throat in late winter of that year.

At any rate, he likewise submitted to a "drinking" treatment in Bad Reinerz, although he himself did not feel extremely ill during this treatment period at the spa, which lasted from 3 August to 11 September 1826. The drinking of whey was at that time a favorite and esteemed medication for persons suffering from tuberculosis and we have a graphic, detailed picture from Chopin's pen on how this spa activity was conducted. In a letter of 18 August 1826 to a friend in Warsaw he says:

> For two weeks now I have conscientiously been drinking whey and the local water, and I am said to be looking somewhat better, apparently fatter and lazier. Early in the morning, by six o'clock at the latest, all the patients are assembled by the well; here miserable wind instruments strike up slow music…for the strolling guests. This promenade on the charming avenue that links the institute [Magolla's Whey Institute] with the city, usually lasts until eight o'clock, depending on the number of cups each person must drink in the morning. After breakfast I generally go for a walk, promenading until 12 o'clock, at which time lunch must

BAD REINERZ. IN THIS FAMOUS SPA IN LOWER SAXONY, SIXTEEN-YEAR-OLD CHOPIN UNDERWENT A MINERAL WATER CURE TOGETHER WITH HIS SISTER EMILIA.

be eaten, because after the meal one goes back to the well. After lunch—again this abominable music, and so the day passes until evening. Now, because afternoons I drink only two glasses of lukewarm spring water, I go home early for dinner, then after dinner to bed.

All in all, however, treatment seems to have done him some good, for in August 1826 he wrote to his teacher Josef Elsner:

The fresh air and the whey I have been drinking busily have restored me so much that I am a completely different person than I was in Warsaw.

So he returned to Warsaw, recovered and visibly strengthened. Yet he still had to remain subject to the treatment prescribed by Dr. Malcz, the family doctor. It consisted essentially of unspecific invigorating measures, such as physical movement outdoors, eating oatmeal, and drinking mineral waters. Another stay at a spa was planned for the coming year, but Frédéric felt no great longing for it, as can be gathered from a letter to his friend Jan Bialoblocki of 26 November 1826:

> I've been told that perhaps next year I would have to return to the warm springs, at least pro forma, but it is still a long time until then and perhaps it would be better to go to Paris rather than to the Bohemian border.

His sister Emilia was not cured by the treatment. On the contrary, five months after returning from Bad Reinerz, her condition worsened acutely. In a letter of 14 March 1827 addressed to his friend Jan Bialoblocki, who was meanwhile also mortally ill, Frédéric described her condition vividly:

> My sister Emilia has been bedridden now for four weeks. She had begun to cough, then she spat blood, and Mama is scared. So Malcz ordered a bleeding. It was done once...then a second time: countless leeches, blistering plasters, mustard plasters, belladonna, excitement after excitement. During the whole time she has eaten nothing; she has deteriorated so much that one cannot recognize her; now she gradually is recovering a little. You can imagine how things were going in our house....

Emilia did not recover and despite all medical efforts she died on 10 April 1827. And a few months later his friend Jan Bialoblocki, too, was buried. These seemingly inhuman medical steps and their obvious futility are surely the reason for Chopin's distrustful and negative attitude all his life toward similar treatments recommended by the doctors and why he favored homeopathy.

After returning from Bad Reinerz, the family had consulted together and agreed that from then on Frédéric would dedicate himself exclusively to music. He enrolled in the Warsaw Central School for Music, which since its reestablishment stood under the directorship of Josef Elsner. He favored Chopin and took him under his wing, teaching him the foundations of composition techniques and the main problems in creating artistic form. Significantly, under Elsner's influence, Chopin at this time eagerly turned his attention to piano music with orchestra. Works conceived at this time were: Variations for piano and orchestra op. 2, on the theme *"Là ci darem la mano"* from Mozart's *Don Giovanni,* the Trio op. 8 for piano, violin, and cello and, as crowning pieces, the two piano concertos, op. 21 in F Minor and op. 11 in E Minor, written in the years 1829 and 1830. In addition, he continued as before to compose waltzes, mazurkas and polonaises, which were assigned opus titles only later by his friend Fontana.

In the summer of 1827, after Emilia's death, which had been a major emotional shock for the close-knit family, Chopin went out to the country to visit Prince Radziwill at Antonin Manor, a very beneficial diversion from his deeply felt grief. The Prince was very musical, played the cello and even tried his own hand at putting Goethe's *Faust* to music, a composition which earned unlimited praise from Liszt. This excellent man, on the occasion of his marriage with a Prussian princess decreed as a bridal gift the release of all Polish soldiers held prisoner in Silesia. Chopin dedicated his piano trio to him, and there he wrote, probably also for the Prince's pleasure, an *alla Polacca* for violoncello.

Meanwhile, Chopin's virtuoso career in Warsaw had taken a significant further development. Besides his first great successes as a piano virtuoso, now his creative activity also was drawing attention, and so understandably his father used every opportunity to ensure a comprehensive musical development for his son, who also began intensively to deal with the field of opera. Since Poland could offer no adequate training in this regard, contacts were sought abroad. One was made in September 1828 when in Berlin a convention of natural scientists was meeting under the chairmanship of Alexander von Humboldt. The Polish zoologist, Jarocki, a friend of the Chopin family, was invited to this convention. He took Frédéric along, hoping that a friend of his, the zoologist Lichtenstein, business manager of the congress, would introduce young Chopin to the prominent musicians of the Prussian capital. Lichtenstein had been a close friend of Carl Maria von Weber, who had died two years previously at a young age. Unfortunately this hope was disappointed and the desired contact did not come about. With a feeling of resignation, Chopin stated in a letter to his parents on 20 September 1828:

> Spontini, Zelter, Mendelssohn-Bartholdy were also there; but I spoke with none of these gentlemen, since I did not feel it appropriate to introduce myself to them.

However, he did have the opportunity, on the occasion of a common meal of the convention participants, to capture a few scholars in a caricature and to make fun of the airs they put on, as a passage from an anecdote seeks to show his parents:

> The common dinner of those scholars took place yesterday. I have assorted them into three classes not under Humboldt's chairmanship (for he has good manners), but under some other guild-master....At table it seemed to me that my neighbor looked askance at me, a profane layman. He was a botany professor from Hamburg. I envied him his high and mighty stature. I had to break the rolls with two hands, while he, a little frog with bear's paws, pressed them flat with one. He conversed across me with Jarocki and forgot himself so much in the conversation that in his enthusiasm he brushed his fat fingers across my plate and swept together the crumbs....I sat on pins and needles during the scraping on my plate and afterwards had to wipe it off with a napkin.

Yet Chopin returned to Warsaw with an abundance of musical impressions, since he made good use of the opportunities to attend the Berliner Theater and the Singakademie. Immediately before his departure, he therefore wrote confidently: "I am healthy and saw what there was to see. I am returning home to you....But travel agrees with me." In the summer of 1829 he ended his studies at the Central School for Music with a final examination, for which Elsner gave him an outstanding grade and noted in the school's records: "A brilliant talent, a musical genius." Chopin thanked his teacher by dedicating to him his Sonata in C Minor for piano, op. 4.

In the spring of 1829, Chopin experienced his first love, which he at first kept secret from everyone. Finally he revealed his secret to his friend Titus Woyciechowski in a letter:

> Six months have gone by and I have not exchanged a word with her of whom I dream every night. She was the inspiration for the adagio in my concerto [referring to the Concerto in F Minor op. 21] and this waltz which I am sending you [referring to the waltz published as Opus 70, no. 3 in D flat].

The name of the woman he adored was still withheld in this letter to his friend, dated 3 October 1829—an expression of his personal need to keep his inner life secret from the surrounding world, a need appearing here for the first time but persisting all his life. Apparently this girl he loved was Konstancja Gladkowska, whom he met at the conservatory and who later also appeared as a singer at the Warsaw Opera. This assumption is, to be sure, based only on a few vague allusions in letters to Titus Woyciechowski, although Konstancja's name is no more mentioned here than in the later Vienna letters or in the Stuttgart diary. His "great love for Konstancja," which many biographers speak of, is thus really not documented in any conclusive source. Even his 1830 confession in his diary retains her anonymity:

> Her image never leaves my mind. I seem not to love her, yet I am always thinking of her.

The entire matter is complicated even further by his unusually close friendship with Titus, since in the aforementioned allusions in Chopin's letters it often remains unclear whether in his confession he did not mean his friend rather than Konstancja. Even taking into account the flowery mode of expression in the letter-writing style of Romanticism—carried almost to the point of exultation—a few passages in Chopin's letters to his friends, especially to Titus Woyciechowski, have set some biographers thinking. For he used expressions such as "my dear," "my darling," and sentences such as "Give your friend your lips" or "I kiss you ardently on the mouth, do you allow it?" Even considering that kissing between men accords with Slavic custom, it is not surprising that when friendly relations with the same sex were stamped with

such passion, the suspected presence of a homoerotic component arose in the mind of some biographers. This suspicion was
also not allayed by the fact that demonstrably there were no homosexuals among Chopin's friends, and especially that his most beloved Titus quite often rejected such tender allusions with the
words: "I don't like to be kissed." Here we have similar conditions as with Robert Schumann, whose rapturous friendship for
the great violinist Joseph Joachim, as well as for Johannes Brahms,
likewise raise the suspicion of a homoerotic component. In both
cases, however, this homoerotically toned relationship had nothing to do with any manifest homosexual inclination. In the light
of more recent psychoanalytical "narcissism-theories," it corresponds rather to a wish for a symbiotic, narcissistic-fusional relationship with a male partner who in his eyes embodies the other
ideal, namely, strength, decisiveness, capability. Apparently a
strengthening of manly identity was expected from such a fusional
relationship, and in fact compared with Titus, who long since was
a man and administered his estates in Poturzyn with great energy,
Frédéric still seemed a mere youth.

Meanwhile his parents and his teachers agreed that the time
had come for Frédéric to gather foreign artistic impressions in the
major cities of Europe and to exploit them for his own creativity.
His father therefore applied to the Polish government to grant
him a scholarship of 5000 guilders to cover the financial expenses
of three years' study abroad. The disappointing answer, however, read: "Monies cannot be squandered on artists of this sort."
And so young Chopin undertook the journey to Vienna, his "spring-
board to the world," at his own expense. And in fact the Austrian
capital, where he arrived on 31 July 1829, first made him known
in the world of art as a virtuoso and as a composer. But shortly
before that, his state of health seemed to give him some cause for
concern, for he wrote:

> I believe the journey abroad will not blossom for
> me this year; instead a fever is blossoming for me,
> then everything will be over.

Contrary to these fears, he arrived in Vienna "happy, joyous, and
healthy," and only a severely swollen nose cast a slight shadow

on these hopeful weeks until his departure on 19 August. His teacher Elsner had provided him with a great number of effective letters of recommendation to facilitate his access to leading Viennese musicians. The famous publisher Haslinger soon gave him the title of the "New Star of the North," and everyone let him know that he would "cause a sensation" if he gave a concert. It was his former teacher Wilhelm Würfel who finally took care of establishing a "musical academy," which took place on 11 August with the collaboration of the Opera's orchestra, "nota bene without charging any fee," as he wrote home. Only a few weeks later, he performed in a second "musical academy" and enjoyed an even greater success. "I was well received the first time, but yesterday was even better. There were three rounds of applause when I appeared on the stage," he wrote to Warsaw, and in the Leipzig Allgemeine Musikalische Zeitung of 18 November 1829 he was praised "as one of the brightest meteors on the musical horizon."

Travel Abroad—The Stuttgart Diary

At least since his return from Vienna, Chopin realized that his career, which had begun so successfully, had prospects of developing further only in a musical metropolis such as Vienna, Paris, or London. He was particularly aware that he had to expand the scope of his compositions, especially in the field of large forms. In a relatively short time he completed two concertos, namely, the Grand Polonaise with orchestra and the *Fantasia on Polish Airs*; and to convince himself of what impression his compositions were making on the public, on 7 March 1830 he organized a great public concert under the directorship of Kurpinski, in which besides the allegro from the Piano Concerto in F Minor he also first performed his *Fantasia on Polish Airs*. The Warsaw public was enthusiastic, and the critics too gave him outstanding reviews, so that just five days later he gave a second concert with an even more smashing success.

On the occasion of Czar Nicholas I's arrival in Warsaw for the opening of the Imperial Congress in May 1830, Chopin met the famous singer Henriette Sontag, who was to enrich the festive concert program and he was captivated by her with regard to more than her singing technique. "She is a thousand times more charming in a house coat than in an evening gown," he reported to Titus. And this enthusiasm probably made it easier for him to remain a secret lover in his relationship to Konstancja Gladkowska and to function as her musical accompaniment in her first appearance as a singer at the Warsaw Opera.

After the close of the concert season, Chopin finished his next Piano Concerto in E Minor in a relatively short time and finally rode to his friend Titus in Poturzyn for rest. Meanwhile the decision was made at last to begin the planned longer journey abroad, and Titus was to accompany him at least as far as Vienna. At first a resurgent feverish illness seemed to imperil their travel plans, but these fears proved to be unfounded. The final months before leaving his familiar homeland, his family, and his friends were a severe psychological burden on the young artist, who feared he would experience loneliness in his voluntary exile. In his reports to Titus, he even spoke of an "unbearable melancholy" which "made him cold and dry as a stone" and repeatedly led him to postpone his departure date.

> I am still sitting here. I don't have enough strength to set the date. I fear I am leaving my homeland forever. How sad it must be to die abroad and not where one was born. How terrible it would be for me to see around me at my deathbed, instead of my beloved relatives, only the coldhearted doctor or the paid servant.

Such words clearly stem from a depressive mood which was later interpreted after the fact as a premonition of his fate.

Before his departure, at a farewell concert given on 11 October 1830 the just completed Piano Concerto in E Minor got its premiere performance and Konstancja, too, participated in it. On 2 November 1830, Chopin left Warsaw after a moving farewell from his friends. The legend reports that they gave him a silver cup containing earth from the homeland as a reminder of Poland. He was supposed to take it with him to his grave, as if it were certain he would never return and would be buried in foreign soil. This pious legend has meanwhile been conclusively disproved by Bronarski and Hedley, but it still hovers about in Chopin biographies, apparently because of its sentimental content. What motives ultimately led him to begin his journey abroad is less clear. No doubt the son's artistic ambitions and the father's striving to facilitate a comprehensive musical education for him were in the foreground. This may not have been the only reason. For after the July Revolution in Paris in 1830, unrest flared up in Europe on all sides and threatened to spread even to Poland, giving the inhabitants of Warsaw the feeling that they were sitting virtually on a powder keg. It is quite possible, then, that Chopin's father, considering his son's delicate state of health, urged him to depart from Warsaw soon.

So young Chopin set out, first for Vienna, where he arrived on 20 November 1830. On the way he was joined by his friend Titus, who, sitting beside him in the carriage, soon helped him banish his pain at parting. In Dresden he participated in a soirée at the house of a physician, Dr. Friedrich Kreyssig, frequently consulted by many Russians and Poles of elegant society, whose main work *Die Krankheiten des Herzens* (*Diseases of the Heart*) won an imperishable place for him in the history of medicine. Unfortunately Chopin's second stay in Vienna brought some disappointments, although he had fatherly friends at his side. First, he again sought out his former teacher at the Warsaw Conservatory, Wilhelm Würfel, who was employed as music director at the Kärntnertor Theater, but meanwhile was suffering from a progressive pulmonary tuberculosis and was already gravely ill. Nonetheless, he wanted to make all preparations for his pupil's concert without delay. On 1 December 1830, Chopin wrote to his parents:

> When I visited our friend Würfel, he immediately spoke of arranging a concert. He is a remarkable man. Although he is too sick to go out, he gives lessons in his apartment. He is spitting blood, and this has greatly weakened him, yet he is talking of a concert.

Subsequently Chopin was often Würfel's guest, and to what extent he comes in question as a possible source of infection for Chopin cannot be decided after the fact, but it lies within the realm of possibilities.

Another fatherly friend was Dr. Johann Malfatti, personal physician of the Austrian Emperor and the doctor who treated Ludwig van Beethoven. Immediately after arriving in Vienna, Chopin was introduced by him to the leading musical circles of the Danube metropolis. This respected doctor spoiled his young friend, who frequently was his guest, not only with dishes prepared in Polish style, but he also gave him valuable medical advice, as can be gathered from Chopin's letters:

> Malfatti really loves me, and I am quite proud of that....I am also healthy as a lion, and people say I have gained weight. On the whole, things are going well with me and I hope to God, who has sent Malfatti as a help to me—oh, magnificent Malfatti!—that they will go even better.

This last remark suggests that Chopin even then was fully aware of his extremely delicate health. This also is evident from the wording of the first letter written immediately after his arrival in Vienna to Jan Matuszynski, his friend who was studying medicine and his fellow sufferer who would later die of tuberculosis earlier than Chopin, while serving as a doctor at the Military Academy in Paris. "For God's sake," he wrote, "don't force anything, for we are both made of the same clay, and you know how often I have fallen apart."

Meanwhile, word reached Vienna that the long-awaited uprising had broken out in Poland on 29 November. Czar Nicholas I had, in contrast with Alexander I, maintained a harsh policy of repression not only of the Russians but also of all other nationalities in his empire. Inspired by the Revolution in France, Polish officers and intellectuals now revolted against the Russian oppressors, and their uprising was supported by the Polish army, nobility, and democrats. It began with the arson of an old brewery near the Weichsel and with the attempt to kill the tyrannical Grand Prince Konstantin, which was foiled by his premature flight from the Belvedere palace. At first the Russians were driven out. But the Poles failed to introduce measures to free the peasants in time, and so the country populace did not join the struggle against the Russians. Thus, despite brave resistance by the Polish defenders, the Russians reconquered Warsaw in September 1831 and put down the revolt. By a so-called "organic statute" Poland was again incorporated into Russia. The unbroken Polish nationalism lived on, however, and was fed from abroad by participants in the Polish uprising who had escaped to Switzerland or France.

News of the revolution, which broke out in the Polish capital a few days after the two friends arrived in Vienna, was an emotional shock to the two friends. Titus, eager to join the rebels as a fighter, set out for home without delay. Chopin, however, was indecisive and could not make up his mind so quickly to return to Warsaw, especially since his father apparently was urging him *not* to return home under the circumstances. Left behind in Vienna, he found that his situation was made more difficult in two ways by the constantly arriving news on the events of the Polish revolution. First, he was worried about the fate of his family and friends, who were exposed to the daily increasing peril. His depressed mood, coupled with silent self-reproach for not having returned together with Titus, is expressed most clearly in a letter to Jan Matuszynski, which he wrote on Christmas Day of 1830:

> I wish I could mobilize all the tones inspired in me by my blind, raging, excited feelings, to capture a part of the songs...that were sung by Jan's soldiers....And if I did not become a burden on my father, I would return today. Cursed is the moment I decided to leave.

Secondly, the revolution in Poland resulted in increased hostility of the populace against the homeland of the Poles. This was an aggravating factor, and Chopin too was made to feel this anti-Polish mood in Viennese society. Apart from many invitations, which merely bored him, he felt lonely, abandoned, and plagued by homesickness. In such a mood on Christmas Eve toward midnight he entered St. Stephen's cathedral. He told of this visit in one of his letters:

> The size and elevation of this mighty dome is indescribable....Behind me a grave, under me a grave, one was missing only over me. Dismal sounds rose in me, and I felt my solitude more than ever....

From a medical standpoint, during his time in Vienna the dominant factor was the constant worsening of his basic emotional mood, as reflected in passages of his letter to his friend Jan, dated 26 December 1830: "Everything here is so sad, dismal, and melancholy for me." A remark in his notebook sounds familiar: "How strange and sad I feel—I don't know what to do, why am I so alone," and the sadness that came over him can be felt also in his Scherzo in B Minor op. 20, written at that time. This sad, downcast feeling soon was mixed with increasingly real despair, occasionally rising to real weariness with life and to suicidal ideas: "To live, to die, everything seems unimportant to me today," or: "Today is New Year's Day. How sadly I am beginning the New Year! Perhaps I will no longer experience its end." These are clues in his letters from those days justifying such an interpretation. As a cause for his feeling of loneliness and despair, the separation from his family was probably an essential factor, as can be seen from another passage of the letters: "I desire to die, but first I would like to see my parents again."

Nonetheless, in the last months of his stay in Vienna, namely, on 4 April 1831, he took part in musical life by playing his Piano Concerto in E Minor, op. 11, though it met with reserved reception. This very circumstance that artistic recognition was denied him during his second stay in Vienna must have been an additional factor contributing to the deep crisis of his self-esteem. For months, self-reproach and self-recrimination for having failed in life began plaguing him more and more frequently.

> I must rightly complain of ever having been born. Why wasn't I permitted not to come here, since I am inactive. Who is helped at all by my presence? I am useless among men.

So and similarly he complained to his friend. And below the surface, one senses again and again self-accusations for not having taken part in his people's freedom struggle, for instance, when he wrote:

> You are my best friend in the world, you have now achieved what you wanted....You are in the army....Have you thrown up walls? Our poor parents. What are my friends doing? I would gladly die for you, for all of you!...If only I could serve at least as a drummer!

Since he lacked the willpower to change his situation, from which he suffered so much, he was at times beset by strong inner unrest and emotional tensions. While in the salons of Viennese society, he seemed calm and serene, but on returning to his lodgings he felt restless and sometimes so excited internally that he began to play wildly on the piano. An eloquent expression of such mood swings can be found in his cycle of twelve etudes, op. 10, composed alternatively in a major and a minor key, which he finished during his second stay in Vienna. The last etude of the cycle, the "Revolutionary" Etude, reveals the turmoil of Chopin's soul with particular intensity.

How alien the Viennese mentality remained for him can be gauged from his judgment on the waltzes by Lanner and Strauss, which led him to conclude that Viennese taste was spoiled. The people of Vienna also did not seem to him as polite and as eloquent as the Poles, and he wrote to his parents shortly before his departure that during the past months he had learned nothing genuinely Viennese: "For example, I cannot dance waltzes well. My piano has simply gotten to hear only mazurkas." On top of all this, because of Johann Strauss' dominant position, his own prospects in the artistic field offered little hope of success. The Viennese music publishers, moreover, regarded printing the works of a little-known Polish composer as a financial risk. His last performance in Vienna during a benefit presentation in the Kärntnertor Theater on 11 June 1831 was ignored by the Viennese press and mentioned favorably only in a report of the *Allgemeine Musikalische Zeitung* in Leipzig on 21 September 1831. So, understandably, the thought of leaving soon became more firm in his mind. Since meanwhile unrest had also broken out in Italy, he decided to go to Paris. It was mainly Dr. Malfatti who showed the hesitant artist the way to Paris. That city was then the focal point of all European artistic life, where a genius like Chopin could first bring his artistry to full development. Malfatti provided him with a series of letters of recommendation, principally to his friend, Fernando Paer, the music potentate of Paris and longtime Director of the Théatre Italien of that city. Malfatti thus hoped he had opened access to the highest circles of the French capital for his young friend as if with a magic wand. In gratitude, on mid-summer day, Chopin presented a memorable festive concert in Malfatti's splendid country house for his name-day.

Unexpected difficulties were raised by the Russian embassy concerning the issuance of a travel permit, so he followed a friend's advice and applied for a passport to England while actually going to Paris. A further delay ensued from the circumstance that at the time not only in Vienna but also in Bavaria there was great fear of cholera, which was spreading southward from the region of the Russian-Polish war, and so a "health pass" was required by Bavaria for transit travelers. But finally the time came; on 20 July 1831, he boarded a post carriage heading for Paris, via Salzburg, Munich, and Stuttgart. The past eight months had been a bitter disappointment for him, since he had neither won notable artistic fame nor drawn financial gain. So he did not find it hard to say farewell to Vienna, and he left it with a feeling of personal failure. During a required intermediary stop in Munich, where he needed to obtain permission to travel on to Paris, he let himself be persuaded to do a concert before the Philharmonic Society. He performed his Piano Concerto in E Minor and his *Fantasia on Polish Airs* with great success. A few days later he arrived in Stuttgart, where the devastating news reached him that on 7 September 1831 the Warsaw uprising had been totally vanquished and the bravest Polish freedom fighters had been forced to capitulate to the crushing and utterly brutal onslaught of the Russian army. Chopin's successes and disappointments in Vienna had contributed to his falling into a depressive emotional state and now he underwent a complete nervous breakdown. But whereas we are informed almost without gaps about the period of his stay in Vienna from November 1830 to the end of July 1831 from Chopin's detailed letters to his parents and to his friend Jan Matuszynski as well as from entries in his notebook and diary, the period between his painful departure from Vienna and his arrival in Paris is bridged by no news from his own hand. Amid this void stands only one document that sounds like the painful cry of a lonely tormented heart and testifies to the horrid imaginings and thoughts of a person standing at the edge of despair who sees no way out, namely, the so-called "Stuttgart diary." Considering the outstanding significance of this document for a medical assessment of Chopin, it seems indispensable to quote the complete text:

> Stuttgart. —Strange! the bed I am about to lie on has perhaps been slept in by more than one dying person and yet today I am not horrified by this idea. Perhaps more than one corpse has lain here, and for a long time. But how is a corpse less than I? A corpse too knows nothing, whether of its father or mother, or its sisters or Titus! A corpse too has no lover, nor can it speak with the people around it in its own language! A corpse is pale like me. It is as cold as I am at this moment toward all things. A corpse has ceased to live, and I too have had enough of life. Enough? If that were so, the corpse would look satisfied, and yet it is so miserable. Does life really have such great influence on its features, on the facial expression, on a person's physiognomy? Why do we live such a miserable life that consumes us and is there only to make corpses of us! One o'clock is sounding from the clocks on Stuttgart's towers. Ah! How many people are dying on earth at this moment? Children are losing their mothers; mothers, their children. How many ideas are being annihilated; how much sadness this brings and also how many consolations! How many dishonest protectors die and how many oppressed people. The evil and the good are dead. Likewise virtue and crime. All are brothers in death.

Besides these frightful images, these fantasies of death dangled before him by his sensitive artist's soul, a feeling of failure and frustration pulsates through these lines, and the reader is repeatedly astonished at the minutious description of his feelings and his extremely intense inner life.

> You see, death is the best thing there is. What is, then, the worst? Birth, for after all it is the opposite of the best. So I have a right to complain of having come into the world. Why was I not allowed not to come, since I am inactive here, and so what is the use of my life? Among all men I am totally useless, for I am neither fish nor fowl, and if I were more, what difference would it make? Would things be any better for me if I were more substantial? But one must be more substantial! Is a corpse more substantial? No more than I am. One similarity more. So actually I am not far short of feeling like a brother of death. Today I no longer desire death so strongly, unless you were unhappy, my children, and wished for nothing more ardently than death! If not, I would like to see you again. Not for the sake of my direct happiness, but for an indirect one, for I know how very much you love me....Father, mother, children, all you who are dearest to me, where are you? Dead, perhaps? Did the Muscovite play an evil prank on me? Oh! wait, wait....Is that supposed to be tears? It is so long since they have flowed from my eyes. Why? A dry sadness has gripped me for so long. I have been unable to cry for many days. What kind of feeling is this? A good feeling full of longing? It is not good to yield to longing, but it is pleasant! It is a strange condition. But even the dead person feels good and bad at the same time. He is entering a happier life and so he feels good, but he regrets having to leave the past and becomes melancholic. The

corpse must feel like I do, when I have stopped crying. It was surely a transitory dying off of my feeling—for a moment I was dead to my heart. Or perhaps my heart was dead to me. Why not forever? Perhaps that would be more tolerable for me. Alone, alone.

Ah! My misery is hardly describable! My feelings can hardly bear it. My heart is just short of breaking from the "joy" and the "pleasures" it has had to endure this past year. My passport expires next month. I will no longer be able to live abroad—at least not officially. So I will be even more like a dead man.

Fearing for his parents' safety and the state of Warsaw after the destructions of war, he elaborated the most horrible possibilities and scolded cruel fate. His desire for revenge against the victorious Muscovites was as clearly expressed as his doubts about the existence of God. The sketches in the Stuttgart diary on 8 September continue:

I wrote the previous pages without knowing that the enemy was already in the house. The suburbs are destroyed, burned down. Jash [his friend Jan]! Certainly Wilus [Wilhelm Kolberg, a friend of his youth] has died on the ramparts. I see Marcel in captivity. Sowinski [a friend who was a composer and music writer], that good man, in the hands of these criminals! O God, do you exist at all? Yes, you do exist, and you do not avenge us! Are there not yet enough Muscovite crimes, or are you yourself a Muscovite? My poor father, my good father, perhaps he is famished; perhaps he cannot buy bread for my mother! My sisters have perhaps become victims of the rage of the unrestrained Muscovite soldiery! Paszkiewicz [the Russian general in command of the conquest of Warsaw], this dog from Mohilew, occupies the residence of the

> first monarchs of Europe! The Muscovite is lord
> of the world? O my father, these are the joys of
> your old age! Mother, tender suffering mother,
> you survived your daughter only to experience
> how the Muscovite kicks her bones about. Ah!
> Powonski [cemetery with Emilia's grave]. Did they
> spare her grave? It is trodden under foot and a
> thousand other corpses cover it. They have burned
> down the city. Ah! Why was it not my lot to kill
> at least one of these Muscovites! Oh, Titus, Titus!

On another page the self-reproach of looking on inactively
from afar at the gruesome occurrences in his homeland, and
the complaint about his nameless solitude in these, his nation's
fateful hours, and his despair because of his own compulsory
inactivity mingles with worry about his "secret love," Konstancja
Gladkowska:

> Stuttgart. What has come of her [meaning
> Konstancja]? Where is she? The poor woman!
> Maybe she is in the Muscovites' hands! A Musco-
> vite presses her, chokes her, murders her, kills her!
> Ah! my beloved, I am here alone—I dry your
> tears, I will soothe the sounds of the present by
> reminding you of the past—of the time when there
> were not yet any Muscovites. Then some Musco-
> vites did their best trying to please you, but you
> made fun of them, because I was there, I, not
> Grab[owski, her later husband].
>
> You have a mother, and what a nasty one. I have
> such a good mother, but perhaps I no longer have
> one. Perhaps a Muscovite has killed, murdered
> her. My frightened sisters protect themselves. My
> despairing father does not know what will hap-
> pen, and no one is there to pick up my mother's
> body, and I sit inactive here and groan from time
> to time with empty hands and surrender myself to
> my despair at the piano. Why all this? God, my

God, shake the earth so that it may swallow the people of this century and the most terrible torments may befall the French for not having hastened to our aid.

It is strange that these extremely depressive reactions of Chopin's to events have not been evaluated at all in previous pathographies, although they certainly marked his further development as a man and as an artist very essentially. Axel Karenberg first saw these events in Chopin's life as standing in a causal connection with physical changes in the sense of a reactive depression and sought to document this in a monograph well worth reading based also on letters from the Vienna period, but above all on the Stuttgart diary. For these tragic events were experiences that exceeded the barely twenty-year-old artist's strength and necessarily influenced his entire later creativity. From then on, "suffering and struggle" were to remain the most essential traits of his individual style. Biographies repeatedly point out that the aforementioned "Revolutionary" Etude in C Minor, op. 10, no. 12, as well as Preludes in A Minor and D Minor, op. 28, no. 2 and no. 24, reflect his state of mind at that time most clearly. Such an interpretation cannot, however, be proven and must therefore be evaluated only as a suspicion in connection with various passages of his letters.

Paris, His Second Homeland

Chopin was able to breathe a sigh of relief only on arriving in Paris in mid-September 1831 and getting the happy news that his family and his friend Titus were well and healthy. From a political standpoint, he arrived in Paris at a time when after the July Revolution Louis-Philippe's position was firmly established. However, since the great majority of Frenchmen, even under the "bourgeois-king," who received the crown from the hands of parliament with its bourgeois-liberal majority, still were excluded from the right to vote, those who really benefited from the revolution were the upper-bourgeoisie, whose favor the government tried to preserve by opening up new economic possibilities. Under the slogan "Get rich!" individual families, among whom the Rothschilds became best-known, built up enormous fortunes in a short time. In the course of these developments, besides political tensions, soon social dissatisfaction also necessarily resulted and would give rise to early socialism. Chopin described this situation in one of his very first letters to Titus:

> Let me tell you, great misery is widespread here....The lower classes are groaning under the burden and often think of changing their fate, but...no sooner is there the smallest gathering of people on the street, and immediately mounted police scatter them apart.

Despite these signs of unrest, Chopin found in Paris "the most beautiful of all worlds," a lively artistic life. Supported by Malfatti's letters of recommendation from Vienna, he very soon succeeded in becoming acquainted with the musical celebrities of the French capital.

> Through Paer, who is the Court Kapellmeister, I met Rossini, Cherubini, Baillot. I also owe to him my acquaintanceship with Kalkbrenner. You cannot imagine how curious I was to meet Herz, Liszt, Hiller; but they are all nothing, compared with Kalkbrenner.

His enthusiasm for this man would almost have led him to become his pupil for three years, but this plan was blocked not least of all by the energetic intervention of his father and his former teacher Elsner, who suspected a plot on Kalkbrenner's part to exploit a pupil of such genius.

Considering the intense competition in Paris, Chopin's rapid artistic breakthrough was an exceptional phenomenon. By the end of February 1832, he performed in the salons of Camille Pleyel, the famous piano manufacturer and later his friend, his Piano Concerto in F Minor and his Variations *"Là ci darem"* with the greatest success. "The stormy applause," wrote Liszt, "seemed not to suffice for our enthusiasm for this gifted musician, who revealed a new phase of poetic feeling with the most felicitous formal innovations in his art." But public concerts were not alone decisive at that time in Paris; rather, private appearances in the salons played at least as much of a role. Chopin very quickly did this too—not only in the Polish salons of the Czartoryskis and others, but far more also in the circles of the Parisian aristocracy and bourgeoisie. Certainly a contributing factor was the particular popularity and sympathy the Poles then enjoyed among the French people, partly from empathy with their heroic uprising against the Muscovites, partly because the French July Revolution was supported, besides by students, journalists, and workers, not least of all also by numerous Polish immigrants. So as early as January 1833, he could report proudly to his friend Dominik Dziewanowski:

> I found access to the highest society and sit between ambassadors, princes, and ministers and do not even know how this came about, for I did not force myself upon them. But for me that is the most important thing, for that is where good taste supposedly comes from.

His artistic standing in French society also led to his very soon having pupils from the most elegant circles assigned to him for piano lessons and to his being able to charge the respectable amount of 20 francs per hour of instruction. Thus his very insecure financial situation soon improved more and more, so that soon he could absolutely be considered a well-to-do artist. However, he was of a different opinion, for he wrote to his childhood friend, Dominik:

> I have to give five lessons today. Surely you believe this is making me rich. But you are wrong: the cabriolet and white gloves cost more than I earn, but without them I would not live up to "good taste."

One should not mistakenly think that his professional new beginning in Paris was an easy matter for the new arrival from Poland. Although the press praised Chopin's piano playing from the beginning and his delightful improvisations and marvelous compositions soon won him an elite class of admirers, especially among the ladies, at first he still was just one among many in the musical life of Paris. Even the aforementioned first public concert in the Pleyel salon on 26 February 1832 did not yet create the anticipated breakthrough, either artistically or materially, so that his father, from Warsaw, repeatedly expressed concern for his son's precarious financial situation. Moreover, the severe economic crisis caused by the July Revolution, with the resulting unemployment, diminished hope of acquiring numerous pupils in the very near future. To make this hopeless situation even sadder, in the summer of 1832 a cholera epidemic threatened the capital, so that the financially strong noble and upper-bourgeois families fled to their country estates. Antoni Orlowski, a friend of Chopin's, described the conditions then in a letter from early summer 1832 as follows:

> The situation here looks very bad; misery and distress are widespread among the artists. Cholera causes the wealthy to flee to the countryside.

Chopin felt so depressed that he seriously planned to emigrate to America to seek his fortune there. "Tomorrow I will cross the ocean," he wrote. But the very idea of this plan was to bring Chopin a completely unexpected turning point in his existence as an artist. For the next time he met Prince Valentin Radziwill, who had just arrived in Paris, and told him of his plan, the Prince that very same evening took Chopin along to a reception at Baron Rothschild's. His piano playing that evening so delighted all present that the Baroness Rothschild immediately enrolled as his first pupil. The aristocracy followed her example precipitously, and in a few weeks he rose to be one of the most sought-after men in the French metropolis. Certainly, his external appearance helped make him chosen as the darling of the ladies in the elegant salons. Franz Liszt gives us a graphic characterization of the man and the artist:

> His whole personal appearance seemed to need no commentary in its harmony. His blue eyes were more intellectual than dreamy, his smile fine and mild, never bitter. His complexion was delicate and transparent, his blond hair silken, his curved nose expressive, his figure of medium

height, his limbs delicate. His movements were charming. His voice sounded a bit muted, often almost choked. His posture had such an elegant stamp that he was often spontaneously treated like a prince.

Through the more copiously flowing financial resources, he could afford very elegant clothing to set himself apart from the intentionally negligent demeanor of the Bohemians. And now he also established an apartment decorated in uncommonly good taste, which his friends liked to refer to as "Olympus." And soon he also had a private coach with his own coachman as well as several servants.

Meanwhile, since 1832 his works began systematically to appear in print, including compositions he had begun back in Warsaw and now published in final versions. This led, incidentally, to newer works at times receiving lower numbering in his list of works than those written in Warsaw. In part, he also published them simultaneously in Germany and England as well. The publishers began to badger him, offering him for a few waltzes royalties which a few years earlier were paid to Beethoven for his monumental Ninth Symphony. His concerts too were now reviewed enthusiastically in the press as witnessed by a report in the *Gazette Musicale*:

> It is easier to report about the reception he got, about the rapturous delight he aroused, than to describe and analyze the mysteries of his piano playing, which has no equal in our earthly regions.

Chopin did not, however, like to make public appearances, probably due to his weak touch. The weakness of his sound had already been criticized in Vienna, because the critics and the public had misunderstood his specific kind of interpretation, although it was greatly admired by experts such as Hector Berlioz:

> In the mazurkas, there are incredible details, and Chopin knows how to make them doubly interesting. For he renders them with the very highest delicacy, in *pianissimo*, the hammer hardly touching the strings. One would almost like to

> draw closer to the instrument to be able to listen
> better, as one would do at a concert by fairies and
> elves.

But there were also some musicians who expressly disagreed
with Chopin's interpretation. Thus John Field spoke of a "sickroom talent" and Mendelssohn and Moscheles found his mazurkas "unbearably affected" and with a "sentimentality unworthy of
a cultured person and musician." The Berlin editor and magazine
publisher, Ludwig Rellstab, even spoke of a "vandalism in relation to Mozart's melodies" and a "music from a crude Slavic tribe";
and only after the many positive reviews, notably those by Robert
Schumann, did he remark that in Chopin's concerts an admirably
noble style prevailed. Despite all recognition for his pianistic art
of interpretation, practically all critics agreed that Chopin's main
abilities were on the side of composition.

Since his touch was not acoustically ideal for a large concert
hall, he withdrew mainly to the intimate atmosphere of the salons, which exposed him to a new misinterpretation of being "a
salon musician, a musician for women." In fact, he felt best in
such a circle of admirers and enthusiastic listeners. His dislike for
public concerts had yet another reason, namely, stage fright, which
he candidly admitted to his friend Titus in a letter in 1830:

> You wouldn't believe what torments I endure in
> the last three days before a public concert.

He said something similar to Liszt, who had absolutely no complexes in this regard.

> I am unsuited for concerts. People make me self-
> conscious, their breath chokes me, their curious
> looks paralyze me; I am embarrassed by the many
> strange faces.

This dislike for appearing before a wide audience led to his giving only nineteen concerts in all during the eighteen years he
spent in Paris—a tiny number compared with Thalberg or Liszt.
He could afford this because the income from the publication of
his compositions and the profitable music lessons freed him from
having to earn a living as a virtuoso.

During those first years in Paris, we have no suggestions from Chopin's pen that he in any way felt ill—apart from the fact that in the first months after his arrival in the French capital the depressive mood that had so afflicted him in Stuttgart must still clearly have resonated. This is confirmed by a letter he wrote to his friend Titus on 15 December 1831:

> My health is miserable, outwardly I act happy, but inside something is tormenting me. A foreboding uneasiness, dreams, indifference, desire to live, and then again a longing for death, a sweet rest, rigidity, absentmindedness.

This depressed mood must, in view of his anything but rosy artistic and material prospects, have persisted for yet some time. Physically, however, he seems to have felt in good shape, since in the following three years we hear of no health problems. On the contrary, in September 1833 he reported to the famous cellist, Auguste Franchomme, in a letter: "People say I have gained weight and look good." He said something similar to his friends, too. The composer Antoni Orlowski, for instance, wrote in 1834 after a meeting with Chopin that he was "healthy and strong" and was turning "the heads of all the French women." And Jan Matuszynski described him in the same year to his brother-in-law: "He has become big and strong, so that I hardly recognized him." Nonetheless, we know that Chopin's condition was by no means as stable as could be suspected from such reports. Every winter he suffered from respiratory illnesses which considerably diminished his general health and led to the decision to travel in 1835 to the spa Enghien-les-Bains for a rest, after having spent the summer months of 1833 in Coteau in the Touraine district together with Franchomme for the sake of his weakened health. Decisive for the choice of the spa Enghien was probably the fact that a friend of his, Vincenzo Bellini, whom he esteemed highly as a composer, had settled there, though he died that same year at a young age. The most important event of that summer, however, was his parents' announcement that they would be coming to spend a few weeks at the spa in Karlsbad. Immediately he broke off his stay at Enghien in order also to travel to Karlsbad, where on

15 August 1835 he was able to embrace his parents again for the first time after a five-year separation.

"I feel happy beyond measure....I had always merely hoped, and now this happiness has become a reality! In my joy I embrace you and my brother-in-law as my dearest ones in the world," he wrote full of joy, and no one suspected that this would be the last time they would ever see one another. In this joyful Karlsbad mood, he composed Waltz in A flat op. 34, no. 1; Mazurka in C op. 67, no. 3; and Polonaise in C-sharp Minor op. 26. Parting from his parents after three weeks of blissful family happiness, he first spent a week in Dresden, where he met his former school friend, Felix Wodzinski, who was then staying in that city together with his parents and his sister Maria. At the Wodzinski's house, he met that family again and closer contact with Maria, the Count's only daughter, resulted. To what extent this charming interlude, repeated with romantic embellishments in many biographies, corresponds to the truth cannot be decided with certainty. The only thing certain is that Chopin, motivated by the experiences of this one-week visit, decided to spend a month in Marienbad and in Dresden the following year. The alleged "love of Chopin for Maria Wodzinska" is dated in that time and is even supposed to have led to an engagement "in a gray hour." While the Wodzinski's youngest daughter, Josefa Koscielska confirmed this in her memoirs, this matter was paraphrased much more vaguely, indeed almost mysteriously in the letters of Mrs. Teresa Wodzinska: "Don't believe," she wrote to Chopin in 1836, "that I would like to revoke what I said, oh no; but we must choose the way we wish to go. For the time being I ask you to keep silent; pay attention to your health, for everything depends on that." It is very striking that Chopin corresponded with Teresa, the mother, in a very cordial, indeed almost tender, way, while his few letters to Maria were kept in a rather conventional style. Although no doubt the central figure in Teresa's letters was not Maria but her son Antoni who was distinguished by no especially good character traits and who in Paris repeatedly had to be helped out of financial difficulties by Chopin, still the relationship between Teresa and Chopin gives one pause for thought. The repeated admonition to keep the said "gray hour" a secret, as well as the content of some letters of the older, mature woman to young Chopin cannot always be interpreted to the effect that Teresa regarded the young artist as her fourth child, even though she literally professed this in one of her letters:

> I regret very much that you left us Sunday evening; I was not feeling well that day and could not devote myself adequately to the "gray hour" we spoke of. The next day I had more leisure....Rest assured that I think well of you. However, to test my wishes and feelings, caution is in any case required.

As far as the allegedly promised marriage between Chopin and Maria is concerned, in view of the mores and customs of aristocratic society at that time, it is out of the question that such a match was ever seriously considered. In all the sources at our disposal not a single clue can be found as evidence of a true love between the two young people, and actually neither Maria nor Chopin showed a recognizable emotional feeling from their separation. We will probably never learn what Chopin meant by the label "My Suffering" on the bundle in which he tied together his letters after the final break of his contacts with the Wodzinski family. Certainly, neither the episode in Dresden nor that in Marienbad left any traces in his creations apart from the so-called "Farewell" Waltz, op. 69, no. 1, which he dedicated to Maria before his departure from Dresden in September 1835.

During the journey home, Chopin fell ill and after arriving in Paris in November 1835 he suffered from the symptoms of a severe "grippe" with fever, as Dr. Raciborski, who treated him, discovered. Because his close friend Jan Matuszynski, who meanwhile had finished his medical studies and was a professor at the Medical School in Paris, had temporarily shared Chopin's apartment since the beginning of 1834 and died a few years later of tuberculosis of the lungs at just thirty-three years of age, later biographers assumed that the acute symptoms of the disease with fever, coughing, and allegedly also bloody phlegm were signs of incipient pulmonary tuberculosis in Chopin. Though proofs are missing for such a suspicion, first stated in 1949 by Wierzynski, a few clues point in that direction. First, the sickness in the winter of 1835/36 actually seems to have been of a serious nature, since the rumor of his death soon spread, especially among the Polish *émigrés* and reached all the way to Warsaw. To the relief of his parents, who were scared to death, this rumor was denied by the *Warsaw Courier* in its 8 January 1836 edition. Chopin himself, who during this illness suffered from hearing-hallucinations which gave him the illusion of the ringing of church bells for his impending burial, was extremely depressed and downcast in those weeks, so that he even wrote a last will. After the end of the acute stage, he still felt miserable for a long time. He coughed constantly, often suffered from hoarseness, and lost considerable weight. Even during the following summer of 1836, which he spent in Marienbad with the Wodzinski family, their youngest daughter Josefa Koscielska noticed Chopin's bad state of health:

> He played unusually frequently, without regard for the fact that whenever he got up from the pianoforte, he was always pale and so tired that he did not know what was going on around him, was unable to reply to the enthusiastic praise with a single word, and hardly heard what people were saying to him. He needed a long time to calm down and regain his lost balance. He was in general very sick and nervous, so that on seeing him a person knew that he was one of those chosen by God to die young.

But there is also from Chopin himself a reference to suffering from a severe "grippe" in the winter of 1835/36. For a letter dated May 1837 to Anton Wodzinski, in which he reported of a "recent" grippe during the past winter of 1836/37, states:

> In the winter I was again sick of the grippe. They want to send me to Bad Ems; so far I have no intention of going.

Documentation exists for this serious illness in the winter of 1836/37, establishing beyond doubt the beginning of Frédéric Chopin's tuberculosis of the lungs at least by this point in time. The first certain indications come from Franz Liszt's mistress, the

Countess d'Agoult, who reported to George Sand in two letters dated 26 March and 8 April 1837:

> Chopin coughs with infinite charm....Chopin is an irresistible man; but he is constantly coughing.

The second clue comes from his own hand in the form of a letter of May 1837, to his friend Anton Wodzinski, in which he reports of a doctor's recommendation that he go for treatment to Bad Ems, a favorite spa for persons who had contracted tuberculosis. The doctors, too, must then already have considered him as having tuberculosis. In February 1837 he was bedridden for weeks and extremely weakened by fever and constant coughing accompanied by bloody phlegm. At that time, considerable bleeding from the lungs was occurring, as can be deduced from a recommendation of his doctor-friend, Jan Matuszynski, to swallow pieces of ice during such bleeding. In addition, the doctors treating him prescribed cupping glasses and blistering plasters.

Since, in contrast with the previous winter's "grippe," this time he recovered only very slowly and they wanted to spare him the hot, dry climate of Paris during the summer months, the doctors' advice of a treatment in Bad Ems was very understandable. Instead of this, he resumed his living habits, which were very detrimental to his health, and rather than going to a spa he traveled, on Camille Pleyel's invitation, with him to London—an apparently completely useless journey, during which by his own statements he spent the eleven days "uselessly." Nonetheless, he was introduced in the house of the famous piano manufacturer John Broadwood, where he played in a private circle and was praised in the *Musical World* of 23 February 1838 for his perfect art of improvisation and his extraordinary piano playing as "the most delightful of all salon-pianists." From those days, however, we also have a few important documents of his medical history, showing that his ailment was beginning to take more serious forms. The famous piano virtuoso and composer, Ignaz Moscheles, thus notes in his diary on July 1837:

> Chopin was the only one of the foreign artists who visited no one and also did not want to be visited, since any conversation aggravated his chest ailment.

Felix Mendelssohn wrote in a similar vein in a letter from London, dated 24 August 1837:

> Chopin reportedly suddenly showed up here for two weeks. But he is said to be still very ailing and sick.

And on 1 September Mendelssohn noted that "he was still very sick and unhappy."

From his arrival in Paris until 1837 Chopin was artistically remarkably productive. Despite the influence of the "*style brillant*" in the very first years of his stay in Paris, he had now attained the full development of his ability as a composer. He began to distance himself quite distinctly from the traditional classical forms and to turn to the form of nocturne typical of his style, in which the repeated tonal influence of Polish folk music is recognizable here and there, for instance in Nocturne in G Minor op. 15, no. 3. His most individual creations are, however, without a doubt the mazurkas, in which melodies from Polish folk music are transformed into a stylized dance and whose narrowly limited melodic sequences (*Tonfolgen*) tend to be interpreted as reflections of experienced feelings—of sadness or loneliness. While his mazurkas transmit a lyrical statement, the form of polonaise developed to artistic maturity by Chopin has a heroic character, which "as the symbol of the national spirit and the patriotic struggle for freedom" reflects national traditions as well as the tragic historical events of his fatherland. Chopin, however, also reached back to another genre of piano music typical of the Romantic era, namely, the impromptu and the ballad which as a work of fantasy was subject to no restrictions. Finally, the stylistic change which Chopin underwent during his first years in Paris is most clearly expressed in the form of the scherzo; for the Scherzo in B Minor op. 20 was really one of his first works that initiated the breakthrough in Chopin's compositional activity. Most typical of his break with the foundation of Classicism and his method of dissolving the sonata-cycle is, in this regard, however, without a doubt the Scherzo in B-flat Minor op. 31, which appeared in 1837. This originality of Chopin's in composition and piano playing was recognized very early on and honestly appreciated by his German friends, Ferdinand

Hiller, with whom he traveled together to a music festival in Aachen in May 1834, Felix Mendelssohn-Bartholdy, and Robert Schumann. Schumann, who erected a permanent monument to Chopin in a movement of his *Carnaval* and also met him in person in the years 1835 and 1836, admired not only the lyricism in Chopin's works, but also the powerful dramatic force of some of his compositions. By the frequently quoted words "cannons installed among flowers," Schumann wanted to express "what a dangerous enemy of the mighty Czar and autocrat was hidden behind the seemingly simple melodies of Chopin's mazurkas."

Yet Chopin still had not reached the peak of his accomplishments in composition, for two-thirds of his total works still lay ahead of him and were to originate in the years 1838 to 1847. These nine years of creativity, in which his best works saw the light of day, were strongly influenced by a famous French author, who in Chopin's work can be equated with a symbol, while her real name Aurore Dudevant is known to only a few. Her artist's name, for which she chose the pseudonym George Sand, is on the contrary today still on everyone's lips. Only a few writers have ever had to endure so many negative comments about themselves as that woman, who was accused of lying, immorality, depravity, verbosity, and of whom some doctors spoke with the learned words of "sexual an-aphrodisia," "nymphomania," etc. Meanwhile new, previously unpublished documents and texts have been discovered that provide a more faithful picture of the personality of this "great woman," as the French essayist and philosopher Alain once called her. But the literary historians of our day have also contributed to a more objective image of this writer and deprived some sensational revelations from the life of a *"femme fatale"* of their truth content.

The Years with George Sand

George Sand was born in Paris on 1 July 1804, the last year of the Republic and the first year of the Empire, as the daughter of a Napoleonic officer by the name of Dupin. On her father's side she was a grandniece of Marshal Moritz of Saxony, who in turn was an illegitimate son of August the Strong, King of Saxony and

Poland. It is remarkable enough to have been the grandniece of a real monarch and a descendent of the King of Poland, but on her mother's side, she was, moreover, a cousin of Louis XVI and Charles X and, as if that were not enough, also related to the German Kaiser Wilhelm I and to his grandson Wilhelm II. She was baptized Aurore Dupin, raised in a convent, and in 1821 at only seventeen years of age she was, in her grandmother's will, made the owner of the feudal estate Nohant and the main heiress of a considerable fortune in cash. Disagreements with her mother, who took her along to Paris, led her to believe that the only way to break free permanently was by quickly getting married. So at the age of eighteen she married Mr. Dudevant, a cultivated young man but with an extremely crude disposition. After only a short time, she realized that this marriage was a troubling mistake both intellectually, but above all, also physically. "My heart outlasted my senses, and I turned pale and gave myself with eyes closed," she later confessed in her philosophical novel *Lélia*, which is the single scream of despair of a frigid woman. But even after she began seeking the satisfaction denied her in marriage outside the matrimonial partnership and for eleven years tried love in all its forms, she still met with the same disappointment: "How shall I free myself from the marble that reaches to my knees?" After eight years, during which she became the mother of two children, she decided to free herself from the oppressive bonds of her marriage, which long since no longer was a marriage, and she finally succeeded in getting the divorce she wanted. Both her children and her properties in Nohant and Paris were awarded to her, and soon she was able to demonstrate her writing talent in Paris with the autobiographic novel *Indiana*, published in 1832 under the pseudonym George Sand. To match the masculine first name, she wore men's clothes and a hat under which she could easily hide her hair and she preferably smoked cigars. Thus Baroness Aurore Dudevant became the bourgeois woman George Sand, by far the most successful female French writer of the 19th century.

When Chopin met her in early December 1836 at an evening party given by Liszt, she was already divorced from her husband; indeed, she had separated from him back in 1831. Her

GEORGE SAND (1804-1876). CHOPIN'S COMPANION IN LIFE FOR NINE YEARS.

emphatically masculine way and his sensitivity to cigar smoke at first aroused in Chopin a lively aversion to her, and on the way home he expressed this antipathy to Ferdinand Hiller:

> What a disagreeable woman, that Sand! Is she, then, really a woman? I doubt it!

But within a short time he too was under the spell of this mysterious "woman with eyes of the night," as she was called by her friend Alfred de Musset, the talented young poet, with whom she had a passionate and eventful love affair from 1833 to 1835. Chopin, to be sure, at first made no effort to get close to her. Perhaps what kept him from doing so were the many innuendoes and arguments made against her in the aristocratic and bourgeois society of Paris. Besides the enumeration of her many admirers and friends, among whom were to be found such resounding names as Sainte-Beuve, the "prince of criticism," Prosper Mérimée, the writer, and Alfred de Musset, who was considered the most ingenious representative of French Romanticism, there were, moreover, her friendly relations with the actress, Marie Dorval, with whom she must have had a sexual relationship, according to George Sand research based on a study of the two women's correspondence. An eyewitness report by the French writer, Arsène Houssaye, suggests the same:

> Then Sappho had resurrected in Paris. Every evening after the actress had charmed all hearts with her acting,....she came to her quarters in the little blue, totally upholstered room in which the woman, wrapped in tobacco clouds, awaited her victim.

Most probably George Sand's passionate nature occasionally entered the path to the lesbian garden, but such love encounters were for her merely fleeting episodes, ever compatible with simultaneous love affairs with men. At any rate, contemporary society considered such behavior deviant and perverse, even though some curious ladies of the elegant salons may not have been absolutely disinclined to experience the paroxysms of Baudelaire's "femmes damnées."

So it is not surprising that Balzac, when he saw her in Nohant in March 1837, had the impression that "the type of man she needed was hard to find." George Sand herself was in a serious psychological crisis in 1837. After many disappointments, she was seeking perfect love and the ideal lover, in whose existence she still believed despite all her negative experiences. "If I could submit to a man, I would be saved," she had remarked shortly before. But now after attending several piano soirées at which Chopin played, she felt more and more attracted by the melancholy beauty and peculiar charm of this Polish musical genius. Since at the time he met Sand he seemed mentally and physically severely debilitated by the aforementioned "grippe," it was the motherliness within her that he appealed to. She acknowledged this with the words:

> I have to be able to suffer for someone. I have to nourish in myself this motherly care which likes to watch over a suffering, weak creature.

Vice versa, in his miserable condition he must have seen the being he most needed as a woman with motherly feelings, who moreover seemed to understand the language of his music, which expressed his sorrow. But, though his feeling toward her must have meanwhile changed considerably, he had not given up his cautious reserve during the whole year 1837. Only in the spring of 1838 did he finally become inflamed with love for her, although they both still could not make up their minds once and for all. As Liszt stated in his psychologically interesting portrayal of Chopin's character, it was generally his habit not to reveal what was going on inside him by a single word, so that even when most deeply moved he could merely turn pale with a corpse-like pallor while still maintaining his self-control. Then finally he overcame his inhibitions after all and tried to explain his hesitation to her. Yet the reasons he gave must have puzzled her. For he hinted that he despised sensual desires out of fear that sexual temptations could soil the happiness of them both.

George Sand, in her tormenting uncertainty, consulted Chopin's closest friend and intimate, Count Albert Grzymala, who after the collapse of the Revolution of 1830 had been sent on a diplomatic mission to Paris by the Polish government and had stayed there permanently. In a long-winded report she described to him with astonishing force and candor all the details of her incipient relationship with Chopin and her certainty that in the long run it could not remain platonic. Alluding to Chopin's inhibitions, she wrote:

> Who on earth is the unhappy woman who gave him such impressions of physical love? Did he have a lover who was undeserving of him?

Actually there seems to have been such an "unworthy lover" with whom young Frédéric must have had an obviously bitter experience. For in Chopin's correspondence we find a letter to Kumelski, in which he reported of a Therese who, in his own words, had brought him to the point of no longer daring to taste "the forbidden fruit" for a long time. Whether this experience had to do with his Dresden or Marienbad sojourn with the Wodzinski family is probably a question that can no longer be answered. We do not know what Grzymala answered to her demand that "this angel who has lost his way among us" should accept the right to earthly happiness. But the answer must have been very reassuring to her, for by the beginning of June 1838 she wrote to Grzymala:

> Come to my place, but in such a way that the "little one" does not learn of it. We want to surprise him.

A short time thereafter, Chopin and George Sand presumably became lovers, for in a letter to a friend of hers, the painter Eugène Delacroix, dated September 1838, her happiness can be heard in every line:

> If God sent me death in one hour I would not complain about it, for now I have already been experiencing three months of untroubled happiness.

They had agreed on "the poem of a free association" that soon brought back Chopin's psychological balance. Anyway the hectic Parisian life did not allow much time for reflection. Chopin's entrance into her life also brought her a mental serenity such as she had not known for years.

In October the opportunity for a longer journey together presented itself. George Sand had, as she wrote in her *Story of My Life*, originally planned this journey for the sake of her son Maurice, who suffered from rheumatic ailments, and doctors had recommended the Balearic Islands because of the favorable warm climate. "While I was pursuing this plan," her autobiography reads, "and making my preparations for the trip, Chopin, whom I saw every day and whose genius and character I loved tenderly, said to me that he too would soon be cured if he could be in Maurice's place." As a matter of fact, his friends, fearing that he was suffering from consumption, had long been urging him to spend the winter months in the sunny south. This fear was well-grounded, for since his severe illness during the past winter he suffered from

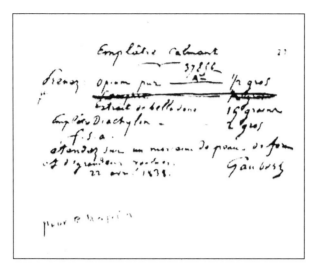

PRESCRIPTION FOR FRÉDÉRIC CHOPIN WRITTEN BY DR. GAUBERT IN PARIS ON
22 APRIL 1838. THE SOOTHING OINTMENT INCLUDES PURE OPIUM, EXTRACT OF
BELLADONNA, AND DIACHYLON.

a chronic cough, copious phlegm, and increasing difficulty in
breathing. George Sand therefore saw the invitation for him to
join them as a chance to be of service for his recovery. Like a
responsible mother, however, she first had him undergo a medical examination by her Parisian physician, Dr. Pierre Marcel
Gaubert, who swore to her on the one hand that he was not
consumptive but on the other confided to her: "You can at any
rate save him, if you give him fresh air, rest, and movement."
This apparent contradiction surely allows for only one interpretation, namely, that by his statement Dr. Gaubert merely wanted to
reassure George Sand.

On 18 October, George Sand left Paris in the company of
Maurice and her daughter Solange in the direction of Perpignan,
where they arrived safely on Tuesday, 30 October 1838. Chopin
set out from Paris only on the morning of 27 October and arrived
in the late afternoon of 31 October in a good state of health,
"fresh as a rose and rosy as a beet." It is astonishing that he
survived so well the nine hundred kilometers from Paris to
Perpignan without interruption in somewhat more than four days

and four nights on rather bad roads covered with pot holes and it represents an admirably withstood test of strength for this delicate, weakly artist. To estimate this achievement of a patient manifestly suffering from tuberculosis of the lungs, one must picture what a journey by express coach meant at that time. Resting places with overnighting possibilities were pre-planned for mail-carriage travelers; but for the postilion of the express mail, only one goal mattered, namely, the punctual delivery of the mail according to a fixed timetable. Every twelve kilometers the change was made with already harnessed horses, a process that lasted hardly more than one or two minutes. Nor was a longer stop foreseen for loading and unloading the mail bags, which would have allowed time for eating or even for sleeping. It thus seems important to point out what endurance Chopin, though already suffering from pulmonary tuberculosis, showed, when drawn by the joy of seeing a beloved person again.

On 1 November the little group reached Port Vendres by mail coach, and from there on the next day they reached Barcelona on the ship "Phénicien." The travel schedule then finally provided for them to reach Palma di Mallorca on the "Mallorquin" only on 7 November, where their first disappointment awaited them. Despite a long quest, not one hotel could be found to give them lodging; and so they provisionally had to settle for two private rooms above a noisy barrel-maker's work shop. Only the French consul's intercession made it possible to rent a whole house from a Señor Gomez and in addition to find a small temporary lodging about which George wrote enthusiastically to her friend Mrs. Marliani:

> Besides, two miles from here I have rented a cell
> belonging to the large monastery Valdemosa for
> thirty-five francs, consisting of three rooms and a
> garden with lemon trees.

Chopin too seemed to be feeling splendidly as is shown by a letter of 15 November 1838 to his friend Julian Fontana, who since fleeing from Warsaw in 1830 was then living in Paris as a piano teacher:

THE VILLA "SON VENT" ON MALLORCA TODAY IN ITS ALMOST UNCHANGED CONDITION. HERE CHOPIN'S TUBERCULOSIS TOOK ITS DECISIVE TURN FOR THE WORSE IN THE WINTER OF 1838/39.

I am in Palma amid palms, cedars, cactuses, aloes, and olive, orange, lemon, fig, and pomegranate trees...in short, among all the trees found in the greenhouses of a botanical garden. The sky is turquoise-blue, the sea lapis lazuli, the mountains emerald and the air like paradise....Oh, my friend, I am revivified! I am close to the most beautiful thing the world has to offer. I am feeling better.

But just a few days later the looming crisis struck. The exertions of the last weeks and the start of torrential rains lasting for two months caused a relapse of Chopin's "bronchitic symptoms," which tormented the patient with coughing day and night. George Sand was apparently not aware of the seriousness of the situation. For in a letter to Grzymala of 3 December 1838 she added the post-script:

> Chopin was sick recently. Now he is feeling much better, but he is suffering a little under the frequent temperature shifts.

The truth looked a lot different, as we gather from Chopin's letter to Fontana, sent the same day; its content sounds far less reassuring:

> In recent weeks I was sick as a dog! Despite balmy 60 degree temperatures, despite roses, orange, palm, and fig trees, I had caught a cold. Three doctors, the most famous ones on the whole island met in consultation. One smelled what I spat out, the other tapped here, and the third felt me and listened while I spat out. The first claimed I would die; the second, that I was already dying; and the third, that I was already dead. But I cannot forgive Jash [Jan Matuszynski] for not having given me any instructions for the case of an acute bronchitis which he would always have had to suspect in me.

This report shows that the doctors called in by George Sand because of Chopin's terrible general state—for he lay in bed with high fever and incessant coughing—were indeed already familiar with the modern investigation methods of percussion and auscultation—tapping and listening to the chest—but still could make little of the phenomena observed thereby. Otherwise it would be inexplicable that after a thorough examination of the patient they diagnosed not pulmonary tuberculosis but consumption of the larynx. As an excuse on their behalf, however, it must be granted that the method of percussion of the chest, invented in 1761 by the Austrian physician, Dr. Leopold Auenbrugger, took almost five decades before it finally gained general acceptance despite silent opposition and contradiction. As the son of a simple innkeeper in Steiermark, who was led to his percussion method by the simple custom of innkeepers to check the quantity of wine in their barrels by tapping them, he apparently did not have the necessary eloquence to convince the learned men of the first

Vienna Medical School, such as van Swieten or de Haen. Only when the French clinician Jean Nicolas Corvisart published a French translation of Auenbrugger's *Inventum novum* of 1761 was the spell finally broken. Since Spanish doctors also probably were able to get their hands on this French version only after some delay, their inadequate practical experience with this method is understandable. The same is true of auscultation, which was developed by the important French physician René Théophile Hyacinthe Laennec and published in 1819 under the title *De l'auscultation médiate*. This method, too, was still in its infant stage in the days when Chopin was being examined on Mallorca, since decades of pathological-anatomic comparative studies were necessary to systematically coordinate the findings that were heard with corresponding changes in the lung. But what made Chopin dubious was not just the lack of knowledge of these methods of investigation and the strange diagnostic conclusion obtained thereby but also the treatment measures recommended by these doctors in the form of diet, blistering plasters, poultices, and, above all, bleedings. He promptly resisted any bleeding therapy and the application of blistering plasters, as we again learn from the aforementioned letter to Fontana:

> Only with effort was I able to prevent them from bleeding me and applying vesicatories and blistering plasters, and thanks to Providence today I feel as usual.

This determined rejection had its good reason in the fact that in his youth he had had to watch how his sister Emilia, with tuberculosis of the lungs, was literally treated to death with bleedings and leeches. Here it should also be mentioned, to exonerate the doctors, that influenced by French medicine they were convinced adherents of so-called "Broussaiism." François Joseph Broussais, who died in 1838, was a fanatical advocate of the use of leeches to draw blood for the most varied diseases, and at that time he exerted a strong influence on medical thinking in France. The massive bleedings he recommended sometimes reached an alarming scale and had disastrous effects on many patients. But fortunately they were soon brought back to a reasonable scale by the

victorious advance of homeopathy. George Sand, too, stood firmly
against the proposed bleeding therapy, though less from knowl-
edgeable medical considerations than out of an instinctive attitude. Even when told by the doctors that a bloodletting would
save the patient and that he would die unless she gave her consent, she persisted firmly in rejecting the idea. In her book,
A Winter in Mallorca, she commented on this:

> However a voice said to me even in my sleep: "A
> bloodletting would kill him, and if you preserve
> him from it, he will not die." I am convinced that
> this was the voice of Providence.

An aggravating factor for Chopin's condition was the fact that
the "house of winds," as the villa rented from Señor Gomez was
called by the local inhabitants because of its loose construction,
was cold and drafty in the rainy season and the walls soon became covered with fungus under the strong rain. Since there
were neither stoves nor fireplaces in this house, coal basins had
to be lit and their choking smoke added intensity to the poor
patient's coughing. So the coal basins were removed. And with
complete rest and the application of a few poultices, the fever
began to decline. Although still extremely weak, Chopin had
survived this first great crisis more or less well.

But soon a further misfortune appeared. For when the doctors learned that Chopin was suffering from tuberculosis, the surrounding populace became suspicious and almost hostile in their
attitude of rejection. When Señor Gomez learned that a man with
tuberculosis was living in the rooms of his villa, he fell into virtual
panic and wrote a letter demanding in no uncertain terms that his
house be vacated in the shortest possible time and that he be
paid the cost for renovating the whole house and the price of the
linens used. Gomez based this brutal eviction on Chopin's having a disgusting infectious disease that threatened his children's
life. In his fear he even wanted to go so far as to charge George
Sand for the furniture they had used, so that he could have it
burned. She described the reaction of the local inhabitants to
Chopin's tuberculosis as follows:

> From then on we instilled horror and disgust in
> the populace. They were convinced that we were
> afflicted with consumption of the lungs, which,
> given the Spaniards' experiences with epidemics,
> is synonymous with the plague.

The news of Chopin's tuberculosis spread due to the doctors' official report to the mayor after the examination. In this regard, it must be pointed out that at that time every doctor in Spain was legally bound under the threat of losing his medical license and of very high fines, indeed even a prison sentence, "to report all consumptive patients and all deaths from consumption."

Since even for gold they had no hope of finding lodging even for a single night, the French consul Fleury offered them a temporary place to stay in his house, until after the diluvial rains stopped and they could move to Valdemosa. By a fortunate circumstance, a married couple living in that monastery suddenly had to leave the country, probably for political reasons, and they were willing to sell their furniture, including a local—rather shoddy—piano. Chopin wrote to his friend Fontana about this upcoming move to the monastery:

> In a few days I will be living in the most beautiful
> part of the world; the ocean, the mountains…
> everything one could want. We will have our quar-
> ters in a large old dilapidated Carthusian monas-
> tery…near Palma. Nothing could be more
> wonderful: arcades, very poetic cemeteries. In
> sum, I feel that here my health will improve.

Unfortunately this expectation was not fulfilled. For very soon torrential rains began again, and the constant dampness was not exactly suited to making the stone-floored former monastic cells a pleasant or even a healthy habitation for a person in Chopin's condition. On top of all this, the stove, which had hastily been given a fresh coat of plaster, gave off, when lit, a nauseating odor that irritated the air passages and aggravated Chopin's coughing again. Difficulties in obtaining food also set in. The peasantry soon learned that the new dwellers in the lonely, remote monastery had to rely on them to satisfy their daily needs, and since the news had spread that they did not attend church, they decided to exploit the awkward situation and sell them their vital necessities only at exorbitant and usurious prices. As believing Christians, they also saw nothing wrong with such behavior.

All these complications and repeated mishaps swiftly worsened the state of Chopin's health. Fever, coughing, and bloody sputum had so weakened him that he was hardly able to leave his cell. "I can't sleep, all I do is cough and for a long time now I am covered with blistering plasters," he wrote on 14 December 1838 to Fontana. But subsequently he recovered enough to be able to play on the piano and he was also thinking again of composing. He reported of this apparent improvement to Fontana on 28 December:

> It is not possible for me to send you the preludes. They are not yet finished. As far as health, I am doing better.

Just imagine under what unsatisfactory local conditions he resumed his work on the preludes, despite his gravely damaged health. George Sand gives a graphic description of this:

> He bore the pains very bravely; but he could not control the uneasiness that gripped his mind. For him the monastery was full of ghosts and horrors....When I returned from the evening strolls I took with the children amid the ruins, I found him at his piano, pale, hollow-eyed, his hair literally standing on end. It took some time for him to recognize us....Thus he created the most beautiful of those little pieces which he modestly called "Preludes." They are masterpieces....Among the preludes is one that he conceived on a dismal rainy night and that plunges the soul into horror. Maurice and I had left him that day, since he was feeling tolerably well, to go to Palma to buy things necessary for our household. It had been raining hard, the brooks were swollen over their banks....The

coachman had abandoned us, and finally we arrived back at Valdemosa late in the night after incredible difficulties, without shoes....When he saw us enter, he jumped up with a loud scream; then he said with a confused countenance and strange voice: "Ah, I knew very well that you were dead." Later he admitted to me that while waiting for us he had seen everything in a kind of dream, and since he had no longer been capable of separating dream from reality, he had calmed down and as it were lulled himself by playing the piano, convinced that he himself, too, was dead. He saw himself drowned in a lake; heavy ice-cold drops of water fell in a uniform rhythm on his breast.

Three preludes have been mentioned in the literature as possibly the one in question: no. 6 in B Minor; no. 8 in F-sharp Minor; and no. 15 in D flat, and the last is probably the right one. Besides the preludes, in Valdemosa he also worked on the second ballad, the third scherzo and the two polonaises, in F-sharp Minor and in A flat. George Sand soon realized that the longed-for stay in Valdemosa was becoming "in many ways a fiasco" for all concerned. Nor did she hide the disastrous consequences for Chopin's health and mental state:

> Our stay at the hermitage of Valdemosa was one single torment for Chopin and me....There could be no more delicate, selfless, truer and more loyal friend than he....Unfortunately also no one more unbalanced, and more entangled in strange fantasies....He was innocent in everything, for all that was a consequence of his sickness. He gave the impression as if his psyche had been skinned alive.

In all these difficult situations, George Sand behaved admirably at his side, and her concern and love during his sickness truly deserves the highest recognition. Her great wish to be a protectress and a second mother to him was fulfilled in Valdemosa for the first time.

In view of the mortally ill state in which he had to spend the last weeks almost without any treatment, they sought any opportunity to return to France. George Sand was, of course, aware that this return trip with all its difficulties would involve considerable risk for him, and so she was plagued with grave qualms of conscience:

> Our patient did not seem strong enough to withstand the crossing, but he also seemed just as incapable of enduring another week on Mallorca. The situation was terrible; there were days in which I lost hope and courage.

Finally, when the weather improved, on 12 February 1839 she decided to set out for Palma, where with the return of beautiful days the ship resumed its daily crossing to Barcelona. Even the short three-mile journey on bad roads was made under grueling conditions, since "no one wanted to lend us his carriage. We had to make the trip in a rented wagon without springs, so that Chopin was spitting blood terribly, when we arrived in Palma." But the crossing on a small freighter also was hazardous enough to further weaken the patient's already catastrophic condition. The captain of the "Mallorquin" was at least as afraid of the danger of infection as Señor Gomez had been and so he provided the patient the worst and most remotely located cabin, which he had to accept for lack of any other possibility. Moreover, pigs were being transported on the ship that day and they were seasick and spread a horrid stench. According to Spanish custom they were therefore whipped by the ship's crew through the whole crossing since otherwise they allegedly would have died from exhaustion. This noise and the loud, pained shrieks of the poor animals was almost unendurable for Chopin's sensitive nature and he spat "wash basins full of blood," as George Sand reports. In her anxiety on arriving at the port of Barcelona, she begged the commander of a French warship "Méléagre," lying at anchor there to be allowed to take Chopin aboard, where he was touchingly cared for by the ship's doctor and the captain. In a few days, the sick man recovered from the hemorrhaging, which meanwhile was brought to a stop. The result of the naval doctor's examination was reported to Paris by George Sand:

> The ship's doctor examined Chopin and reassured me concerning the coughing of blood, which still continued and finally came to a halt this past night in the hotel. He said that he had an extraordinarily tender lung; there was no cause for despair, and given rest and care he would soon regain his weak health.

This letter written on 15 February 1839 to the Countess Marliani was mailed from the hotel in Barcelona where they had to await the arrival of the "Phénicien," which was not scheduled to leave for Marseilles until 25 February. Before leaving Spanish soil they had another annoyance, this time with the owner of the hotel. Like Señor Gomez, he too wanted to draw financial advantage from Chopin's sufferings by trying to charge extra for the bed the patient had slept in. Beside herself with rage, George Sand vowed in her whole life never to speak another word with a Spaniard. She wrote:

> Anyone who coughs is considered consumptive in Spain, and whoever is consumptive is treated like a plague-ridden, scabby leper....For they believe that consumption is infectious and that the sick person must be killed just as two hundred years ago the mentally ill were eradicated. What I am saying is literally true. In Mallorca we were treated as pariahs.

These harsh words referred, of course, mainly to the insults they had had to endure in Mallorca where on their strolls they actually were "persecuted by people throwing stones." But they do not take sufficiently into account the fear of infection and of falling ill of consumption of the lungs, which then was snatching away so many people in the blossom of their years, not only in Spain. For the doctors were quite helpless until finally, after the discovery of

the pathogenic agent of pulmonary tuberculosis by Robert Koch
in 1882, this scourge could be brought under control step by step.

At last, on 25 February 1839 the hour arrived when the trip
home could be continued. Chopin survived the thirty-six-hour
journey to Marseilles very well and he was awaited on the dock
by François Cauvière, Professor of the Medical Faculty of Marseilles
and Chief Surgeon of the hospital there. Cauvière, who enjoyed
an outstanding reputation as an excellent clinician, was at first
very worried by the patient's serious condition. But when from
day to day a visible improvement set in, he believed himself justified in excluding tuberculosis of the lungs. Full of confidence,
George Sand therefore informed the Countess Marliani on 5 March:

> Chopin is now doing much better....On his face I
> noticed that he was not very worried and has no
> doubt of the success of his treatment.

Chopin, too, was in an optimistic mood and wrote to Julian
Fontana on 7 March:

> Embrace Jash and tell him...I am coughing only a
> little in the morning and I am still not at all consid-
> ered a consumptive. I drink neither coffee nor
> wine, only milk, I keep warm and I look like a
> young lady.

These lines confirm that Cauvière's plan of treatment was aimed
mainly at strengthening the quite weakened patient and consisted,
besides strict confinement to his bed, mainly of dietetic,
hydrotherapeutic, and medicinal measures. This is confirmed by
a report of Chopin's dated 12 March to Grzymala in Paris:

> My state of health is getting better from day to
> day. The blistering plasters, the diet, the pills, the
> baths, and—more than anything else—the infinite
> care of my angel [George Sand] have put me back
> on my feet, on somewhat emaciated legs.

Again and again he mentioned with gratitude his "angel's self-
sacrificing care," as in the following lines of the letter describing
the bad situation in Valdemosa:

She had to care for me all by herself, for God
preserve us from the doctors there! She made my
bed, cleaned my room, prepared the medications,
and gave up everything for my sake.

The incompetence of the doctors consulted in Mallorca must in
fact have been horrifying, for we know from Sand's book *A Win-*
ter on Mallorca that one of these doctors had an assistant who
was so filthy that Chopin did not let him feel his pulse!

Within a few weeks Chopin's ailments clearly diminished. He
was developing an appetite and he joyfully noticed a steady weight
gain, and so by the end of March he could write to his friend
Fontana:

I am doing much better, I am beginning to play,
eat, walk, and speak like other people.

He wrote something similarly to Grzymala, and everything indicated that his bad mental state and the humiliations endured in
Mallorca had played an essential part in his miserable condition
there, for these things had struck and wounded him in his deepest soul. In the pleasant surroundings in which he now found
himself in Marseilles, his cultural interests revived, whether it was
his ideas on composition or his lively interest in George Sand's
works, for she was now passing the time in Marseilles working
on an ingenious study of Goethe, Byron, and the Polish writer
Mickiewicz. Chopin's improvement continued, and his state of
health was finally so strengthened that in May he could even dare
go on an excursion to Genoa, which, despite a violent storm on
the return journey, he survived surprisingly well. The only mental shock during his three-month stay in Marseilles was the news
of the death of his friend, the singer Adolphe Nourrit, who committed suicide in Naples. Chopin played the organ at his funeral
mass.

At the end of May, Dr. Cauvière finally gave permission for
Chopin to continue on the journey to Paris, but not without first
giving strict instructions that he was to spend the summer of 1839
at George Sand's country estate Nohant in the region of Barry.
When they arrived in Nohant in late afternoon on 1 June, all
friends in the vicinity showed up to greet them. Most of them

were seeing the famous Frédéric Chopin for the first time. However, after all the indescribable hardships of the past months, a
beneficial melancholic peace now descended on him from the
tall trees of the parklike garden of this comfortable country
mansion.

Nohant and Their Parting

In Nohant, because of Chopin's state of health as a chronic
patient, Dr. Gustave Papet, a country doctor, who was a friend of
George Sand's, took over his further medical care. Papet, who
was very wealthy and who carried on his practice only for the
poor and for his closer friends, was a very caring and insightful
doctor for Chopin. After a first examination, he reassured George
Sand that the patient showed no signs of a lung ailment and
merely had a slight chronic inflammation of the larynx. Since it
can hardly be assumed that Papet was not convinced of Chopin's
pulmonary tuberculosis, his trivialization of Chopin's disease may
have served the purpose of putting the mistress of Nohant at
ease. For the peaceful country life, the regained joy in work, and
Chopin's gradual recovery were reasons enough to look optimis-
tically into the future. For the first time in his life Chopin had
something resembling a home of his own, where he felt secure.
He went strolling a lot, played music industriously, and enjoyed
taking part in a quickly improvised theater, where he again displayed great acting talent such as he had demonstrated in his
youth by various arts of imitation.

A drop of bitterness fell into this idyll—at least for George
Sand—from the realization which began to dawn on her that her
desperate quest for the perfect lover was threatening to fail once
again. For Chopin's chronic illness imposed a reserve bordering
on abstinence, which no doubt was a severe test for this passionate young woman. Since we know that during the eight years of
living together with Chopin she persisted in faithfulness to him,
her motherly feeling seems to have gained the upper hand over
her passionate feelings:

After the stay in Mallorca…I was moved internally by a serious problem. I asked myself whether I should favor the idea of binding Chopin's life with mine….I was blinded by no passion. I felt for the artist a kind of very lively, truly motherly adulation.

Yesterday's lover thus was to be spoiled like a third child in the family and live in a domestic atmosphere where he could realize his creative ideas and dreams. Chopin seems to have approved the new situation, for from then on he called George Sand almost only "hostess," "mistress of the house," or "Mrs. Sand." Probably the decision on this new modus operandi was made as early as eighteen days after their return from Mallorca, as the significant date of 19 June 1839, written on the wall in her room next to the left window suggests. Since she burned all her love letters and not a single line from Chopin about his relationship with her has come down to us, it can no longer be verified whether she then actually filled only the role of a maternal caring nurse and "denied" herself sexually, which incidentally, according to her own words, supposedly meant a great torment to Chopin. This last statement does not seem quite credible; for Chopin, as is known, never was an artist of the sort plagued by sexual desire; rather, he was one of the spiritual or "seraphic" poets, as Heinrich Heine once expressed it.

Chopin then used the solitude of country life at Nohant copiously for composing. He first busied himself mainly with the Sonata in B-flat Minor op. 35, which French interpreters like to call the "*Sonate funèbre*" [Funeral Sonata], since the funeral march completed in 1837 comprises the core and point of departure of this work. Whereas in Beethoven's case we know exactly for whom he was grieving in his funeral march, the Sonata in A flat op. 26, in Chopin's case we have not a clue. But we would not go wrong to presume that his funeral march must have sprung from patriotic feelings. His disinclination to share his inner experiences with others, here too allows for only vague suspicions, as was confirmed, among other things, by George Sand:

> Chopin speaks little and seldom about his art....He
> even remains reserved in the circle of those clos-
> est to him and confides solely in the piano.

Besides the sonata, he also finished the nocturnes, op. 37, as well
as the mazurkas, op. 41, but then the monotonous life in the
country gradually began to make him restless. Thus in October
1839, physically recovered and animated by the wish to resume
his old living habits, he started out for Paris, where meanwhile his
friend Fontana had rented a new room for him.

Arriving in Paris, he was immediately again drawn into the
whirlpool of the social life of the capital, so that he rarely found
time for personal contacts with George Sand, who had also rented
an apartment nearby. Since they both soon began to suffer from
their separation, Chopin moved in with her in the Rue Pigalle,
where he lived in one of her pavilions. George Sand devoted
herself more strongly to her auctorial inclinations, associated in
her house with the most varied representatives of literature and
art, such as Honoré de Balzac or Eugène Delacroix, and most
recently was completely filled with a particular passion, namely,
socialist mysticism. The cause for this passionate interest in politics may have resided in her compulsory sexual "castigation" due
to Chopin's chronic illness.

> Since it was impossible for her to feel absolute
> love for another man, she loved man as such, man-
> kind.

Moreover, in early youth she had felt drawn to the ideas of Jean-
Jacques Rousseau.

Besides lively cultivation of social life in the Parisian salons,
Chopin again began giving piano lessons. All his activities should
not mislead one to draw the false conclusion that his physical
condition was in the best shape. Especially during the winter
months his state of health worsened considerably, and his well-
known clinical symptoms again made themselves more strongly
noticeable. His pupil Friederike Streicher, a German girl, in her
diary under October 1839 described Chopin's physical condition
very clearly:

> He scheduled two hours of instruction per week,
> excusing himself in advance if he should have to
> change the day and hour of the lesson due to his
> sickness.

And in another passage she noted:

> Ah, he was so ailing, weakly and pale, coughing
> much and frequently taking opium drops on sugar
> or syrup, rubbing his forehead with cologne, and
> yet he taught with admirable patience, endurance
> and zeal.

But he himself reported of morning fits of coughing with sputum
of phlegm and pus, which may possibly have been caused also
by a secondary bronchitis of unspecific nature. This chronic coughing at times apparently took almost unbearable forms, although
he seemed to assign little importance to that circumstance:

> I am suffering from an unbearable cough, which
> is however nothing extraordinary.

It is astonishing that he could give his lessons under such condi-
tions, though at times they reached the limit of his endurance.
His pupil, the famous pianist and later publisher of his works,
Karol Mikuli, described this as follows:

> A sacred zeal for art inflamed him, every word
> from his lips was exciting and inspiring. Often
> individual lessons lasted for several hours in a row
> until exhaustion overpowered teacher and pupil.

Despite it all, he found sufficient time and strength to compose the works that originated in the years from 1839 to 1841,
from the Sonata in B-flat Minor, op. 35, to the three mazurkas of
Opus 50. This series contains, among other things, the second
and third ballads, three polonaises, the third scherzo, as well as
various nocturnes and mazurkas. Finally, now and then he appeared in public concerts, and each time critics found words of
complete praise. The most essential statements related to the
difference in style of interpretation between Chopin and Thalberg
or Liszt, which the reviewers noticed to the effect that the other

virtuosos mainly sought to achieve orchestral effects on the piano, while Chopin's advantage lay in subtle nuances and in his unequaled timbre.

Since 1839 Chopin lived in Paris only during fall and winter months, while in spring and summer he preferred to stay in Nohant, where he could compose undisturbedly in peace and quiet. From the summer of 1841 we hear from George Sand: "Chopin just keeps on coughing," and he himself remarked in a letter that as a rule it took him until ten in the morning finally to finish coughing. Nonetheless, the artist should not be pictured as a constantly seriously ill patient. Rather, relatively long phases with general absence of ailments alternated somewhat equally with phases of acute complaints. Such acute aggravations were then also mostly characterized by bloody sputum, as Chopin reported in a letter to his banker Auguste Léo from 1841: "I spit out blood, and my doctor has forbidden me to speak." On the whole, a steady, though often almost unnoticeable progression of his chronic lung ailment was unmistakable.

Previously, as can be gathered from various statements of Chopin's, apparently Jan Matuszynski, a friend from his youth, had usually acted as his medical adviser, but at the beginning of 1842 he put himself under the care of Dr. Adam Raciborski, who was widely known in Paris and especially familiar with lung diseases. The reason for this must have been that Matuszynski, who since 1841 had been living together with Chopin on the Rue Pigalle, was likewise severely ill. Whereas Chopin at first wrote to Camille Pleyel: "I am doing better, but I feel very weak and am going to bed," indicating a new worsening of his condition in the winter of 1841/42, we learn from a letter of April 1842 to Grzymala not only that he was still not doing very much better, but at the same time also that his friend Jan lay ill:

> All day long I have to lie in bed, my mouth and glands hurt so much. If tomorrow Raciborski allows me out (Jash has already been bled and he is bedridden himself), I will drive over to see you right away.

How hard it was at that time to accomplish such a purpose, is shown by the very next letter to the same addressee:

> I would have driven to your place, but that is possible only very early in the morning, and by the time I finish coughing it is already ten o'clock.

Nonetheless, the year 1842 began under a good star in an artistic sense, for despite his weakened condition, Chopin was able, on 21 February, together with a friend, the cellist Franchomme, and the recently married singer, Pauline Viardot, to present a very successful concert. He was affected all the worse on 20 April by the death of his bosom friend, Jan Matuszynski, after repeated hemorrhages. This death was a real blow to him. The emotional shock contributed not merely to a further deterioration of his general state of health, but it also led to a deeply depressive mood, so that George Sand decided to leave with him for Nohant as swiftly as possible, where different surroundings might distract him from the place of the grizzly event. The loss of Jan, with whom the few memories of their common youth and their native Warsaw linked him most intimately, aroused in him death fantasies like the one he had previously experienced. On 11 August 1841, he wrote from Nohant to Julian Fontana in Paris:

> I once dreamed I had died in a hospital, and that is as vividly present to me as if it were yesterday.

With the help and consolation of friends who had accompanied him to Nohant, Delacroix and Witwicki, as well as Pauline Viardot-Garcia, Chopin gradually regained his inner calm and he again began to devote himself more intensely to composing. Works that appeared that summer were Opus 50 to 54: three mazurkas, the Ballade in F Minor, the Polonaise in A flat, the Impromptu in G flat and the Scherzo in E.

Nonetheless, in the fall he was still emotionally not up to returning to his old apartment in Paris and so Fontana found new lodgings for him, separated from George Sand's apartment by only one house, in which lived their common friend, Charlotte Marliani, the wife of the Spanish consul. In the summer months he devoted himself mainly to composition, while in Paris he was occupied mainly with piano lessons, as well as many social obligations which he eagerly met. Meanwhile, however, his illness had progressed so far that every slightest bodily exertion brought him considerable breathing difficulty and therefore as early as the winter of 1843/44 he had to be carried up the house stairs. An eyewitness, namely, the sister of Chopin's pupil Gutmann, described this as follows: "To have climbed the stairs would have been impossible for him, even with assistance." Here it must be mentioned that his condition that winter was particularly worrisome and that just about no one got to see him, as Heinrich Heine reported in 1847 in *Lewalds Theaterrevue*.

The year 1844 seems in any case to have brought an improvement, as we are again informed by an entry in the diary of his pupil Friederike Streicher:

> At the end of 1844 I came to Paris several times
> and found Chopin looking somewhat stronger....
> His friends were then hoping for a recovery of his
> health or at least a significant improvement of how
> he felt.

Some claim to see in *Berçeuse* op. 57, which originated at that time, how sick and weak its creator already was. Lenz, who on Liszt's recommendation wanted to enroll as Chopin's pupil, describes him as follows:

> A young man of medium height, slender, consumed
> by care and of uncommonly elegant Parisian ap-
> pearance.

He had no idea that the composer often, out of weakness, had to give the music lessons not sitting, but lying on a divan. If he did not agree with a pupil's execution, he got up briefly to model the passage in question, and then he lay down on the divan again.

On 3 May 1844, Chopin was struck a further severe blow of fate by the unexpected death of his father. With him he lost his spiritual support and the fatherly friend who stood at his side with advice and deed in every emergency. How despairing and downcast he was for weeks and what anxious states of mind tormented him was described impressively by George Sand in her *Story of My Life*:

> He became visibly more miserable, and I knew of no means to combat the growing overexcitation of his nerves. The death of his friend, the medical doctor Jan Matuszynski, and, shortly afterwards, that of his own father had been terrible blows for him. Instead of picturing these pure souls in a better world, he had only dreadful visions. I was forced to spend many nights in a room close to his, always ready…to chase away the specters that pursued him in delusion and sleep. The thought of death was for him bound up with all the superstitious ideas of the Slavic legendary world….The ghosts called him, grabbed at him…and he shrank back from their fleshless faces and tried to ward off the choking grip of their icy hands.

When George Sand realized how severely Chopin was suffering from the loss of his father and that he was not even able to write in person to his relatives in Warsaw, she wrote to his sister Ludwika Jedrzejewiczowa asking her to visit them in Nohant after she had written a rather reassuring letter to his mother. To Ludwika, however, she wrote:

> You will find my dear child very ailing and completely different from the time you last saw him; but do not be too alarmed at the state of his health. He has remained essentially the same in the more than six years in which I have been seeing him daily. Every morning a rather strong fit of coughing; every winter two or three greater crises, lasting however only a few days; and from time to time neuralgic pains—that is his usual condition. Otherwise his lungs are healthy and his delicate constitution without serious damage. I still am

hoping that in time he will get stronger, but I am at least certain that with an orderly way of life and appropriate care he will survive like anyone else.

Chopin himself saw things quite similarly, when he remarked:

I have outlived so many stronger and younger people that I almost consider myself immortal.

The joy of seeing his sister again gave him renewed energy. When Ludwika, who together with her husband, spent a few weeks in August and September at Nohant castle, returned to Moscow, Chopin accompanied them to Paris, from where he reported in the best of moods to George Sand on 23 September 1844:

I say only that I am well and remain your most fossilized fossil, Chopin.

Apparently his tuberculosis of the lungs remained relatively quiet at this time. No doubt the moderate, pleasant climate of Nohant had a favorable influence on the course of his sickness, which George Sand repeatedly emphasized:

Two weeks of beneficial warmth are worth more to him than all medications.

But when Dr. Papet, on the occasion of a medical examination in 1845 declared Chopin's organs healthy and believed he noticed in Chopin's complaints "a tendency to hypochondria," this certainly did not agree with the truth. But that his mental attitude influenced his subjective sense of wellness considerably is beyond any doubt and can be seen from the way he regained courage and strength from the visit by his beloved sister, so that George Sand also confided to her:

I assure you that you are the best doctor he ever has had, for it is enough just to speak of you to give him back the desire to live.

The winter months in Paris became increasingly more burdensome to him. At that time he felt worried mainly about a peculiar inner coldness, so that in a melancholic moment he once said: "I will probably be able to warm up only in the grave." For

that reason the doctors strictly instructed him to wear warm clothing and apparently he followed this advice meticulously. A letter
of 5 December 1844 reported whimsically of a common lunch
with friends, one of whom had a fat little son with him:

> He was rosy, fresh, warm, and had bare little feet.
> I was yellow, wilted, frozen through, and wore
> three layers of flannel under my trousers.

The winter of 1844/45 was especially harsh and cold in Paris. A
wave of influenza raced through the capital and Chopin fell ill of
a severe bronchitis, which probably must be interpreted in the
framework of that kind of viral infection as nonspecific.

After the diagnosis of Dr. Papet, who, in George Sand's words,
"palpated and auscultated him with the greatest care and found
all organs completely healthy," George Sand lost her confidence
in this doctor. Chopin now consulted a certain Dr. Molin, a homeopath, toward whom he developed confidence. At this time the
homeopathic school, whose founder Samuel Hahnemann was living in Paris, stood at the very peak of its reputation in the French
metropolis, although there were serious doctors, such as Gabriel
Andral, who could not believe that the effect of a useful drug
could be intensified by infinite dilution. In artist circles, such
controversies were unknown and so they continued undeterred
to hold to their faith in homeopathy and often even went one
step further by changing from the path of conventional medicine
to magnetism. Such magnetic methods of healing as were practiced with special success in Paris in those days by the charlatan
Koreff also enjoyed the greatest popularity. Although those kinds
of treatment could achieve no objective effect, at least they were
completely harmless, which probably cannot be said of the approach followed by the Parisian orthodox school of a Broussais,
with its hunger cures and massive bleedings. Molin's symptomatic measures, at any rate, seemed to have had a mitigating effect
on Chopin's increasing ailments, otherwise the patient and George
Sand would not have called on his assistance so often. A few
such swiftly scribbled notifications from the years until 1848, which
a messenger had to deliver to him, read: "Dear Doctor, would
you come and visit Chopin, who although he is at this moment

not in so severe a crisis as last year, has been suffering from a severe cough and great breathing difficulty," or: "My dear Doctor, Chopin has caught a horrible cold and has been coughing terribly for two days. Bring him something for relief and come this morning!" The patient himself also occasionally scribbled down a few words hastily on a scrap of paper, as a message to Molin: "Dear Doctor. Be so good as to visit me today. I am suffering." Although we have no knowledge as to what kind of medications were prescribed, Dr. Molin in any case did not do without opium as a cough-suppressant. This is clear from two letters that allude to such application: "I believe that my drug tones me down too much; I will ask Molin for a different medication," Chopin wrote on 26 November 1843 to George Sand, which simultaneously confirms that Molin must occasionally have been consulted earlier. In a letter of George Sand's, in turn, it is said:

> We ask you to help us. Mr. Chopin has sent for
> his medicine bottle, but the druggists refused to
> refill it without a prescription.

During the summer of 1845, in addition to a few mazurkas, he composed the Barcarole op. 60, which is convincingly free of any premonition of death and, rather, lets the joy of life break forth in an overpowering way. The strictly rhythmic form and the title of the work often led to picturesque intentions being heard in this music such as the rendition of rowing movements, which naturally must be left to the subjective perception of each individual. In truth, we know as little about Chopin's motives for his compositions as about his mode of creation itself. If we believe George Sand's description, his way of working at composition was rather complicated and toilsome:

> Chopin's creation was direct and miraculous. The
> ideas came to him at the piano unsought and sud-
> denly, or they hummed around in his head during
> a walk, so that he had to hurry home and make
> them audible on the instrument. But then began

> the most painstaking work I have ever seen! A
> series of exertions, doubts, and impatient attempts
> to rediscover and capture certain details of what
> he had heard internally....He shut himself up in
> his room, walked back and forth, broke his pens
> in two, repeated and changed a hundred times....
> Thus he could at times spend six weeks on a single
> page, only then finally to write it down exactly the
> way he had put it on paper the first day.

Subtracting poetic frills from this report, the impression remains that Chopin worked at his compositions extremely critically and occasionally also with great doubts.

The summer of 1846 in Nohant was so beautiful that a similar one could scarcely be remembered, and as to his health Chopin seemed to feel correspondingly well, although he usually felt too weak to take part in the excursions to the closer vicinity of the manor. "I did not go along, for these things tire me more than they are worth," he wrote on 11 October 1846 from Nohant to his relatives in Warsaw, and he also seemed to be anticipating the coming winter with a certain anxiety, as the same letter shows:

> I feel quite well, for the weather is beautiful. Win-
> ter is not getting such a bad start, and if I spare
> myself, it will also go by like the past one. God
> grant that it does not get worse!

He did not yet know that it was the last summer he was to spend in Nohant when he returned to Paris in November 1846—alone as usual. For in these months the situation in George Sand's house was undergoing some difficult changes. Besides her six-teen-year-old daughter Solange, who had till then been living in a boarding school, she received into her house a distant relative called Augustine Brault, who soon became engaged to her twenty-four-year-old son, Maurice. In this way two hostile camps arose, since Sand always preferred her son Maurice, whom she loved tenderly, while Chopin, who believed that the many years of living together with George Sand gave him the right to interfere in family matters, sided with the temperamental Solange. On top of that, came Chopin's increasing irritability and jealousy, for he longed to be everything for George Sand and did not want to accept that "the true source of her strength flowed from her son," or a certain increasing cooling of George Sand's relationship to Chopin. Despite his neat appearance, the chronically ill, irritable artist, with his frequent fits of coughing, accompanied by abundant phlegm, necessarily was becoming more and more of a burden, although her tender motherly love for him was as deep-rooted now as before and she had remained a faithful companion despite many years of abstinence. That this had not been a sacrifice for her can be seen from a letter of 1847, which she wrote with remarkable candor to their common close friend Grzymala:

> For seven years I have been living like a virgin with him and the others. I have grown prematurely old, without it having cost me any effort or sacrifice, so much was I surfeited with passions and robbed of illusions....I knew that many accuse me; some saying that I exhausted him with my tumultuousness, others saying that I drove him to despair with my mischievous pranks....He, in turn, complains to me that I killed him by denying myself to him, whereas I would surely have killed him, had my behavior been different.

At that time, when dark clouds were beginning to tower over Nohant, a new novel by the authoress appeared, *Lucrezia Floriani*, and its publication elicited mixed reactions. For many believed they could recognize in it autobiographical features that would allow the conclusion that George Sand wanted to tarnish Chopin's personal image and character. Indeed, they virtually accused her of having so freely expatiated on the secrets of her private life in these autobiographical depictions for the express purpose of causing the break with Chopin, whom she had tired of. However, such an insinuation lacks any objective foundations. For we know from Delacroix that she wrote this novel, which Heinrich Heine called a "divinely written romance," at the same time as she was still living closely with Chopin, and that before its publication she had read it aloud to Chopin in full length. He had not for a moment gotten the idea of seeing it as a copy of their relationship, and so George Sand can probably rightly be believed that she wanted to mirror neither herself nor Chopin in the characters portrayed in the novel.

Undeniably, her great love cooled under the burden of repeated disagreements and family tensions. Painful scenes between Chopin and Maurice occurred more and more often, and in their reconciliation she more clearly than ever used to side with her son. But ultimately Solange's behavior was more decisive than anything else for the irremediable and final break between George Sand and Chopin. She had become engaged with Fernand Préaulx, a poor nobleman from the neighborhood of Nohant and in February 1847 she arrived in Paris together with her mother to prepare for the wedding, of which Chopin too approved. But now Auguste Clésinger, a "former dragoon, who had become a great sculptor," was supposed to make a bust of mother and daughter. On that occasion Solange became his lover, and when George Sand withheld her approval for their marriage, he forced her to give her consent by the brutal threat of abduction. Maurice, who was staying in Paris and had regular contact with Chopin, then received the following notification from his mother: "Not a word of all this to Chopin; it is no concern of his." When the young couple, who were married on 6 May and one day later thrown out of the house because of a violent dispute with George Sand, drove to Paris to Chopin, he found out that this time he had been bypassed and out-trumped. In his sympathy for Solange, whom he had always liked, he openly sided with her in a letter to George Sand, and this led to the final break in August 1847. As several letters show, George Sand was convinced that Chopin's protection really stemmed from a love for Solange that had long been germinating. "The mere sight of her and he dares to do anything, he breaks everything apart with imperturbable calmness," she wrote to Emmanuel Arago, and in that light Chopin's conduct amounted to a spiritual betrayal. Her letter, kept in a cutting tone, which Chopin never answered, closed with the bitter words:

> Farewell, my friend, may you soon recover from all your ailments, and I hope so now; and I will thank God for the grotesque end of a nine-year exclusive friendship. Let us hear from you now and then. It is useless to come back to the other matter.

We will probably never fathom the secret of the love in Chopin's heart for George Sand. Certain is only that by speaking up for Solange, who was an egoistic person thinking only of her own advantage and who knew how to entice him with her coquetry, he lost a true friend in George Sand. Simultaneously this brought an end to the happiest period of his life, in which he could pursue his composition work undisturbed, for from now on his life meant just vegetating along. It is worth noting that there are proofs that George Sand was still interested in him and still thought of him in a heartfelt way. But he too could never banish her

GEORGE SAND'S FAREWELL LETTER TO CHOPIN ON 28 JULY 1847. SHE FEELS THAT HE HAS ENCROACHED UPON HER AUTHORITY AND DIGNITY AS A MOTHER. ALTHOUGH SHE FORGIVES HIM BECAUSE HIS "COMPASSION IS SINCERE," STILL THE BREAK IS FINAL.

completely from his heart, as is proven by the fate of those locks of hair she had once given him and which he moved each year from the old notebook to the new one—including his last one from the year 1849!

The Last Years

Chopin's state of health deteriorated steadily from then on. In 1846 he was already so gravely ill that they seriously feared for his life, but in early May 1847 there was a new worrisome advance of the disease. Eugène Delacroix jotted in his notebook under the date of 9 and 10 May:

> The poor child has been ill for a week, indeed very gravely ill. At the moment he is doing a little better....This morning I went to Chopin's and was not received.

These attacks, generally called a "grippe" or an "asthma attack," sometimes subsided again after just a few days. Apparently this time after hardly a week he began feeling distinctly better. Gradually he seems almost to have grown accustomed to it, for in December 1847 he reported to his family in Warsaw:

> This winter is not so bitter. There are many cases of grippe, but my coughing has become habitual for me, and I am less afraid of the grippe than of cholera. Now and then I sip at my little bottle of homeopathic medicines, give many piano lessons at home and so manage to keep my head above water.

He expressed himself similarly to Solange:

> I cough and am all taken up with my piano lessons. I go out but little, for I find it cold outside. Aside from this I have my usual breathing complaints.

After the break with George Sand he remained alone for the short remainder of his life and had to rely completely on his own resources in such situations, more or less at the mercy of whoever his servants happened to be at the time. According to a description by his pupil, G. Mathias, Chopin's external appearance then was a "painful sight. His stride became dragging, his back was bent, the head pushed forward." Moreover, during the coughing spells, which often lasted for hours, he could hardly speak. He became more and more aware of how hopeless his condition was and how closely death loomed. His letters to Solange from November and December 1847 give alarming expression to his trouble in breathing, as when he complains: "I am choking, my head hurts," or, "I am choking and wish you all conceivable happiness." All biographies agree that his suffering's final turn for the worse coincided chronologically with the definitive separation from George Sand. From that moment on, his life's path led steeply downward.

In February 1848 there came a new advance of illness, as we learn from a letter to Solange:

> Since your last letter I lay in bed for several days
> with a terrible grippe and gave a concert at Pleyel's.

This concert took place on 16 February and was his last one in Paris. Artistically it was a triumph for him, but physically it almost exceeded his strength:

> The maestro played with his usual mastery and
> bravado, as at his earlier concerts, but at the end
> of his performance he was then in the artists' ward-
> robe so exhausted by the excessive physical and
> mental exertion that he was almost close to faint-
> ing.

But by March he had recovered enough to leave the house and even to climb the stairs with his servant's assistance. We can draw this conclusion from an incident that occurred on 4 March 1848. For on that date George Sand and Chopin met—for the last time in their life—purely by accident in the lobby of the Countess Marliani, a mutual friend, and Chopin communicated the following information to Solange:

> I said "Good morning," to your Lady Mother, and
> my second words were, whether it was long since

CHOPIN'S LETTER TO HIS MOTHER ON 11 FEBRUARY 1848. IT STATED "I HAD THE GRIPPE, WHICH INCIDENTALLY EVERYONE AROUND HERE HAS, AND IF I AM WRITING ONLY BRIEFLY TODAY, IT IS SIMPLY BECAUSE MY THOUGHTS ARE COMPLETELY ON MY CONCERT..." THIS WAS SURELY AN UNDERSTATEMENT OF HIS SERIOUS CONDITION.

she had gotten a letter from you. "A week ago," she answered...."Then I inform you that you are a grandmother. Solange has had a little daughter." Then I said farewell and went down the stairs....But I had forgotten to tell your Lady Mother that you are well...so I told Combes [his servant], since I was unable to drag myself back, to go up and tell your Lady Mother you are well, and the child likewise.

This letter is evidence that apparently he could climb stairs only with his servant's assistance and that even then it must have been possible only with great effort.

Slowly financial worries also became pressing, for the doctors' and druggists' bills, the servants, his carriage, and the expensive salon life swallowed considerable sums of money. His entire hope was now England, where he saw his only chance to improve his precarious financial situation in view of political events in France. As early as April 1848, he therefore dove into the "abyss called London" after the Poles had already left Paris in March hoping that the hour of freedom had struck for their homeland. After the catastrophe of 1831, the Polish people had been left with only the Republic of Krakau as their last remnant of an independent state, and now in 1846 a rebellion began in Galicia and Posen. Social divisions weakened the forces attempting this revolt and so it met with failure. As a result, Krakau too, as the starting point of the Polish Revolution, was deprived of its independence and annexed to the Austrian monarchy in 1846. But, the real heart of the revolutionary movement in Europe, from which the conflagration spread, was incontestably Paris. There the July Revolution of 1830 had sowed the seeds for a strong opposition by two decisions that continued working constantly below the surface. First, it had at the last moment deflected the development to a republic—something which had been quite within the realm of possibilities. And, secondly, it created the monarchy of King Louis Philippe, which exemplified an upper-bourgeois class rule, hardly to be outdone later. But Paris, the city of the Jacobins and their successors, had the forces needed by any revolution, namely, revolutionaries. For in Paris, any revolution might get support from the workers, who stood in the tradition of the Jacobins and represented an element of unpredictability in every political upheaval. The events of February 1848 actually were determined by such unpredictability through the intervention of the masses. On 24 February bloody clashes occurred between the army and rebellious masses of people, and the uprising got out of control, forcing Louis Philippe to resign and flee abroad precipitously. In the proclaimed provisional government, besides the leftist Republicans, the socialists with Louis Blanc were also represented, and their primary objective was to achieve a social revolution. But since the bulk of the petit-bourgeoisie were not willing to support socialist experiments, the moderate Republicans came out with a two-thirds majority in the elections on 23 April and the social revolution seemed defeated from the start. This led to a renewed uprising of the masses of craftsmen and workers of Paris in June 1848, the first socialist uprising in Europe. It was put down bloodily by the military on 26 June and, with its three thousand dead, went down in history as the bloodiest revolutionary event of the 19th century.

More and more people were leaving Paris because of these political events, which extended over half of Europe and left almost untouched only the marginal regions of the continental European core, including Great Britain. Besides the politicians, many artists also abandoned the French capital and chose the way to England. Chopin was among these artists. Two of his pupils, the "Scottish ladies," Jane Stirling and her sister Lady Erskine, had urged him to make this journey, which was very much to his liking because of the revolutionary turmoils that had broken out in France. After crossing the Channel without getting seasick, he arrived in London on 20 April 1848.

Jane Stirling and Lady Catherine Erskine occupy a special position among the women who played a kind of protective role for Chopin. Immediately after his break with George Sand, Jane concerned herself with him in a touching way. Nor did she abandon him when most of his friends had left Paris during the cholera epidemic in the summer of 1847 and after the February revolution of 1848. Since Chopin was feeling especially miserable and ill at that time, he had to rely particularly on this woman's self-sacrificing and concerned care. Now, too, these two ladies tried with all their strength to make his stay in England as pleasant as possible. On 21 April, a day after his arrival in London, he wrote to Grzymala:

> The two Erskines had thought of everything, even
> of chocolate, but especially of an apartment, al-
> though I intend to move.

The reason he gave for always changing apartments was that in London everything was so expensive. The two ladies, of course, immediately began organizing an ever-increasing number of social gatherings. These appearances in various salons brought him honorariums and helped him obtain pupils for lucrative music lessons. Jane Stirling also saw to it that a suitable piano was always at his disposal in his apartment—for a time there were even three pianos at the same time, namely, a Pleyel, an Erard,

and a Broadwood. Thus the rumor is not surprising that he had
intended to marry Jane Stirling in the near future. He commented
on this in a letter to Grzymala:

> They might as well marry me right away with
> death....One may be poor only alone; for by twos
> it is the greatest misfortune. I would like to die in
> the hospital, but I would not want to leave a wife
> behind in misery. Actually I feel closer to the cof-
> fin than to the marriage bed. I have resigned
> myself....I don't even know how to sing in the
> house anymore.

With this resignation, his creative energy also dried up, for it had
previously been maintained only by his memories of his Polish
homeland and was additionally paralyzed by the failure of his
people's striving for independence in those days. This can be
seen from a letter of 13 May 1848 to Grzymala, expressing his
thoughts and his bitterness:

> The terrible news from the Grand-Duchy of Posen
> reached me here....Misfortune upon misfortune!
> My soul takes pleasure in nothing more.

How much the exhausting social obligations affected his weak,
disease-consumed body was reported in a letter of 2 June 1848 to
his friend Grzymala:

> If I had not been spitting blood for a few days, if I
> were younger, the memory of the past would not
> depress me so much, for I could perhaps begin a
> new life....My good Scottish ladies show me so
> much friendship. But they are accustomed to roam
> and wander around London all day long with their
> calling cards, and they would like me to go visit-
> ing all their acquaintances—and yet I am just barely
> alive.

In early July, he sent two more letters to the same addressee,
replete with the same desolate mood:

For hours I feel better, but often in the morning I think that I am coughing out my soul....I can no longer be sad, nor glad, I have completely exhausted my feelings and am merely vegetating and waiting for it to come to a quick end.

In this condition, early in August he followed Jane Stirling's invitation to Scotland, where he lived in various houses and performed a public concert in Manchester on 29 August 1848. Besides the merits of his piano playing, the *Manchester Guardian* also referred to his worrisome physical condition:

Chopin appears to be about thirty years of age. He is very spare in frame, and there is an almost painful air of feebleness in his appearance and gait. This vanishes when he seats himself at the instrument, in which he seems for the time perfectly absorbed.

This description accorded perfectly with Chopin's health at the time, as we can gather from his communication to Grzymala of 18 August, that is, in the month he spent in Calder House near Edinburgh as a guest of Lord Torphichen, a relative of Jane Stirling's:

The climate does not agree particularly with me. Yesterday and today I have been spitting blood, but in my case that doesn't mean very much, as you know.

In a letter mailed to his friend Fontana on the same day, he adds:

I can hardly breathe any more; I am about to kick the bucket; and you are surely getting balder and balder and will yet bow your bald head over my grave....I am vegetating and patiently awaiting winter.

He felt most well in Edinburgh with Doctor Lyszczynski, a homeopath who cared for him with the greatest diligence and in whose house he found a hospitable resting place. This physician had come to England as a Polish refugee, had studied medicine in Edinburgh, also had married there, and in this way had become a regular Englishman. Although the treatment failed, these days meant a resting place on his journey to Scotland. Chopin was so weak by then that Dr. Lyszczynski had to carry him up the stairs every time; but in view of the patient's body weight of hardly more than a hundred pounds this must not have required too much effort. Even before the fireplace he was still trembling with cold and only at the piano could he gradually warm up by his playing. In Edinburgh he also met again with the Czartoryski family and was given valuable moral support in the person of Princess Marcellina, who enjoyed his full confidence. This had a soothing effect on his mental state and was a help in mobilizing his depleted energies for his concerts. At the concerts in Manchester, Edinburgh, and Glasgow, to be sure, his soft and weak playing was nonetheless noticed, and so people were not as delighted with his playing as formerly. Before his concert in Edinburgh, Jane Stirling was therefore worried of not being able to sell all the tickets, and to spare Chopin the depressing impression of a possibly half-empty hall, she bought up the remaining tickets herself to distribute among her acquaintances and friends.

The exertions resulting from moving around restlessly from city to city and palace to palace with his "Scottish ladies" increasingly became an unimaginable burden for him—after all, during his eight-month stay in England he changed quarters more than sixty times. It is hard to grasp how in his run-down state he was able to withstand the hardships of the journey at all, including a carriage accident without serious injury. Moreover, there were the incessant deadlines, which were set for him in an imperious manner, as well as the evening socials at various Scottish princely manors, where he was bored by people's exaggerated concern. But above all he felt more and more unspeakably alone. He could never relax and breathe a sigh of relief, not to mention compose, and he suffered from his tormenting coughing with accompanying bloody phlegm, which he tried to fight with lemons and ice water. He also suffered from increasing difficulty in breathing. On 1 October 1848 he described his condition to Grzymala:

I am feeling weaker, and can compose nothing. This whole morning, for instance, I was unable to do anything until two o'clock, and when I get dressed, everything bothers me, and so I pant until dinner, when one has to sit with the men for two hours....Then my good Daniel carries me upstairs to my bedroom, undresses me, brings me to bed, lights the candles—and now I may catch my breath and dream until the moment when the same thing starts all over again.

At the end of October he returned to London, where on the first day he was prostrated by a violent "catarrh attack." On 30 October 1848, one day before his return journey, he reported from Edinburgh:

On the return journey from Hamilton palace...I caught a cold and have not gone out for five days. I am living here with Dr. Lyszczynski, who is treating me with homeopathic methods. I don't want to go visiting anywhere else.

We learn about the further course of this "cold" from a letter to Grzymala from London, dated 18 November:

I have been ill for eighteen days, not leaving the house at all; I had such a catarrh attack, with headache, breathing difficulty, and all my bad symptoms. The doctor (Dr. Mallan, a homeopath) visits me every day. He has restored me so much that yesterday I was able to play at the Polish concert and ball (a splendid affair); but immediately after my playing I returned home and could not sleep all night. I am suffering from a severe headache, besides coughing and breathing difficulty. Till now the dense fogs have not started, yet despite the cold weather I have to leave the windows open in the morning in order to swallow some air.

This Dr. Mallan was acquainted with his "Scottish ladies," and his wife was a niece of Lady Gainsborough. How miserable Chopin must then have felt is shown by the aforementioned letter of 30 October, in which he remarked in full knowledge of his situation:

> On the day I received your dear good letter, I made a kind of inventory of my things in case I should perish somewhere.

After his return from Scotland, new symptoms announced the beginning of the end of his disease, namely, a swelling of the legs, which he himself attributed to a "neuralgia." Shortly before leaving for Paris, he told Solange in a letter of 22 November 1848:

> I am leaving for Paris tomorrow; I can barely drag myself and I am weaker than I have ever been. The doctors here are chasing me away. I am completely swollen with neuralgia, can neither breathe nor sleep and have not left my room since 1 November.

Because of the acute change for the worse he was examined before leaving for France by Sir James Clark, Queen Victoria's personal physician, a famous tuberculosis specialist, apparently after having first consulted several other doctors in London. Chopin reported on the result of this consultation with James Clark as follows:

> Sir James Clark, the Queen's personal physician, visited me a while ago and gave me his blessing. I am choking in Scott's beautiful country—maybe I will get my health back.

This last sentence shows that he was still deceiving himself about the seriousness of his condition and held hope of recovery, as is typical of consumptives. He wrote to Grzymala:

> One more day here and I will be not exactly dead, but crazy. My Scottish ladies are getting on my nerves....Today I lay in bed almost all day, but the day after tomorrow at this hour I am leaving London, this dog of a city....I ask you to take care that

the bed linens and pillows are dry, so that I can warm up after my arrival....And on Friday order a bouquet of violets so that the parlor will have a good aroma.

On 23 November, Chopin left London and he arrived in Paris the next day. With dismay he learned that Dr. Molin, his physician of many years, had died during his stay in England. Chopin had special confidence in this homeopath, since he apparently knew how to deal correctly with him psychologically, as can be seen from a letter to Solange Clésinger dated 30 January 1849:

In recent days I was much too sick to write to you....Here we are having real March weather. So I have to lie in bed ten times per day. Molin alone had the secret of getting me up again. For two months I had Mr. Louis and Doctor Roth; now Mr. Simon, a very famous homeopath, is treating me again; but they do a lot of guessing and are no help. They all agree about the climate, taking it easy, and resting. I will have rest someday even without them!...I will try to be more intellectual in my next letter, after some "sulfates" or other that Mr. Simon will give me to inhale.

Of all these doctors who stood at Chopin's bedside, among whom a certain Dr. Fraenkel should be mentioned, Dr. Pierre Charles Alexandre Louis was without a doubt the most serious authority in the field of pulmonary tuberculosis. When Chopin told him how the deceased homeopath Molin had helped him, Louis replied that this had not been achieved through the particular methods of treatment but through omitting various blood-removal methods prescribed by the academic medicine of that time. But since a man with the medical qualifications of Dr. Louis also could not help him noticeably, Chopin soon returned to the homeopathic doctors with whom he was familiar and in whose hands he felt safer. But gradually his confidence even in them seems to have declined, as his description of Dr. Fraenkel and his uncertainty proves:

> He has again stopped his tisane [an emulsion of
> medicinal herbs] and prescribed a different medi-
> cine; again I do not want to take it, and if I ask
> him about hygiene, he says that I need no regular
> way of life. In a word, he belongs in an insane
> asylum. All joking aside, perhaps he is a very
> good consultation doctor, like Koreff, for example,
> but he has no consistent line of action in his mind
> as does Koreff.

From these lines, but also from other sources we learn that among
the "no less than fifty doctors who struggled with Chopin's weak
health during his short lifetime," one was the Serapion's brother
and magnetizer David Ferdinand Koreff. The description of his
homeopathic doctor continues:

> My Jew, Fraenkel, has not been here for a week
> now; he did not insert any more pieces of paper
> in my urine after all. He told me of an Englishman
> he saved from cholera with a medicine which the
> reactionary French government did not even per-
> mit him to introduce.

And when Fraenkel finally gave up completely, Chopin said the
reason was "that he had finally realized there is something beyond his knowledge. Left to myself, I will perhaps recover more
quickly."

Among his other homeopathic doctors, there was a relatively
great number of German doctors. Aside from Dr. Gruby they
included the aforementioned Dr. Roth, who occasionally had to
endure critical remarks and many a joke from his patient. This
same Dr. Roth was once lampooned as "the mocker from Lyon"
by Heinrich Heine. The violinist Ernst had given the poet a magnificent bar of salami to deliver to his physician Dr. Roth, but
Heine and other hungry travelers ate the whole thing on the way
except for one paper-thin slice. Heine then wrote the following
accompanying note for the doctor:

> Your researches have determined that millionth
> parts show the greatest efficacy. Receive the mil-
> lionth part of a Lyonese salami, given to me by
> Mr. Ernst for you. If homeopathy is true, it will
> have the same effect for you as a whole salami.

On the severely ill Chopin's changing state of health during
the winter months of 1948/49, aside from numerous entries in
Eugène Delacroix's diary, we get a revealing picture from a letter
of the singer Pauline Viardot to George Sand, dated 15 February
1849:

> You ask me about Chopin's condition. His health
> is slowly deteriorating; there are better days when
> he can drive out in the carriage, and others when
> he spits blood and suffers from choking coughing
> attacks. He no longer goes out in the evening.
> But he can still give a few lessons, and on good
> days it even happens that he is happy. That is
> how it looks now. Incidentally it is a long time
> since I have seen him.

The daguerreotype of Chopin taken at this time conveys the sick
man's pitiful situation impressively by the tired resigned-looking
facial expression, the languid position of the body and arms, the
eyes sunken deep into their hollows, and the clothing too large
from his loss of weight. Especially striking in this picture is the
vertical fold in the forehead typical of depressive persons.

"Chopin is prevented by his ailment from interesting himself
in anything, never mind working," Delacroix noted in his diary
on 29 January 1849. And in fact composing was becoming more
and more difficult for him. Most of what he created during the
last two years of his life he destroyed again and finally he admitted "not being able to write a single note more. Only two mazurkas have been preserved: no. 2 in G Minor op. 67 and no. 4 in
F Minor op. 68. More and more he lost all hope of ever being
healthy again. In a phase of despair he wrote:

> Am already at the end of my life. I've reached the
> fourth doctor; they charge me 10 francs per visit,
> sometimes come twice per day, and all that with-
> out giving me any considerable relief. I hope that
> the springtime sun will be my best doctor.

And it actually achieved a minor miracle. From his new apartment near the Champs-Elysées, which permitted him a marvelously beautiful view of Paris, in spring on beautiful days he was
able to ride out to the Bois de Boulognes a few times, and already
a new optimism germinated in him:

> I feel stronger because I am eating well and have
> thrown away the medications.

Especially beneficial were the visits of friends, above all of
Grzymala, the princely family Czartoryski, Countess Delfina
Potocka, the Franchomme family, Gutmann, Pleyel, and Delacroix.
Then it could happen that he told them full of joy:

> Thank God, I have no fever, which dejects and
> annoys all decent doctors.

And he began planning new concert tours.

Of course, piano lessons and, even more, concert tours were
out of the question due to his illness, and since his scanty mon-
etary reserves were soon exhausted, a further misfortune was
imminent, namely, a financial catastrophe. When Jane Stirling
heard of these difficulties, she tried diplomatically to send him
25,000 francs through his housekeeper, wisely knowing that his
pride would never have allowed him to accept such a generous
contribution. For very obvious reasons, however, this money did
not reach Chopin. Only after engaging the psychic Alexis was it
possible to discover the location of this considerable sum and to
transfer it to Chopin, although he at first did not want to accept it.
Finally he decided to keep half of the amount after all, hoping to
be able to return it later.

In early spring a cholera epidemic broke out in Paris and the
majority of his friends fled to the country, so that Chopin was left
behind almost alone with his servant. When Solange, with whom
he was then corresponding a great deal, learned of the bad state

of his health, she invited him to her house in Guillery. But he could not accept this offer, since he was physically no longer up to leaving Paris. In June he was assailed by a new violent coughing of blood, as we learn from a letter to Grzymala of 22 June 1849:

> Last night I hemorrhaged twice. Today, however, I did nothing and was spitting blood, but already much less.

At the same time there came a great swelling of the legs, though it must not have persisted long. For by 2 July he reported to Grzymala:

> Since yesterday I have not been spitting up any more blood—the swelling in my legs has gone down—yet I am still weak and lazy; I cannot walk—I gasp for breath—and your stairs!!!

In view of this ominous development, Chopin decided at the end of June finally to inform his relatives in Warsaw about the seriousness of his sickness, after having previously always spared them about his condition. With an intimation of his imminent death, in a letter dated 25 June 1849 he asked his sister Ludwika almost pleadingly to come to him in Paris:

> My life, if you are coming, then come! I feel weak and no doctor will help me as you do....If you are short of money, I will lend it to you. Once I am feeling better, I will easily earn it and give it back to the one who lent it to you; but now I am too poor to send it to you....My friends and all other well-wishers believe that Louise's [Ludwika's] coming would be the best medicine for me...I don't know myself why I have such a desire to see Louise near me, but it is as if I were pregnant!...I hope that my letter for Mother's name day arrived, so that I was not missing from your midst. I don't want to give any thought to all that, for otherwise the fever will seize me right away....Your faithful, but weak brother.

Ludwika immediately applied for a passport, but the matter was delayed so long that she did not arrive in Paris with her husband and daughter until August 19. Meanwhile in July 1849 a completely new symptom appeared, signaling the beginning of the approaching end, namely, diarrhea. It was not so massive as to be attributed to cholera, then still rampaging in Paris. Chopin's statement to Grzymala, dated 10 July, points in the same direction:

> I have some sort of diarrhea. Yesterday I consulted Cruveilhier, who has me ingest almost nothing, but only has me sit quietly.

Jean Cruveilhier, who numbered among the famous personalities of the 19th century and was considered a particularly competent expert in the field of stomach and intestinal diseases, among other things, actually prescribed nothing but rest and the ingestion of a harmless sulfur mixture. At the same time he explained to the patient the nature of his disease and the best possibilities for treating it. Whether he pointed out the circumstance that these diarrheas were probably caused by the spread of tuberculosis to the intestine, is not known to us. The only thing certain is that he told the patient he was suffering from consumption.

A few weeks later Chopin was hardly able to speak loudly and audibly any more, so that at times he could communicate only with sighs and gestures. Possibly this was conditioned by the spread of tuberculosis to the larynx, an event that occurs quite often when an active or "open" pulmonary tuberculosis has existed for a rather long time. However, the losses of fluid, with the resulting desiccating phenomena, may additionally have made speaking difficult, as earlier could frequently be observed in persistent diarrheas, especially when accompanied by other factors, such as severe sweating spells. Chopin was affected by this very thing in those stiflingly hot days in Paris during the summer of 1849, when he had to spend the greatest part of the day in bed with fever and "sweated thick drops behind the heavy bedcurtains."

Ludwika, aware of the seriousness of the situation, in a last desperate effort to save him, in early September called for a consultation between the most important doctors in France, Jean Cruveilhier, Pierre Louis, and Jean-Gaston Blache, the most famous doctor for childhood diseases at that time. Chopin seemed to place his greatest hopes precisely on the last-mentioned doctor, for he said: "He will most likely help me, for there is in me somewhat of a child." We learn, among other things, the results of this consultation in a letter to Franchomme of 17 September 1849:

> As far as I am concerned, I feel worse rather than better. The gentlemen Cruveilhier, Louis, and Blache held a council and decided that I must not travel, but rather should take a room with windows facing south and stay in Paris....I love you, and this is for now all I can tell you, for I feel close to fainting from weariness and weakness.

Furthermore, the doctors determined that the patient's condition was hopeless.

At the end of September, he made the move to the "apartment at Place Vendôme Nr. 12, which was more expensive but met all conditions." There he was now tended by his sister with untiring concern. She was assisted by the fellow caretakers most welcome to the patient: Princess Marcellina Czartoryska and Adolph Gutmann, but many others from his great circle of friends also offered their services with heartfelt sympathy. Meanwhile the disease had progressed so much that in the first days of October he could no longer sit up in bed without recourse to a nurse's help or supporting cushions. He had also become too weak to write letters to his friends and acquaintances and his voice was lost more and more in an unresonant whisper.

Chopin's death is described in many reports, partly very embellished and often contradictory, based almost exclusively on more or less questionable eyewitness accounts. The reason for the strikingly divergent statements of persons present during Chopin's last hours is that a huge number of persons were admitted to his dying chamber and many of them later wanted to emphasize how closely they were associated with the composer during his lifetime and how very much he wanted precisely them by him in his last moments. On the other hand, some were present who in their later reports wanted to underscore especially their own personal merits—whether of a friendly or a spiritual kind. After all, Chopin's dying seemed to have been a kind of social event, and to be in attendance at it must have been of special interest to the ladies, as can be gathered from Pauline Viardot's letter to George Sand:

> All the great ladies of Paris felt obligated to faint in his room, where a group of artists quickly drew sketches, and a daguerrotypist even wanted to place the bed by the window so that the dying man would lie in the sunlight.

It is therefore today hardly possible to reconstruct the last days and hours of Chopin's life accurately in all details. The only certain thing is that Poland's great son breathed forth his soul at 3 A.M. on 17 October 1849. His pupil Gavard's report, though meanwhile also doubted on some points, probably comes closest to the truth, when he writes:

> The whole evening of 16 October went by with the praying of litanies, Chopin remaining silent. Only by the congestion in his chest could one recognize that he was still alive. On that long evening, two doctors examined him. One of them, Dr. Cruveilhier, took a candle and held it close to Chopin's face, which had already turned black from the most recent suffocating spells, and he remarked to us that the senses were already failing to function; but when he asked him if he was suffering, we heard still very distinctly the answer: "No longer." That was his last word. He died without torment between 3 and 4 o'clock in the morning, surrounded by faithful friends, countesses and princesses.

Far less credible is the report in a letter from the priest, Alexander Jelowicki, to the wife of a well-known, wealthy property owner, which was published in the *Illustrierte Zeitschrift* of the year 1897. This letter was concerned most of all with emphasizing his own

FRÉDÉRIC CHOPIN ON HIS DEATHBED, WITH HIS SISTER LUDWIKA AT HIS SIDE.
PAINTING BY TEOFIL KWIATKOWSKI.

merit. This merit consisted in having convinced Chopin, who at first refused both confession and the sacraments, finally after all to receive the holy sacrament on his deathbed. The flowery embellishment and strange anecdotes drummed up in this writing were supposed to prove to posterity that Chopin breathed forth his life happily and gratefully in the bosom of the Catholic Church and could hardly wait to be united with God.

Even more strange seems the description of Chopin's last moments in a letter from Gutmann, his pupil and friend, to a songstress in Mannheim:

> At the last grave moment when his soul was already turning toward the countenance of the Almighty and he no longer had the strength to open his eyes, he asked, "Who will lift my hand?" When he recognized my voice, he wanted to lift mine to his lips, we embraced and he pressed a farewell kiss on my cheeks with the words, "Cher ami!!!" His head sank, and his soul had fled.

Reverend Jelowicki's portrayal was incredible in view of Pauline Viardot's remark shortly after Chopin's death that "the poor lad died tormented by priests who forced him to kiss a relic for six hours until his last breath." Yet Gutmann's story is even more peculiar. For a letter by Chopin's niece Ludwika Ciechomska of 7 August 1882 states that Chopin could not have died in Gutmann's arms for the simple reason that Gutmann was not even in Paris in those days. This letter also unmasks as false a statement of Jelowicki's relating to Chopin's last words. Whereas according to Jelowicki, they were supposed to have been: "I am happy! I feel death drawing near. Pray for me. We will see one another again in heaven," the truth is that Chopin in his last moments turned to his mother with the words: "Mother, my poor mother!" Thus his niece Ludwika confirmed Mrs. Erskine's report which she sent in a letter to Chopin's sister:

> I am certain that the heartrending cry I heard on
> that last night will remain stuck in my memory
> forever: "Mother! My mother!"

Finally his niece's document also refuted a few items of information concerning Countess Delphine Potocka, who belonged to the circle of great ladies, whose favor Chopin courted in his lifetime and to whom he used to dedicate his compositions. A few days before he passed away, she hurried to him from Nice, and it is documented that Delphine, who was very musical and had a marvelously beautiful voice, sang a few of his favorite melodies to the dying man—but not in his dying hour, as was often asserted, but rather, a few days before his death, as Ludwika Ciechomska testifies in the aforementioned letter. In view of the strongly differing data on the songs themselves, today we no longer know what she sang, but that Delphine sang at Chopin's deathbed is established beyond doubt, not least of all because this scene was immortalized and documented in a painting by the French artist Barrias.

One more detail mentioned in almost all biographies is contested today by modern Chopin research, namely, a note of Chopin's first published in 1904, in which out of fear of possibly

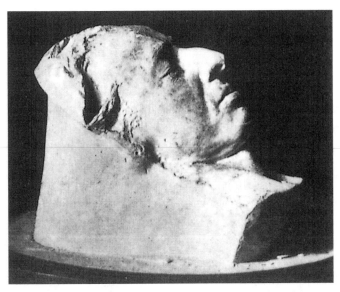

FRÉDÉRIC CHOPIN'S DEATH MASK, TAKEN BY GEORGE SAND'S SON-IN-LAW,
A. CLÉSINGER.

being buried alive he supposedly begged and pleaded to have
his corpse dissected. This note, which has been preserved, reads:

> And since the coughing is killing me, I urge you to
> open my body so that I may not be buried alive.

Because this note could also easily have stemmed from Chopin's
father, who likewise died of tuberculosis and out of this kind of
fears expressly stated his wish to have his body opened after
death, the authenticity of this note has recently been cast at least
into doubt. After Clésinger had made the death mask and Chopin
had been sketched on his deathbed by E. Barrias, A. Graefle, and
T. Kwiatkowski with drawing pencils, Cruveilhier undertook the
autopsy. Unfortunately the very exact autopsy record later was
destroyed by a fire in police archives, and since no copy was
made, we can only rely on an oral communication of Cruveilhier
to Jane Stirling. According to him, the autopsy is said not to have
brought any additional conclusions "on the main cause of his
death," but surprisingly the heart had been more affected by the

disease than the lungs. But this statement of Stirling's does not sound very credible, since it seems quite conceivable that she did not want to worry her own family by a truthful description of the tubercular lesions in Chopin's lungs, because she had had such close contact with him during the months in England. Since it was the deceased man's wish for his heart to rest in Warsaw, it was removed during the autopsy and taken by Chopin's sister to the Polish capital, where it has since been preserved in Holy Cross Church. The embalmed corpse, on the other hand, was transported to the vault of the Magdelene Church in Paris, from where it was brought for final burial to the Père Lachoise cemetery only on 30 October 1849 after a thirteen-day delay. The reason for this delay was Chopin's last will that the funeral festivities begin with Mozart's *Requiem*. But since the collaboration of female soloists was absolutely necessary for its performance and females at that time were generally forbidden any admittance to the Magdalene, the complicated bureaucratic process for obtaining an exceptional permit took considerable time.

The funeral procession was led by Prince Czartoryski and Giacomo Meyerbeer, amid a great show of sympathy by the people of Paris. Close to the graves of Cherubini, Bellini, and other important musicians, the coffin was lowered into the ground of the country he had loved so much and which had become a second homeland for him. Only a few days later, under the chairmanship of his friend Delacroix, a committee was formed for the erection of a monument and to give the sculptor Clésinger the assignment of making out of marble a worthy monument for Chopin that would be unveiled on the anniversary of his death on 17 October 1850.

Final Diagnosis

In the medical observation of Chopin's biography, what one first notices is that he came from an apparently very healthy family, whose medical history shows little that is noteworthy. Considering that the average life expectancy of people around 1800 was only about forty years, both parents lived to an above-average age, the father to seventy-three years and the mother to eighty years. Judging from sources in letters, his mother, apart from occasional "rheumatic complaints" and in later years a decline of her eyesight, apparently almost always remained healthy. His father, however, is said to have suffered in the last years of his life from heart ailments and frequent coughing and allegedly to have died from the effects of tuberculosis. Chopin's sisters, Ludwika and Isabella, who reached ages of forty-eight and seventy, respectively, displayed no medical particularities in their life history. It is therefore completely incomprehensible why J. Willms and F. Blume tried to link Chopin's later illness with a hereditary defect.

The role played by illnesses in Chopin's youth has previously been given very differing interpretations from a medical point of view. An exact study of his medical biography, however, leads with considerable certainty to the conclusion that they were the first signs of his later tuberculosis. For we know that at the beginning of the 19th century ninety percent of all youths had already undergone a tuberculosis infection by their eighteenth birthday. As a rule the doctors diagnosed this illness as an unspecified inflammation of the throat and upper air passages. Chopin, too, in his youth repeatedly became sick with bronchial catarrhs, so that by his fourteenth year he was instructed to eat plenty of oatmeal, drink an extract of burned acorns, pay attention to fresh air and sufficient sleep. Whether the two family doctors, Dr. Roemer and Dr. Malcz, however, due to his very delicate constitution in childhood and early youth, even then thought of the possibility of a tuberculosis infection is beyond our knowledge.

More probably, they must have considered this possibility on the occasion of Chopin's first serious illness in February 1826. At that time, in the context of a "catarrhal affection," for which he had to stay in bed for a longer time, there occurred a "swelling of the neck glands," which the doctors treated, among other things, by the application of leeches. That it hardly could have been a harmless side-effect of a throat infection can be seen from the mode of treatment plus the circumstance that he still felt weak and ill in the summer of that year and was instructed to avoid physical strain. The suspicion is therefore plausible that these lymph gland swellings in the neck areas must have been tubercular in nature and also that his family doctors took that into consideration. This assumption is confirmed by the fact that Chopin was sent for treatment to Bad Reinerz, together with his sister Emilia who was ill with an "open" tuberculosis, in order to undergo a drinking treatment at Dr. Magolla's Health Institute, located there. But he survived that illness with no other treatment than drinking whey, then considered a valuable medication for persons who had contracted tuberculosis. Assuming correctly that Chopin's illness was a tubercular infection of the lymph glands, then a primary pulmonary infection must have preceded this occurrence, and chronologically it must have been months or years back. For the regular course of tuberculosis is that after the tubercle bacilli penetrate the lungs—whether by a so-called droplet infection by breathing or coughing or by contact with a person infected with an open pulmonary tuberculosis—a regional core of infection, called the primary complex, results. This event can subside again within a few weeks, if the organism's resistance is good, and not be noticed at all by the patient due to a lack of symptoms, since only a barely detectable scar is left. If the body's power of resistance declines or a reinfection follows, then the infection can spread further, whether via the lymph canals or through the blood, and then more and more new settlements of tubercle bacilli can result. One of these possibilities seldom found today and therefore described more precisely only in old textbooks is tuberculosis of the lymph glands of the neck. In such cases, it could happen that the primary lung site has mostly healed, while the lymph gland tuberculosis spreads so extensively that under certain circumstances whole groups of lymph glands could be transformed into crude knotted lumps. If this process was not limited to the lymph glands located along the large bronchia and the windpipe but spread to the glands of the neck and lower jaw, then in the worst case it could even lead to severe external disfigurement. Because this disfigurement resembles a pig's head, it was called scrofula (*scrofa*: Lat.: "pig"). The majority of these cases led to the formation of an abscess or a scar from the long healing process, and if resistance was strong, a surprisingly rapid diminution of the lymph swellings was observed, especially if they were not too massive. In Chopin's case, a relatively mild form of tuberculosis of the lymphatic glands in the neck must have been the case.

This was probably also why he recovered relatively swiftly after returning from Bad Reinerz in the autumn of 1826, while his sister Emilia experienced a rapid deterioration of her condition. In her case, an increasingly tormenting cough, which emitted vast quantities of bloody phlegm, led within a few months to extreme emaciation from exhaustion and total loss of appetite, and the symptoms leave no doubt that Emilia wasted away from a galloping consumption of the lungs. What was understood by this term was a progressive tubercular pulmonary disease in which the affected lung tissue is destroyed and the dead tatters of tissue are caught in the bronchial passages. This then leaves smaller or larger hollows in the lung, so-called "caverns," in which there can likewise be bleeding from destroyed blood vessels. The coughing up of larger quantities of blood, also called a "hemorrhage," then results. But her death in April 1827 makes it possible to assume that Emilia's case probably involved the spread of tuberculosis via the blood in the sense of a so-called "miliary metastasis" permeating the entire lung and often affecting other organs, too, especially the meninges [tuberculous meningitis]. Without a doubt, however, medical treatment in the form of copious bleedings, blistering cups, and leeches also contributed greatly to her rapid end. Since those days when Chopin saw with his own eyes these seemingly inhuman and completely useless methods of treatment, he developed a deep lifelong repugnance for all modes of procedure of contemporary medicine, and that is surely the reason why he later preferred homeopathy in his choice of doctors.

To make out a sure source of infection for Chopin's reinfection with tuberculosis is hardly possible, given the tremendous dissemination of this disease at that time. But since he lived in the same house with his sister Emilia who was suffering from open tuberculosis, the assumption seems justified that he was reinfected in 1826. Kapellmeister Würfel would also come into consideration as a source of infection, for he repeatedly met with him during his second stay in Vienna in 1830/31 and he too was already suffering from advanced open tuberculosis at the time. Finally, Chopin lived for quite a long time in 1834 in his Parisian apartment together with his friend Matuszynski, who died of pulmonary tuberculosis in 1842. It therefore does not seem very sensible to search for Chopin's specific source of infection, since we cannot get beyond suspicions from the existing sources.

Certainly, however, in contrast with his little sister's case, in Chopin the disease assumed a pronouncedly chronic character as a result apparently of his sufficient physical resistance, and for years it was not at all noticeable in the patient. On the contrary, from the first years in Paris, all sources assert that Chopin looked healthy and strong and even gained weight. However, when most pathographies report that the years 1832 to 1837 went completely free of diseases, that does not fit the facts. Closer examination of the sources shows that almost every winter Chopin suffered from colds and bronchitis, so that because of his weakened health in 1833 he spent a recovery vacation in the country and in 1835 he went for treatment to Enghien les Bains, one of the most favored spas for tubercular patients.

The first certain indications of tuberculosis are, however, not found until the winter of 1835/36, when he had to spend a longer period in bed because of a severe, highly feverish "grippe." That was also when, during persistent coughing, bloody phlegm first was seen. Indeed, because of his strongly damaged general condition, characterized among other things by an alarming weight loss, the rumor spread even as far as Warsaw that Chopin had died. The winter of 1836/37 again brought a severe "grippe" with high fever, tormenting coughing, and bloody phlegm, which he tried to mitigate with pieces of ice. This time he seems to have recovered very slowly, since in August 1837 Mendelssohn-Bartholdy still reported from London of an "ailing and sick" Chopin. Thus it can be accepted as certain that by 1836 his chronic pulmonary tuberculosis had progressed so far that it now made itself distinctly recognizable by its typical symptoms. The bloody cough, repeatedly observed, moreover, indicates that by this time cavernous lesions must already have formed. But it is remarkable how astonishingly well he at first repeatedly recovered from these spells of the disease, although from then on the coughing hardly ever left him.

A lot of thinking has gone into trying to explain what actually caused the outbreak of his pulmonary tuberculosis in 1836. Regardless of whether a new infection from outside or a renewed flare-up by reactivation of older tuberculous sites in the lung is seen as the cause—though the second possibility certainly is more probable at an adult age—the role of factors causing diminished resistance on the part of the organism must also be considered, since this leads to an intensified virulence of tubercle bacilli previously dormant for years in encapsulated sites. Disregarding the aforementioned active sources of infection in his immediate circle, his social, hygienic, and professional environmental conditions during his first Paris years provide no explanation as to what could have caused the sudden outbreak of the disease. Attempts to make his personality structure responsible for it are also more than problematic. Chopin was, indeed, described by his contemporaries quite unanimously as a pale, frail, and very thin young man, a portrayal that agrees with the data in the passport he needed for his voyage to England during the summer of 1837: "Height 1,70 meters [5 feet, 7 inches], Weight 97 pounds." Although a constitution weakened by undernourishment or physical overexertion can promote the reactivation of tuberculosis, it has to date not been possible to attribute the origin of tuberculosis to a particularly premorbid personality. Attempts have therefore been made to search through the biographical forefield before the chronological beginning of Chopin's sickness for crisis-like events and conflict situations that could come in question as triggering factors. Karenberg came to the conclusion that the conflictual tension leading to the breakup of Chopin's love relationship with Maria Wodzinska was the essential factor triggering the disease and causing a massive flare-up of his dormant tuberculosis by diminishing his resistance capacity. A counterargument to this, however, is that the manifestation of his pulmonary tuberculosis, with the greatest certainty, must have occurred a full year before the breakup of his relationship with Maria, namely, in the winter of 1835/36, so that such psychosomatic connections with his tuberculosis surely seem rather speculative.

The fact remains, at any rate, that Chopin just about certainly was infected with tuberculosis in his youth, with a flare-up in 1826—whether by a renewed infection from his mortally ill sister Emilia or by a reinfection via an activation of a primary site—which made its appearance under the clinical picture of tuberculosis of the lymph glands of the neck. In 1835/36, finally, there was a renewed activation of the tubercular sites in the lung, dormant for years and now already forming caverns.

After this reactivation of the organic sites during the winter months of 1835/36 and 1836/37, an especially severe spell of his chronic, recidivous pulmonary tuberculosis showed up in the winter of 1838/39, which he spent on Mallorca; and it took him to the edge of the grave. Aside from the physical exertions connected with the journey, this was unleashed by a feverish cold with "bronchitic symptoms" he caught at the beginning of the rainy season. Chopin's general condition had deteriorated alarmingly in Palma, where he lay in bed with high fever and coughing incessantly; but his health got even worse during his stay in Valdemosa. Constant fever, tormenting, incessant coughing, and bloody phlegm so weakened the patient that he could hardly leave his cell. When the return journey was begun in February 1839 because of his life-threatening condition, during the ship voyage a severe hemorrhage occurred, in which Chopin "spit washbasins full of blood," as the result of a massive bleeding from a lung cavern.

Although he arrived in France as a man marked by death, he recovered from this severe crisis astonishingly fast in Marseilles under the medical supervision of the chief surgeon there. It is surprising how differently this Mallorca crisis is evaluated by various doctors. Some authors even held the view that Chopin's illness first made its appearance in Mallorca. Beside the French doctor and Chopin scholar, E. Ganche, it was mainly the Australian doctor K. Barry, who said:

It is significant that every doctor who saw him before his first acute bronchitis or pulmonary infection in Palma insisted on the fact that he showed no signs of tuberculosis. Until he went to Palma, absolutely no proof of tuberculosis is present.

Such an idea leaves out of consideration the whole aspect of the history of medicine: namely, that doctors at that time were still hardly capable, with the examination methods of tapping and auscultation of the chest, of diagnostically evaluating organic changes in the lung. To discuss such interpretations is thus superfluous.

In the following years, Chopin's advanced chronic pulmonary tuberculosis again behaved relatively peacefully, apart from repeated spells of fever and his permanent cough. Surely he owed this generally inactive behavior of his disease for many years to a considerable extent to George Sand who offered him, along with her self-sacrificing care during the summer months at her estate in Nohant, the necessary rest and relaxation. Nonetheless, since the Mallorca crisis, Chopin's state of health could no longer be compared with that of the previous years in Paris. He remained a chronically ill patient, in need of constant treatment, and his slowly progressing pulmonary tuberculosis determined his daily schedule. It began with morning coughing attacks, often lasting for hours, in which copious slime and pus were coughed up, repeatedly accompanied by bloody phlegm. Yet Chopin must not be imagined at that time as constantly severely ill. Rather, longer intervals free of complaints alternated with acutely worsened states, accompanied especially during the winter months with violent ailments. On the whole, however, the chronically progressive course of the disease cannot be overlooked; by liquefying processes it led to ever new cavernous lesions, out of which further disseminations to other, previously spared sectors of the lungs occurred in spells via the bronchial tubes. This process was generally manifested in the image of a "grippe," while the development of caverns was characterized by the start of bloody coughing. Moreover, destruction of the connective tissue of the lungs

gradually occurred, although this first became clinically noticeable in 1847 by increasing difficulty in breathing.

When a few biographers accuse the doctors who treated
Chopin of ineptitude, this is, as Franken rightly stresses, not merely
unjust, but it also is evidence of complete ignorance of the background in the history of medicine. For at that time there were
practically no effective possibilities for treating tuberculosis, since—
its cause being unknown—reliance had to focus solely on so-
called counterirritant measures, which were supposed to cleanse
the organism of pathogenic materials and humors. One of these
measures, besides sweating, vomiting, and purging was, in particular, the drawing of blood, whether by opening a vein or by
the application of leeches. This treatment was propagated most
strongly by Broussais in France, where, in its extreme aberrations,
it became famous, or notorious, as "Broussaiism." In addition,
the use of opiates and other alkaloids was recommended to di-
minish the coughing, and the patient was advised to drink mineral water containing sulfates, alkalines, and antimony. Finally
dietetic prescriptions in the form of sufficient nourishment and
milk, especially as whey or asses' milk, played a decisive role,
complemented by a change of climate and treatment in spas.
Under such conditions, it is remarkably to the credit of Chopin's
doctors, almost all recruited from renowned representatives of
their profession, that they preserved their patient from the bloodletting methods by opening the veins or with leeches, a treatment
then widespread, although it is not merely senseless, but dangerous. By this abstention from drawing blood, they surely prolonged his life by years. Moreover, since his sister Emilia's death,
Chopin himself had an insurmountable repugnance for blood-
drawings of any kind; and this must not have remained without
influence on his doctors' actions and have led him more and
more to the homeopaths. Homeopathy was precisely the movement that vehemently opposed academic medicine in France,
which was so strongly influenced by Broussais, and it is remarkable that so serious and famous a physician as Cruveilhier apparently recognized clearly that patients were thereby saved from
death. Otherwise it would be inconceivable that Chopin stated
about the homeopath Molin that in Molin's time homeopathy had

done him good because the doctor did not overload him with medications and left a great deal to nature.

In the summer of 1847 there came a new flare-up of his tuberculosis. To what extent this beginning of the final worsening of his disease had a psychological background and possibly was triggered by the tremendous mental strain of the breakup with George Sand that occurred at this time is a question that must be left unanswered. However, it is clinically significant that now among his customary complaints one system dominated the scene more and more, namely, his difficulty in breathing. Causally, what it primarily resulted from was the progressive decrease of breathing surface, which in turn was an effect of repeated and ongoing infections and cavernomatose processes with the resulting constant destruction of functioning lung tissue. His breathing difficulty was, however, essentially intensified in the last phase of his sickness by yet another factor, namely, progressive scarred lesions in the connecting tissues of the lungs formed during years of sporadic tubercular spells and leading to an overburdening of the right heart which is responsible for blood circulation in the lung.

Thus it is not surprising that during the second journey to England in the summer of 1848, his shortness of breath was so intensified by the tremendous physical exertions involved in the journey that he had to be carried up stairs he had once occasionally managed to ascend with only his servant's help. Nor is the noticeable reduction in the strength of his heart surprising, here again mainly of the right ventricle of the heart. After returning from Scotland, therefore, edema (swelling of the legs) showed up for the first time. Ascites, that is, the accumulation of fluid in the abdominal area, allegedly observed in the last year of his sickness, would also fit readily within this framework. Finally the continuous headache that Chopin complained about in the final phase of the disease requires an explanation and it can probably be found in the increasing impeding of gas exchange in the lung. For we know that when the oxygen pressure in the arterial blood is lowered its carbon dioxide content increases and an enrichment of carbon dioxide in the blood often is linked with headaches. Of course, in Chopin the situation of oxygen shortage is not just the expression of a "respiratory insufficiency," but surely must also be seen in connection with the anemia which necessarily had to follow from the repeated hemorrhaging and the frequent coughing of blood.

The persistent diarrheas that began three months before his demise must surely be explained by a complicating tubercular infection of the intestine. Such an abdominal tuberculosis was not rare in the 19th century, which did not yet know of any medication to treat tuberculosis. Even in a textbook on intestinal diseases of the end of the 19th century we can read:

> Whereas tuberculosis most rarely occurs in the stomach, it is a common occurrence in the intestine and the most frequent of all infectious diseases afflicting it. This is understandable from the wide dissemination of pulmonary tuberculosis, along with which intestinal tuberculosis so often occurs as a complication....In the vast majority of cases the tubercular intestinal ulcers arise through swallowing the sputum containing tubercle bacilli, when the air passages are infected with tuberculosis....If signs of an intestinal ailment are present in a consumptive, then from the start nothing is more probable than that the pathological processes in the intestine are equivalent to those in the lung....The stool can in many cases be completely normal, but often there are also unquenchable diarrheas....The stools can occur preferably at night, but they are mostly painless or accompanied by a slight cramping sensation; they are uniformly thin; their number is at most six per day....Finally, we observe a category of severely ill patients, who suffer from profuse, unquenchable diarrhea.

It can thus rightly be assumed that Chopin's diarrheas were a symptom of an intestinal tuberculosis as a complication of his lung disease.

A few weeks later, speech difficulties finally set in, suggesting that he had in addition developed a tubercular infection of the larynx. Chopin had been suffering from hoarseness for a rather long time. Now his voice failed to such a degree that he could communicate only in a whisper or even only by hand signals. Wild hypotheses have in part been made to explain this hoarseness. For instance, for a long time its cause was seen as the continuous coughing and the production of abundant secretion. Meneses Hoyos, however, questioned the existence of tuberculosis at all and held that Chopin had suffered a mitral stenosis (a narrowing of the valve guarding the opening between the left auricle and the left ventricle of the heart), which supposedly led finally to terminal hoarseness through the pressure of the massively expanded left auricle of the heart on the efferent nerve responsible for supplying blood to the vocal cords. Here too, as with interpretation of the diarrheas, some fail to consider completely different courses of the disease due to the medical-history aspects of tuberculosis in the 19th century with its lack of effective methods of treatment. Consulting a 19th-century medical text once again, one reads the following:

> A chronic laryngeal tuberculosis occurs considerably more rarely than pulmonary consumption. While the latter is most frequently of primary nature, chronic laryngeal tuberculosis is almost always a secondary ailment generally following a prior pulmonary consumption. As a rule the infection of the larynx results when the phlegm containing tubercle bacilli adheres to the laryngeal membrane....Disturbances of voice formation generally set in, varying in form from a muffled and hoarse voice to total loss of voice. Speaking frequently not only tires the patient, but it also induces pain in the larynx....The patients are plagued day and night by violent coughing....Recoveries from laryngeal tuberculosis occur only very rarely, so that the prognosis is in every respect unfavorable.

This detailed description shows that in Chopin a laryngeal tuberculosis surely must have existed much earlier, while in the last
phase of the disease a radical worsening set in. At any rate, there
seems hardly any justification to doubt that Chopin's laryngeal
tuberculosis was a complication of his pulmonary tuberculosis.

Thus the final medical diagnosis would have to read: Chronic
pulmonary tuberculosis with cavernous lesions and connective
tissue destruction processes in the lung, chronic laryngeal tuberculosis, with a terminally ensuing tuberculosis of the small intestine, overburdening of the right heart with signs of heart muscle
failure, high level of chronic blood-loss anemia.

A completely new version, though one surely untenable medically on any point, has recently been presented by O'Shea to
explain Chopin's disease and its fatal outcome. O'Shea raised the
hypothesis that Chopin could have suffered from *mucoviscidosis*,
a genetic metabolic disease, in which extremely viscous secretions are produced in the mucous glands of the pancreas and the
airways, leading to a massive blockage of normal secretions with
subsequent inflammation and permeation of the connective tissues of the pancreas and the lungs. The blockage in the glandu-
lar ducts and bronchial tubes, moreover, results in their cystic
widening, for which reason the term cystic fibrosis is also used.
Apart from the fact that there are absolutely no indications of this
hereditary disease in the Chopin family and that in his life any
signs are missing of dysfunctionality of the pancreatic gland, obliga-
tory in such cases and with most serious consequences for digestion, this hypothesis seems incredible for yet another reason. For
prior to the antibiotic era, the fully developed syndrome generally led to death in earliest childhood, and even as late as 1950
four out of five victims died in childhood. Only in mildly developed cases, which do exist, could the patients reach adulthood.
But for Chopin, with his years of feverish spells and hemorrhages,
the assumption of such a mildly developing image of a
mucoviscidosis is absolutely unimaginable.

A second aspect, to which too little attention has been paid in
pathographies of Chopin, consists in the various mental crisis situations in the artist's life, which in part influenced and shaped his

artistic development and to which Axel Karenberg first referred. Essentially this involves depressive moods, which appeared in two different forms and must be evaluated variously as to their causes.

We first meet a depressive phase in Chopin's life during his second stay in Vienna in 1830/31 and his Stuttgart time in autumn of 1831. At that time he experienced a psychic shock from the bloody defeat of the Polish freedom struggle, accompanied by severe self-reproach, since he had not, like Titus, returned to Warsaw immediately to fight with his compatriots. This crisis in his self-value was intensified, moreover, by the failure to achieve outward success as an artist. Separation conflicts also existed, and very soon after parting from his family, friends, and native soil, these emotions mounted and reached full development in the solitude of his new environment. We cited information about this mental crisis almost without gaps from his diary, his note-book entries, and various letters, in which he spoke of an "un-bearable melancholy" that made him "cold and dry as a stone." In fact, his underlying mental state worsened so much that in his genuine weariness with life he reached the point of actually con-templating suicide. The most important document from this time is the Stuttgart diary, from which we could glean all the important symptoms of his psychic depression: self-reproach, feelings of frustration, hopeless despair, weariness with life accompanied by suicidal ideas and death fantasies, insomnia, apathy and a moti-vational deficit, disinterest to the point of dulled feelings toward other people, as well as a feeling of desolation about his whole situation in life. On the other hand, he was tormented by inner uneasiness and unbearable states of tension, from which he gen-erally could free himself only by transposing them into music.

Some doctors have tried to explain these mental states by the presence of a cyclothyme or schizoid component in Chopin's personality. It must be conceded that Chopin was extremely sen-sitive even in his earliest youth; but during his whole life we never find indications of his being a depressive personality. This thesis must, accordingly, be rejected. The same is true of psychoanalytical attempts to explain his mental despondency as the manifestation of a depressive neurosis in the sense that a previously latent neurotic attitude was activated by the events of 1831. For such an interpretation overestimates certain neurotic traits recognizable now and then in Chopin as in other artists. This interpretation too is therefore not acceptable.

The mental crisis of 1830/31 involved, rather, a reversible experienced reaction to mental conflict situations in the sense of a reactive depression. It differs from a "normal" grief reaction to external events both by the intensity of Chopin's depressive mood and by its relatively long duration. For his state of mental despondency is still clearly recognizable during the first, artistically rather unsatisfactory months in Paris, as can be gathered from various letters and from statements of his Polish countrymen. Only with the start of his artistic ascent and his social integration did this reactive depression gradually subside and yield to a sense of well-being, which continued until 1838.

With the final outbreak of his pulmonary tuberculosis in Mallorca, he again fell into a state of mental depression beginning in the winter of 1838/39 and characterized by insomnia, weak motivation, indecision, a dejected, sad state of mind marked by "melancholy," apathy, and resignation to an inescapable fate. Once again it was a matter of a depressive mood, a secondary one this time, caused by disease and irreversible in view of his chronic and incurable disease. The depressive moods, which appeared alternatively at periodic intervals from then on, were correlated with the recurrent spells of his progressive pulmonary tuberculosis. The depressive character of his frame of mind reached its peak after the break with George Sand or respectively during the strenuous stay in England in 1848, where he finally realized that his condition was hopeless. Besides the guilt feelings and tormenting thoughts of having failed in life, resignation became more pervasive in the knowledge that he could not go on. His indifference and his apathy, even toward his benefactors intensified to the point of a deep feeling of alienation from the outside world. Strangely, even to explain these phenomena, some doctors have again tried to draw upon essential organic changes. Thus,

Lange-Eichbaum, for instance, spoke of "a very bio-negative schizoid personality, stamped mainly by physical illness"; and Rocchietta even believed he had to diagnose schizophrenia or at least a "pseudo-schizophrenia." However, arguments to prove such statements were not provided.

Understandably, such periodic depressive moods are frequently found as a reaction to a chronic progressive disease. And Chopin too, innately very sensitive and scarred by a mild neurosis, had to endure this martyrdom. It is all the more astonishing that the artist's most productive creative period must be set between 1839 and 1846 and could be impeded neither by the critical worsenings of his organic disease nor by the accompanying depressive moods. Possibly the premonition of an early death due to the progressive incurable disease even created the inner tension so necessary for his creative activity, since he could free himself from it only by transposing his emotions into music. Such a view was corroborated by Chopin's own admission: "On the piano I expressed my despair."

Only in the last two years of his life did his creative energies finally run out. With a "country dance" that conjures up the soul of his tortured nation, he said farewell to his beloved homeland which, as the Polish writer, Cyprian Norwid, wrote after Chopin's death, owes it to him alone "that the tears of the Polish people shed far and wide were united in crystalline form into the diadem of mankind."

Chopin's Doctors

Dr. Jean Gaston Marie Blache (1799-1871)

Dr. Blache worked as an intern in the children's division of the Cochin Hospital in Paris, where in 1822 he received a prize from the Medical Faculty of Lyons for a treatise on whooping cough. In 1824 he published his *Research on the Particular Production of the Mucous Membranes of the Mouth*, and a few years later he wrote, together with Guersant, the textbook *Treatise on Children's Diseases*.

Dr. François Joseph Victor Broussais (1772-1838)

The founder of "physiological medicine," Dr. Broussais was the son of a doctor murdered during the turmoils of the French Revolution. Broussais first became a soldier, then a naval doctor. He had brilliant intellectual abilities and was a very eloquent and convincing speaker. He was Chief Surgeon at the Military Hospital in Paris and after 1831 Professor of General Pathology at the University of Paris.

Broussais's doctrine is closely connected with Brownianism on the one hand, and with the movement led by Corvisart and Laennec on the other. In his time, the justification for assuming an "essential fever" was one of the most important topics under discussion. Since typhoid fevers were so frequent precisely in Paris, pathological anatomy had proven the frequent occurrence of inflammatory processes and ulcers. Broussais therefore believed that "gastroenteritis" was not merely the basis of all diseases of the intestinal canal, but also of all other diseases. In accord with this idea he knew no other treatment than the removal of the omnipresent "gastroenteritis" by diet, warm cataplasms, and especially the use of incredible quantities of leeches. His doctrine, known by the name of "Broussaiism," won a great number of adherents, mainly through his genial mode of presentation. On the other hand, his opponents were no less numerous, and they could prove that the mortality rate of patients so treated in the department of Val de Grace headed by Broussais was higher than in other departments.

In the last years of his life he was one of the adherents of phrenology. One of his most important writings is a publication of 1821 titled *Examination of Medical Doctrines and Systems of Nosology.*

Dr. A. L. F. C. Cauvière (1780-1858)

This physician, born in Marseilles, studied in Paris where he graduated as a Doctor of Medicine in 1803. Later he worked as Professor and Director of the Medical School in Marseilles. There he was considered a respected and much-sought clinician. Of his scientific works, the *Report of the Medical Commission Sent to Paris*, published in 1832, should be mentioned.

Dr. Sir James C. Clark (1788-1870)

Dr. Clark studied in Aberdeen and Edinburgh, where in 1809 he became a member of the College of Surgeons, and subsequently served with the English fleet until 1815. Then he continued his studies in Edinburgh and received a degree there in 1817. Since 1818 he turned his attention particularly to consumption and the favorable influence a mild climate had on it. He settled in Rome and in 1820 he summed up his experiences under the title: *Medical Notes on Climates, Diseases, Hospitals and Medical Schools in France, Italy and Switzerland.* After Dr. Clark met Prince Leopold von Coburg—who later became King of Belgium—in Rome, he was named his personal physician. In 1826, however, he moved back to London, where he published his most important work: *The Influence of Climate in the Prevention and Cure of Chronic Diseases, More Particularly of the Chest and Digestive Organs.* With this book and one published in 1835 dealing with the treatment of tuberculosis and scrofula, his fame and recognition rose mightily in English society. As a result he was appointed Queen Victoria's personal physician and given the title of baronet. His great influence at the court was of help in establishing the Medical Department of the University of London. The queen put at his disposal for his lifetime a wonderful estate in Bagshot Park, where he lived in high honor until his death.

Dr. Jean C. Cruveilhier (1791-1874)

Born in Limoges, the boy was brought up almost exclusively by his mother, since his father as a military doctor had to follow the Republican troops. This probably explains his deep religious fervor. Only the energetic father's command caused the lad to study medicine, since he was fully drawn to the clerical state. But he was so horrified by the first sight of the dissections of a corpse, which he experienced at the University of Paris as a nineteen-year-old, that, following his original inclinations, he entered St. Sulpice Seminary. His father soon forced him back into medicine, so that finally he graduated as a Doctor of Medicine in 1816. Following in the footsteps of his teacher, Dupuytren, in his thesis he used not the organs as principle of division, but the pathological-anatomical changes. After working as a general practitioner until 1823, he won first prize in a contest for an extraordinary professorship and soon afterwards was named Professor at the Chirurgical Clinic in Montpelier. Just two years later he held his inaugural lecture as Professor of Descriptive Anatomy in Paris; and when in 1836 an independent teaching chair for Pathological

Anatomy was opened at the University of Paris he was given the appointment. He held that position for thirty years.

As early as 1830 he was Chief Surgeon and Director of the Maternity Hospital in Paris, later also of the Salpetrière and the Charité. He was much in demand as a doctor, and was personal physician of the Tallyrand family, among others. Of his many writings, his *Pathological Anatomy of the Human Body,* published between 1830 and 1842, occupies a special place as one of the most detailed, artistic, and outstandingly designed atlases of pathological anatomy. His *Treatise of General Pathological Anatomy* appeared in five volumes between 1849 and 1864. Because of the illustrations of his dissection findings and case histories, he is often compared with Morgagni, whose three-volume work published in 1770, *De sedibus et causis morborum,* created the foundation of pathological anatomy.

Dr. René Théophile Hyacinthe Laennec (1781-1826)

Born in Brittany, Laennec studied in Nantes under the guidance of his uncle. He entered the Medical School of Paris in 1800 and graduated from there in 1804 with his thesis *Proposition on Hippocrates' Medical Doctrine Relative to Practical Medicine,* which already revealed his comprehensive scientific education and his focus on the generally applicable particularities of diseases. In 1812 he took a position as doctor at Beaujon Hospital and published a series of highly important works on a great variety of pathological-anatomical themes. In 1823, after working at the Salpetrière and at Necker Hospital, he obtained a professorship at the Medical Clinic of the Charité and became a titular member of the Royal Academy of Medicine. After his first signs of tuberculosis had appeared as early as 1820, repeatedly forcing him to interrupt his teaching activity, he succumbed to this treacherous disease at just forty-five years of age.

His main claim to fame is his invention of the stethoscope, which made it possible for him to conduct a series of observations on patients with heart or lung disorders. He summed up those findings in his immortal work: *On Mediate Auscultation, or Treatise on the Diagnosis of Lung and Heart Ailments, Based Mainly on this New Means of Exploration.* This two-volume fundamental and revolutionary work was published in 1819 in Paris, after he had first demonstrated his experiments with the stethoscope before the Medical Society as early as 1815. Along with the Steirmark doctor, Auenbrugger, who inaugurated the percussion method, Laennec, with his method of auscultation, laid the foundation for an exact physical diagnosis of diseases of the chest organs. A monument erected in 1868 in his birthplace Quimper in Brittany commemorates the extraordinary medical achievements of this great doctor.

Dr. Pierre Charles Alexandre Louis (1787-1872)

This famous medical clinician was born in Champagne and graduated as a Doctor of Medicine in Paris in 1813. He worked for several years at the Charité Hospital, where he made extremely careful clinical and pathological-anatomical observations, resulting in his two immortal masterpieces, whose knowledge is based on more than five thousand autopsies. His *Anatomical, Pathological, and Therapeutic Researches on Phthisis*, published in 1825 in Paris, and his comparative investigations of the most frequent acute disease profiles, published four years later, not only drew tremendous attention in medical circles, but at the same time dealt a death blow to Broussais's "physiological medicine."

He was a member of the medical academy since 1826, and his clinical lectures which he held as a doctor at the Pitié and at the Hôtel-Dieu hospitals, attracted a good number of hearers. So it was not hard for him to win a group of young doctors for his "numerical method," medical statistics with which he wanted to oppose wild speculation in all questions of clinical medicine. As a proponent of clinical research supported by statistical methods, he occupied the position of a true reformer of practical medicine and founded a school that gave France a series of outstanding clinicians. He was almost broken by the death of his only son in 1854. He resigned from all his posts, but continued always to be a self-sacrificing helper.

Dr. Gustav Papet

Country practitioner and family doctor, a friend of the Sand family in Nohant.

Bedrich Smetana

(1824–1884)

Smetana's composition activity took place during a period
when Czech music still stood completely under the shadow of
German and Italian music. With its typical Czech sound, his music
must have struck his contemporaries as something new. Yet his
unmistakable style was inseparably linked with the modern
achievements of the so-called "neo-German school" in the manner of Franz Liszt and Richard Wagner, and so inevitably he was
drawn into the quarrel raging bitterly between two parties—the
"Brahmsians" on the one hand, and the "Wagnerians" on the other.
Indeed, opposition from his conservative opponents at times
reached almost defamatory proportions. Although he never had
a personal relationship with Wagner, they made him suffer a great
deal by associating him with that name. What he did admire
about Wagner's new dramatic style was its striving to integrate the
orchestra with the polyphonics and its empathetic insight into the
psychology of the leading figures in the operatic material. He
tried to enrich Wagnerian style by the newly discovered melodiousness of the Czech language. Thus, he was absolutely not a
genuine "Wagnerian," but rather an artist whose intentions for
modern music drama corresponded to a certain extent with those
of Richard Wagner.

In contrast with Wagner, Franz Liszt remained for Smetana all
his life his "master and unattainable model," much as Wagner was
for Anton Bruckner. Liszt's innovations in tonal composition, which
meant an unsuspected enrichment of the eloquence and expressive force of his music, were the basis of Smetana's instrumental

composition. In contrast with Anton Dvorák's symphonies, Smetana's music was never "an absolute playing with tones" but always a very personal communication of poetic ideas in the sense of a poem in sound. Actually Smetana's orchestral creativity contains not a single important symphony, but only symphonic compositions in Franz Liszt's sense. In fact, even Smetana's piano compositions would be inconceivable without Liszt's technical innovations.

Typical of the new appreciation of Smetana outside his more immediate homeland is the fact that recently even his opera *Dalibor*, in its tragic depth, or his two string quartets have found their due recognition. His striving for monumentality in his symphonic compositions and serious operas and his attempt to synthesize the essence of Czech folk music with the symphonic images of Franz Liszt or the music drama of Richard Wagner seem more important today than the clowning, lighthearted joyfulness of his *Bartered Bride*, which won him his great breakthrough and world recognition in his own time. His life's work led Czech music to its highest point within European art, and so Smetana's countrymen rightly consider him to be the creator of Czech national music. That the Czech voice within the reawakened European nations was first heard in the second half of the 19th century with Smetana's operas and symphonic compositions or with Dvorák's symphonies is all the more remarkable since Bohemia and Moravia have had considerable artistic music since ancient times. Its written documents go back to the eleventh century. That is why the English musical writer Charles Burney referred to 18th century Bohemia, with its numerous musical talents, as "Europe's conservatory." A major cause for this delayed recognition was the Counter-Reformation centralism of the Habsburgers at the end of the Thirty Years War. This led not only to Bohemia's loss of political independence but also to the loss of Czech national and cultural identity. The time for the Czech renaissance came only with the pre-March restoration in the early 19th century. Interestingly, German cultural movements played a more decisive part in the Czech reawakening than revolutionary ideas from France. During the Prague revolution of 1848/49, the Czechs fought on the barricades together with German Bohemians against

Metternich's reactionary system. But after that struggle was over, the paths of the liberal Bohemian Germans and the Czechs began to separate, for the long oppressed Czechs began to understand the nationalistic signs of the times. Only in the course of these changes did the Czechs become aware of how much their music was stamped by a foreign-dominated conservative tradition. That Smetana was able in a short time to lead the music of mediocre provincial composers to the height of a magnificent Czech national music is a great creative act motivated by a compelling conviction. In Smetana's case it was, however, not only the emotional fire fanned by the spring showers of the national awakening that gave him the capacity for such a supreme creative achievement, but also rational creative forces whereby he knew how to insert the developments of the modern art of his time into his own idiom. From this perspective Smetana is, in Vaclav Helfert's words, a thinker "who in relentless, strict intellectual work shaped his great artistic organism with an unquenchable fire of creative passion."

Childhood and Musical Training

Bedrich Smetana was born on 2 March 1824, in Leitomischl, a dreamy little town east of Prague, as the eleventh child of the lessor of the castle brewery, Frontisek Smetana and his wife Barbara. The world of his parental house was essentially shaped by his father, who through his industriousness, intelligence, and prudent management was able to purchase a house of his own on the town's marketplace. Besides his business activity, his father was an ardent hunter but also an enthusiastic amateur musician. His respected position not only assured his son Bedrich a carefree childhood in domestic security, but also many inspirations, especially in the musical field. Extremely patriotic-minded, his father certainly contributed to arousing Bedrich's interest in Czech folk music in his childhood, and his father also encouraged him to learn to play the violin at an early age in connection with house music, featuring especially quartets. Yet his preference for the piano must soon have become noticeable, for he writes in his diary:

> When I reached the age of four, my father taught
> me the beat for music. At five years of age I went
> to school and learned violin and pianoforte.

By the age of seven he was able to demonstrate his outstanding talent as a piano player in a piano performance at the "Academy of Philosophers," arranged in Leitomischl in October 1830 and earning him the reputation of a Wunderkind or "child prodigy."

His father's commercially inclined personality did not permit the least thought of his son's pursuing an artistic career. The desired goal he saw for his son's education was to be an official or a merchant. Despite his striking musical talent, the boy thus received only basic instruction in piano playing. For the father, it was enough that Bedrich could play very well and enjoy music. Smetana's development into a professional musician and creative artist had to follow upon an advanced dilettantism, a hard and stormy path he mastered only by his unusual talent, strong will, and unbending perseverance.

An important change for little Bedrich resulted from the family's move from Leitomischl to Neuhaus in the southern Bohemian lake region. There his father leased a lucrative beer brewery in 1831, and four years later he acquired a landed estate that was to become the family's home for almost ten years. The four years before they bought land in Ruschkolhotitz, which Bedrich spent in the somewhat livelier town of Neuhaus, enabled him to receive regular lessons in violin and piano, but also singing instructions in the church choir. But since in high school he failed in the natural sciences, his father sent him together with his younger brother Anton to nearby Iglau to improve his knowledge of German. For to get ahead in Bohemia at that time one had to attend a German or Latin school, since there were not yet any Czech schools of higher learning in the first half of the 19th century. But here too he could stand it for only half a year. Only in Deutsch-Brod, where he subsequently spent three years at the German-language Premonstratensian high school, did he feel somewhat comfortable. All the more so, since his class teacher showed a warm understanding for his musical intentions. The music-loving priest familiarized him with important modern compositions, including Weber's *Freischütz*, and there were frequent occasions to play in quartet with comrades, so that Bedrich made considerable progress in music autodidactically.

When most of his comrades went to Prague after passing the final examinations, Smetana's father also consented to his son's wish to move to the Bohemian capital. In 1839 Bedrich thus entered the fourth class at the Prague Academic High School, which had an outstanding educator and scientist as director. But Bedrich was far more fascinated with the theater and concert hall than with the school. Besides various operas, he also heard for the first time of Franz Liszt, who was then performing his own compositions in Prague. More recent investigations, however, contradict the long-expressed suspicion that Bedrich had personally attended one of these concerts given by Liszt. In reality, Smetana seems to have followed this event with great interest but only as an outsider, although Liszt would later influence the young man's artistic development so significantly. In Prague, aside from artistic inspirations, Bedrich experienced his first rapturous love. To be sure, even earlier in Neuhaus he had had a childhood playmate, "wild Kathy" who was later to become his wife. But this time he felt other, more exciting feelings for a cousin of the same age, and this inspired him, among other things, to compose a *Louisina Polka*. In his diary listings of April 1841 is found a first listing of his compositions till then, showing that quartet music predominated among his compositions at this time. The reason is surely that since childhood he had again and again gotten his most important ideas from chamber music. Otherwise, Bedrich, despite lessons with a Prague music teacher, remained as autodidactic as ever in his further musical training without any recognizable systematic procedure.

Fascinated more and more by music, he decided to leave high school. This led to a serious dispute with his father. When his father came to visit him in Prague after Easter of 1840 and was informed of his son's plan by the director of the school, he gave Bedrich "a hard slap, the first and last gift of this kind ever given me by my father." After stubbornly refusing to help with the family business, he was finally given one last chance by his father to finish his academic education. Decisive for this was the intercession of a cousin twenty years older than himself, Dr. Franz Josef Smetana, a Premonstratensian priest who taught at the high school in Pilsen and was a noteworthy historian and natural scientist. This very cultured and art-loving man not only inspired him to serious study, but he also introduced him to the bourgeois society of the city. His musical talent and his virtuosity at the piano soon opened for him the doors of the most prestigious salons, where he could also play his own compositions. These works included a string quartet and several polkas, but also the somewhat more demanding impromptus, that is, conventional music composed "in complete ignorance of intellectual musical training."

Since music was moving more and more strongly to the center of his life, he was determined after finishing high school to devote himself exclusively to it and become a musician. "With God's help and grace, someday I'll be a Liszt in technique, a Mozart in composing," he wrote in his diary at the beginning of 1843. Such high-soaring, romantic ideas were too much for his father to follow, especially since he was forced by financial reasons to sell his property and start all over again by leasing a brewery in Lamberk, north of Prague. Worried about his son's uncertain future, he therefore gave in to Bedrich's urging only after long hesitation. All he could give him for the road was 20 guilders. When Bedrich arrived in Prague in October 1843, he experienced his first disappointment, for he was refused admission to the conservatory because he was over the prescribed age limit. The second disappointment was that the scanty income from giving piano lessons was not enough to live on. What a desolate existence he had to eke out can be seen from his own description:

> I ate my meals at the restaurant for 21 florins daily—
> as long as there was money. Very often I went to
> bed hungry; once I ate nothing for three days in a
> row except for a cup of coffee and a roll for break-
> fast, then nothing more. I had already been in
> Prague for two months without being able to ob-
> tain a piano.

In this situation, Mrs. Anna Kolarova, mother of "his wild Kathy" intervened as his saving angel, after meeting him by chance and recognizing the gravity of his situation. Even during his stay in Pilsen he again saw Kathy, who meanwhile was a grown-up young lady and an excellent pianist. In his susceptibility to feminine charms, he soon was afire with passionate love for his former playmate, as his diary reveals:

> It is Katerina, Kathy, that girl virtuoso, who has fascinated me by her art as well as by her love. She is and will remain the one.

At first this enthusiastic affection found little response from the demure object of his devotion, perhaps because of his unattractive personal appearance. Of slight build and an almost dwarfish height of only five feet, four inches, and wearing plain wire spectacles since his school days to correct myopia, not much about him must have been seductive. He was all the happier and more grateful to Mrs. Kolarova for coming to his assistance and through her mediation getting him accepted as a pupil in the famous and highly reputed Josef Proksch Music School. Proksch, blind since the age of thirteen, recognized the young student's outstanding talent immediately and he set the direction for his further musical training, but above all also for his later development as a productive artist. For, along with the classical tradition of Robert Schumann, Frédéric Chopin, and Franz Liszt, he also included in his instruction prominent representatives of modern music. Following his teacher's pedagogic principle that "the whole person comprises and represents the artistic idea," young Smetana thus did not receive a one-sided further education as a virtuoso, but a comprehensive, versatile development as a musician that enabled him even now to develop the basis for his later individual style in the sense of a classical and Romantic synthesis.

Smetana's enthusiasm was intensified even more by the fact that his adored Kathy was on the faculty of the Proksch Music School as a piano teacher, so that he enjoyed constant contact with her and they could also play music together. His first public appearance as a pianist in the spring of 1845 then was together with Katerina Kolarova. But in early January 1844, just a few months after his entry into the Proksch Music School, his luck almost ran out when he had to come up with one guilder per hour tuition. Weakened by constant hunger and despairing at his hopeless situation, he had only one desire, namely, to die. The unexpected turn of his destiny therefore seemed to him like a miracle when an offer came from the Count Leopold Thun-Hohenstein for him to become the music teacher for his five children in return for an apartment, food, and 300 guilders per year.

The following three and a half years as a pupil with Proksch and tutor for Count Thun's household were a carefree, happy time for Smetana. He was "never seen in a bad mood—always cheerful and inclined to every childish prank," Countess Elise Thun later reported. Physically he was also in the best of health. There is only one single reference in his diary to any illnesses. It states that as a child in 1835 and again in 1839 he had undergone infectious diseases. But we have no details as to their nature. These illnesses seem to have been rather serious events—perhaps scarlet fever or diphtheria— since the wording in his diary is "During that time I was mortally ill twice."

Besides instruction by Proksch, based on the composition textbook by A.B. Marx, which was standard at that time and whose most important basic foundation was represented by J.S. Bach and Beethoven, young Smetana also received valuable inspirations from the blossoming concert life in Prague. He experienced Hector Berlioz, with his *Symphonie fantastique*, as well as the enthusiastically celebrated Franz Liszt, and he became personally acquainted with the Schumann couple in Count Thun's house. Although he always remained mainly a self-taught man as a pianist, his piano playing must by then already have attained a considerable mastery, since it was admired even by Proksch. Accordingly, even his composition studies already took the form of piano works worth taking seriously. Besides the album pages dedicated to various friends, among which the one in B Major written for Katerina stands out for its especially heartfelt expression, the beautiful cycle *Bagatelles and Impromptus* particularly deserves to be singled out. This cycle of eight piano pieces published only after Smetana's death and corresponding fully to the typical genre

SMETANA'S FIRST WIFE KATERINA KOLAROVA DIED OF TUBERCULOSIS IN 1859.
THREE OF SMETANA'S FOUR DAUGHTERS FROM THIS MARRIAGE DIED IN CHILDHOOD.

of miniature painting of small program compositions of the first half of the 19th century, reflects passionate love and lyrical devoted enthusiasm. The eight-line poem written in German on the back of the dedication page identifies the woman to whom the musical composition was addressed in its ending: "Oh look down at me and choose—yes, choose what delights your heart." Smetana's mastery of the piano and his creative development inspired in his at first coy beloved, his "Kathy," increasing respect for this artist's future greatness, signs of which could already be seen, so that budding affection soon changed to love.

Smetana successfully completed his training with Proksch with the Piano Sonata in G Minor from 1846, a voluminous four-movement work of remarkable technical maturity and certainty of structure. Looking back on the path of his development, he proudly asserted: "I can today not imagine any technical problem that would give me real difficulties." Equipped with such theoretical tools, Smetana felt the time had come to go out into the world independently and finally go the route he had longed for since his youth, namely, to devote himself exclusively to the work of composition.

Artistic Rise and Family Mishaps

Smetana was well aware that he could not earn a living as a composer, so he first tried to acquire a financial basis as a pianist. But his very first concert tour to western Bohemia, in which his program of contemporary music surely must have been too demanding for the audience in question, turned out to be a bitter experience for the young, unknown artist. His plan to form an orchestra met the same fate, so that very soon the only available means of financial support was again teaching music. So he decided in January 1848 to file an application to establish his own music school. Unfortunately, the bureaucratic channels took almost six months to approve the permit on 8 June 1848. Deeply depressed because of his seriously threatened livelihood, Smetana, with the courage of desperation, resorted to an almost rash idea—to seek help from Franz Liszt, whom he so admired and who was so highly esteemed by the contemporary musical world. In that letter of 23 March 1848, whose basic tone, despite all respect and esteem for the famous master, is absolutely self-confident and, convinced of his own value as an artist, he expressed not only his entire existential distress, but also his depressive mood and despondency at that time, all the way to suicidal thoughts. He enclosed with the letter the manuscript of his *Six morceaux caractéristiques*, op. 1, to move the master more favorably. Excerpts of this document read:

> Fully confident in your world-famous magnanimity and kindness, I dare dedicate this little intellectual product to you....My conditions bring me only 12 guilders per month, so I have just enough to avoid starvation. I cannot have my compositions printed, because I would have to pay in advance....

Until now no one has done anything for me. Indeed, I must say I was close to despair when I got the news that my parents had sunk so low as to become almost beggars....Now I stand before you, begging you to kindly accept this work and have it printed! Your name will give this work access to the public. Your name will be the cause of my future happiness, my eternal gratitude....But I venture one more request....It would be so easy for me to obtain a livelihood that would make me the happiest man on earth....It consists in establishing a music school....I am therefore so bold as to run the danger of seeming impertinent in your eyes by asking you for a loan of 400 guilders which I pledge even with my life to pay back....In greatest uneasiness I ask you again, hopefully not in vain, not to delay your answer, whether it contain my happiness or my misfortune, but to snatch me from my doubt; for in a few weeks perhaps—Smetana might be no more....

Basically, this letter was a seemingly crazy act of desperation, including the suicidal threat of a petitioner, who was absolutely unknown to the addressee. But Liszt, who was always willing to help, also did not deny his help to Smetana in his distress and within a week he sent him the following reply:

Above all, I express to you my most sincere gratitude for the dedication and I accept it with all the greater delight because the pieces are really some of the most excellent, beautifully felt, and finely worked I have come across recently.

Liszt apologized that he could not scrape up the requested sum of money himself, but promised to do his best "to find a good publisher for a good work," and to see "that a suitable royalty will be paid to you that will cheer you up and establish a more active rapport with the publisher." Although Smetana's request for a loan was not fulfilled, Liszt gave him a great deal of self-confidence by his artistic recognition and was a real help in obtaining the publisher F. Kistner, where Smetana's first published works appeared in Leipzig in 1851.

Meanwhile young Smetana was drawn into the political turmoils of 1848. What had happened in July 1830 was repeated in the spring of 1848: Paris again gave the signal for great changes not only in France but also in wide expanses of Europe. That the wave of revolution could spread so fast was a sign that an inner readiness was present in other countries, too. The revolution was a European event actually only in its external course and only at the moment it spread to the states of the German Federation, and especially to Austria. For thus the German question was raised as a national problem as well as a constitutional problem. The decisive event of the first phase of the Vienna Revolution occurred on 13 March 1848, when State Chancellor Prince Metternich, the incarnation of the Austrian system, was forced to step down. From that moment on, the revolutionary movement in Vienna became increasingly radical. In Bohemia, too, events went precipitously once the Emperor had fled from Vienna and abdicated. Civil guards were formed and the Czechs hoped to get back their political independence within the framework of the monarchy. Although Smetana at first bothered neither with politics nor with the question of nationalities, he was drawn more and more into the general revolutionary fervor in the artists' club "Concordia," where Germans and Czechs associated together in friendship. He composed marches for the student legion and for the national guard, which he finally also joined. But the victory of Prince Windischgrätz over rebellious Prague in the bloody Pentecostal days of June split apart the liberal Germans and the Czechs, who had recently been fighting side by side on the barricades, and segregated them into two separate peoples of Bohemia, since from then on the Czechs simply equated the Germans with Habsburg rule.

Although Smetana did not stand fully outside these events, he seems not to have taken part directly in the battles in Prague, since his memoirs do not contain the slightest reference to that. But as an artist he visibly sympathized with the revolutionary events in Prague, as witnessed by his *Song of Freedom*, which originated under the emotional impact of the bloody battles. His inner sympathy with the revolution in Prague can, however, most clearly be sensed in his first great composition for orchestra, the "Festive" Overture in D, which he began to write in his parent's house in Lamberk, to which he withdrew after the failed Pentecost uprising. That the composer was actually reacting to the revolutionary events with this powerful work is evidenced by an entry in his own hand at the end of the score: "Prague, completed on 5 March 1849. Begun in Obristvi [Lamberk] after the Pentecost events of 1848."

After defeating the revolution, the absolutist government began to repress or eliminate completely all political and cultural achievements connected with the short-lived upswing of the young Czech bourgeoisie. In this atmosphere Smetana returned to Prague in the summer of 1848 to open his own private music school, which had meanwhile been approved by the magistrates and by the archiepiscopal consistory. He began instruction with fifteen pupils and three pianos obtained on credit, with the goal of striving for a well-rounded musical development of his pupils similarly to his former teacher Proksch. In the very next year his school occupied a respected position in the music life of Prague, and it soon began to develop a profitable financial basis, allowing him to think of establishing a family. His marriage with his childhood sweetheart, Katerina Kolarova, finally took place on 27 August 1849. She became a loving and understanding partner, and as an excellent pianist she helped actively in the continued growth of the music school.

Smetana must have had quite extraordinary qualities as a pianist, although not with the acrobatics of a Thalberg, Kalkbrenner, or Liszt, as his daughter Sophie actually wrote:

> It is, to be sure, true that he could not compete with the other great artists in loudness of playing; on the other hand, his execution and his technique were perfect and unique. I never heard any other artist play Chopin the way my father did.

Chopin was one of Smetana's most important models, without whose mazurkas his comparable polkas surely would never have attained such perfection. The Three Poetic Polkas from 1855 come to mind; they render most impressively the partly virtuoso, partly delicate charm, with all his modulatory nuances, and show that this is far from being dance music, but rather poems in sound. The only large orchestra composition that originated in this period was the *Triumph Symphony* in E, completed in 1853 on the occasion of the Emperor Franz Joseph's wedding with the Bavarian princess, Elizabeth, in which he cited Haydn's famous "*Emperor Song*" in three of its four movements. This is the only classical, absolute symphony Smetana ever wrote. Its dedication to the Emperor was rejected by the Viennese court. And when in 1855 he directed it himself in its maiden performance, that was, at the same time, his first appearance as a director.

Smetana's family life was soon enriched by the birth of several children. The firstborn Friederika or Bedriska aroused particular hopes, for she seems to have inherited his unusual musical talent and, in her parents' tradition, to have displayed this talent in earliest childhood: "At three years of age she was already singing songs to texts with very good intonation and she played the C major scale even in countermovement with both hands. She knew all the pieces played in the school and the names of their authors," the proud father noted in his diary. The harsh blows of fate that struck the family in the mid-1850s were all the more painful. At that time, within three years, three of his four daughters died: in December 1854 Gabriela, the second-born; in September 1855, Bedriska, the firstborn; and in June 1856, Katerina, the third-born. Bedriska died of the effects of a severe diphtheria, Katerina of scarlet fever.

Scarlet fever is caused, as we know today, by a certain kind of bacteria from the group of hemolytic streptococci and is typically accompanied by an angina and atypical skin rash that heals by forming scales. From Galen we know that this disease was already known in antiquity, but could not be delimited from similar infectious diseases. A precise description was first presented by the English physician Sydenham, who first coined the term "scarlet fever" at the beginning of the 18th century and at first regarded this sickness as harmless. Not until fifteen years later, during a severe epidemic, did he experience that the same disease can occur with a malignancy hardly inferior to the plague. The ages of three to eight years proved to be most susceptible. In such children it could take the horrifying toxic form called "blue scarlet fever," which I myself observed as a student at the Charité in Berlin in 1940. After the sudden onset of a shivering chill with vomiting and high fever, it can lead to unconsciousness in a few hours and shortly afterwards to the fatal coma. In such cases, because of the swift onset of a weakening of the heart, the rash takes on a bluish tint. However, this toxic form of scarlet fever does not always bring death with such lightning speed; a few days can go by before the patient dies of heart failure. Since the discovery of penicillin, scarlet fever has become much less terrifying, for with this medication the streptococci can usually be eliminated from the nose and throat area within twenty-four hours, thus achieving clinical improvement and lowering of fever, so that penicillin treatment can be ended after just ten days. Around the middle of the 19th century, however, the pathogenic agent of scarlet fever was still unknown, and even in the most severe cases treatment had to be limited solely to symptomatic measures, consisting mainly of the prescribed fever-reducing poultices or cooling baths. The mortality rate of this infectious disease in the 19th century accordingly was extremely high in some epidemic periods, and multiple cases of death in families with many children were not infrequent when scarlet fever struck, as the example of little Katerina Smetana shows.

Diphtheria, which little Bedriska died of, was always an extremely dangerous disease and was likewise already known to the doctors of antiquity who spoke of a *morbus aegyptiacus* or *morbus syriacus*. Since the middle of the 18th century, greater epidemics were described in Germany, too, and were characterized by the choking phenomena associated with laryngeal involvement. A precise description of diphtheria with its various forms of disease in the areas of the throat, the nose and the larynx, was first made, however, in 1825 by the French physician Brétonneau, who gave this infectious disease its name. His description received a valuable addition by Trousseau, who also described the severe toxic general symptoms in the malignant forms of development. The boundary stone in the history of diphtheria is, however, the discovery of the bacterial pathogen by

Löffler in 1884, since only with knowledge of the pathogen and the poison it produces was a discovery of a specific medication for diphtheria possible. This great medical feat was accomplished by Behring ten years later. Around the middle of the 19th century, mortality from diphtheria began to rise alarmingly, whereby the ages from two to five years were most endangered. The main pathological disturbance caused by the diphtheria bacilli is poisoning by the toxin they emit which causes localized damage mainly in the area of the larynx and the upper respiratory tract, but can also lead to dangerous general consequences, here again mainly to the heart muscle. Laryngeal diphtheria can lead to choking attacks, whose fatal outcomes can sometimes be prevented only by performing a tracheotomy in time, or a progressive difficulty in breathing can develop which in serious cases can lead to coma and death due to severe carbon dioxide poisoning. But the most dangerous quality of the diphtheria poison is its damaging effect on the heart, which can often instantaneously and without warning lead to the dreaded sudden heart death. Today the patient's fate depends mostly on the point in time when the antitoxin is administered, since the diphtheria antitoxin can neutralize only free toxin and not toxin bound in the tissues. Moreover, today all children should be immunized against diphtheria by the age of one and a half, in order to forestall the occurrence of this dangerous infectious disease. Unfortunately, even today a high percentage of youths and adults still have insufficient immunity to diphtheria or none at all. The mortality rate for primary toxic diphtheria even today, therefore, is still above thirty percent. Around the mid-19th century, that is, at the time little Bedriska fell sick, when diphtheria epidemics went especially badly in Germany, the affected children were exposed without protection to this deadly disease, so that the fatal outcome of a toxic diphtheria tended to be the rule.

When little "Fritzchen," as Bedriska was also called, died of diphtheria at the age of four and a half, a world collapsed for her parents and the pain Smetana suffered from the loss of his adored little daughter also flowed into his music. His first important chamber music work, the Trio in G Minor for piano, violin and violoncello, was written while he was mourning Bedriska's death.

TRIO

I

Friedrich Smetana, Op.15.

IN HIS PIANO
TRIO IN G MINOR
WRITTEN IN 1855,
SMETANA EXPRESSED
HIS PAIN AT THE
LOSS OF HIS DAUGH-
TER BEDRISKA.

In the list of his compositions it is written that this Trio presents the "memory of his first child Bedriska, who delighted us with her unusual musical talent, but was soon snatched away from us by a relentless death, when only four and a half years old." Smetana also mentioned the causal context of the origin of this trio several times in other places, likewise expressly remarking that his "genius child Friederika died of diphtheria." In his later creations there is no other remark indicating such a direct connection of a work with an external event. This chamber music work of Smetana's, embodying a heartrending musical composition of experienced suffering, became not only a boundary marker of his creative career, but also the first example of modern Czech chamber music from the mid-19th century.

Meanwhile, in the late summer of 1856, on the occasion of the performance of Liszt's "Gran Mass" in St. Vitus Cathedral in Prague, Smetana had the opportunity to begin a personal friendship with the adulated master. Making music together for hours and lively discussion with the experienced and worldly-wise master musician led Smetana suddenly to see in a depressing light the musical conditions and chances for a successful future as an artist in the stuffy atmosphere of Prague. Thus an informal invitation to the Swedish city of Göteborg came at just the right time, although at first it held out no great prospects. A drop of bitterness in it was that he had to leave his family behind, since his wife had already been ailing for some time with the symptoms of a progressive pulmonary tuberculosis. But since he hoped that a sojourn abroad would enhance his reputation in his homeland and be advantageous to his family, too, he rejected all reservations about the old familiar adage "that the fatherland does not want to recognize its children, and so an artist must make a name for himself and earn his bread abroad. I, too, met this fate."

On 17 October 1856 he arrived in Göteborg, that important Swedish harbor city that would become a kind of second homeland for Smetana in the next five years. The motives for this move were probably not financial in nature. Rather, it was the fact that this city, though not comparable with Prague musically, was more open and presented a freer field for creativity and did not oppose the modern, progressive schools of art. By his piano performances and his successful activity as a conductor, he soon became the musical center of the city, as we can gather from a letter to the Danish publisher C.V. Lose:

> My two concerts had the result that I was showered with opportunities to give lessons; and in addition appointed to the directorship of a musical association with a fixed salary, so that my future here promises to become pleasant.

In fact, Smetana earned up to 12,000 talers per year in his later Göteborg years! Early on, he also developed several friendly contacts, among whom should be mentioned especially the Czech violinist and composer Josef Czapek, the synagogue cantor

A. Nissen, and his pretty young niece Fröjda Benecke. This beautiful woman, just twenty years old, had a sick husband to take care of and thus a similar destiny to Smetana's, whose wife, ill with pulmonary disease, had remained in Prague. We do not know how far the relationship between these two people developed. For Smetana, at any rate, this woman became his strongest love relationship during his Göteborg period and led to a bond of friendship that stood the test even in the artist's later crisis years.

Full of impatience, Smetana waited for the summer that gave him opportunities to visit his family in his homeland. His father died at the age of seventy-six in Neustadt in June 1857, and so he was able only to attend his funeral. But other cares also awaited him at home. His little daughter Sophie fell ill with scarlet fever and his wife was still suffering unchanged from pulmonary tuberculosis. Despite her bad state of health, however, she set out on the journey back to Göteborg with her husband in September 1857, together with Sophie, who had meanwhile recovered. They stopped for a time in Weimar, where Smetana, as Liszt's guest of honor, lodged in the latter's princely residence Altenburg. The musical works *Faust* and *The Ideals* of his idolized master, which he had the opportunity to hear there, made a tremendous impression on him, and they also stimulated his own composition works. In October 1858 he wrote in a letter to Liszt:

> Regard me as one of the most zealous disciples of our art movement; I stand up for and work for its sacred truth in word and deed.

As proof of his honest intentions he could point to his first symphonic composition, *Richard III*, to be followed in rapid succession by *Wallenstein's Camp* and *Hakon Jarl*. These symphonic works, together with a few piano pieces, among them the two completed polkas *Souvenir de Bohême en forme de Polkas*, are the most important products of his creative activity in Göteborg. They cannot yet count among his masterpieces, but represent an important prior stage for the development of his individual "New German" style, for which Franz Liszt incontestably showed the way. Smetana was always gratefully aware of this, as proven by

a letter written many years later, on 23 May 1880, in which he
affirmed:

> I owe him everything I have been able to achieve
> till now, for he showed me the only true way I
> could go. Since then he has been my master, my
> model, and for everyone probably an unattainable
> ideal.

During the now almost two years Smetana had spent in
Göteborg together with his family, his wife's disease progressed,
so that he had to ask her mother to come to Sweden to provide
better attendance and care for the sick woman. The only wish of
the meanwhile mortally ill woman was to see her homeland once
more. It was not to be fulfilled. They hastened to travel home as
fast as possible, but because of the patient's extreme weakness
the trip had to be interrupted in Dresden, where on 19 April
death released her from her sufferings. In Smetana's diary one
finds the following entry for that date:

> It is completed—Kathy, my dear, warmly loved
> wife, died this morning, gently without us know-
> ing anything, until the silence caught my atten-
> tion. Good-bye, angel!

Katerina was buried in her children's grave in Prague, as she
wished. Smetana sought consolation among his relatives in order
at least not to be completely alone in his pain. Perhaps he also
was saddened by feelings of guilt for not having concerned himself enough about his sick wife during his stay in Sweden, for he
confided suggestively to his diary in the following words:

> I feel completely alone and abandoned. I often
> feel very, very anxious. Now I feel how dear she
> was to me!

But life and the care of his daughter required his attention.
He accepted an invitation of Liszt's to Weimar, where he introduced his host to his new symphonic works. More significant for
the future was his visit to the former economic director Ferdinandi,
which gave him the opportunity to meet Ferdinandi's younger
daughter Bettyna in Prague. Smetana had known Bettyna as a

little girl. Meanwhile, at nineteen she had grown up into a dazzling beauty, moreover, with a remarkable intellectual culture. She mastered several foreign languages, had a beautiful singing voice and considerable talent as a painter, and she was an excellent chess player. While Bettyna acted rather reserved and cool toward him, Smetana, lonesome and sixteen years her senior, flared up in passionate love for her, as can be read in a letter of 3 August 1859:

> Good, good Betty! Grace, mercy for me in my misery! Let me see your beautiful face again! I have no other wishes in this world. She went and died! The world has died for me! I want nothing else but deathlike rest, rest in the midst of life, that my destroyed temperament be wrapped in the icy cover of death, that I could finally achieve this desired coldness in my heart, where I have suffered so much....Adored! Incomparable! My angel, my world, my happiness, my all!!! What have I done wrong to suffer so much?

Bettyna surrendered to such ardent urging, although she did not feign any great love for him. Her promise to become his wife in the coming year was attributable more to his artistic aura and his warmhearted lovable nature than to his external appearance. His servant Jan Rys, whom he then took along to Sweden to manage his orphaned household, described him as follows:

> The slight, but solid figure was clad in a gray-brown shirt-like jacket with very wide sleeves.... Smetana was by then wearing gold-rimmed glasses. His chestnut-brown hair hung down to the shoulders and was shiny as if oiled, although that was not the case. His facial hair consisted of three groups: over the lips a dark chestnut brown mustache with a slight tinge of red, on his chin a goatee, and sideburns. Smetana's personality caught one's interest; indeed, he was even said to be "handsome" when he smiled. His charming smile was enhanced by two rows of beautiful white teeth.

On 22 September 1859, Smetana again arrived with his young servant in Göteborg, where sad memories and melancholy traces of his deceased Kathy awaited him in his apartment. While the sketches of his programmatic piano composition for *Macbeth* were written while he was still mourning her death, after a rather long interval his creative inspiration was steered into new channels by Betty. By the beginning of 1860, he had completed two great polka cycles, dedicating the first one to his Swedish friend Fröjda Benecke and the second one to Bettyna. In May 1860 he again took leave of Göteborg and on 10 July he married Betty, who accompanied him back to Sweden in the fall and, with her attractive appearance, quickly conquered the salons of the city.

Meanwhile, changes came to his homeland through the "October Diploma" of 20 October 1860 and they strengthened his desire to be active as an artist back home. This political development gave room for hope that the Czechs might possibly fulfill their demand to restore "Bohemian independence" and give the same status to the "lands of Wenzel's crown" as Hungary was demanding. For, among the various possibilities of an Imperial constitution in the multinational state [the Austro-Hungarian Monarchy], the October Diploma of 1860 held out the hope of a constitution rather on the federalist side with strong autonomy of the states. Smetana was especially concerned with the related cultural changes in his homeland, and when he learned that in Prague in the aftermath of these events finally a new Czech theater was to be founded, he could no longer stay in Sweden. On 31 March 1861, he noted in his diary:

> I cannot bury myself in Göteborg; I must try to have my compositions published and seek a chance for new activity and an incentive for more comprehensive work. So I have to get out into the wide world, as soon as possible! My Betty is glad she will be living in the homeland again, and I am too.

Disregarding his Swedish friends' pleas, urging him to change his mind, on 11 May 1861 he said farewell to Göteborg once and for all. And finally on 19 May, he arrived in Prague where the decisive period of his career began.

SMETANA WITH HIS SECOND WIFE BETTYNA, WHOM HE MARRIED IN 1860.

At first, however, Smetana's new beginning in Prague was a bitter disappointment. Both his first solo concert as a pianist and his conducting of the first orchestral concert with his own works in January 1862 went almost unnoticed, as he wrote in his diary:

> What cold weather that was and the hall almost empty....I was forced to pay 208 guilders out of pocket.

He soon saw himself compelled to turn to teaching again; and so in August 1863 he established his second private music school. The active participation of the conductor and violinist Ferdinand Heller in this institute enabled Smetana to devote himself mostly to composition. As shown by his two choruses, presented to the Prague public in 1862 and 1863 by the great singing club "Hlahol," Smetana, too, was caught up by the general wave of enthusiasm that marked the rise of Czech national activities. The establishment of the art association "Umelecka beseda" in 1863, the musical section of which was assigned to Smetana, gave him new possibilities in his struggle to create a modern Czech music; for "the writer's pen and the conductor's lectern" seemed to him the most effective means of achieving this goal. On 2 May 1864, his first discussion of an opera in his role as music critic of the Prague *Volksblatt*, the most important of the newly founded newspapers, appeared in that newspaper. In addition, he also wrote programmatic essays, calling for separate Czech subscription concerts. In an article on 1 October 1862, for instance, he had written:

> The programs will contain masterpieces of our music heroes of whatever nation; however, works of Slavic composers are given special consideration....As a Czech I arrange Czech concerts. Surely, we Czechs will be permitted to have our own concerts.

As a conductor he also put this plan into action in the form of three subscription concerts, which first took place in 1864 and 1865 and which he later expanded as Kapellmeister of the theater.

But soon Smetana was obsessed with the *idée fixe* that the first foundation for developing a modern national music could be laid only by the opera, and so his creative interest began to be focused completely on the opera. Something that accommodated this striving in a virtually ideal way was the "Harrach Contest for a New Czech National Opera." In the quest for a suitable libretto he discovered the writer Karel Sabina, coauthor of the most famous Czech dramatic work of art, *The Bartered Bride*, who in just a few weeks wrote the text for his first opera *The Brandenburgers in Bohemia*. This opera was something completely new, insofar as the traditional "opera comprised of separate solos" was abandoned and the score, composed as a scenic unity, showed distinct features of Richard Wagner's music drama. Smetana confirmed this in his article of 15 July 1864: "Operas must not be musical

productions where singing is done for its own sake....Operas
have to be elevated to a drama," and referring to *The Brandenburgers*, he later conceded in retrospect:

> Wagner's trend was indeed already there then, but
> I knew that I must not begin with it, if I did not
> want to block off my own way forever.

The premiere of the opera, which took place on 5 January 1866 in
the Provisional Theater, the first Czech theater, opened in 1862,
was such a success with the public that the jury of the "Harrach
Contest" finally had to award him the prize of 600 guilders.

Because of this success, the theater director was also interested in the performance rights of Smetana's second opera, *The
Bartered Bride*, finished a year earlier. His diary reports of this on
5 July 1863: "Sabina even gave me a comic operetta to put to
music." This work, which later became tremendously popular,
had its premiere performance on 30 May 1866 in Prague's Provisional Theater and at first was so badly received by the public
that it had to be discontinued after only its second performance.
The reason was, however, not the lack of understanding or the
disinterest of the Prague music lovers, but external circumstances.
The Austro-Prussian War was already casting threatening shad-
ows on Prague and, with the Prussian troops approaching, the
inhabitants of this city surely were in no mood for a cheerful
opera. Smetana himself fled out of Prague ahead of the Prussians,
who were already standing close to Königsgrätz, fearing that they
might have him shot as the author of *The Brandenburgers*. But
four weeks later he returned with his family to his Prague apartment where Prussian officers were quartered and they exhibited
correct behavior. Apart from the unfavorable political circumstances leading to the negative reception of the premiere of *The
Bartered Bride*, admittedly it was then still a rather simple two-act
song-play with spoken dialogues and the masterpiece we know
now did not exist until the fourth version performed on 25 September 1870.

On 15 September 1866, overjoyed, he wrote to his wife in
Lamberk that he had been named Kapellmeister at the Provisional
Theater in Prague, although with a yearly income of only

1400 guilders. In the ongoing cultural policy struggle, this meant victory for Smetana, the progressive "freethinking young Czech," over the backward "feudal-clerical Old Czech," Johann Mayr, who had previously held this post. This new era of the following nine Smetana years marked the beginning of the real golden age of the Provisional Theater, which besides German and French operas also gave a chance to the at first rather modest works of an Antonín Dvorák or Zdenek Fibich. As Kapellmeister and an unrestrained admirer of Hans von Bülow, he was able, like Bülow, to enthuse the singers as well as the orchestra's instrumentalists, so that the first years in the position of Kapellmeister are among the happiest in his life. These successes as conductor and as a composer, however, were increasingly becoming a thorn in the eye for his conservative opponents. His most bitter enemy was Frantisek Pivoda, one of the most influential critics of the Prague music scene who belonged to an arch-conservative movement similar to Eduard Hanslick's in Vienna and saw the rise of the modern school of a Berlioz, Liszt, or Wagner as the doom of all music. It was inconceivable that he could do anything but thoroughly reject Smetana's mature works. And with the predisposition of some critics he did not shy away from unfair and insulting personal attacks. Pivoda contributed more than anyone else to Smetana's late isolation, since, unlike Hanslick, he knew no restraint and his insults transformed issues of musical aesthetics into material for national politics. For the reactionary "Old Czechs," to be a follower of Richard Wagner meant not to be a "New German" progressive in the musical sense; rather, it was considered tantamount to alienation from one's country and treason to the Old Czech principle. Smetana was an ardent patriot, and if he had more clearly demarcated himself from "Wagnerism" outwardly, he would have been spared many insults and much mental suffering.

The start of Pivoda's massive offensive against Smetana was his opera *Dalibor*, which was supposed to be the tragic counterpart to *The Bartered Bride*. After its completion on 29 December 1867, this opera was selected as the national opera for the celebration at the laying of the cornerstone for the future National Theater—the building that was regarded symbolically as the home of future Czech political independence. The premiere of this

opera on 16 May 1868 received stormy applause, apparently ascribable more to the festive occasion, for after only a few repeti-
tions it had to close for lack of interest on the part of the public.
This tragic fate of his work, which he had written with his heart's
blood, was something he never was able completely to overcome, and artistically it was the most bitter disappointment in his
life.

Ignoring the hateful critics, he turned to composing *Libuse*, a
type of opera corresponding completely to a celebratory music
drama, and of all his eight operas it is the one that most clearly
displays the stylistic elements of Richard Wagner. On the other
hand, textually *Libuse* is Smetana's most Czech opera, to a certain
extent an "apotheosis of the Czech nation," in whose musical
transposition Smetana decidedly wanted to distance himself from
any dependence on Wagner. He underscored this in a letter to
Ludwig Prochazka of 29 September 1877:

> I regard Libuse, which I wrote in full health, as my
> most successful work in the field of higher drama,
> and, as I would like to emphasize expressly, it is a
> completely independent work—neither Wagner
> nor Offenbach....Music and oratory both occupy
> their logical place.

Actually, this unique work, not to be found in any other operatic
culture, has remained down to this day what Smetana wanted it
to be, namely, a national holiday celebration opera intended for
certain occasions. Its premiere performance on 11 June 1881,
almost nine years after it was finished, on the occasion of the
dedication of the Prague National Theater, was therefore the proud-
est day in his life, even though by this point in time he was
completely deaf.

Despite all this, the reactionary Old Czech critics continued
relentlessly with their unfair attacks, directed both against his activity as conductor and manager of the opera and against his
allegedly depleted creativity. With the composition of the opera
The Two Widows for the text of the one-act comedy by Felicien
Malefille, the French author and former lover of George Sand, he
proved the falsity of such discrediting slurs. The elegant, refined

style of this comic opera almost reminds one of Mozart, and although it did not achieve any lasting effect in Prague, not least of all surely because of Pivoda's poisoned darts, it was even praised by Hans Richter after a performance in Hamburg in 1881 as the best opera of the 19th century.

The Progression of a Fatal Disease

The constant attacks by the Old Czech Party, against whose "defamations" he repeatedly tried in vain to defend himself, were an ever-increasing and almost unbearable burden on Smetana's nerves. Nevertheless, since the end of 1872 he began working on the plan for a large-scale cyclical musical composition for orchestra, the first parts of which were titled *Vysehrad* and *The Moldau*. The undermined state of his nerves was first manifested in an extremely disturbing auditory hypersensitivity. If he heard the sound of a hurdy-gurdy or a band from down the street, he had to shut the windows of his room, since such "false tones," as he called them, hurt him physically. "Such noise" quite often put him practically in an aggressive state. The only joy that helped him forget all his everyday cares for a short time was the wedding of his oldest daughter Sophie from his first marriage in the spring of 1874, with Josef Schwarz, the chief forester of the domain of Thurn and Taxis. A few days after the premiere of the opera *The Two Widows,* he visited the young couple, who were now living in the forester's house of the manorial estate in the vicinity of Jungbunzlau. In a letter of 12 May to his daughter, Smetana's longing for rest can be felt, when he wrote:

> I have to thank you for the care you both devoted to me during my visit. Although it was only a few days, their effect was very beneficial....How offended I am by my current position, and I would most prefer to creep into some corner where none of those artists could find me. I long for peace and quiet. For the time being, however, the struggle goes on.

But the rest he longed for would never be his for the remainder of his life. That spring an event occurred as the first signal of his impending baneful fate and it was noted in his diary on 30 April 1874 with the laconic words: "Since the 12th I have been ill with a pus-oozing ulcer." Soon throat complaints, not further described, were added, as can be gathered from a diary entry of 11 June:

> My throat ailments persist uninterruptedly, and I've had that now for about two weeks.

On 28 June the diary reports without change that he is "constantly sick in the throat," and when in the first half of July a skin rash was added to all that, he decided to consult Professor Zaufal, a well-known specialist in the field of ear, nose, and throat medicine in Prague at that time. On 14 July he noted in his diary:

> I am going to Prague for a consultation with the doctor. I got a rash on my body. The doctor assured me that it was nothing bad.

But on 24 July we read in Smetana's diary of new complaints of a different kind, which must have especially worried him:

> At times I have stopped-up ears, and my head spins at the same time, as if I were having spells of dizziness. The illness began after a little duck hunt while the weather suddenly changed. At that time I treated myself mainly with "inhalations."

According to a diary entry of 8 August, these "air inhalations" were prescribed to him by Professor Zaufal, who associated the patient's ailments with the presence of a "tube catarrh," that is, an infection of the Eustachian tube.

But in July, further symptoms not explainable by a tube catarrh had manifested themselves. For Smetana reported of strange auditory hallucinations which he thought he heard during walks in the form of "peculiarly beautiful flute tones." At the same time he discovered to his dismay that the tones of the higher octave had a different pitch in his right ear than in the left ear, which he called healthy. These ear disturbances apparently had nothing to do with those temporary acoustic sensory illusions he had described to his wife twelve years earlier in a letter of March 1862 as follows:

> I heard, probably as an affection of overstrained nerves continually the double singing of two male voices in G major with deep organ sounds, which stopped when I stuck my head outside the carriage, but began again as soon as I sat down.

At that time it was probably a matter of so-called neurasthenic complaints in the framework of an over-irritation of the nerves during his early career difficulties and strains in Prague after his return from Sweden, while the present hearing disturbances seem to be of organic nature with progressive tendency. The deterioration of his condition took such a rapid turn that during September he was as good as deaf in the left ear.

Because of anticipated difficulties from this ailment in his functioning as Kapellmeister, Smetana felt obliged to report his condition to the Director of the Landestheater in Prague, and, in the hope of recovery, to request that he be released from his duties as conductor for an indefinite period. From his letter to the Director of 7 September, we learn a few additional details about the previous course of his disease:

> It is my duty to inform you of the hard blow fate has dealt me: it must be feared that I am losing my hearing. As early as last July, right after the public rehearsal, I noticed that in one ear I heard the tones of the higher octaves at a different pitch than in the other ear and that at times a roaring began in the stopped-up ears, as if I were standing near a strong waterfall. This state was constantly changing, But by the end of July it remained permanently and was accompanied by spells of dizziness, so that I began to totter and when walking I was able to keep my balance only with effort. I hastened back to Prague to be treated by Dr. Zaufal, the famous ear specialist. I have been

under his care to this day. He forbids me any
activity in music; I must not play and must not and
cannot listen to anyone play. Great masses of
sound congeal for me into a knot, and I can no
longer distinguish the individual voices. And so I
ask you, then, Doctor...,to release me for an indefinite period from my duty to direct and hold
rehearsals, since I can temporarily not perform this
service. If my condition should become worse in
the course of the next three months I would obviously be forced to give up my position at the
theater and accept my sad lot.

A characteristic light is cast on the kind of people around
Mr. Pivoda, himself mostly a failure as a musician but all the louder
as a critic, that even this terrible fate for a musician, of having to
look ahead to deafness, was used for hateful comments in the
press, such as:

> So that is the top personality who regards the Czech
> theater as a medical asylum, a veteran's hospital, a
> pathological institute.

Beethoven, who with his "Heiligenstadt Testament" wrote a
similarly heartrending document of hopeless despair about his
impending deafness as did Smetana with his letter to the Director
of the Prague Provisional Theater, still had several years ahead of
him to gradually become accustomed to his increasing loss of
hearing. For Smetana, however, this misfortune broke in, so to
speak, overnight. Almost instantaneously, in the night of
19 October his previously healthy ear became deaf. In his diary
on 20 October 1874 is found the entry: "My ear disease has
gotten worse; now I can no longer hear with my left ear either."
This is followed by an entry on 30 October, suggesting his bad
premonitions about his expected fate:

> I fear the worst, am completely deaf, hearing ab-
> solutely nothing. How long will this continue?
> Am I not to become healthy at all?

Only now, after the onset of complete deafness, did Smetana give up and resign his office of Kapellmeister of the theater once and for all on 31 October 1874. Since he could expect a pension of only 1200 guilders per year and in compensation had to cede to the theater without charge all rights to his previous operas, from now on he found himself at the limits of the minimum needed to subsist. Nor was it possible to think any longer of any piano performance, or even piano lessons, so that actually he had to rely on the support of his friends. On his doctors' instructions, he lived for weeks in darkened rooms, lined with sound-absorbing carpets, so that no noises could reach him. "I have to keep my ears wrapped in cotton wadding and to maintain complete quiet," he wrote in his diary in October. A month later his condition was completely unchanged, as can be gathered from a diary entry:

> My ear ailment is in the same condition as at the beginning of the month. I hear nothing, neither from the right ear, nor from the left one. If only at least the whistling would stop.

Smetana accepted this heaviest blow of fate with admirable strength; he began to immerse himself ardently into composing— for at first the most important thing was not affected, namely, the ability for creative activity. By the end of September he was absorbed in working on the symphonic composition *Vyschehrad*, which he had finished by 18 November. Two days later he began composing the second symphonic work, *The Moldau*, and according to a note in his handwriting he was able to complete its score in the unimaginably short time of only nineteen days.

Professor Zaufal's methods of treatment still remained ineffective. Smetana was not allowed to speak, and even his friends and family members were instructed to converse with him only in a whisper. In view of these disconsolate prospects of any improvement, they were generally of the opinion that Smetana should seek foreign medical experts in order to exhaust all conceivable possibilities. Since he himself was too poor to afford such expensive consultations, his friends and students tried to cover the travel expenses and doctors' fees financially by donations and collections. A charity concert organized by a former pupil of his, the daughter of Count Leopold Thun, brought in 1800 guilders. And his Swedish lady-friend, Fröjda Rubenson, who had meanwhile married, organized a collection and sent him the 1244 guilders received without delay. Thus supplied with financial means, Smetana could begin his journey abroad in April 1875. It took him first to the famous otologist, Friedrich von Troeltsch, then employed as a professor at the University Clinic in Würzburg. Since he was able to tell him no more than had Professor Zaufal in Prague except to recommend that he have his eardrums opened, Smetana went to Vienna to the famous ear specialist, Professor Adam Politzer, to whom he wrote the following medical history of his illness:

> Since June 1874 I have been suffering from hearing disturbances, temporary ringing now in the left ear, now in the right one, mostly containing the highest tones of the four ledger-line octaves. —In July a stronger humming like breaking waves was added; and later dizziness with ever stronger turning of the head. I began losing hearing, namely, on the right side. At the end of July I asked the advice of Dr. Zaufal, Professor of Ear Medicine in Prague. After a close examination he found that both ears were affected. For the time being, he recommended rest and protection of my hearing, forbade piano playing, and once per day, for five minutes, I had to put the end of a rubber hose—I don't recall the name of it—into my ear. For in the whole month of August I was living in the country in my daughter's house in order to have the necessary quiet. Meanwhile back in Prague, at the beginning of September, Dr. Zaufal applied an air douche by means of a catheter. In October my condition improved on the left side. There I could hear perfectly well. But the right ear has remained completely deaf. At the end of October I became completely deaf within two or three days, could it be a result of my resumption

of piano playing, though moderate? Or from some other cause? —I now remained, as is said, "deaf as a stick," until the end of February, despite all medical help. Then at that time Professor Zaufal applied the air douche with balloon in both ears.—Since March of this year I find an improvement in the left ear, insofar as I can distinctly hear all strong high sounds, such as whistling, high voices, sibilant sounds, etc., but with one undifferentiated coloration like crackling thin wood. I cannot distinguish words, but hear only the clear vowels, "e," "a," and "ah," and the sibilants "s," "sh," etc.

Professor Politzer's diagnosis after a thorough examination on 5 and 6 May 1875 was a "labyrinth laming" that should be treated with "electrisation." Yet Politzer must also have given the patient other therapeutic recommendations, since from a calendar entry of Smetana's for 24 May we learn of a smear treatment, though without any clue as to the ingredients of the salve used. Strangely, this salve had to be applied not just locally behind the ears but on the whole body, a circumstance that will be of significance in discussing the definitive diagnosis of Smetana's disease. This manner of treatment makes it possible to conclude that it must even then have been clear to Professor Politzer that the sickness could not be a disease of the middle ear, as previously assumed, but must have been a disease of the inner ear or of the auditory nerve.

Unfortunately, these measures, too, led to no recognizable improvement, as can be seen from a diary entry of 30 June 1875: "Examination of my hearing capacity. I notice no progress. The doctor was satisfied." Neither the smear treatment nor the subsequent exercises in the manner of hearing exercises—by striking a series of notes on the piano or loud reading of consonants and syllables—could give the despairing patient any hope. The last anchor of hope he saw was the electrotherapy which Professor Zaufal began to perform on 25 October, after having obtained his own equipment for this purpose. But this treatment attempt also remained without success. "The last attempt!—Then my fate is

AFTER 1876, SMETANA LIVED IN RECLUSION IN THE HOUSE OF HIS DAUGHTER
SOPHIE'S FAMILY IN JABKENICE.

sealed!" he wrote in his diary before beginning this electrotherapy.
Soon he knew once and for all: he was and would remain deaf
for the rest of his life. Deep resignation settled over his disposition, as is shown by an entry of 2 March 1876, his birthday: "If my
disease is incurable, I would rather be released from this painful
existence." He had meanwhile moved to the forester's house of
Jabkenice, where his daughter Sophie and his son-in-law wel-
comed him heartily and where he spent the rest of his life in
rustic solitude.

Basically, life in the forester's house went quite joyfully. Smetana loved his two daughters [Sophie and Bozena, his daughter by
Bettyna] and Sophie's four children above all else and he was
treated with love and exquisite respect by all members of the
household. If he nonetheless fell more and more frequently into
a depressive state, it was his deafness which forced him in any
conversation to have the words addressed to him written down—
a process we are also acquainted with from Beethoven's conversation notebooks. But beyond this inevitable misfortune, there

came another circumstance that made him downcast, namely, the increasing alienation from his second wife Bettyna. She bore her lot of having to live with a deaf husband in constant financial distress with the dutifulness of a faithful but dispassionate comrade. But she was unable to come up with loving sympathy as the wife of a suffering genius, while Smetana never ceased hoping to rekindle her love and to court her. His piano cycle *Dreams*, completed in 1875, by its elegiac, dreamy basic mood and its melancholy reminiscence of happy days gone by, reveals how much he suffered from this perceptible alienation of his wife. This piano cycle, *Dreams*, is in many respects the subjective counterpart of Smetana's great orchestra cycle *Má Vlast (My Fatherland)*, the likes of which cannot be found in all music literature and whose fourth symphonic composition *From Bohemian Fields and Groves*, as opposed to the first three parts, was likewise written in the forester's house in Jabkenice.

The first opera that originated after Smetana's loss of hearing was *Hubicka (The Kiss)*. This work, completed at the end of July 1876, betrays no sign of the inner struggles with which he had wrested it out of his deep depressions. Of all his eight operas it had the most uncontested success from the first, as can be seen from the diary entry of 7 November 1876 on the occasion of its premiere:

> First performance of Kiss, full theater, two encores after the first act, three after the last one...there was a lot of applause.

In that same month the opera was repeated seven times with the house all sold out. This noticeably alleviated Smetana's financial troubles at least temporarily. More important for Smetana, however, were the enthusiastic ovations from a public that at first was waiting curiously to see whether the deaf composer was still at all able to create an opera. An eyewitness reported: "Wreaths were thrown from the balconies over the heads of the parterre to his feet, flowers were showered on him from all sides, the jubilation did not come to an end," until finally the deaf composer, deeply touched and gesticulating helplessly with his arms appeared on the stage.

SMETANA'S OFFICE IN JABKENICE.

Soon after completing the score to the opera *The Kiss* and two years after the onset of his deafness, Smetana began composing his First String Quartet in E Minor. The title itself, *From My Life,* shows that this is an autobiographical work. Since this form of program music was unusual in chamber music, Smetana felt compelled to provide various verbal explanations for the musical portrayal of his life. He explained this to his friend Josef Srb-Debrnov in April 1878 as follows:

> I did not have in mind to write just any quartet according to the recipe and sages of the customary forms....For me the form of every composition arises from its subject. And so this quartet too created the form it has.

Smetana had once before, in a state of deep mental pain, fled to the intimacy of chamber music, when the death of his beloved little daughter had occasioned the Piano Trio in G Minor.

In the String Quartet in E Minor, *From My Life,* which originated in the short work period between October and December

1876 in the seclusion of Jabkenice, Smetana describes the decisive stations of his life in four movements. In a letter to Srb-
Debrnov, he summarizes them as follows:

> First movement: inclination to art in my youth,
> romantically dominated, unspeakable longing for
> something I can neither express nor imagine but,
> as it were, also a warning of coming misfortune;
> the long resounding tone in the finale stemmed
> from this beginning; it is that fateful whistling of
> the highest tones in my ear, announcing my deaf-
> ness in 1874. Second movement: a kind of polka,
> accompanies me back in reminiscence to the happy
> life of my youth, when as a composer of dance
> pieces I showered the young people with music.
> Third movement: largo sostenuto, reminds me of
> my blissful love for a girl who later became my
> faithful wife. Fourth movement: describes the
> knowledge of the element of national music, joy
> in the route taken until interrupted by my omi-
> nous catastrophe; beginning of deafness, look into
> the sad future, a little ray of hope, but the memory
> of the beginnings of my career still a painful feel-
> ing. That, then, was the meaning of this composi-
> tion, which was, so to speak, of a private nature
> and therefore is intentionally written for four in-
> struments, which are supposed to speak with one
> another in an intimate circle of friends about what
> so depresses me. Nothing further.

This program is most realistically elaborated in the final movement, where the main theme suddenly breaks off and over a
horrible deep bass *tremolo* a shrill four-stroked E resounds—a
motif Smetana explained to August Kömpel in Weimar as follows:

> I believed I had to portray the beginning of my
> deafness and I sought to depict it as happens in
> the finale of the quartet with the E of the first vio-
> lin stroked four times. For before the onset of my

THE FOUR-STROKED E THAT TORMENTED SMETANA AT THE BEGINNING OF HIS EAR AILMENT WAS CAPTURED BY HIM IN THE FINAL MOVEMENT OF HIS STRING QUARTET IN E MINOR, *FROM MY LIFE*, COMPOSED IN 1876.

complete deafness for many weeks in the evenings between 6 and 7 o'clock I was always pur-
sued by the strong whistle of the A-flat major
chords, A flat, E flat, and C, in the highest piccolo
key, uninterrupted for a half hour, indeed often

for a whole hour, and there was no way to free myself of it. This happened regularly each day, as it were, as a warning cry for the future! I therefore have tried to portray this horrible catastrophe in my destiny with the high-pitched E in the finale. Therefore the E must be played fortissimo the whole time through.

Still not fully convinced that there could be no possibility of his recovery, in November 1877 he went to Lamberk, where a Kapellmeister called Klíma, who held a position in Russia, proposed to improve his hearing with his more than dubious methods of treatment. Smetana, in his desperation, allowed this obvious charlatan to puncture him in several places behind the ear and on the neck, perhaps similarly to the serious use of acupuncture today. Smetana commented on the outcome of this treatment: "The result was null; instead of regaining my hearing I got a sore neck." A few years later, in March 1880, Smetana again saw a glimmer of hope on the horizon by the announcement of a new kind of hearing aid with the trademark "Dentiphon." It was a voluminous gadget that did not improve his hearing at all and that he rejected because it was so awkward to use: "In order to hear I would have to run around everywhere with a very large box on my back."

The new year 1877 began relatively joyfully and full of hope. After completing a composition assignment for a great Prague chorus, an *a capella* men's chorus *Song of the Sea*, which is one of Smetana's most important choral works, in April in a state of high spirits and euphoric creative joy he began composing four polkas, which he "wrote directly in finished version with the pen and also played through on the piano right away." But soon his difficulties in working kept increasing. Besides deafness with all its physical burdens, in June 1877 additional symptoms appeared and made composition more and more difficult for him. In his diary we read:

> Three days in a row I suffered dizzy spells, associated with vomiting....Dizzy spells from morning to night, reduced energy.

Until then in Jabkenice he had composed for several hours each day divided between morning and evening; but now after just one hour, the "humming in his head" and the frequent dizzy states prevented him from further work by a lack of concentration.

Yet amid this mental and physical distress, he still found the strength, after the success of his opera *The Kiss*, to compose a new operatic work by the title *The Secret*. In a letter to the lady writing the libretto, dated 2 October, he wrote:

> I am working as well as I can, when the dizzy spells plaguing me now more than ever permit, on our last opera The Secret....I am afraid, however, that my music is not cheerful enough! Where should I get it when my mind is full of pain and care....I have not been receiving any salary since May....But when I plunge into musical reverie, I forget at least for a while all that pursues me in old age.

Yet *The Secret,* too, became a great success. It is the first opera composed as a unity through and through and polyphonically permeated from the prelude, via the great ensemble and choral scenes, all the way to the finale. After the premiere, the overjoyed composer wrote in his diary on 23 September 1878: "Overfilled house. Wreaths, encores. My children were here." Smetana had finally been accepted by the Prague public, so that even his archenemy Pivoda could not help finding words of recognition for the composer in his newspaper.

Smetana's productive stream came to a halt. By March 1879, when he finished the symphonic compositions *Tabor* and *Blanik*, the great cycle *My Fatherland* was complete. This "National Shrine of Czech Music" marked the creation of a portrayal of a nation's landscape and history in the form of a musical composition, the likes of which no other music culture can show. The first complete performance of the cycle on 5 November 1882 was then also a unique kind of festive event, as we can see from a review of this concert published in the journal *Dalibor:*

Since the opening of the National Museum, there
never were in a Czech gathering such high spirits
as last Sunday...immediately after the heart-
gripping finale, hundreds of lips shouted "Maestro
Smetana," and on that day he was celebrating one
of his greatest triumphs....The same unending
storms of applause were repeated after each following piece of the six-part cycle....After *Blanik*,
the public went wild and could not part from the
composer who could not hear his work but was
happy in the awareness that it made others happy.

Right after finishing this grandiose cycle, Smetana completed
a further piano-cycle, *Czech Dances*, consisting of four polkas,
less virtuoso than those from his piano-playing days, but in return
more mature and poetic, and representing this typical folk music,
as it were, on a higher level of artistic reflection. They thus differ
in principle from the more elementary portrayal of Dvořák's
Slavonic Dances or Brahms' *Hungarian Dances*. In a letter of
2 March 1879, Smetana spelled out his very personal idea of a
Czech polka for a better understanding of this composition: "My
intention is to idealize the polka, as Chopin formerly did with the
mazurka." Incidentally he himself considered this cycle to be the
best he wrote for the piano in his life.

Apart from his deafness, with its depressing accompanying
circumstances, gradually other symptoms appeared and gave him
increasing difficulties in composing, as he described them:

Just imagine the turmoil of music in a person who
has lost his hearing. No one has any idea how a
deaf person's thoughts run away. If I do not write
things down immediately, after a while I no longer
know how they were; and yet my memory was
once acclaimed as phenomenal.

This declining memory was disturbing, not merely for composing, but also for personal contacts with his surrounding world.
When on the occasion of the festive opening of the National

Theater with his opera *Libuse* on 11 June 1881 he had to give a festive speech, he stated this openly:

> I am supposed to thank you for all this and I must admit to you that I am trembling, for nothing is so difficult for me as to speak coherently. Hardly do I speak one sentence, and the next moment I no longer know what I had just been thinking because I no longer hear it. I am lacking the "copia verborum" [eloquence] that accompanied me throughout my whole life.

This painful existence in the seclusion of the forester's house in Jabkenice was enlivened by side tours to Prague, where he attended theater performances and concerts of various kinds but also paid tribute to lighter entertainment. In answer to the puzzled question of his libretto writer, Krasnohorska, he tried to explain the reasons for this:

> Just picture a deaf, so to speak, dead head into which penetrates no sound of an instrument or human word, indeed no echo of life! I therefore want at least to see something, to feast my eyes like a child, and the wilder it is, the less I miss the sense of hearing.

But the most important form of diversion from his cruel destiny was again and again composing. Inspired by the successes of the opera *The Secret*, soon the plan for a new operatic work *The Devil's Wall* developed; and its premiere took place on 29 October 1882. Here Smetana broke with tradition with his plan to design a "speaking symphonic painting" that gave equal weight to the vocal and the instrumental components. In an analysis of the work intended for conductors, he stressed the "unity of the whole opera, as if it were one single great…symphony, although combined with text." As could be expected, the novelty of this opera was understood neither by the audience nor by his friends; therefore it had little success. Smetana, already seriously ill, was deeply disappointed by this failure. Behind the scenes, with tears in his eyes, he is said to have spoken the resigned words:

> So apparently I am already too old and should
> give up composing. No one wants anything to do
> with me anymore!

This opera gave him particular difficulties, since the work was made difficult by various health problems. Besides the humming in his ears and the dizzy spells, it was the loss of memory, increasingly felt as embarrassing, that most bothered and depressed him. How hard composing had already become for him is shown in a letter of 24 February 1882:

> If I write merely for a short hour, a noise rushes
> through my head, and the world spins before my
> eyes, so that I must abandon any writing, step back
> from the table and wait until everything calms
> down! In such a complicated work as the opera I
> am now working on, since not a single tone reaches
> me from the outside I have all I can do to retain in
> my memory the context of the whole organism.

Even more than in the composition of the opera *The Devil's Wall*, Smetana had to struggle with his physical complaints and disturbances when he was working on his Second String Quartet in D Minor. This chamber music work, too, became again a personal, autobiographical confession, whose form he himself characterized as follows:

> This quartet moves forward from where the first
> one left off, after the catastrophe. It depicts the
> turmoil of music in a person who has lost his hear-
> ing.

And in the list of his compositions he added:

> String quartet (continuation of From My Life in
> D Minor). Composed in the nervous disease re-
> sulting from deafness.

The work on this quartet dragged on until March 1883, since it had to be interrupted again and again due to the exhaustion of his mental and physical energies. A few weeks earlier, on 18 February 1883, he once again gave detailed depiction of the origin and course of his hearing disturbance to the Prague music psychologist Carl Stumpf:

> The year I became completely deaf, first in the right ear, and two and a half months later in the left one, without any alleviation to the right one, was 1874. Since October 1874 I have been totally deaf in both ears....When the disease first began and only the left side was receptive to any external sound impression, in the evenings outside the closed room, out in the grove, there sounded a wonderfully beautiful flute playing every evening. Only after my arrival in Prague did it disappear, never more to return through all the years. During the day I was plagued by long-lasting chords in A-flat major kept at the highest piccolo-pitch...which resounded alternatively, and which I believe I expressed in the E-tone (stroked four times) of the finale of my string quartet....And in this lamentable condition I have composed works of the greatest scope, without ever having heard them....For me to critique my works is out of the question. I see them before me, but I have never heard one tone of all the works listed here, and yet they live in me, and their mere imaging aroused in me: tearful emotion, an ecstatic revelry, astonishment and admiration of the mystery of the creative psyche!

In the last years of his life, however, Smetana's creative activity was impeded more by the onset of psychic and mental changes than by his hearing disturbance. Approximately since the end of 1881, complaints of heightened nervousness and lowered ability to concentrate when composing became frequent. Although his works therefore advanced only at a snail's pace, since he often forgot what he had written from one moment to the next and repeatedly had to read it over again, he could not be deterred from his work for the following reason: "I really want to give my people all I owe them and carry in my heart." These lines written on 24 February 1882 still point to his unbroken industriousness, while a letter of 4 December 1882 clearly describes the conditions that gave him more and more difficulties in composing:

> The work generally leaves me quite confused; I have to write very attentively and slowly and constantly seek the earlier motifs.

On 9 December, finally, a letter gives us a truly moving insight into his physical and mental state and a premonition of the whole extent of an abrupt mental breakdown:

> I have undergone a great change. About three weeks ago toward evening I suddenly lost my voice, that is, the possibility and ability to express my thoughts. Indeed, even reading became difficult for me. I could not recall the names of living and historical persons; I kept screaming only "tye-tye-tye," and in between were long pauses where I sat there with an open mouth. No one knew what to do with me, they wanted to send for the doctor—it was already late in the evening when the affliction gradually subsided. I could read again and recall all names again. —After a few days, perhaps a week, the incident was repeated on an even worse scale; I couldn't get out even the smallest word. They immediately put me to bed where I slowly recovered. The doctor forbade me any drop of wine, beer, or alcohol, and declared that this was blood pressure in the brain and I could happen to lose consciousness, indeed even my mind. The intellectual work of the brain in grasping new musical ideas, the persistent deafness, the overburdening of the auditory nerves allegedly were driving a strong current of blood into the brain, which froze up, so to speak, and at that moment could grasp nothing. — The doctor forbade all reading for longer than a quarter of an hour at most, and absolutely any occupation with

music at all. I must not even think of music, neither reading my own compositions, nor those of
others, nor picturing them in my thoughts, even if
this should last for a year. —It was high time and
even in Prague signs of it were noticeable; I was
ever dissatisfied, my new compositions were re-
pugnant to me and sometimes so depressed me
that my whole body trembled. The whole summer I suffered from feeling cold, and delight in
jokes vanished day by day.

Still Smetana did not give up. Around the middle of 1883, he
began writing the score for an opera, *Viola*, whose text, based on
Shakespeare, had already fascinated him ten years earlier. He
told his friends:

I keep on composing only so that people will know
what goes on in a musician's head when he is in a
condition like mine.

Whenever pains or spells of excitation allowed, he tried to continue with his work, which sometimes rose to a real euphoria.
For instance, on 8 January 1884 he wrote to his friend Srb-Debrnov:
"On Viola, tell the gentlemen in Prague how moved my soul is,
tears—tears!" And a few days later, he inscribed on a page of the
score the confused words: "Fame! Viola! Eternally shall she—
famously (sic) bear the fame! Fame to her!" The course of the
disease was still changeable, with short-term improvements and
even complaint-free intervals. But signs of mental confusion came
more and more to the foreground. Optical and acoustic hallucinations began. He waved from his window to persons on the
street who did not exist at all but whom in his fantasy he very
clearly saw passing by. Another time he thought he saw:

...a long row of completely unknown and various
persons entering his room, in particular a crowd
of very beautiful and expensively dressed ladies,
and he could not understand from where this large
company so suddenly came and what it was

seeking there in his solitude and how he sent especially the ladies to Prague, remarking that they
could entertain themselves better there.

In the first weeks of 1884, Smetana fell increasingly into a complete mental darkness. A letter written partly in German, partly in
Czech on 19 January 1884 shows this heartrendingly:

Dear friend! I write in the greatest haste to you to
buy me 20 to 30 postage stamps, red with a big
five; when I come to Prague, I will pay you the
30 florins back. I have such a rage I would most
prefer to shoot in with cannons….Oh Viola! I send
you the divine melodies of the first Act, so that
you can enjoy these passages with delight. Many
make me—into an angel.

This opera-fragment, *Viola*, mentioned by him again, which he
was working on until February 1884, ended with the 365th measure. With an unconscious premonition of his further destiny he
wrote on the upper border of this page a handwritten remark:
"Last sheet." Surprisingly, this torso of his last opera shows hardly
any signs of his confusion, although at this point in time he was,
with his creative activity, already at the edge of insanity.

Smetana, incidentally, had had a vague premonition of the
coming disaster, even years before. For, as early as 1879 while
composing his cycle *My Fatherland*, he had jotted down the prophetic words:

I am afraid of insanity. I have become so melancholic that I sit there doing nothing for hours, thinking of nothing but my misfortune.

Now, in the spring of 1884 insanity broke out into the open. He
wrote more and more confused letters to unknown addressees;
on his birthday on 2 March, he even sent a postcard to himself. But he also carried on an irrational correspondence with
Mozart and Beethoven. Frequently, incoherent word fragments,
such as "in the country," "in the woods," "by the lake," "it was
good too," were found on loose snippets of paper—their meaning no longer decipherable. His stride became dragging and

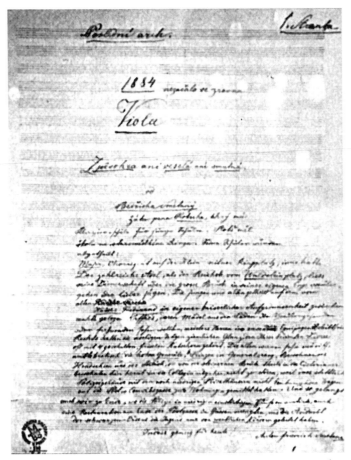

SMETANA'S LAST MANUSCRIPT BOOKLET OF HIS PLANNED OPERA *Viola*. THE
WORK BREAKS OFF IN FEBRUARY 1884.

his comprehension was so impaired that he no longer could per-
ceive the premiere of his *Prague Carnival* performed in Prague
in honor of his birthday on 2 March, this being his last complete
composition, finished in September 1883.

Finally he reached the point where he could no longer recognize his friends on the street, indeed even his own children and
family members. He used to babble senselessly to himself, and
only exceptionally could words like "Wagner" or "Liszt" be understood by people around him. Moreover, states of agitation began, in which he smashed furniture and window panes of his

living room and even threatened his relatives with a revolver, so that he had to be watched day and night. After an especially serious fit of rage, the family therefore decided on April 22, with a heavy heart, to have him committed to the mental institute in Prague for inpatient observation and care. Frantisek Moucha, a servant of Smetana's son-in-law, Chief Forester Schwarz, describes in moving words the sad farewell of the composer from Jabkenice, never to return again:

> The dismal, rainy day of 23 April 1884 dawned....
> The carriage stood ready, before the wooden stairs
> leading to the lobby....Tears were running down
> the Forester's face as I handed him the blankets to
> cover Smetana. Smetana sat completely absent-
> minded in the carriage....Everyone was weeping.

In the following three weeks, in which the destructive process was bringing the life of this important artist to an end, only the closest relatives were granted access to the barred little room in which Smetana spent his last days. How he spent them can be read in the case history preserved in the institute's archives:

> The patient is badly nourished, his body trembles,
> extreme feebleness prevents him from standing
> upright. The patient lies curled up in bed, wakes
> up at night screaming and speaking incomprehen-
> sibly. He has difficulty in swallowing, can swal-
> low only liquids. His articulation is impaired, the
> tongue hard to move, the voice deep, strong; fre-
> quently the patient makes movements, as if he
> were directing an orchestra; his hands tremble as
> he does this. The pulse is sparse and weak; the
> right corner of his mouth hangs down somewhat.
> When he speaks or screams, the left half of his
> face remains immobile. He gets out of bed, drags
> himself along the floor with lots of screaming. He
> seems to be pursued by unpleasant fantasies. The
> patient makes peculiar motions with his right hand.
> His speech is incomprehensible.

SMETANA DIED IN THIS ROOM IN A PRAGUE CLINIC.

This medical report was completed by a detailed description of the further course of the disease until the patient's death, written by the doctor-in-charge, Dr. Vaclav Walter, which states:

On the chaise longue, a chattering old man slides back and forth. Smetana's illness has been long drawn out and actually began with his deafness. He was of completely turbid consciousness and yet very restless. Although he could no longer maintain himself, in his constantly expansive affects he allowed neither himself nor those around him even a moment's rest. It was impossible to say anything to him. He did not hear. Fortunately he was not strong and could easily be overpowered. He rejected all nourishment, and it was necessary to feed him. Smetana's speech, paralytically blurred from the very first, worsened to incomprehensibility. He no longer recognized any of the visitors. He had no lucid intervals. Only fainting and hallucinations. There was absolutely no hope of a decline of the disease, not to mention recovery. Physically, he was just skin and bones, frailty incarnated. He was expiring slowly. Keeping beat with his right hand, he bellowed as he did so, trying to imitate musical instruments, and in disharmonious sequence he suddenly gave a tone with unusual force like a heavy blow on a Turkish drum: boom! Sometimes he laughed with the broken, groan-like laughter of the paralytic. On 12 May 1884 we expected Smetana's death that morning....At 4:30 P.M. he breathed his last.

Diagnostic Evaluation

An autopsy of the corpse was performed on 13 May 1884 in the Pathological-Anatomical Institute in Prague with the consent of Smetana's family members by Professor Dr. Jan Hlava with the assistance of five doctors. The finding in the autopsy report read as follows:

> The corpse of an approximately sixty-year-old man is of small stature, delicate bone-structure, badly nourished. The epidermis of the torso is shrunken, the face reddened, likewise the mucous membrane of the lips, but the conjunctiva is pale. The neck short, wide enough, the thoracic cage flat, short; the abdomen sunken; abrasions around the knee caps on both sides. The skull is well-proportioned, oval, 17 cm. long, 14 cm. wide, about 1 1/2 cm. thick. Porosity is predominant. The inner surface completely smooth. The pericranium very taut, pale; in the longitudinal fissure freshly coagulated blood. The meninges [cerebral membranes] are thickened, mostly above the left frontal lobe, then on the parietal area, where an insignificant amount of Pacchionian granulations are also found. Above the occipital lobe, the soft parts of the brain are fine. The convolutions of the brain show these

changes compared with a normal brain: mainly, it is striking that they are more massive and less numerous than in other brains. The central convolution of the brain, usually about 1 cm. wide, here has a width of 2 cm. Particularly developed is the third left convolution of the brain (locus Broci); the meninges lie very close to the brain surface. Indeed, they cannot be separated at the thickened places. In dissection we find that the lateral ventricles are widened and contain a clear fluid; the ependyma is smooth, but firm. The cerebral cortex completely narrowed, at most 3 mm. in thickness, browned, shiny and almost as if sclerotic. The central ganglia are flattened, solid enough. Nucleus caudatus and nucleus lentiformis are a black-brown color. Claustrum strikingly wide, ca. 4 mm. [the normal width for this layer of gray matter outside the external capsule of the brain is 2 mm.]. The third ventricle is widened, the ependyma fine, rough, pale, the small veins wide and rough, grainy, shiny, of browned color. The striae acusticae very insignificant, on the right side two, on the left only three, and these notably narrow, grayed. The cerebellum soft and pale. Pons and medulla oblongata solid. The gray matter pigmented, similarly also in the extended spinal cord. The nervi acustici on both sides thin, grayed, and narrower than the norm. The veins at the base of the brain are atheromatous. The brain weighs 1250 g.

In both lungs, lobular hepatization, the left side of the heart somewhat enlarged. Widespread atheroma of the pericardium and almost all arteries. Brown atrophy of the liver and kidneys. Nothing special in the abdomen. In the arteriosclerotic upper thigh artery a solidly attached thrombus.

Diagnosis: Chronic inflammation of the soft meninges, particularly above the frontal lobes. Partial fusion of the soft meninges with the surface of the brain. Water content in the brain ventricles. Red nucleus atrophy. Grainy inflammations of the inner lining of the fourth ventricle with consumption of the acoustic fibers. Inflammation of both lungs, scattered in the lower lobes. Arteriosclerosis, discolored coagulation on the wall of the left thigh artery. General collapse of the body and organs.

This complete rendition of the autopsy report is given because at first highly different views were given about the true cause of Smetana's death, which also led to heated scientific discussions. The autopsy report is therefore an especially important document for establishing the correct diagnosis of Smetana's sickness. Other most important primary sources for an objective and dispassionate medical evaluation of his disease from a medical perspective are his letters and diaries, which were first examined and evaluated expertly from an otological standpoint by H. Feldmann in 1963. Once these documents became known, this put an end not only to all speculations about his hearing ailment, but also to those about his final mental decline and fatal disease.

The key event, from which all later symptoms began, occurred in the weeks of March 1874. At that time there occurred, as must be deduced from a retrospective examination of his diary, an infection that was very frequent in large cities at that time, namely, syphilis. Since the incubation period between infection and the appearance of the first visible lesion, the so-called primary affect, must be set at three to six weeks on the average and this primary affect is dated by Smetana himself as 12 April, the point in time of the infection can be reconstructed with some precision as the beginning or middle of March. For on 30 April we find in his diary the at first seemingly banal remark: "Since the 12th I have been ill with a pus-oozing ulcer." We do not know the exact location of this ulcer, but given Smetana's obviously heterosexual disposition, it must surely have been either in the genital region or around the lips or mouth cavity. The primary affect which begins as a painless crude swelling and soon erupts into an ulcer, generally heals by itself after two to six weeks. But after a further six weeks the disease enters its second stage, the secondary lues, whose clinical picture can be extremely varied. Various organs, such as the throat, the tonsils, or the Eustachian tubes, can be affected, and persistent difficulties in swallowing, as in an anginous throat inflammation, can follow. But the most frequent manifestation of the secondary stage is, no doubt, a characteristic skin rash, which is generally symmetrical and sometimes spreads over the whole body. Again we find in Smetana's diary entries corresponding in time and content with the beginning of a secondary luetic stage. On 11 June 1874 he wrote: "I am constantly sick in the throat," and on 14 July he entered the remark: "I got a rash on my body."

Unfortunately in the course of a lues, the nervous system, too, is often greatly affected even in the early stage, especially in the area of the cerebral membranes and cranial nerves. The eighth cranial nerve, the *nervus acusticus* or hearing nerve, is especially susceptible. Therefore, frequently in the early stage of lues, hearing disturbances, mostly of a mild nature are found, but occasionally they can also progress all the way to complete deafness. This latter event is, however, not observed before the sixth month after the beginning of the disease. Again, data corresponding in time and content can be read from Smetana's diary. By 24 July he complained: "At times I have blocked-up ears and at the same time my head spins as if I were having dizzy spells"—typical effects of a syphilitic infection of the hearing and balance nerves. They are frequently accompanied by tormenting noises in the ears, about which Smetana first complained in a letter of 7 September: "At times it begins to roar in my blocked-up ears, as if I were standing next to a strong waterfall." As a rule the disease is developed to a different degree in the two ears. Smetana also reported about this on the occasion of a consultation with Professor Politzer: "In October my condition improved on the left; I heard perfectly well there. The right ear, however, has become completely deaf." Finally, one finds in the diary in mid-November 1874, typically six months after the beginning of the disease, the entry filled with resignation: "I hear nothing, neither by the right ear, nor by the left one." The date of the onset of his complete deafness was given definitely by Smetana once again later, when in 1881 during an intermission in his *Libuse* at the opening of the Prague National Theater he was summoned to the royal loge of Crown Prince Rudolf and he addressed him as follows: "Imperial Highness, I am so unfortunate not to hear anything....I have been totally deaf for six years."

Today it is beyond doubt that Smetana fell ill of syphilis in March 1874 and that at an early secondary stage of the disease it led to a typical affection of the cochlea of the inner ear and, via a specific infection and later degenerative deterioration of the eighth cranial nerve, had complete deafness as a consequence. Apart from the virtually classic medical history, this diagnosis is confirmed by the autopsy findings which speak decidedly of a consumption of the auditory fiber and a paralysis of the auditory nerves, which appear "grayed" because of erosion of the myelin sheath and atrophy of the nerves. It can be assumed that Professor Politzer on the occasion of Smetana's consultation in Vienna had no doubt about the true diagnosis of the hearing disturbance when he determined a "labyrinth laming" and recommended several weeks of salve treatment. For syphilis was known in otological literature since 1868 as the triggering factor of damage to the inner ear with accompanying disturbances of the balance mechanism and subsequent deafness. The only effective method of treatment was still the salve treatment with a mercury salve, which the patient after a bath rubbed into the skin, one area of the body each day in regular sequence. In view of the source documents available today, it therefore seems incomprehensible to want to interpret Smetana's symptoms with a double-sided Menière's disease combined with bleeding of the inner ear, as the Prague psychiatrist, Professor A. Heveroch, tried to do in 1924 on the occasion of a ceremonial speech for the composer's one hundredth birthday. Aside from the fact that the classic Menière's disease always occurs on one side, all the other above-described symptoms cannot be incorporated into this absurd diagnostic structure.

Still greater confusion resulted from the question whether the composer's final mental breakdown can be understood as the consequence of the relentless destructive process of syphilis or whether it can be explained by arteriosclerotic changes of the brain. The latter version was given new currency through findings concerning Smetana's daughter Bozena, who died in 1941 in a Viennese mental institution at the age of seventy-eight years showing the signs of mental confusion caused by arteriosclerosis and allegedly displayed symptoms similar to those her father had in the last stage of his life. On closer examination, however, the daughter's ailment was a state of confusion and mental degeneration corresponding to today's concept of a "multi-infarct dementia," caused by pronounced multiple narrowings in the arteries of the brain due to arteriosclerotic deposits which in turn result in numerous sites of necrotic brain tissue. The variant of a so-called vertebro-basilar syndrome agrees even less with the course of Smetana's disease and the last part of his life, since like multi-infarct dementia it leaves essential symptoms of Smetana's medical history completely out of consideration.

The first depressive psychic symptoms accompanying his deafness made themselves known around 1880, when a decline of his memory began to make composing noticeably more difficult. If he did not put his ideas down on paper immediately, so he then wrote, "after a while I don't know how they were." Similar difficulties also occurred more and more in personal association with his fellowmen. In 1881 he admitted candidly that he found nothing so hard as "to speak coherently. Hardly do I pronounce a sentence, when in the next moment I don't know what I was just thinking." Just a year later, the exhaustion of his mental energies had advanced so much that he often had to break off his composing activity after a short time. He wrote, as we can read in a letter of February 1882, "only for a little hour, then this roaring in the head pursues me, and the world spins before my eyes, so that I must abandon all writing." This at first rather atypical beginning of a mental disease with increasing nervousness, decline of memory, and disturbances of concentration then led in November 1882 to a breakdown with dramatic symptoms. One evening without any warning, he lost his voice and the capacity to clothe his thoughts in words. Even reading became difficult for him, and he had completely forgotten the names of his historical persons. He emitted unarticulated syllables and sat there confused with his mouth open. As fast as this condition came, so rapidly did it disappear again, only to return even more dramatically just a few days later. At first short-term improvements, indeed even complaint-free intervals could be observed, but soon his state of mental confusion took on threatening forms. Smetana began to suffer from constantly feeling cold, and he experienced disturbances in walking, making it hard for him to set one foot in front of the other. Visual and auditory hallucinations began, and by the beginning of 1884 Smetana fell increasingly into mental darkness with only very brief periods of lucidity. Finally he was no longer able to recognize his closest family members. He babbled incomprehensible nonsense to himself, and more and more frequently he became aggressive in his actions. After such a fit of rage, on 22 April he was finally committed to an institute for mental patients. According to the doctors' description he "wandered about in his four walls like a caged animal," refused food, often screamed for hours, urinated on himself, and laughed intermittently like the "groaning of paralytics." He could no longer stand up, and when he spoke or screamed "the left half of his face remained immobile." His voice, "paralytically blurred" from the first, finally degenerated to complete incomprehensibility.

Based on this clinical picture, the doctors of the Prague mental institute assumed the presence of a progressive taboparalysis, a syphilitic disease of the brain and the spinal cord, for in describing the course of the disease they used the term "paralytic" several times and based it on the symptomatology of this disease profile, which was already known to doctors at that time. In a textbook from the late 19th century, the involvement of the brain, one of the characteristics of tertiary syphilis, was described as follows:

> Brain syphilis [*Hirnsyphilis*] is unfortunately a very
> frequent disease. The danger of falling ill of brain
> syphilis is all the greater the more superficially an
> anti-syphilitic treatment was carried out. The rule is
> that five, ten, and sometimes more than twenty years

of complete health have gone by until suddenly signs of brain syphilis make themselves known. Brain syphilis is manifested either in purely functional disturbances, or by the formation of rubbery knots on the meninges or in the brain matter, or finally by the development of an endarteritis obliterans (infection of the inner wall of the blood vessels) in the arteries of the brain, leading as such or by formation of thrombi (blood clots) to a blockage of the vessel and causing a softening of the corresponding brain sectors.

The conviction is gaining ground more and more today that progressive demented paralysis in the vast majority of cases depends on a previous syphilis. Rubbery changes at the base of the brain often condition laming of the cranial nerves, frequently affecting especially the optic nerve but also the facial nerve. Endarteritic lesions most often affect the vessels at the base of the brain so that speech disturbances are almost always to be found. It is especially peculiar to brain syphilis that the disturbances often come repeatedly and disappear again.

But the proof for the actual presence of a neurosyphilis was provided by Professor Dr. Jan Hlava's detailed autopsy report describing definitively the changes of the brain visible to the naked eye in a progressive paralysis and thus making any later discussion of Smetana's disease moot. For the findings he stressed (chronic inflammation of the soft meninges, in particular over the frontal lobe, partial fusion of the soft meninges with the surface of the brain, watery content in the ventricles of the brain, red nucleus atrophy and grainy inflammation of the inner lining of the fourth ventricle with consumption of the acoustic fibers and paralysis of the auditory nerves) are such a clear description of the changes of the brain typical of a progressive paralysis in the context of a tertiary syphilis, that only national and political motives could have led the Director of the Prague Psychiatric

Clinic, Professor Dr. A. Heveroch to accuse doctors who held this diagnosis of being "desecrators of Smetana's honor," so that—reportedly, under pressure from persons unnamed—Professor Hlava saw himself compelled to revise his diagnosis of a syphilitic disease.

To underscore the exactness of Professor Hlava's pathological-anatomical descriptions and the rightness of the diagnostic conclusions he drew from them, it might be well to cite a modern standard work of specialized pathology on this theme. The morphological picture of a progressive paralysis is there described as follows:

> The inflammation of the meninges...can be clearly recognized by the turgidness and the scarred calluses of the soft meninges, especially at the frontal lobe of the brain....The inflammatory lesions prefer the cerebral cortex....In advanced stages of paralysis, atrophy of the convolutions of the brain is noticeable.... The thickened soft meninges can be peeled from the narrowed convolutions of the brain only with difficulty. The atrophy of the convolutions of the brain is counterbalanced by an enlarging of the ventricles of the brain. But here, besides atrophy of the brain, ependymitis granularis [grainy constitution of the inflamed inner lining of the brain ventricles] plays an additional role. A complication of meningitis syphilitica is neuritis of the basal ganglia....Losses of functioning are observed in the optic nerve, the auditory nerves, and the facial nerve.

In the subsequent discussion of progressive paralysis, this modern textbook then states literally:

> In the early stages, the collateral inflammation damages the ganglia cells without causing them to atrophy or die. In this stage occasionally accompanied by manic over-excitability...intellectual productivity can be heightened to genial levels. The classic example of this is the time of Nietzsche's

great philosophical creativity. In late stages, with increasing atrophy of the cerebral cortex in the affected brain sectors, a decline of the personality and increasing stultification follows.

This text not only rehabilitates Professor Hlava's autopsy finding, but it also provides a morphological basis to explain the symptoms manifested in the last stage of Smetana's disease—loss of memory and mental decline after prior creative activity heightened to levels of genius, manic overexcitability all the way to fits of rage, speech disturbances, one-sided laming of the face, and finally total deterioration of the personality.

The anamnestic reference to the point in time of the primary infection, the chronologically typical beginning of the second phase with the appearance of a general skin rash, the characteristic affection of the auditory nerves with total deafness of both ears occurring after the passage of at least six weeks, as is typical for this disease, and finally the process starting after an interval of at least ten years, leading to the development of a progressive paralysis in the tertiary stage of the disease, and the total decline of the personality of this previously so brilliant musical creator—all this allows for no other diagnosis than that of syphilis, which on top of all these evils was also treated totally inadequately.

Investigations of the European and North American population around the turn of the century show that between ten and fifteen percent of people underwent a syphilitic infection, and that the socioeconomically underprivileged classes clearly were more frequently affected thereby. In Europe's larger cities it was estimated that in the prosperous strata of society less than one percent were infected. Since in recent times voices have loudly pointed out the endemic occurrence of this disease in Asia Minor and wanted to displace the origin of this disease to the Asiatic area, it may be useful to take a look back at the history of this fear-instilling infectious disease.

Actually, to this day the question has not been definitively answered whether this venereal disease, which was first called the "French disease" and since the end of the 16th century "lues venerea," already occurred before Columbus discovered America.

For four centuries people believed the incontestably dominant portrayal that the disease was brought into Europe by Columbus' crew. Even the second edition of Jean Astruc's book on *The Venereal Diseases* in 1736 says:

> I can prove that this disease, unknown in antiq-
> uity among Jews, Greeks, and Arabs, first occurred
> on our continent toward the end of the fifteenth
> century. It was unfortunately brought into Europe
> from the Antilles, especially from the island of Haiti.
> The Spaniards who had landed on these islands in
> 1492 and 1493 under command of Christopher Co-
> lumbus were first infected by unhygienic sexual
> intercourse with the women of the country. Fi-
> nally they infected the Neapolitans when they came
> to their assistance there in 1494. Here the disease
> was transmitted to the French during the war, so
> that finally three nations were infected, and they
> carried the disease to the rest of Europe and in
> part also to Asia and Africa. There are thus good
> grounds for saying that with this deadly disease
> America brought ruin to its conquerors, the Euro-
> peans.

Not until 1912 was doubt cast on this view by the important medical historian Karl Sudhoff from Leipzig. He stated that this disease, later called syphilis, had existed in Europe long before Columbus and merely appeared to a greater extent toward the end of the 15th century. This interpretation was accepted not only by outstanding German scientists, but also by American scientists, among whom MacCurdy even came to the astonishing conclusion: "The existence of syphilis in the New World before Columbus cannot be proven." This surprising assertion, which indirectly made the transmission of syphilis from Europe to America seem possible, was, however, definitively refuted around thirty years later by the famous pathological anatomist, Ludwig Aschoff. For he was able to demonstrate the typical syphilitic damages to bones in skeletons from newly discovered graves in Alabama from pre-Columbian times, whereas the oldest syphilitic bone damages found in Europe belong to the time after Columbus. These findings are proof that, at least in America, syphilis already existed before the arrival of Columbus.

The question still remains whether or not this disease was not dispersed worldwide even before the discovery of America in a form that was clinically scarcely recognizable. A discovery in 1927 from a Neolithic cave in the Marne valley, in which bones with the typical syphilitic damages were found, would seem to suggest this. But it is hard to imagine that the doctors of antiquity, who were very careful observers, would have overlooked such impressive late damages as consumption of the spinal cord or progressive paralysis. The same is true of medieval doctors and of those from the Arab countries. A clear resolution of this question will also hardly be possible in the future, because an exact separation of the four venereal diseases under consideration became clinically possible only since 1838 and a certain diagnosis of syphilis even only since 1905, after Fritz Schaudinn had discovered the *Spirochaeta pallida* as its pathogenic agent and one year later a serological method of detection had been developed by August Wassermann.

The first cases of syphilis showed up in central Europe around 1495. As can be read in a chronicle from 1510, "this abominable disease, which no one had ever seen before, was brought back from the war by the mercenaries." Everywhere in Germany, and a little later also in Spain and Italy, little booklets appeared, describing this "malignant pox" and calling it by various names. An especially important book about this new disease was published in 1530 by Girolamo Fracastoro, in the form of an artistically significant didactic poem that has been compared with Virgil's *Georgica*. This poem treats of a shepherd called Syphilus, who had so damaged the temple of the sun that Apollo punished him with a new, terrible sickness that could be cured only with *guajak*. This work is important not only because the shepherd Syphilus gave the disease its name, but also because it already indicates a possible successful treatment for this horrible disease.

When syphilis first occurred in masses around 1500, it is understandable that desperate attempts were made to find a suitable cure. The wood of the guajak tree, recommended as specific medication against this disease and therefore first imported to Europe in 1514 rapidly acquired great popularity—it is the same medication Fracastoro reported of in his book. The trading houses of the Welsers and Fuggers in Augsburg were the major distributors of the medicine praised as a wonder drug. The famous humanist Ulrich von Hutten was among the first grateful patients who believed they were cured by this guajak wood. But besides guajak wood, mercury, introduced into medicine by Arab doctors, soon acquired increasing recognition as a medication for syphilis and toward the end of the 16th century, despite its considerable side effects, it almost completely replaced guajak wood. One of the first patients apparently successfully healed by quicksilver poultices was the young scholar, Joseph Grünpeck, a canon and confessor of the Emperor Maximilian, who described his painful experiences vividly in his little book published in 1503 about *Mentulagra, Also Called the French Disease.*

One should be restrained in moral judgments about historical persons who demonstrably contracted syphilis, as I emphasized in the chapter on "Franz Schubert." Since even as late as the 19th century there was still a great lack of clarity about the origin and possibilities of infection, people were much more likely to contract syphilis than today when the populace is almost totally informed about these matters. That Schubert or Smetana fell sick with syphilis does not at all mean a moral condemnation of these artists as to their sexual life. For at all times since its appearance, this disease has not spared the prosperous, so-called good society any more than it did artists, intellectuals, or politicians. Hans Bankl enumerated with laudable candor not only the musicians Schubert, Smetana, E.T.A. Hoffmann, Paganini, and Hugo Wolf in the ranks of famous syphilitics, but he also gave examples from painting and literature. Famous painters like Édouard Manet, Hans Makart, and Paul Gauguin were affected, as were the writers and philosophers, Friedrich Nietzsche, Heinrich Heine, Arthur Schopenhauer, Nikolaus Lenau, Gustave Flaubert, Charles Baudelaire, and Guy de Maupassant, as well as the earlier humanists, Ulrich von Hutten and Erasmus of Rotterdam. But scientists like Semmelweis or politicians and potentates like Lord Randolph Churchill, King Francis I of France, or Henry VIII of

England join their company. Indeed even the higher clergy was not spared; besides the aforementioned Canon Grünpeck, the Popes Alexander VI, Julius II, and Leo X were afflicted with this scourge. The named personalities did not all die of this disease, and only a few suffered the horrible fate of having to perish from progressive paralysis of the brain, as did Nietzsche or Smetana. But they all more or less got to feel the frightful mental and physical ravages of this disease.

So in Smetana's case, too, we once again stand before a tragic fate that was caused by a disease whose course and fateful outcome could certainly have been averted with the means available to modern medicine today. For today a single injection with a high dose of long-acting penicillin can heal this disease with a success rate of more than ninety-five percent.

Smetana, however, lived at a time when the possibilities of treating syphilis were very restricted, so that he had to walk the horrible way of this disease to the bitter end. His mortal remains found their last resting place in the cemetery of that fabulously unique castle, Vyschehrad, which the founder of the new Czech music glorified so uniquely in his cycle *My Fatherland*. Before the coffin was closed forever, the eulogist pronounced the warning words: "Pride of the Czech people—the victim of Czech conditions."

Smetana's Doctors

Dr. Jaroslav Hlava (1855–1924)

Born in Unterkralovic in Bohemia, Jaroslav Hlava studied in Prague and graduated in 1879. After he had rounded out his studies in Germany and France, he was able to qualify as a university lecturer in 1883 at the Pathological-Anatomical Institute in Prague. In 1887 he was appointed Professor on the faculty of this Institute.

His main interest was the etiology of infectious diseases, as well as bacteriological and epidemiological questions in this field. The problem of cancer claimed his special interest. As a university professor he initiated an important school of medicine.

Dr. Adam Politzer (1835–1920)

Dr. Politzer was born in Alberti, Hungary. He studied at the University of Vienna, where he was especially a student of Skoda, Rokitansky, and Oppolzer. He graduated in 1859. He continued his training in foreign clinics under Claude Bernard, Carl Ludwig, Toynbee, and Troeltsch, and he was the first person in Vienna to qualify in the field of otology. He taught as a lecturer starting in 1861 and as an Associate Professor since 1870. Then in 1873 he became Director of the University Clinic for Ear Diseases at the Vienna General Hospital—since 1895 with the rank of Professor.

His scientific research dealt mainly with the anatomy and pathology of the ear, as well as the physiology and therapy of the hearing organ. He developed particular treatment methods for infections of the middle ear and introduced the approach of blowing air into the auditory canal. His *Textbook on Medicine of the Ear* was especially well known. He assembled a large collection of pathological specimens of the auditory organ, the likes of which cannot be found in any other clinic. Among his students were Heinrich Neumann and Gustav Alexander.

Dr. Anton Friedrich Freiherr von Troeltsch (1829–1890)

Dr. von Troeltsch was born in Schwabach near Nürnberg. He studied law in Erlangen starting in 1847, then changed to the natural sciences in Munich in 1848, and studied medicine from 1849 to 1853. His thesis for an advanced degree in 1853 was *On the Case History of Complex Bone Fractures*. Finally he studied ophthalmology in Berlin and Prague. Only then did he begin to devote himself to otology. After stays in Dublin, London, and Paris, he returned to Würzburg to open a general practice and on the side to engage intensely in anatomical investigations of the auditory organs. In 1860 he qualified in this special field and in 1864 he was appointed Extraordinary Professor for Oto-Rhino-Laryngology.

Among his numerous publications is his *Textbook for Medicine of the Ears*, first published in Würzburg in 1862 under the title *The Diseases of the Ear, their Recognition and Treatment*, and later translated into English, French, Dutch, and Italian. In 1864 he founded the Archive for Otology, which he directed until 1890. His main merit consists in having developed various methods of investigation, mainly by improved illumination of the eardrum and the outer ear with natural and artificial light.

Dr. Emanuel Zaufal (1837–1910)

Dr. Zaufal was born in Puschwitz in German Bohemia. He studied at the Josephinum in Vienna. In 1859 he qualified as lecturer in otology at the University of Prague, and in 1873 was appointed Professor of Otology and assigned the task of establishing a state Ear Clinic. His publications are mainly in the field of otology and rhinology. His merit consists mainly in having perfected methods of examination of the interior of the nose and throat by means of various funnels. His bacteriological studies brought proof of the most important pathogens for acute middle ear infections. But he also perfected the radical puncturing of the middle ear areas by indicating his own operative procedure whereby the fatal outcome of a septic sinus thrombosis could be prevented. Finally, in his clinic more major intrusive operations, such as the emptying of brain abscesses, were undertaken.

Peter Ilyich Tchaikovsky

(1840–1893)

In the eyes of his Russian contemporaries, especially the so-called St. Petersburg "mighty little group," Tchaikovsky was a composer oriented mainly by Western patterns, who only occasionally bared his soul, when he used folk melodies from his own homeland. Indeed, in contrast with the national Russian group headed by Rimsky-Korsakov, his music cannot be measured by national standards. From the very first, he sought access to the great European music tradition, and so his musical roots can be found preponderantly in the German Romantics and in 19th century Italian and French music, while his Russian teachers hardly influenced him. Tchaikovsky is therefore today considered Russia's first great composer who used an international music language without thereby denying his national origin. For the Russian element in his music is preserved even where no similarity with Russian folk melodies is directly recognizable; and so his works always radiate an atmosphere felt to be "typically Russian." He himself expressed this in a letter of 17 March 1878:

> The Russian element generally present in my works…can be attributed mainly to the fact that I…was permeated with the incredible charm of genuinely Russian folk music since my earliest childhood, that I passionately love the Russian element in all its manifestations, in a word that I am a Russian in the truest sense.

This was also the way Igor Stravinsky felt, who considered Tchaikovsky to be "the most Russian of us all" and whose muse he felt to be more Russian than the music that "has long been labeled as picturesque Muscovite."

What is evaluated either as the indecisiveness of his character as an artist or else as a cosmopolitan trait of his creative activity, is, in truth, the utterly immeasurable richness of his musical nature, which gives form to subjective impressions with perfect emotional honesty. Some authors even believe all his works have a purely "autobiographical" character, since they perfectly reflect his personality and in them he "bared to the whole world the self he otherwise revealed only to his most intimate friends and relatives." So, understandably, the emotional side of his music, along with its features of lyrical tenderness, can sometimes erupt explosively, and Tchaikovsky has been criticized for allegedly overemphasizing feelings. This strongly subjective emotional component stemmed, as will be shown later, from the composer's mental state at any particular time, which could easily be tilted out of balance due to his hypersensitive and easily excitable nature. Yet, to experience Tchaikovsky's music as an undisciplined outpouring of feeling for that reason is unjustified and practically unpardonable in a critic like Eduard Hanslick. Reviewing Tchaikovsky's violin concerto, Hanslick indulged in a kind of "aesthetic snobbism" when he wrote:

> In discussing lascivious drawings, Friedrich Vischer somewhere says there are pictures "one sees stinking." Tchaikovsky's violin concerto first leads us to the ghastly notion there might also be musical pieces one hears stinking.

To evaluate Tchaikovsky's music more objectively, closer attention must be paid to the posthumous aftereffects of his music than to such regrettable word games. His Sixth Symphony, in particular, exercised lasting influence on later composers. Donald Tovey wrote about its last slow movement as follows:

The slow finale with its perfect simplicity of despair is a stroke of genius that solves all artistic problems standing in the way of most symphony-composers after Beethoven.

Gustav Mahler must have shared this opinion; for he likewise closed his Third Symphony with a slow finale. Mahler, as Alban Berg reported, had, like Tchaikovsky, had a premonition of his impending death and clearly expressed it in the basic mood of inconsolable resignation. But a similar slow finale is also found in Alban Berg's own works, namely, in the "*largo desolato*" of his *Lyric Suite*, which in this work for string quartet marks the heart-rending divide between madness and despair. Influences of Tchaikovsky's music can also be demonstrated in the musical creation of Puccini, Sibelius, and Stravinsky, although these three composers in their extreme independence otherwise have little in common. That is surely also why Stravinsky was more devoted to Tchaikovsky's music than to Rimsky-Korsakov, whose pupil he was early in the 20th century, and he expressed his admiration for his teacher in an open letter of 18 October 1921 to Diaghilev on the occasion of a new production of *Sleeping Beauty* with the words:

> It makes me very happy to know that you are producing this masterpiece.....Tchaikovsky's music, which does not seem typically Russian to everyone, is often more deeply Russian than the music which has long been perceived as Moscow's frivolously picturesque side. That music is just as Russian as Pushkin's literature or Glinka's songs....And how revealing it is to see whom he valued among the musicians of the past and also of his own time! He honored Mozart, Couperin, Glinka, Bizet; that leaves no doubt about his taste.

Statements like Stravinsky's finally found more acceptance among the art-loving public than the critiques and commentaries of so-called "scholarly personalities." That is why Tchaikovsky is

surely even more famous and loved in our times than in the outgoing 19th century of an Eduard Hanslick, and we are happy
today that, besides his symphonies, operas, instrumental concertos,
ballets, and overtures, other works that would have deserved to
be presented to the public long ago are also being performed
more often.

Tchaikovsky no doubt regarded composing as the only possibility of coming to terms with his extremely complicated mental
life or at least freeing himself from the pressure of psychic problems to make his existence bearable. He saw compositional works
as the most suitable means to give form to his urgent ideas and
feelings. It gave him a language far more expressive than the
spoken word, and it compelled him—by creatively transposing
sometimes uncontrollable emotional outbreaks into music—to
subject himself to a spiritual discipline he often could not maintain in mastering problems of daily life. Since he was not very
innovative in creating new musical forms, very early on he relied
on the "classical" forms, although it took hard work even in this
to bring form and content into harmony. "Only through iron-
willed industriousness did I gradually get the form of my works
to match their content," he later admitted in a letter to Mrs. von
Meck, and no doubt his music's reliance on classical models worked
to his advantage, because they acted as a safety valve preventing
emotional discharges from overflowing beyond a bearable extent.

To penetrate the mystery of this Russian artist, whose life was
filled with constant internal contradiction and mental tensions,
one must always try to analyze his musical creation as strongly
influenced by states of mental tension and spiritual crises. For
this reason it seems of special interest to pursue the deeper causes
of such crises and to elaborate the peculiar mental qualities and
character traits of this man as an artist and a human being, although we will probably never completely fathom the inner life
of this strongly introverted personality even from his many letters
and diary entries. Sergei Rachmaninov spoke of a mask he wore
apparently since childhood and must never have taken off. But
more recent documents allow interesting insights into many of
Tchaikovsky's psychic problems, just as today statements by Nina

Berberova make it possible to take a clearer stand on the medical questions concerning the artist's death.

Formative Events in His Childhood and Youth

Peter Ilyich Tchaikovsky was born on 7 May 1840 in Votkinsk, a little town in the Province of Vyatka in the Urals. His father, Ilya Petrovich, came to this world in 1800 as the twentieth child of a governor of this province, on whom a title of nobility had been conveyed at the beginning of the century. Tchaikovsky's father then served as chief inspector of mines in that province's iron mining center. He had graduated from the military mining academy and was a well-respected citizen, of pleasant and honorable character. But due to his mediocre intelligence, he never got very far in his career. Although he played some flute in his youth, he lacked any inclination for music. His first wife, who bore him a daughter named Sinaida, died in 1833.

His second wife, Alexandra, Peter's mother, was twenty years younger than he and stemmed from a Huguenot family who had left France and settled in Russia. Her father, André Ossier, is said to have been a cultivated man who ultimately occupied a relatively high position as a government official with the customs office, but he died in 1830. He reportedly had been an epileptic and had inherited this sickness from his grandfather. All we know of him otherwise is that he was supposed to have been a nervous and very impulsive man; and it surely is beyond all doubt that Peter's neurotic heredity came from his maternal side. Alexandra herself received a good education in a boarding school for female semi-orphans, including arithmetic, rhetoric, and geography, as well as literary history and foreign languages. She too had no very great penchant for music, although she is said to have had a pleasant singing voice.

When Ilya Petrovich became director of the great iron mines in 1837 and, as the manager of a huge enterprise, had at his disposal a comfortable house with many servants and even a private army consisting of a hundred Cossacks, he could give thought to enlarging his family. Two years before Peter's birth, Nicolai was born, and two years after him his sister Alexandra, who was nicknamed Sasha. Later the family was increased by Hippolyt in 1844 and the twins Anatoly and Modest, who were born in 1850.

To make her work easier, Madame Tchaikovsky decided in November 1844 to hire a governess for the education of the older brother Nicolai and his cousin Lydia, who lived with the Tchaikovsky family. The arrival of twenty-two-year-old Fanny Dürbach, a Protestant woman from French Switzerland, was the first decisive turning point in Peter's life. Peter, whose heart even then threatened to explode with ecstatic feelings, clung to Fanny from the first moment and insisted stubbornly on being allowed to join in the instruction hours. As an excellent and empathetic educator, Fanny also soon recognized the silent and somewhat strange child's thirst for knowledge and his sensitive receptivity, and she knew better than his adored mother, who was less ready to understand emotional reactions, how to deal with Peter's strong outbreaks of feeling and exaggerated sensitivity to any criticism. Thus her "porcelain child," as she tenderly called him, could develop quickly under her care, so that by the age of six years he was already able to speak and write in his mother tongue, in French, and some German. Even at that early age, the extremely sensitive child vented his innermost emotional urges, which sometimes threatened to choke him, by writing very sentimental Russian and French poems. Strangely, Fanny Dürbach did not notice what an extraordinary attraction music had on little Peter, probably because she herself was indifferent to music. Although he became visibly excited when guests sang or played music in the Tchaikovsky household and he once said to Fanny: "Music sits in my head and gives me no rest," his parents, as well as the family doctor, were of the opinion that it was still too early to begin with music lessons. So the only possibility left for him was to constantly replay the opera program of the orchestrion [a mechanical musical instrument with an orchestra-like sound] the family owned, which also contained a melody from Mozart's *Don Giovanni* and to follow the melodies he heard with two fingers on the piano. Sometimes the child could be removed from the piano only with difficulty, and when this succeeded he drummed the beat on the tables or on a window pane, which once broke and injured him when he was trying to play a *"forte."* Not until the end of 1845 did Peter receive his first piano lessons from a young lady freed from serfdom, called Maria Markovna, whom he soon equaled in reading notes.

On 8 October 1848 little Peter experienced his first psychic shock. His father, retired with a pension as a major general and now hoping for a suitable position in Moscow, left Votkinsk with his family to move to St. Petersburg; and so Fanny Dürbach had to be let go. A farewell letter to Fanny failed because his tears made the ink-writing completely illegible. This abrupt end of a life in familiar surroundings and constant proximity to his beloved Fanny had an almost traumatic effect on him; all the more so, since now his unfriendly and tyrannical half-sister, Sinaida, replaced Fanny in supervising her brothers and sisters. Entrance into the preparatory class for high school meant hard work and so worsened the state of his health that even the piano lessons he was receiving from a Mr. Filippov had to be suspended. If he was taken to a concert or an opera, the music could trigger veritable hallucinations in him. He suffered from insomnia, and all these impressions so changed him that he was hardly recognizable any more as the delicate young boy he had been.

FANNY DÜRBACH, TCHAIKOVSKY'S
GOVERNESS FROM 1844 TO 1848.

On top of all this, he and his brother Nicolai fell ill with the measles in December 1848. While his brother recovered quickly from the disease, for Peter it took a long-lasting course with complications that apparently affected mainly his nervous system and was therefore diagnosed by the doctor as "spinal cord consumption." In his brother Modest's biography one reads on this subject:

> In Nicolai the disease took a normal course, but not in Peter. His hypersensitivity became more aggravated and caused nervous fits. The doctors discovered a spinal cord ailment.

At any rate, the family doctor prescribed six months of absolute rest. From this, Modest drew the conclusion:

> How terribly those nervous fits must have manifested themselves. The measures taken in time had a healing effect on the boy's physical health, but his character could never return to its former equanimity and clarity.

In fact, in June 1849, when his state of health was improving rapidly, his irritability increased. An attention deficit caused learning difficulties, and a certain apathy to the world around him led his mother to report to Fanny Dürbach:

> He is like a different person, loitering around. I don't know what to do with him. Sometimes I feel like crying.

Unfortunately, the sensitive child's psychological misdevelopment, promoted by the long-lasting course of the infectious disease, was also aggravated by his mother's attitude; for on the one hand she was surprisingly not very empathetic, and on the other she was overly concerned. Only toward the end of the year, when a new governess by the name of Petrovna Petrova was hired, did Peter seem to have become "more reasonable," as his mother wrote to Fanny Dürbach.

Meanwhile, Peter's father found a new and acceptable position as mining administrator of privately owned mines located

THE TCHAIKOVSKY FAMILY IN 1848. FROM LEFT TO RIGHT: PETER ILYICH, HIS
MOTHER ALEXANDRA A., ALEXANDRA, SINAIDA, NICOLAI, HIPPOLYT, AND HIS
FATHER ILYA P.

beyond the Urals on the Siberian border near Ekaterinburg, and
the family moved there, with the exception of Nicolai, who stayed
in St. Petersburg for his studies. A desolate and sad existence
now began for Peter in the remote village of Alapayevsk, where
the Tchaikovsky family now lived, not to be compared with the
"golden age" of his life in Votkinsk. There Fanny Dürbach had
taken loving care of him, while now he was taught by his stepsister Sinaida, whom he did not like very much. Peter had already been alarmingly disturbed by separation from Fanny and
by the severe attack of measles; but now he became more insecure and his temperament changed completely. He became malicious, recalcitrant, and envious of his brother Nicolai's successes.
And since the music lessons were discontinued, he began playing

the piano all by himself in the hours when he felt particularly sad. Early in 1850 he wrote to Fanny Dürbach: "I am always at the piano. I find solace there, when I am sad." The ten-year-old boy became more and more introverted, and his self-preoccupation grew into a regular egocentric attitude. In return for the indifference of those around him, he kept his passion for music hidden from the others, and when he undertook his first attempts at composition, that too remained a secret. He began to idealize more and more the four and a half years he had lived in Votkinsk together with Fanny Dürbach, and these formative impressions from his earliest childhood would become greatly significant for his further life. This glorification of his past was accompanied by an idealization of the female persons around him, above all Fanny Dürbach and his mother, whom he virtually idolized. Some psychoanalysts have tried to portray Peter's love for his mother as "a lover's passion, revealing the subconscious desire to flee from the world and return to the womb from which he came." Even if one does not want to follow this attempt at an interpretation, the fact remains that, as in his childlike reverence for Fanny or his mother, even later in life he meticulously avoided any intimacy with the few women whom he loved or for whom he felt affection. No doubt, Peter's early inclination toward homosexuality, already recognizable even before puberty, played a role here and was passed on to his brother Modest and his nephew Bob—possibly favored by an antiquated educational ritual traditionally practiced in the family.

   This also casts a light on the unusual psychic shock that was to strike him in October 1850. In August of that year, it was believed that the time had come to undertake something against Peter's nervousness and his excessive sensitivity, and it was decided to take him to St. Petersburg to the preparatory class for law school, where he was admitted as one of the best prospective students. His mother accompanied him to St. Petersburg and spent several weeks together with him to make it easier for him to become accustomed to his new environment. But when the time came for her to leave and return to Alapayevsk in mid-October, a heartrending farewell scene resulted. It was customary for passengers traveling to Moscow to be accompanied by family members as far as the city-gate of St. Petersburg. Thus Peter traveled this good distance with his mother, clinging firmly to her skirt with both hands. When she was supposed finally to say farewell, he lost all self-control. He clung so frantically to his mother that he had to be pulled away from her by force and held back while the carriage started moving. In a kind of hysterical fit he broke free, ran after the carriage with bloodcurdling screams, and tried desperately to grab the spokes of a wheel in order to stop the vehicle. The memory of these horrible moments followed him until the end of his life. This event was the first visible symptom of a glowing and passionate identification with his mother, from which he could never free himself.

A second unhappy incident soon occurred that increased his incipient guilt feelings. When a scarlet fever epidemic broke out in the school in November 1850 Peter was temporarily taken in by the family of his guardian, Modest Vakar. Peter was spared by the scarlet fever, while his guardian's oldest son fell victim to this infectious disease on 6 December. Peter felt responsible for his death, and all attempts to convince him of his innocence failed. His depressive mood cleared up only gradually after his return to school. His piano playing or "coloratura improvising" soon opened the way to his school comrades' hearts, and while he did not want to disappoint his parents, who had destined him for a law career, with his increasing inclination to study music, he even then confided to a school comrade in a letter: "I can feel it, I am going to be a composer."

When Peter's father retired in 1852, the whole family moved to St. Petersburg, and so a happier time for Peter began. Since he did not mention his earlier enthusiasm for music at all, his mother thought this problem was done with and she felt reassured. In this period of harmony fell Peter's first severe blow of destiny: his adored mother died on 25 June 1854 from a cholera epidemic raging in St. Petersburg at that time. Since, until the end of the 19th century, the water of the Neva, into which most of the city's sewerage flowed, also was the source of water for basins and pitchers, the door was repeatedly open to such epidemics. The doctors were hoping that they had warded off danger for his mother, when on the fourth day of illness, after a bath recommended by the doctor, she fell into a coma from which she never recovered. Moreover, on the day of her burial, his father too fell ill but survived the disease. This event struck Peter with a shock. We have no witnesses of the immediate effect on the fourteen-year-old's mental state, but we know from letters written many years later that he was never able to overcome this loss his whole life long. Thus, he once wrote:

> Exactly twenty-five years ago on this day my mother died. It was the first great sorrow I endured. Her death had the greatest influence on my fate and my family's. She died in the full bloom of her years, very suddenly, of cholera, followed by an-other disease. Every minute of that terrible day is present to me as vividly as if it had happened yes-terday.

And in a letter he wrote two years earlier, philosophizing about the insignificance of immortality, he suddenly contradicted his own arguments by asserting:

> I will never accept the thought that my dear mother whom I loved so much no longer exists and that I will never again have the possibility to tell her that after twenty-three years of separation I still love her as ardently as ever.

It is medically revealing that Tchaikovsky's first composition attempt dates from the month after his mother died. When he admitted many years later that he "no doubt would have lost his mind without music," this admission must be taken literally and at the same time valued as one of the most convincing examples of the fact that an internal emotional conflict can successfully be projected out into artistic channels. His love for his adored mother persisted in his youth so overpoweringly that her death actually would have gravely threatened the stability of his emotional state had it not found release by translation of the pent-up passionate feelings into music. Proof that this assumption is right cannot be produced from the fourteen-year-old's compositions, since they have been lost. But we do have convincing evidence from his later life that similarly grave mental crises seriously threatening his psychic stability all the way to a real danger of suicide could be overcome only by creative transposition into music—for example, his Fourth Symphony or *Eugene Onegin*. For his spiritual landscape extended dangerously between the boundaries of genius and madness.

Music, however, remained his strongest consolation not only in the sad time after the loss of his mother; rather, for the whole rest of his life, it remained the escape valve for his emotional life and an effective substitute for dispersed wishful dreams and insufficiently satisfied sexual passions. In the fall of 1854, he took singing lessons from Gabriel Lomatkin, since he was already beginning to play with the idea of composing an opera. Early in 1855 he finally got his first serious lessons in piano playing from the pianist Rudolf Kündinger, who allegedly, however, could discover no outstanding musical talent in young Tchaikovsky, for he wrote to his father that he "firstly, can recognize no genial traits in Tchaikovsky and, secondly, it is my view that a musician's fate in Russia customarily can only be difficult." Nonetheless, Peter was undeterred and continued to busy himself intensively with music while still studying law. At sixteen years of age he was introduced to an Italian singing teacher by the name of Luigi Piccioli, who directed his interest mainly to Italian opera. Piccioli himself was a strange personality; out of vanity, he tried to give the impression of being a younger man by dyeing his gray hair and putting makeup on his cheeks; and we do not know what other influence he may have had on Peter, who had just emerged from puberty. At any rate, the youth then composed a song titled *My Genius, My Angel, My Friend*, but later his brother Modest avowed that "the main bond that held the two together was music."

After graduating from law school in 1859, Tchaikovsky was employed as a titular councilor by the Justice Ministry. He had meanwhile developed into a handsome young man; and feeling free of all scholastic constraints he eagerly immersed himself in the social and artistic events of the big city. Along with frequent attendance at the opera and the theater, he liked to participate in private celebrations, where he occasionally also provided dance music and also had abundant opportunities for many flirtations. Although at this time he is described almost as "vainly elegant to the point of dandyism," still he even then kept the young ladies at a safe distance. He had taken up smoking in law school and all his life it served to satisfy his wish for a narcotic.

When his sister Sasha married Leo Davidov in 1860 and moved to Kamenka in the Ukraine, Peter's correspondence, which soon reached immeasurable proportions, first began with letters addressed to her. On 22 March 1861 he reported to her that their father, meanwhile reduced to almost total poverty, no longer rejected a musical career for his son and that he would now begin studying thorough-bass with Nicolai Zaremba, who was versed in German music theory and from whom he hoped to learn the regular technique of composition writing. In September 1862, when the first St. Petersburg Conservatory opened under the directorship of Anton Rubinstein, even before the end of that year Tchaikovsky enrolled in Rubinstein's composition class. Soon the master called his attention to the fact that in view of his talent he should pursue the profession with greater zeal. And since the uninteresting work at the Ministry was becoming an increasingly heavy burden for him anyway, he was thinking more and more frequently of quitting his career as a government official. His disinterest in this work and his distraction during service sometimes assumed grotesque dimensions and could lead him absentmindedly to tear up an important document and shape it into paper balls which he swallowed out of a habit acquired in his childhood. No wonder he was always being deliberately passed over for promotions at the Ministry. Disappointed about this, in spring 1863 he therefore made the final decision to end his governmental career, which he had so disliked. His family was outraged at his resigning from the Justice Ministry, for according to his uncle's words he had exchanged the Ministry for a trombone. He himself was convinced that he had taken the right step, and he wrote reassuringly to his sister: "At least I am convinced of one thing, that after my training I will be a good musician." Outwardly he was hardly recognizable. A short time previously, influenced by the questionable Piccioli and his ambiguous affection—which no doubt strengthened an inclination in him that had been aroused in puberty by his friendship with his fellow pupil Alexei Apuchtin—he had been absorbed in the unrestrained activities of St. Petersburg society, but now a remarkable change took place. With the 50 rubles per month he earned by giving music lessons, his life had to be regulated more modestly. He now wore a beard and a strikingly broad-rimmed hat, which gave him a more serious look, and his already too obviously displayed indifference toward women led his sister Alexandra to remark that he surely was a failure in love. His entire interest now was focused on music and the zealous striving to become a recognized composer someday.

First Years as a Musician

Tchaikovsky's decision to become a musician appalled his brother Nicolai, who contributed little to Peter's self-confidence by his statement that Peter Ilyich could never become a second Glinka. Therefore it was all the more important that Tchaikovsky met Hermann Laroche, with whom he became friends at the conservatory and who knew how to strengthen his feeling of self-esteem. In this friendship, which was also important for the future, as opposed to that with his school friend Apuchtin or with the Italian singing teacher Piccioli, any kind of emotionality was avoided and replaced by mutual respect. Tchaikovsky immersed himself in the study of theory and wrote two compositions per week for practice. His orchestral work *Dances of the Hay Maidens* was even performed with some success by Johann Strauss in Kiev. Yet, although his music profession and the personal freedom it brought decisively shaped the development of his personality, within this development the characteristic symptoms of a complex neurotic disposition were already beginning to show. He displayed an unusual sensitivity, and he suffered under it since he tried to hide it from his fellowmen in order not to be taken for an effeminate enthusiast. Yet upon hearing the music of his adored idol Mozart, or even the mere mention of his name, he could not prevent tears from coming to his eyes. In general, the experience of music in the conservatory and especially the state of his own creative activity transformed him into strange states of excitement he himself called "shock." Yet before going to sleep he could lose all sensation in his arms and legs or fall into a trembling in his whole body, followed by exhaustion and insomnia. Occasionally there were episodes of real hallucinations—which he mentioned only to two of his brothers, who were quite alarmed by them. It went worst of all for him during the composition of his First Symphony, when he had a real nervous breakdown, which he had apparently anticipated. For three months earlier he had written to his brother Anatoly:

> My nerves are totally undermined. The reasons for this are, first, the symphony, which doesn't sound satisfactory. Secondly, Rubinstein and Tarnovsky have discovered that I am easily startled and therefore have been amusing themselves by giving me every kind of shock all day long. Finally, I cannot shake off the thought that I do not have long to live and therefore will leave my symphony unfinished. I long for summer and for Kamenka [his sister Sasha's house] as for the Promised Land, and I hope to find peace and rest there and to forget all my cares here....I hate people in masses and would be happy if I could withdraw to some wilderness or other with very few inhabitants.

These continual fears, which made social life unbearable for him, as well as his discouragement and self-pity, are signs that he was unable to transpose his energies completely into music. He struggled constantly, but no matter how much he tried, a part of his spiritual energies remained caught, and so he was unable to overcome completely the worst of his fears. The original world of his feelings, so strangely stamped by his early ties to his mother and his sister, soon developed into a distorted image characterized by homosexual conflicts, which he never would be able to escape. His life would have been difficult enough, if he had had to master his unusual passion as an artist with its intrinsic danger of impending madness. This struggle would simply have had to be endured as the price for his creative activity. Tchaikovsky's real tragedy, however, was the compulsive rejection of a normal love. His neurotic disposition, of which he was aware at an early age, prevented not only intimate relationships with the female sex, but it drove him to homosexuality with all the accompanying difficulties resulting from the constant need for secrecy and deceptive maneuvers, but also mounting guilt feelings and fear of prosecution. His fertile artistic productivity must probably be explained by the fact that he stood constantly under the pressure to produce incessantly in order to find a kind of balance between his work and his unsatisfied and insatiable passions. In some artists, their neurotic elements are hardly detectable in their works— for instance, Verlaine's delicate, restrained, and reserved poetry would never suggest the repulsive ugliness of his neurotic character. Homosexuality, too, in all its forms of manifestation and degrees of intensity, is by no means always recognizable as a psychological disturbance. In Tchaikovsky's character, however, neurotic elements are inseparable from his development into a creative musician. It is therefore not surprising that neurotic symptoms showed up in his directing and could be overcome only after many years.

> He claims that standing on an elevated podium before the orchestra instills in him such a nervous anxiety that he feels the whole time as if his head must fall off his shoulders. To forestall this catastrophe he braced his chin with his left hand and directed only with the right.

When Tchaikovsky, after spending a refreshing summer at his sister's home in Kamenka, returned to St. Petersburg, where his father and his brother were about to set out to his stepsister Sinaida's in the Urals, he was gripped by a deep depression in the empty apartment left for him by his school friend Apuchtin. He felt unneeded by anyone and had a sense of failure, since by the age of twenty-five he had still really produced nothing tangible. His depressive state even caused him at night to dream of a pistol to shoot himself with. Then it happened that in 1865 Nicolai Rubinstein, the grandiose pianist and director and brother of his instructor Anton Rubinstein, came to St. Petersburg to recruit suitable professors for the institute he had established in Moscow in 1860, out of which would develop the second Russian

Conservatory. And Anton Rubinstein suggested his pupil Tchaikovsky, who had just successfully passed his final examination at
the conservatory with a cantata, although young César Cui from
the national St. Petersburg school had written a very negative
critique:

> Tchaikovsky was mediocre through and through.
> Not for a moment did his talent break the chains
> of the conservatory.

This disappointment, but also his bad financial situation led him
to accept the offer despite his aversion to teaching. Moreover,
except for his young twin brothers, Modest and Anatoly, to whom—
to a certain extent as a mother-substitute—he gave his whole love
and affection, there was nothing keeping him in St. Petersburg.
For this city in the end gave him only a feeling of lonely solitude,
lack of artistic recognition, and melancholic reminiscence on happier bygone days, which led not only to an increasingly depressive mood, but also to various psychosomatically conditioned
ailments, as can be seen from something he wrote shortly before
his departure:

> Since the time I have been living here, I feel unin-
> terruptedly ill: now my arms ache, now my feet,
> constant coughing.

In Moscow, Nicolai Rubinstein arranged a room in his house
for Tchaikovsky, provided him food and clothing appropriate for
his station, and in the very first days introduced him to his circle
of colleagues. Of course, with his 50 rubles per month he could
not, by his own financial means, meet the social demands called
for by the lifestyle of the circle around Nicolai Rubinstein; therefore the director took him along to the opera and to concerts and,
if necessary, lent him his own tuxedo. "Rubinstein looks after me
as if he were my baby-sitter," he wrote to his family, and the ten
letters written to them from Moscow during the first four weeks
resound with his homesickness and his pain of separation—especially for his twin brothers. The immediate proximity to the all-
dominant Nicolai Rubinstein, who often returned noisily from his
English Club late at night or practiced for a piano concert in the

nighttime, increasingly disturbed the calm that Tchaikovsky needed for composing. In addition, there were Rubinstein's weakness for the female sex, gambling, and especially alcohol, which he consumed in incredible quantities. Gambling meant little to Tchaikovsky, apart from occasional card parties at the English Club or in circles of artists; and women, too, as always, left him completely indifferent. However, Tchaikovsky's personality was not absolutely such as to enable him successfully to resist the appeal of alcohol, and we know from the later diary entries that he sometimes got very drunk in the last decades of his life, indeed much more frequently than he admitted to the people around him.

Thus it is not surprising that more and more often there appeared various ailments, mainly of a psychic nature, described to his brother Anatoly as follows:

> Recently I have been sleeping very badly; my apoplectic symptoms have come back, indeed with greater intensity than ever, so that I always know in advance whether they will return in the coming night or not, and if so, then I don't try at all to fall asleep. The day before yesterday, for example, I did not sleep all night. My nerves are all shattered again....Since yesterday I have resolved not to drink any brandy, any wine, or any strong tea any more.

Yet one has to agree with Modest when he stated:

> No one played a greater role in the composer's destiny, no one was more supportive—both as an artist and as a friend—to the blossoming of his fame, no one took better care of Peter and gave him effective support in his first dreadful beginnings than did the Director of the Moscow Conservatory.

In fact, only Nicolai Rubinstein had any idea that behind this pleasant external appearance, with its gentleness and its beauty, something independent was developing and beginning to seek its course relentlessly and indomitably. Besides Rubinstein, a few friends in the Conservatory were of almost vital importance by always encouraging him and helping him establish his reputation as a composer. Moreover, even later on they were an invaluable support to him in his isolated aloofness and tormenting loneliness, in which a homosexually inclined person was forced to live at that time, incapable of a lasting love relationship with a woman, hence unable to establish a family, and living constantly in lies and secrecy from fear of prosecution. Among his closer circle of friends were: Konstantin Albrecht, Inspector of the Conservatory, Peter Jürgenson, his later publisher, the family of the musician Nicolai Kashkin, as well as his friends from St. Petersburg, Hermann Laroche and Nicolai Hubert, who later became Director of the Conservatory. He also maintained close contact with his favorite pupil Vladimir Shilovsky, with whom he spent the summer of 1868 in Paris.

On the day he finished his First Symphony, titled *Winter Daydreams*, Tchaikovsky wrote to his brother Anatoly:

> I work a lot, especially at night. Today I have completed my first symphony. I am nervous, often tormented by anxious ideas and fear of death. The doctor advised me to work less, otherwise I would finally end up in an insane asylum.

Actually, as Modest reports, "not a single one of his compositions cost him so much effort and torment as did precisely this symphony. And allegedly he later never wrote a single note of his compositions in the night hours." About the crises which first appeared during work on his first symphony, but also repeatedly later on, and which he himself used to call "apoplectic spells" and "heart cramps," Herbert Weinstock writes:

> We have no knowledge of his having had a serious disease....Apparently he was neurasthenic.... Facts and allusions lead to the suspicion that the essential cause of his mental shocks and nervous disturbances was the toilsome repression of the sexual drive, the futile attempts to fall in love like other people, and the incessant fear that a

malicious and heartless society could discover his secret nature and his genuine erotic inclinations.... Gossip linked him with some conservatory students....But all these names would change nothing about the significant fact that Peter's erotic nature and his way of dealing with it affected his whole adult life and gave his personality and sometimes also his music that dark, sensual, introspective and melancholic character.

Tchaikovsky's shame for his "unnatural" disposition and his guilt feelings at being a contemptible person because of his "secret" accelerated the onset of depressive states. In a letter to his sister Sasha in the summer of 1867, typical references in this direction are detectable:

Perhaps you have already yourself observed that I long passionately for a quiet, peaceful life as it is lived in the country, in the village. The reason is because, although I am still far from old age, I am already weary of life....People around me often wonder about my taciturnity, about the depressions I often suffer from, while basically I do not lead a bad life at all....And yet I avoid parties, am incapable of entertaining acquaintances, I like solitude, enjoy silence. All this can be explained by my surfeit with life. You may believe that such moods generally lead to thoughts of marriage. No, my dear! Again out of weariness with life I am too lazy to form new relationships, too comfortable to establish a family.

Such statements written during a depression characterize exactly those typical symptoms clinically indicative of this pathological image. Weariness with life, taciturnity, and groundlessly depressed moods are typical symptoms, just as is drive deficiency, which he called laziness. It is all the more remarkable that he succeeded in overcoming this latent lethargy by his own strength through a renewed urge for creative activity. If, in his unconscious tendency to self-abasement, he considered himself unable to form new relationships or establish a family, this is contradicted by a strange episode that befell him in 1868. An outstanding soprano singer, Désirée Artôt, was then giving a guest performance in Moscow, and although she is said not to have been a great beauty, he was seized with such affection for her that he was determined to marry her, as can be read in a letter to his father on 7 January 1869:

> Very soon we flared up in mutual tender affection
> and avowals followed immediately. Naturally, we
> immediately discussed the idea of a legal marriage
> and if nothing prevents it the wedding is to take
> place in the coming summer.

For the first time the presence of a woman, indeed even the idea of a marriage did not seem absurd to him. Probably it was not her charm, however, that fascinated him, but rather the strength that radiated from this woman, five years his senior, with her self-confidence and her free manner, which arose from her professional successes and gave her whole demeanor, indeed her entire being, an element of the masculine. He wrote for her the *Romance* op. 5 and was "very much in love with her," as he confided to his brother Modest in December 1868. But a few months after her departure from Moscow, Madame Artôt married the Spanish baritone Padilla. The reason seems to be a conversation that Nicolai Rubinstein had with her before she left Moscow, in which he seems to have informed her about certain inclinations of Tchaikovsky's. Since Peter received no letters from her, his feelings seem to have cooled remarkably rapidly, even before the news that Madame Artôt had married. For he remarked in a letter to Anatoly:

> As for my love intermezzo....I can tell you only
> that I do not know whether I will enter the realm
> of marriage; the matter is not going according to
> plan.

Despite these reservations, he apparently had felt that he could enter an intimate relationship with Désirée Artôt. Indeed we know that homosexuals are definitely capable of heterosexual liaisons. On the other hand, his heart does not seem to have been broken by the news brought by Rubinstein of the marriage of "his" fiancée, although his pride seems to have been deeply hurt for a rather long time.

Shortly before the unhappy love affair with Désirée Artôt, he had begun writing the overture *Romeo and Juliet*, the inspiration for which he owed to Balakirev. Together with Cui, Rimsky-Korsakov, Mussorgsky, and Borodin, Balakirev was part of the so-called "mighty little group" in St. Petersburg, whose goal it was to continue Glinka's efforts to create a national artistic language by exploiting the peculiarities of the Russian folk song. Tchaikovsky had met Balakirev in 1868 when Balakirev, as director of the Russian Music Society, invited Hector Berlioz to Moscow. Although Balakirev was not completely satisfied with this overture dedicated to him, Tchaikovsky attained his first fame with this work; indeed, his fame extended even beyond Russia's borders. Almost at the same time, he published a first collection of his own songs as Opus 6. These songs, like most Russian songs composed at that time, were for the most part strongly influenced by Schumann. Finally, he undertook a job Laroche had gotten for him as music critic for the *Russian News*, resulting in deeper involvement with various realms of music and compelling him to drastically revise his preference for Italian opera, acquired from his former teacher Piccioli, so that in the end he came to regard Italian music virtually as "anti-music."

Tchaikovsky was incessantly composing and he loved this grueling way of working, just as he was beginning to feel more and more at home in Moscow. And yet an inexplicable melancholic mood once again took hold of him. According to his brother Modest's depiction, he lost "his strength little by little all the way to complete exhaustion." And Tchaikovsky himself reported:

I have become an unbearable hypochondriac as a result of serious nervous disorders. I don't know why I feel pressed by unspeakable melancholic longings. I would like to go away somewhere and hide in an unreachable God-forsaken place.

The wish to free himself became more and more urgent and his loneliness and the feeling of being alone in the world over-shadowed his temperament. His twin brothers were long since going their own ways, and his sister was completely occupied by a growing family. So he was left only with his musical friends in various taverns in Moscow and his own four walls, in which he did not have to fear the existential threat of his inclinations be-coming known. In May 1870 he gave the following report of his situation:

> 1. Sickness—I am becoming quite dull-witted, and
> my nerves are completely ruined. 2. My finances
> are in bad shape. 3. The Conservatory bores me
> to the point of nausea.

And how lonesome and alone he felt can be seen from a letter to his sister of 17 February, complaining to her that there was no one in Moscow with whom he "lived in genuine close friendship. I often think how happy I would be if you or at least someone like you were here." Because of his rundown condition, absolute rest was prescribed by the doctor and a treatment at the seaside or at least at a mineral spa was recommended.

While he was working on his opera *The Oprichnik*, the news arrived that his young friend Vladimir Shilovsky had become gravely ill in Paris. This close friendship had begun at a time when his pupil Volodya, as he called him, was only fourteen years old. From the first, Tchaikovsky was very fond of "this little man, who is destined to delight the whole world, and the boy, too, clung with extraordinary love to his teacher. Since the boy was of delicate constitution and often ailing, Tchaikovsky repeat-edly had accompanied him on journeys that took him for pur-poses of recovery to the country estate of Volodya's parents or even abroad. In his company, Tchaikovsky had been happy ev-erywhere, and because of this, during the summer holidays he neglected even his brothers. Of course, it had not gone unno-ticed that teacher and pupil sometimes suddenly left Moscow for no apparent reason to spend a few happy days together. Be-cause of these circumstances, it is understandable that Tchaikovsky without delay hastened to Paris to Volodya's bedside upon receiving the news that he had fallen ill of tuberculosis. His state of health had meanwhile improved to the point that the two of them could travel together to Bad Soden in June 1870 for a spa treatment. Because of its warm springs rich in carbon dioxide and sodium chloride, Bad Soden on the Taunus river had, since the 18th century, been a favorite spa for patients suffering from asthma or sicknesses of the breathing passages. This stay at the spa was "terribly boring" for the two men, as can be seen from a letter of Tchaikovsky's:

> Life in Soden is very simple. We get up at six o'clock, Volodya drinks his spring water, while I (on the doctor's advice) take my salt-bath....But I am struggling energetically against dismal moods and console myself with the thought that my presence will save Volodya and that the way of life in Soden will help me too.

In the meantime, the Franco-Prussian War had broken out, so the two fled to Interlaken in Switzerland, and from there after several weeks they arrived refreshed in Moscow.

Meanwhile with his opera *The Oprichnik* and with the just completed Second Symphony, Tchaikovsky attained in St. Petersburg candid recognition by the critical "mighty little group," which nominated him the first musician of Russia. In a concert featuring for the first time exclusively his own works, the high point was the String Quartet op. 11 with its dreamlike *andante cantabile*, and everyone agreed that he had thereby reached his full maturity. But despite the great success achieved by the Tchaikovsky concert on 28 March 1871, reports of melancholy moods gradually resumed. The feeling of exclusion he felt because of the ever emerging rumors about his inclinations and the related behavior instilled in him not only a painful loneliness and isolation within the society of the city, but it also made him anxious and distrustful. This was no doubt also the main reason why he was so extraordinarily hypersensitive and easily offended by critical reviews of his works.

After returning to Moscow, he decided to lead his life from then on independently both as an artist and as a person. As a professor at the Conservatory he was earning 2000 rubles per year, and the royalties from his concerts and his review-writing activity brought him another 1000 rubles, so that he now definitely could afford to rent a three-room apartment of his own. He moved out of Nicolai Rubinstein's house and hired a servant Mikhail Sofronov, who however soon passed his job on to his brother Alexei, who, according to statements by Modest, "played a not insignificant role in Peter Ilyich's life." The joy at finally having gained his independence is reflected in a letter to his brother Nicolai:

> As for myself, I can only report that I am over-joyed with my decision to leave N. Rubinstein. Despite my friendship with him, I found living together with him very burdensome.

Since his yearly salary at the Conservatory was meanwhile increased, he could have lived a carefree life had he not been so careless in managing his money. Whenever he could accumulate some savings, he gave money away generously or spent it in the shortest time on his journeys. For example, during the Christmas holidays in the winter of 1871/72, he traveled with Volodya through Germany to Nice and spent three weeks there. Also in the summer of 1873 he took a long journey to the West, mainly visiting various cities in Germany. This journey is noteworthy because in those weeks he began writing a diary. Although his brother Modest, after Tchaikovsky's death, destroyed many remarks and sketches that were probably interesting medically, still the relatively few passages of the diary that are important for creating a psychograph of the artist cast some situations in his life in a new light. Above all, we learn from it how very much his homosexuality made his existence harder and how very much his guilt feelings at times threatened to crush him. Although his compendious correspondence no doubt displays far more substantial content, providing insight into the composer's intellectual world, it cannot give us an idea of the many contradictions in his most secret inner life and of his typical surges, indeed outbursts, of feeling. All this he entrusted only to his diaries, very personal documents not meant for eventual publication, in which he could vent his feelings under the direct influence of momentary moods or emotions by quickly jotting down various notes. These diaries, in which with complete freedom and unrestricted candor toward himself he gave information both about his relation to the "gods" of his aesthetic Olympus—Glinka, Tolstoy, and Mozart—and also about his most intimate private sphere, are therefore, despite many irrelevant banalities they contain, an especially valuable source. For we find in them not only important allusions to his sexual activities, which he incidentally indicated by a special abbreviation, or to the significance in his life of alcohol, which played a far greater role than was admitted outwardly, but also numerous references to mental or physical ailments that are interesting from a medical perspective.

The first entries written during his journey to Germany and Switzerland in the summer of 1873 report about a "horrible condition of his nerves" and "excessive wishes" to attend a circus in Vervey, which he saw no possibility of fulfilling. With every fiber of his heart, he longed to be back in Russia with its splendid forests and steppes. On the return journey in Milan, he complained of pains in his upper abdomen, especially noticeable in the mornings; he mentioned difficulty finding a pain-soothing oil in a pharmacy. Arriving in Russia in August 1873, he spent a few weeks on Volodya Shilovsky's estate Ussovo, where he composed his symphonic work *The Storm*, based on Shakespeare's play by the same title. Gradually he became fed up with the friendship with the extremely moody Shilovsky, who became more and more bothersome and particularly disturbed his composition work. In a letter of December 1873, he complained to his brother Modest that there was no one with whom he could have a genuine and deep friendship and that he had also just broken his tie with Volodya.

But his depressed mood did not last long. The triumphal success of *The Storm* in December and of the Second String Quartet, which premiered in March 1874 gave him a powerful boost, and when on the occasion of the premiere of his opera *The Oprichnik* in St. Petersburg he was awarded the Kondratiev Prize with 300 rubles, he set out on a journey to Italy, visiting Venice, Florence, Rome, and Naples. Much as he later loved this country, so sadly was he moved by impressions on this first journey. In letters to Modest, one reads:

> ...Venice is a city, in which—if I had to stay here for a longer time—I would have hanged myself by the fifth day....In Naples I reached the point that I wept bitter tears daily from sheer homesickness....In such moments of black melancholy I am ready to give up everything to see one dear face near me....I hate Rome...may the devil take it! There is only one city in the world, and that is—Moscow.

As he wrote this, he was probably thinking of his Alyosha, the fourteen-year-old peasant boy with round eyes and blond bushy hair, whom he had hired as servant and whom he loved at first sight. This Alyosha, whom he showered with an expensive fur coat and other presents, on the other hand also caused him torments, because he constantly sought to hide his love for him meticulously from the surrounding world. But his thoughts were no doubt also of his young brother, whom he knew to be his double, with all his good and bad qualities, and whom he therefore repeatedly worried about:

> I am really appalled when I think that you could not free yourself from a single one of my defects...you have taken the role of my mirror image, holding all my defects to view.

While an apparently rather severe diphtheria in the autumn of 1873 left no detectable traces, various mental complaints came more and more frequently and lastingly to the foreground. He complained about melancholic impulses which he tried to oppose by more intensive works. He therefore plunged feverishly into the composition of another opera, *Vakula the Smith*, with which he wanted to enter a competition in St. Petersburg and whose draft he began to elaborate in May. Then in June 1874, he began a six-week mineral-water treatment with Karlsbad spring water in the hope of improving his condition. The work, reappearing in a new version nine years later with the title *Cherevichki*, was however first performed on the stage in December 1876. His psychogenic complaints were not improved either by intensive work on the opera or by the drinking treatment in Nisy, so that in January 1875 he complained in a letter:

> I feel lonesome and abandoned, I am quite afraid of people, am sad and constantly thinking of death. For days I sit in my room, breaking my head about a theme, smoking cigarettes....It would probably be best for me to enter a monastery.

Perhaps contributing to this depressive mood was disappointment he experienced precisely about the composition that stands at the beginning of his great career, namely, the First Piano Concerto in B-flat Minor, op. 23. Originally he had planned to dedicate it to Nicolai Rubinstein, whose critique however was so devastating that he finally dedicated the score to Hans von Bülow, who performed it in Boston on 23 October 1875 and had a triumphal success with this premiere. At this time, Tchaikovsky experienced another deep sorrow, namely, the death of a friend, the violinist Ferdinand Laub, in whose memory he composed the Third String Quartet in E-flat Minor, whose quality excels even that of his two chamber music works. Finally, he was troubled somewhat by criticism of his world-famous ballet, *Swan Lake*, written in 1876, which depreciated this music as "monotonous and boring" apart from a few successful passages.

Because of the progressive deterioration of his mental state and his psychosomatic complaints, for which even his intensive composition activity provided no effective antidote, although generally it always meant for him a kind of "psychic salvation," his doctors again recommended a spa treatment. It was to be carried out in "damned, repulsive Vichy," where he arrived on 13 July 1876. But since a few days later the mineral water led to diarrhea accompanied by intestinal colic, he left the prominent spa just ten days later to attend the Wagner music festival in Bayreuth in his capacity as reviewer for the *Russian News*. But even experiencing the *Ring of the Nibelung* apparently did not contribute very positively to his recovery, for he wrote to Modest:

The *Nibelung* may in fact be a magnificent work,
but it is also certain that never was there such an
endless and boring nonsensical chatter. All this
has tired my nerves to the nth degree.

Although he expressed himself more cautiously in his reviews,
they indicate that Wagner's music obviously had nothing to do
with what he himself was seeking in music. It was thus understandably difficult for him to report objectively on the Bayreuth
Music Festival for the readers of his newspaper. Physically exhausted and worn out by mental convulsions, he returned via
Vienna to Moscow.

Two Crucial Female Figures

Depression had been tormenting Tchaikovsky almost unin-
terruptedly since November 1875, and the *idée fixe* had gradually
taken hold of him that his recovery could be achieved only by the
presence of a loving person, who alone could lead him out of his
agonizing solitude by being constantly present. He longed more
and more ardently to free himself of that burden of his "moral
ailment," as Modest expressed it, until in 1877 Tchaikovsky was
misled into taking a nearly disastrous step. He announced to his
brother Modest in the fall of 1876 the following irrevocable decision:

> From this day on I will do everything possible to
> marry someone or other. I know that my inclina-
> tions are the greatest and most insurmountable
> impediment to my happiness, and I must fight
> against my disposition with all my strength. I will
> bring about the impossible to marry before the
> year is over, and if I cannot muster courage enough
> for this, I will in any case give up my habits. The
> thought that those who love me are sometimes
> ashamed of me offends me mortally. It has hap-
> pened a hundred times and will happen a hun-
> dred more times....I would like to silence the whole
> pack by a marriage or an official tie with a woman.

I despise their rumors but they cause worry to the people close to me. But I am too deeply caught in my habits and preferences to cast them away like an old glove all at once. I have no solid character, and since my last struggle I have already given in to my inclinations three times.

This step may have been preceded by a certain disgust with his increasing sexual activity, which in all probability consisted less in active homosexual action than in an intensive sexual preoccupation with his own person. At any rate, he was convinced that his previous life, with its anxieties and melancholic impulses and its guilt feelings which pressed him deeper and deeper into isolation, could not continue that way. How much his passionate desires at this time drew him into a downward whirlpool is reflected in his composition *Francesca da Rimini*, in which he most movingly portrayed in music the most secret and wildest dreams of a love he could himself never experience.

When in September 1876 he informed his brother Modest of his firm decision "to enter the married state with anyone whatever," he was apparently unaware of what catastrophic consequences such a step might entail. It is hard to imagine what would have become of him if an unusual woman, Mrs. Nadezhda Philaretovna von Meck, had not stood by him during this critical phase of his life. This cultured, tall and slender, but not exactly beautiful lady, was considered extremely extravagant and in her eccentric personality she resembled Tchaikovsky in many respects. She was the widow of a railroad engineer who had acquired a huge fortune by constructing railway lines. Karl von Meck had left her property that ranked among the richest in all Russia and comprised, besides two railway lines, a magnificent house in Moscow, the Brailov estate, as well as several mills and textile and sugar factories. Her huge fortune allowed her to go on extensive journeys with her family in her private car on her own trains and to give numerous social performances and receptions in her house. She came from a music-loving family, played piano very well; and this otherwise rather sober and extremely capable business woman could be set into an almost ecstatic rapture by music. When her husband died in 1876 at the age of forty-five from the results of a heart attack suffered on receiving the news that his wife had been unfaithful, she was the mother of eleven surviving children, seven of whom still lived in her house. Probably plagued by self-reproach and guilt feelings, after her husband's death she withdrew completely from the outside world to devote herself exclusively to her children and the management of her property. The only contact she continued to maintain was with Nicolai Rubinstein, who represented for her a kind of gateway to the musical world. He was also the person who recommended that she take into her household a young musician Josif Kotek, a violinist and pupil of Tchaikovsky's. No one could have suspected that this would be the start of a decisive turning point in Tchaikovsky's life.

Mrs. von Meck, who, like Kotek, ardently revered this composer and became ecstatic on hearing his overture *The Storm*, decided to ask Tchaikovsky to rewrite a few of his smaller compositions in a version for violin and piano, in order to play them in her house together with Kotek. She offered him an unusually high honorarium for this. This assignment, which Tchaikovsky gladly accepted, would mark the beginning of a fourteen-year friendly correspondence, for which there is no comparable example in the entire history of music and which is also unique from a medical perspective. This strange and unique correspondence, with its 1200 letters, provides insight into the intimate and yet unreal relationship between the two partners. It was possible only because both had agreed never to meet and to reply to not a word, a look, or even a greeting of the other. Surely the idea would not be farfetched that Tchaikovsky maintained this strange correspondence with a lady nine years his senior only for the sake of money. For her considerable financial subventions enabled him to get rid of his duties as professor at the Moscow Conservatory, which had long since become burdensome to him. In reality, however, this grotesque relationship, without parallel in history since the time of the *Minnesänger* in the early Middle Ages, may have had a different motive for Tchaikovsky, namely, finally to create a relationship of maternal dependency once again. Having suffered from a mother complex all his life, he found in

NADEZHDA VON MECK (1831-1894). SHE WAS TCHAIKOVSKY'S PLATONIC FRIEND AND GENEROUS PATRONESS FROM 1876 TO 1890.

Nadezhda a woman who was always intimately close to him like a mother, whom he could revere, and who in turn would also revere him. Moreover, since she always stayed at a safe distance, he did not need to fear the physical proximity of a woman, which made him quite uncomfortable. But when this correspondence lasting many years is correlated chronologically with letters to Modest, many proofs are found that he was not always free of hypocrisy and insincerity. He also was aware of this when he wrote to his brother:

> I confess with regret that our relationship is not normal and sometimes I am very much aware of its abnormality.

During his frequent despondent states he complained to his brothers of Nadezhda's exaggerated concern for his personal welfare, which he felt to be an unwarranted intrusion into his private sphere, or he made fun of Mrs. von Meck's tender feelings with rather unrefined words. Another time he spoke of fearing that Nadezhda intended to cross the boundaries of his personal intimate sphere, and many such things. All this stands in glaring contrast to what he wrote in his letters to his generous patroness, which virtually overflow with assurances of his love, reverence, and gratitude. He was also fully aware of his duplicity and made no secret of it when he openly admitted the duality of his nature with the words: "I think in one direction and act in another."

It must be admitted on Tchaikovsky's behalf that Mrs. von Meck in her voluntary seclusion apparently had a sick fantasy and in her enthusiasm for Tchaikovsky she could be transported to an almost rapturous state by his music. A few months after the beginning of their correspondence on 30 March 1877, after receiving the reworking of an aria from his opera *The Oprichnik*, she wrote:

> Your music is so wonderful that it sends me into a state of blissful ecstasy....I seem to hover above all earthly things, my temples throb, my heart beats wildly, a fog swims before my eyes, and my ears drown in the magic of this music....Oh God, how great is the man who has the ability to give others such moments of bliss.

The famous *andante cantabile* from the First String Quartet, which moved even Leo Tolstoy to tears at its premiere, got similar professions from her:

> ...I feel transported by this music into a state of exhilaration that moves through my body like an earthquake.

The initiative for this unique esoteric liaison between them both had been going on for several weeks before these written "love confessions" from Nadezhda, who on 27 February 1877 made a confession almost in the form of a challenge:

> I would like to report to you on an unusual affection I feel for you, but I am afraid to steal your valuable time. So I will tell you only that these feelings—may they be ever so abstract—mean very much to me, for they are the best and purest of all that a human being knows. For that reason you can, Peter Ilyich, if you want, call me a visionary

or even an insane woman, but you must not make fun of me, for all this would seem ridiculous only if it were not felt so sincerely and deeply.

Three weeks after writing these pathetic lines, she wrote to him that she took every opportunity to read all reviews and remarks about his compositions; and he found it consoling that in this woman's eyes even his less successful works always were given full recognition. From the very beginning, however, she also made it clear that a personal acquaintanceship, of whatever kind, was out of the question, even if that should be desirable for one of the parties. She expressly told him that it was not necessary for her to see him and that she would also never invite him to arrange a meeting with her, for, as she explained, "The fascination you exercise over me is as great as my fear to make your acquaintance." Since fortunately both of them, in their shyness and "misanthropy" were afraid of disillusionment, which "frequently follows on the heels of all intimacy," they actually never met in person, which would no doubt have led to a cruel disappointment. Nadezhda expressed her fear of this with the words: "I feel that I am all the more afraid of a personal acquaintanceship, the more you fascinate me." How happy Tchaikovsky was about this kind of mutual affection can be seen from a letter sent to Mrs. von Meck on 28 March 1877:

> ...I have always esteemed you as a person whose moral principles and character traits display many features in common with my own nature. The fact that we both are suffering from one and the same condition, binds us to one another. This condition can be called misanthropy, but it is a very particular kind of misanthropy, which is not aimed at people in the form of disdain or hatred. People who suffer from it fear...disappointment and the longing for the ideal that follows upon every intimacy. There was a time when this fear of people took such a hold of me that I came close to losing my mind. The circumstances of my life were such that I could neither hide nor

find a way out. I had to carry on the struggle with my own self, and God only knows what it cost me. Now I have come out of it so victoriously that life, long since, no longer seems unbearable to me....Thanks to a few successes I managed to achieve, I have regained courage; and depression, which could intensify to the point of hallucinations and delusionary ideas, now seldom afflicts me....From all this you will understand that I am not at all surprised when despite all your love for my music you do not feel the need to make the acquaintanceship of its composer. You are afraid not to rediscover in me the qualities with which you have endowed me in your fantasy and its tendency to idealization. And you are absolutely right. I am sure that on closer acquaintance with me you would not find complete agreement and harmony between the musician and the person you dream of....If you only knew how consoling it is for an artist to know a soul who feels just as strongly and deeply as he himself does when working out his composition.

It can easily be seen from these passages extracted from his letters that in Mrs. von Meck he had found a woman who in a certain regard was a mother-substitute with whom he could always find refuge when he needed solace. Under her protective wings he could not only feel secure when oppressed by his vital fears, but rather this woman, in her generous affection, at the same time removed from him all material cares. As early as 1 May he received from her the considerable sum of 3000 rubles to pay off his debts. He therefore saw it as appropriate to dedicate his Fourth Symphony to her, announcing it to Nadezhda as "our symphony." The opening theme of this work, he explained to her, represents that "power which incessantly hangs over our heads like a Damocles sword and constantly grips our heart." It seems quite interesting that in his letter to Modest by the "Damocles sword that incessantly hangs over my head" he is referring to his fear that his homosexual tendencies could be exposed in public.

Poor Tchaikovsky felt as if transfixed by a barrage of guilt-ridden poisoned arrows because of this vice he never spoke of expressly, but always referred to enigmatically as "this."

The question of why he wanted to marry just then at any price seems to provide its own answer in view of these guilt complexes. As Modest rightly noted, Tchaikovsky apparently saw an official marriage as the only means "to save his soul from the moral ailment which had so tormented him through all these last years." On 2 October he told his brother Anatoly:

> I am still standing before this turning point. I often think of it and am waiting for something to spur me to action.

It would not be very long before without any of his own doing an event caused him to act. At the end of April 1877, while he happened to be working on the letter-scene of his opera *Eugene Onegin*, out of the clear blue sky he received a letter from a certain Antonina Ivanovna Milyukova, telling him that she had admired him for a long time in the Conservatory and "will never stop loving him." At first, he wanted to ignore this over-emotional letter, but then at last he forced himself to reply, since the declarations in this letter were "so warm and open," as he wrote in a letter to Mrs. von Meck on 15 July 1877. Later the opinion was often expressed that Tchaikovsky at that time saw similarities between the fate of the young letter-writer and that of Tatyana, the heroine in Pushkin's drama *Eugene Onegin*, which however is certainly an impermissible simplification of the problem. At first, only a purely idealized love for Tchaikovsky was involved in Antonina's case, just as in Mrs. von Meck's. The difference was that Antonina did not want to be satisfied with life in a fantasy world. When Tchaikovsky on 1 June 1877 accepted her invitation to visit her and became aware of what this approximately thirty-year-old, charming, and well-built woman would expect of him, he told her of his defects, his moody and melancholic character, his nervous irritability, and his delicate health in general. For he felt no real love for this woman, but only a friendly affection. When Antonina saw that the fulfillment of her dreams was in jeopardy, she assured him that his defects could not upset her and that she loved him all the more because of them, and finally she even threatened to commit suicide if he rejected her:

> You have visited a solitary young girl and in this
> way bound our destinies together. If you do not
> want to make me your wife, I will kill myself.

After this threat he visited her again and proposed marriage to her, perhaps really in order not to behave as coldly and unfeelingly as Onegin.

For him marriage could mean only a platonic relationship, and he let her know clearly that his only purpose in this marriage would be to conceal the problems connected with his homosexuality from the public once and for all. Moreover, he was naive enough to hope that he could thus perhaps also succeed in mastering his abnormal disposition. In a letter to Mrs. von Meck of 15 July 1877, he described not only the cruel alternative he faced— either preservation of his personal freedom at the price of Antonina's death or consenting to a marriage—but also the grotesque situation of a bridegroom who could not offer his bride even the slightest feeling of love. But the storms raging inside him in those days and weeks could be most clearly intimated in his music. In his Fourth Symphony, whose final movement he had just finished, his untrammeled passions, which sometimes mounted to really hysterical outbreaks, cannot be overheard. On the other hand, he was able to transpose Tatyana's fate in his opera *Eugene Onegin*, with whom he identified to the highest degree, into almost insuperable lyrical expression.

In July 1877, after some self-overcoming, he decided to inform his family of his intention to marry. Characteristically, he wrote neither to his homosexual brother Modest, nor to his beloved sister Sasha, but only to Anatoly and his eighty-two-year-old father, to whom he wrote on 5 July 1877:

> My bride's name is Antonina Ivanovna Milyukova.
> She is a poor, but good and innocent girl who
> loves me very much. Dear father, you know that
> at my age one doesn't marry rashly, therefore don't
> worry.

Tchaikovsky with his wife Antonina in 1877. This marriage of convenience brought the composer to the edge of madness.

Modest and Sasha received the news only immediately after the wedding, which took place on 18 July 1877. While his family sincerely wished him happiness, for Mrs. von Meck this turn of events was "bitter and unbearable," as she confided to Tchaikovsky two years later. For she loved him "more than anyone else," and so naturally she had to hate Antonina, who was now so close to him, "because she did not make you happy; but I would have hated her a hundred times more if you had been happy with her"—words she wrote only in September 1879.

In a letter dated 18 October 1876, Tchaikovsky had first mentioned to his sister Sasha his intention to prepare himself for the
married state, assuring her that he "would not incautiously plunge
into the abyss of an unhappy relationship." But the very opposite
happened, for according to Modest's description of the "insane
undertaking" of 18 July 1877, Peter Ilyich "had to atone most
grievously for the whole frivolity, the whole folly of his deed
from the first days, indeed the first hour, and was deeply unhappy." Actually only a few days after the wedding Tchaikovsky
reported to his brother Anatoly about the "horrible ecclesiastical
torture" he had gone through and his wife's "absolutely repulsive
behavior" toward him. This contrasts to some extent with his
description of their seven-day "honeymoon":

> We had conversations that clarified our mutual
> relations in more detail. She is in total agreement
> with everything and will never be dissatisfied. She
> only wants to spoil and mother me....She is very
> simple-minded, but that is good so.

But in the same letter he alludes to his insurmountable aversion
to this woman, about which he had become completely clear
after only a few days.

> It would be completely unbearable and inexcus-
> able if I had deceived my wife in any way, but I
> informed her that all she could count on was my
> brotherly love. Physically my wife has become
> totally repulsive to me.

The consequences of this "insane enterprise" became clearer and
clearer. He had expected by the demonstration of a natural married life before the public to calm his mind concerning all the
fears and self-reproaches of recent years, but now it was driving
him to the edge of madness. Incapable of enduring this condition even for a short time longer, he saw as the only possibility a
hasty departure for Kamenka, to his sister Sasha, where he hoped
to relax. To his soul-friend Mrs. von Meck he admitted all his
despair in a letter of 9 August, and she also financed the spa

treatment in the Caucasus region, which he used as pretext to his wife. He wrote in his letter:

> I am leaving in one hour. A few days more—and
> I swear—I would have gone insane.

After having left Moscow, he felt as if "he were awaking from a horrifying dream." As he confessed to Mrs. von Meck, even the mere thought of living in the same room with his wife made him terribly uncomfortable. Not only did he feel Antonina's presence to be repulsive, but it also completely prevented him from composing. His future seemed to him similar to the "life of a plant," from which music, the main component of his existence, was extinguished forever. In these moments of utmost despair he probably really believed this. But by the month of August, which he spent alone at his sister's, while Antonina at this time was making preparations for their home together in Moscow, he began orchestrating the Fourth Symphony and finishing some sections of *Eugene Onegin*. But Tchaikovsky's final breakdown was inevitable. One day after his return to Moscow, he fell into a sort of panic. He jotted into his diary:

> All I long for is a possibility to escape somewhere.
> But how and where to? It is impossible, impossible, impossible!

And to Mrs. von Meck he even wrote in his nameless despair:

> Death seemed to be the only way out, but suicide
> was out of the question.

Two weeks later, this horrible episode culminated in a spell of mental confusion, strangely combined with cowardice in the face of an ultimate resolution to commit suicide. In this way what came about was a grotesque-sounding suicide attempt by intentionally contracting a fatal pulmonary inflammation, which he described to his friend Kashkin as follows:

> Every evening I went for a walk and roamed without destination through the lonesome streets of
> Moscow. On such a night I approached the bank

of the Moscow River, when suddenly the idea
flashed up, to catch a fatal cold. Under cover of
darkness, observed by no one, I waded up to my
waist in the water. I stayed there as long as I
could bear the cold. Then I climbed out of the
water, certain that I had caught a fatal cold. At
home, however, I told my wife that I had been
fishing and had fallen into the water. But my health
proved so strong that the icy water could not
harm me.

Probably this halfhearted suicide attempt actually was meant to
free himself from marriage with a woman whom he found "simply bothersome." How serious his intention was can be seen
from a letter to Mrs. von Meck from those days:

Death is really the best blessing; I plead for it with
the whole strength of my soul.

After the failed suicide attempt or even before, Tchaikovsky
had no doubt that he was close to insanity and that to continue
living with this woman would mean the end of him. According to
a report by Modest, "under the pretext of a telegram calling him
most speedily to St. Petersburg, on 24 September he left Moscow
without delay in a state bordering on madness." When Anatoly
went to meet him at the railroad station the next morning, he saw
coming toward him an old man with trembling hands, thin, pale
yellow face and reddened eyes. Tchaikovsky was hastily taken to
a hotel, where he suffered a nervous breakdown and spent forty-
eight hours in an unconscious state. The doctors, among them
the psychiatrist Dr. Balinsky, were in agreement that a complete
recovery could be achieved only if his tie with Antonina were
broken once and for all. When Anatoly, who traveled to Moscow
for that purpose, told her this, he was surprised at the coldness
and frivolity with which she received this news. Today we know
that Antonina, who was committed to an insane asylum in 1897
and died there in 1917, was already mentally disturbed at the time
of her marriage with Tchaikovsky and must have been
nymphomanically inclined. Surely that is why he wrote to
Nadezhda von Meck the following description of his wife:

For hours she repeated endless tales of the countless men who were in love with her. They were
mostly generals, nephews of famous wealthy persons, famous artists, even members of the Czarist
house. No less often and with an incomprehensible passionate zeal she described to me in detail
her vices, the cruel and base actions...

It is all the more to Tchaikovsky's honor that even later he never
tried to put the blame completely on his wife, and in a letter to
Mrs. von Meck he even remarked:

In retrospect to the short period of our life together, I see that I did not play a beautiful role....My
wife deserves pity, in any case.

On the other hand, one can thus better understand the paradoxi-
cal situation created by the marriage between a sexually perverted
man and a woman sexually aroused to the point of nymphomania, since in this way by chance two persons with completely
opposite dispositions and total sexual incompatibility tried to establish a bond of marriage.

Without ever getting a divorce, Tchaikovsky separated from
his wife, but only to sink even deeper into the world of illusion
that characterized his bond with Mrs. von Meck. If he could write
to Modest: "Gradually I am finding myself again and returning to
life," that was not least of all due to this woman's help, for she
was his closest confidante and in that capacity she contributed
decisively to his regaining his mental balance. But her financial
subventions were another thing that bound him ever more tightly
to his benefactress, and Nadezhda knew only too well how to
bind him even more tightly. When after a short stay in Berlin he
arrived for rest in Clarens on Lake Geneva in October 1877, together with his brother Anatoly, the news reached him that
Mrs. von Meck was granting him a yearly pension of 6000 rubles
and giving him the opportunity at last to relinquish the task of
teaching at the Conservatory to devote himself from then on exclusively to composing. In deep gratitude, he assured her in a
letter of 6 November that "from now on every note flowing from
his pen was dedicated to her." Shortly before he had still written:

> You know, dear friend, that people with some jus-
> tification were whispering that I had lost my mind.
> When I remember all I did, all the wrong things I
> committed, I must involuntarily draw the conclu-
> sion that my reason at intervals is not quite in or-
> der.

Through the financial independence he had acquired, he could
again yield unimpededly to his creative urge, and his joy about
this is clearly expressed in his letter of thanks of 6 November:

> I owe it to you that my love of work is returning
> with double strength. Never for a moment will I
> ever forget that you helped me to continue living
> for my artistic profession.

The changed relationship with Mrs. von Meck can be seen by a
drastic change in the manner of the correspondence between the
two. His letters to her had formerly been stereotypically alike;
but now he was ready to answer her questions about music or
about love candidly. For instance, he answered her question
whether he had ever loved by explaining to her:

> You ask me, dear friend, whether I know any other
> love than a platonic one. Yes and no. If you want
> to know whether I have experienced perfect hap-
> piness in love, then I answer, "No." I even believe
> that my music is an answer to this question. But if
> you ask me whether I know the stormy might of
> this feeling, then I answer you, "Yes." And I also
> tell you that I have many times sought to express
> the torments and delights of love with my music.

The best example of this is the Fourth Symphony, in which he
put his personal world of feeling to music and thereby imprinted
a subjective stamp on it, as later also in his Fifth and Sixth Symphony. In this Fourth Symphony are heard all the disappointments and guilty fears of his strongly ingrained homosexuality as
well as his states of excitement whipped up to a frenzy under the
influence of alcohol, although the antitheses between reality and
repression are recognizable only blurredly as behind a veil. He

himself was deeply convinced of the quality of this work, as he expressed it to Mrs. von Meck:

> In my innermost depths I am convinced that this symphony is the best thing I have created till now.

From Clarens, Tchaikovsky made a short journey to Paris together with his brother Anatoly, yielding to his brother's urging, to undergo a complete examination by the famous internist, Dr. d'Archembault, due to his still unsatisfactory general condition. We have a report from Tchaikovsky's own pen about this rather disappointing examination:

> Hardly had I begun to tell him my medical history when he interrupted me coolly and not without arrogance with the words: "Yes, yes, I know all that by heart. You can spare yourself the effort." Then he named to me the various signs of my sickness, more on his own than by having interrogated me. Finally he wrote down his prescription, got up, and said to me: "Sir, your sickness is incurable, yet you can live to be a hundred years old!" Then I heard his prescription, consisting of four points: "1. I was to ingest a particular kind of chalk before breakfast and lunch; 2. Drink a glass of Haute rive a quarter of an hour before eating; 3. Bathe in Barège; 4. Avoid a tremendous number of foods." I laid the doctor's fee on the table and, by no means reassured, I left him without any confidence in his instructions, aware that I had not been with a doctor practicing medicine, but rather with a salesman of medical advice. My trip to Paris thus turned out to be just about useless....It is most peculiar that d'Archambault did not even ask me what my profession is and why I became so nervous. A doctor would have to know that!

This example shows once again the importance of an extensive conversation between the doctor and his patient in order to gain the patient's confidence, especially when psychic disturbances or psychosomatically conditioned complaints are involved. In the case of this Parisian doctor, it was not at all enough to have excluded an organic ailment, since he simultaneously trivialized the neurotic symptoms that were present.

Since Tchaikovsky in the long run also did not feel happy in Clarens, he decided on a several month long tour touching mainly on various Italian cities. But even Italy could exercise no positive influence on his depression, which still tormented him, as can be seen from the medical reports in his letters to Mrs. von Meck. Thus on 18 November a letter from Florence reads:

> In Clarens, where I was leading a perfectly quiet life, I often sank into melancholy. Incapable of explaining these periods of depression to myself otherwise, I blamed them on the mountains. How childish! I was convinced I needed only to cross the Italian border to begin a life of perfect happiness! Nonsense! I feel a hundred times more miserable here.

And a week later he reported from Rome:

> I am still a very sick man. I can still not endure the slightest noise; yesterday in Florence and today in Rome every carriage rolling past threw me into an insane rage, every sound, every scream tears my nerves to shreds. The masses of people that flood the narrow streets annoy me so much that I look upon every stranger coming toward me as a deadly enemy.

This misanthropic fear of his fellowmen was, in his present mood, surely also the main reason for his being unable to accept the basically honorable proposal that he attend the World's Fair in Paris in January 1878 as the Russian ambassador. To excuse himself, he wrote on 4 January 1878 to his friend Nicolai Rubinstein, who could not understand his negative decision:

> I cannot go to Paris. That is neither pusillanimity nor laziness, but I really cannot. For the last three

days since receiving the news of my appointment, I have been completely sick. I am almost insane. Death is preferable to this. I wanted to overcome myself, but nothing came of it. I know now from my own experience what it means to do violence to oneself, to go against one's nature. Now I cannot stand the sight of any persons; complete isolation from any noise and any excitement is urgently necessary for me. In short, if you want me to return to you completely healthy, don't demand that I go to Paris.

Where he felt best during this winter period was in San Remo, where he stayed for a longer time. Meanwhile, since Anatoly was expected back in Moscow in December 1877, he sent for his young servant Alyosha, who usually had to accompany him on his later journeys. In view of his bad physical constitution, it is surprising that his composition work moved ahead briskly during this winter of 1877/78. He apparently seemed, as he himself noted, "to recover best by working." After having just finished orchestrating the Fourth Symphony, a little later his most famous opera *Eugene Onegin* likewise was swiftly moving toward completion. What especially distinguishes this work is the passionate identification of the composer with the subject of this opera; and although he believed it would appeal to only a small part of the public, still all his life his special love was directed toward this opera. And yet another work finished in a few weeks saw the light of the world in that spring of 1878, namely, his Violin Concerto op. 35. Although this work, too, shows what he had been going through during the previous months, one also senses clearly that his despair and his depressive spells at last were again yielding to a genuine joy in life. The "high mood" he was in since the arrival of the young violinist Kotek in Clarens, where Tchaikovsky had meanwhile returned together with Modest, is evident in a letter of 22 March 1878 to Mrs. von Meck, in which he joyfully declared that such a "fantastic disposition made composing the purest pleasure." He could all too gladly have dedicated this concerto to young Kotek, who meanwhile had become a pupil of

Joseph Joachim and to whom he owed many clues about violin technique for his composition work. But he feared thereby to expose it to "gossip," as he confided to his friend and publisher Jürgenson. The premiere of the violin concerto was presented in December 1881 in Vienna by the young virtuoso Adolf Brodsky, and although the critic Eduard Hanslick apostrophized it as "stinking music," it is numbered today among the "classical" violin concertos.

On 23 April 1878, he finally arrived back in Russia, where his sister Sasha awaited him in Kamenka. So that Tchaikovsky could work "pleasantly" she arranged a separate house for him and his servant Alyosha. Temporarily he also accepted Mrs. von Meck's invitation to spend a few weeks at her vast country estate Brailov, where rooms of his own and the entire personnel stood at his disposal. Intermittently, melancholy came over him, and his most effective means of overcoming it was work. In a letter to Mrs. von Meck he reported on 18 July:

> ...I need work like air to breathe. As soon as I am idle, despondency overcomes me....I am dissatisfied with myself and even hate myself....Indeed, I am very much inclined to melancholy and I know that I must not give in to my desire for idleness. Only work saves me.

Yet alcohol was beginning to play an even greater role, as he had confided to his brother Anatoly the previous winter:

> ...evenings I always drink several brandies. And during the day I drink a good many. I cannot exist without it....I can write letters only after taking a little swallow. All this proves to me that I still am not in the best shape.

Nomadic Period

When Tchaikovsky returned to Moscow in October 1878, he handed in his resignation from his position as professor at the Conservatory, from which he had merely been on leave during the past year. This marked the beginning of his so-called "nomadic period." Since he no longer had his own apartment in Moscow, he commuted restlessly back and forth between Russia and Western Europe, or he visited friends and relatives in Moscow, St. Petersburg, or Kiev. He was still suffering from phobic anxieties and a fear of establishing personal contacts. He therefore was very glad when Mrs. von Meck put one of her houses, namely, the newly acquired landed estate, Pleshtcheyevo, at his disposal, whenever he wanted it, while strict attention would be paid that she herself remained absent during his stays there. Only once, as chance would have it, did they meet in the woods of Brailov in their two coaches, which cast them both into confusion and caused him to merely lift his hat briefly without a greeting. The mere thought of facing her unexpectedly or even the idea that she could notice his deviant sexual disposition instilled horrified panic in him. Yet it can be gathered from Mrs. von Meck's letters that she gradually must have hoped for something more from her "platonic friend." For her initial strict reserve gradually gave way more and more clearly to an open declaration of love, for instance when she assured him:

> All last night I dreamed of you….What happiness it is to feel that I have you near me, that I possess you….If only you knew how much I love you. That is no longer love, that is adoration, adulation, reverence.

How much she strove for a closer personal relationship can also be seen from the fact that in the winter of 1878/79 she invited him to Florence and there rented a splendid apartment for him not far from her luxurious villa. Yet even now letters were merely exchanged each day via the servants, and no personal meeting took place between the two of them. Tchaikovsky probably remembered the shock of the unintentional meeting of their carriages in Brailov, which caused him a loss of appetite and insomnia and would again have cast him into a deep depression, as he described it to Modest: "Yesterday I had my hysterical spell again; I cried the whole evening." In Florence, however, he too occasionally longed for more; for he reported a few days later to his

recently married brother, Anatoly, that he too longed to be loved
by a woman. Perhaps he was not fully aware that he needed not
so much a wife as a mother, and in fact his correspondence with
Mrs. von Meck was almost a real mother-son relationship. In
view of this it was surely a satisfaction for both of them that in
1884 the marriage of Sasha's daughter Anna and Nadezhda's son
Nicolai forged a family bond, at least in that way.

Mrs. von Meck's ongoing subventions, as well as the rising
income from the royalties and the sale of his works made it possible for him to lead the life of a nobleman. In his travels he
always stayed at the most exclusive hotels and munificently gave
invitations and generous tips. Meanwhile in Russia, but also abroad,
he had risen to fame, which on the one hand flattered him, while
on the other it also meant a further psychic burden. In a letter to
Mrs. von Meck of 25 August 1880 he described his mixed feelings:

> Fame! What conflicting feelings this word releases
> in me. On the one hand, I wish and strive for it,
> on the other I hate it since...with my fame, inter-
> est in my person also increases, so that I am ex-
> posed to the public's stares....Sometimes the
> senseless wish seizes me to hide away somewhere
> once and for all, and to be considered dead.

To be able to live with this obvious inner contradiction and achieve
some equanimity, he tried to put on a kind of mask. His inter-
human contacts were characterized by correct, courteous, and
affable forms, and his deportment in society became more self-
confident and occasionally even displayed cheerfulness. This
protective wall he surrounded himself with and his inner life were
also reflected in his letters to Mrs. von Meck, for they not only
became more seldom and laconic, but their content now dealt
mostly with his composition activity. Only in letters to Modest
did he now and then hint that he was still tormented by depressions or various other mental and physical ailments. For the rest
of his life, his ambivalent nature, which was so clearly manifested
in the Fourth Symphony and in *Eugene Onegin*, repeatedly created conflict situations that had to be manifested in one form or
another both artistically and medically. His divided sexuality still

condemned him to indulge in cunning pretexts and lying duplicity, while simultaneously trying outwardly to represent the perfect gentleman, interested only in his composition work, traveling
a great deal professionally and privately, occasionally playing the
role of a benevolent uncle, and otherwise frequently preoccupied
with his own mental and physical ailments. The many pages of
his compendious correspondence with Nadezhda von Meck are
therefore also full of insignificant details and complaints which—
as Olga Bennigsen noted—would have to be addressed more to a
medical adviser than to a lady-friend. In fact, on reading his
letters, it is sometimes hard to picture that "the letters were written by a young man and not by a childish old man whose interests were limited only to his digestion and other slight indispositions
of a senile organism." In fact, Tchaikovsky sometimes made absolutely no effort to conceal a childish sentimentality similar to a
little girl's. Otherwise one learns again and again of insomnia,
feverish headaches, and upper abdominal complaints, which he
sometimes referred to as colic of the gall, other times as a stomachache. Since the fall of 1878, when he reported without misgivings
to his soul-friend that he rather often "tried to strengthen" himself
with wine, and was given severe warnings by her in this regard,
data about his alcohol consumption are given only in letters to his
twin brothers and in his diaries. These data become progres-
sively more detailed in the following years.

In the years between 1878 and 1885 his creativity was not all
too productive. An exception was his *Capriccio italien*, which
stands very close in form to Glinka's First Spanish Overture and
was a tremendous success at its premiere in Moscow at the end of
1880. The utterly joyful nature of this work, whose composition
is dated at the beginning of that year, does not give any clue that
his father had died on 21 January 1880. Since he had hardly any
contact with him in the last years, his death seems not to have
affected him very much, which is confirmed by the very fact that
he did not consider it necessary to return to Russia from Rome,
where he was then staying.

The second masterpiece which he wrote at that time "from an
inner impetus," was the *Serenade for Strings*, which Anton
Rubinstein, who was otherwise very restrained in his criticism,

called Tchaikovsky's best work. Qualitatively not comparable
with these two works is the Second Piano Concerto op. 44, whose
instrumentation he completed in May 1880 and whose themes are
far inferior to the blossoming melodies of the famous First Piano
Concerto in B-flat Minor. And Tchaikovsky's smaller piano pieces
from this time, as well as his Concerto Fantasia op. 56, composed
a few years later, display similar weaknesses. Like Hector Berlioz,
apparently Tchaikovsky, too, could not be inspired by the piano
as instrument.

Little as his father's death affected him, he was all the more
deeply moved by Nicolai Rubinstein's tragic end in Paris in 1881.
At the news that Rubinstein lay dying, he hastened to Paris immediately, where he found his friend already dead. He had succumbed to a perforated intestine, and it cannot be decided whether
the cause was really a perforated tubercular intestinal ulcer, as the
Parisian physician, Dr. Potin, suspected, or whether it was the
effect of an intestinal obstruction caused by a malignant tumor.
The preceding severe emaciation and feebleness would lead one,
rather, to assume the latter possibility. Tchaikovsky, who was
afraid of corpses, ghosts, and burglars, feared he would have to
see his friend disfigured by death. On the occasion of the burial
ceremonies he wrote to Modest:

> To my shame I must admit to not having suffered
> so much under the sad, irretrievable loss as under
> having to see poor Rubinstein's dead body.

In his memory, he composed a two-movement piano trio, in which
the first movement by its sad elegy convincingly and sincerely
mirrors the composer's basic mood. In the second variations
movement, each variation is supposed to correspond to an event
from Rubinstein's life, but one also senses in it a lack of inner
involvement on the composer's part, just as in general this work
of chamber music contains many weak passages. Originally he
feared that contact with death could trigger a similar crisis as the
parting, shortly before, from his beloved Alyosha, who was more
than a servant. Despite all attempts to exempt him, Alyosha was
drafted to military service, and Tchaikovsky from then on had to
get on with his hectic, chaotic life by himself, but he also feared

that his Alyosha, brutalized by military life, would someday return to him changed for the worse. On the day of farewell, Tchaikovsky suffered a severe nervous crisis. Convulsed by cramps, he let out despairing screams and finally fell into an unconscious state. His letters to Alyosha express the whole pain of separation:

> ...Oh, my dear little Lanya! Even if you remained far from me for a hundred years, I would never become disaccustomed to you, and would wait for the happy day when you will return to me. I think of it every day....Everything is hateful to me, because you, my dear little friend, are no longer with me.

During his work on the Third Orchestra Suite op. 55, which he began with Alyosha again by his side—in Kamenka in spring of 1884, numerous remarks are found in his diary about "Bob," his thirteen-year-old nephew Vladimir. Since earliest youth he was especially fond of this lad and in later years this warm affection seems to have taken on a more than platonic character. We know that Bob likewise was homosexually oriented and committed suicide in 1906 at the age of thirty-five. At first, however, Tchaikovsky's love for Bob was still uncomplicated, for instance when his diary for 26 April 1884 states: "What a treasure Bob is....My dear, incomparable and inspiring idol Bob!" And another time he noted: "His unimaginable charm will yet rob me of my reason." This boy's presence brought into his life a real confusion and unrest that were aggravated even more by a certain card game: "Playing Vint [or Russian Whist, a cross between Whist and Bridge] is ruining me." In his exasperated moments, he then turned his anger against himself. "Soon I will be forty-one years old. How long I have already lived, and how little I have achieved." He feared such depressive moods because the inactivity they entailed was the source of his pathological, unsatisfied sexual longings and wishes. The secret symbols z and x, which in his diary indicate homosexual or other activities connected with his strong sexual feelings, give a picture of the compulsion under which he at times lived. The diaries, however, also reveal under what self-reproach and guilt feelings he then suffered. Thus, on three consecutive days in May 1884 he noted:

> Z is less tormenting but more constantly present than x...z torments me unusually strongly today. God spare me such a state....I was extremely irritable and annoyed, not because of the card-playing but because z tormented me.

Similar entries are repeated at irregular intervals, and sometimes he was befallen by fear of himself. Then, feeling guilt-ridden, he admitted:

> What a monster I am! May God forgive me my sinful feelings.

Under such circumstances, it is not surprising that he was often plagued by psychosomatic ailments of the most various kinds. Stomachaches alternated with pressure in the throat or nausea; another time he mentioned in the diary a hemorrhoidal ailment that bothered him; or else he reported on 9 May 1884 that during a walk after the noon meal he suddenly had the feeling "of choking, combined with a pain in the heart area, which very much alarmed me." In early June he seems to have fallen ill of a feverish inflammation of the throat that caused him a "hellish torture" with each swallow. But his mental state was also anything but serene, so that he felt incapable of attending the St. Petersburg premiere of his new opera *Mazepa*. To Mrs. von Meck he wrote: "Fear and excitement are driving me nearly insane," and five weeks later, on 25 March 1884 Tchaikovsky, otherwise not at all religious, made the surprising profession:

> Daily and hourly I thank God that he has given me faith in him. What would I be if I did not believe in him and submit myself to his will, given my pusillanimity and the quality of being shaken to the depths of my soul by the smallest blow and wanting to give up living?

In his depressive phases, as these lines lead one to suspect, suicidal ideas seemed repeatedly to reverberate in his soul, despite his external successes at home and abroad. For in June 1883 he was awarded an honorary doctoral degree by Cambridge University as the foremost Russian composer, and even Czar Alexander III contracted with him for several composition assignments, mainly in the area of church music.

He grew more and more weary of his hectic activity and eternal travels, and he began increasingly to long for inner calm. He admitted to Mrs. von Meck in a letter of 4 April 1884: "I am tired of wandering. I don't know why, but now I am thinking only of a home of my own." He still spent September on the Pleshtcheyevo estate as Mrs. von Meck's guest, but in 1885 the time had come. He rented a house in Maidanovo near Klin, where Alyosha came from, in order at last to put an end to his restless roving existence. Later he moved three times, but till the end of his life he stayed in this region, which he found so attractive. As Modest reports, it was not only the beauty of this region he was enthusiastic about, but rather "its location between the two capital cities." But 1885 marked a turning point in an artistic sense, also. For, after a mental and creative nadir lasting almost seven years, he now began gathering new energies and emerging from the creative paralysis he had fallen into, despite the many works that originated in this period. Modest describes this change in his brother as follows:

> He no longer needs a support anymore. Independence in all details of his life has now become his main necessity. The duties of public activity besides composing no longer frighten him, but rather they attract him, because he feels equal to them.... He no longer flees people, he advances to meet all of them....Since 1885 his business correspondence with publishers, enterprisers, and representatives of various musical institutes of Russia and

Europe has been growing constantly....The biographical material has accumulated very much in
quantity, but qualitatively it offers significantly less
interest.

However much he now participated in international music
life and however much he tried to conceal his fearful timidity
toward people behind his new "mask," his depressions still did
not let go of him. In his biography, Modest, to whom he confided his various physical and mental torments in his letters even
in this phase of new-found strength, expressly refers to these
mood swings:

> After a seven-year recovery period, Peter Ilyich
> seizes everything with gusto and courage. But
> then his courage gradually goes lame; he becomes
> weary and has to muster all his willpower once
> more to continue this way of life. His enthusiasm
> flees, and all that is left, as he himself writes, is a
> weariness with life, at times terrible sorrow, a trace
> of sadness, finality.

Because of a "renewed high degree of nervousness, Tchaikovsky,
during a stay in St. Petersburg, sought out the internist Dr. Vasily
Bertenson, in whom he had great confidence in his later years,
too. He reported to him that recently, in addition to the usual
stomachaches and intestinal ailments, "breathing difficulty" had
set in and was causing him considerable worry. Dr. Bertenson,
too, could discover no organic cause and classified the disturbance as a general neurosis, just as Dr. d'Archambault had formerly done in Paris. Dr. Bertenson advised him to go in the near
future to Vichy for treatment for a diagnosed "stomach and nervous disorder."

In 1885 Tchaikovsky was unanimously elected to the board of
directors of the Moscow branch of the Russian Music Society, and
in this capacity he managed to have his former pupil Sergei Taneyev
appointed Director of the Moscow Conservatory. Later Taneyev
would contribute much to propagating his teacher's works. The

intrigues that had to be overcome to accomplish this appointment weighed especially heavily upon Tchaikovsky, as he told
Mrs. von Meck: "The result—indescribable exhaustion and a
boundless longing for rest and relaxation." He found this rest in
his house in Maidanovo, where in April he began with the composition of *Manfred*, a program symphony of the greatest scale.
The composition of this work, which was already completed by
September and was considered to be Tchaikovsky's master achievement by many specialists, presented tremendous challenges and
thus again led to a state of over-irritated nerves, together with
phases of deepest despondency.

While previously his timidity toward people had prevented
him from thinking of working as a director, by the end of 1886 he
had gathered the necessary courage and self-confidence to prove
his skill as a conductor for the first time since the attempt ten
years earlier. He wrote to Mrs. von Meck that the circumstances
had taken shape in such a way that

> I must try to overcome myself and put myself to
> the test at the conductor's stand....What contrib-
> uted to this decision was an insurmountable wish
> to prove to myself how unfounded are the doubts
> about my ability to conduct.

With the first performance of his opera *Cherevichki*, a reworking
of *Vakula the Smith*, he made a successful comeback as a conductor. He therefore decided to conduct a concert in St. Petersburg, consisting entirely of his own compositions. The success of
this event, which took place on 5 March, was so overwhelming
that he planned a similar concert in November, in which his new
Fourth Orchestra Suite *"Mozartiana"* had its premiere.

But first he was struck by a severe blow of fate. Just as he
was beginning treatment in Borshom to reinvigorate his general
health, the news reached him that his old friend Nicolai Kondratiev
lay severely ill in Aachen. The following six weeks, which he
spent at his dying friend's bedside, imposed a severe mental strain
on him and brought him once again to the brink of depression.
He wrote to Mrs. von Meck on 12 September 1887:

> That was one of the hardest times in my life. I
> became very old and thin at this time. Such a
> weariness with life, despondency and apathy took
> hold of me as if I, too, would soon have to die.

On top of this depressed frame of mind came, in the beginning of
November, the disastrous failure of the premiere of his new opera, *The Sorceress*, in St. Petersburg, whereby his depression became clinically manifested. Despite this mental depression, he
continued directing the rehearsals for his planned great symphony
concert in Moscow, which cost him a great deal of energy, as he
confided to his friend Nadezhda: "I am very tired and afraid of
ruining my health with these worries and excitement." The triumphal success of this concert on 26 November 1887, which made
a repetition necessary the next day, however, gave him back so
much strength that in 1888 he could begin his great concert tour
right across Europe, taking him to Danzig, Dresden, Hamburg,
Prague, Berlin, Geneva, Paris, and London, and enabling him to
establish contact with numerous great musicians. Johannes
Brahms, Antonín Dvorák, Eduard Grieg, and especially France's
leading composers, such as Fauré, Gounod, and Massenet, expressed their admiration for him, giving a great boost to his self-
esteem. His *Diary of My Journey in 1888* made accessible to the
public shortly after his death all his experiences and the magnificent successes of his concerts in great detail. His private diary,
continued parallel with that one, however, reveals that his display
of a self-confident artist accustomed to success was possible only
with the greatest mustering of energy and that behind this mask,
of which his brother Modest so often spoke, was hidden a man
tormented by doubts and self-reproach. More and more frequently
in addition to the mysterious abbreviation "*z*," entries are found
referring to his increased alcohol consumption:

> Drunkenness; I drank so much that I can't remem-
> ber anything more; endless drunkenness and talk-
> ing.

From such remarks one can conclude that Tchaikovsky felt alcohol to be an appropriate means for overcoming his doubts and

self-reproach more easily. However, he generally awoke the next day, as could be expected after drinking too much cognac, grog, or absinthe, with a headache and nausea. Sometimes remarks are also found in his diary leading to the suspicion that he occasionally even tried narcotics, for example on 10 May 1888: "Experienced something like falling in love with Daudet's heroin," or on 2 June in Paris: "Went with Brandukov to Golitzin. Three other men were also there: another handsome, flat-chested man; an elegant gentleman, and a doctor, morphine injection." But we also learn from his diary of phases of "homesickness and weeping in sadness." In addition, there were various complaints on the part of his irritated stomach, especially after drinking all night, as well as repeated toothaches, which sometimes gave him a great deal of pain, especially when an abscessed tooth occurred, as was the case in March 1886. At that time Tchaikovsky noted between 4 and 9 March:

> My cheek caused me unbearable pain the whole night through—suffered all day from pains in the cheek—by this morning a strong swelling of the whole cheek had formed. I am unable to speak; the pain subsided somewhat, but the fever remained unchanged—was totally exhausted from this condition; then suddenly toward four o'clock, as if by a magician's hand, all complaints had vanished.

If one reads through his diary carefully, one becomes convinced that even his stomachaches were not always of a functional nature. Some data suggest that occasionally they must have been conditioned by an organic ailment. For on 13 July 1886 it says, after he had been complaining of a pressure in the stomach region on the preceding days: "I ate something and felt better. I was already thinking the stomachache had disappeared, but toward evening it became worse again," and a little later he noted:

> My stomach aches worse than before. After drinking some cognac with water I feel no more pain. How strange that is!

The description of relief of stomach pain by ingestion of food is just about classical for the presence of an ulcer of the stomach or the duodenum. An additional symptom fits into this picture and is likewise precisely described in the diary, for on 17 July it reads:

> Woke up in the night with indescribable tormenting pains in the chest—could hardly sleep, could not lie down, sat alternatively in one armchair or the other—Golitzin's advice to apply a mustard plaster brought some relief, for then I was able to sleep in the armchair until morning.

These pains, which began in the first hours after midnight, especially after drinking alcohol or after a fatty evening meal, were localized under the sternum and were improved by putting the body in an erect position. They correspond to a so-called reflux disorder, in which acidic stomach fluid flows back into the lower esophagus and causes a violent burning sensation or a piercing pressure.

But Tchaikovsky also described in his diaries the typical symptoms that are the guidelines for diagnosing a real depression. On 31 July he noted with surprise:

> It is strange. I have for a long time observed that I always feel especially bad in the morning. How can that be explained? Why do I in the morning feel, instead of increased energy and efficiency, only dejection, sadness, and aversion to every kind of activity?…A boundless feeling of loneliness and depression.

Of course, such states of mental depression were repeatedly triggered by problems connected with his homosexuality. What feelings of jealousy or what insults he had to endure in that regard can only be read between some lines of his diaries. Thus, on 2 November 1886 he noted: "I hide from the others the circumstance that I am jealous of Bob, because of Vanya"; and six days later he remarked: "I have a very strange feeling that he not only does not love me, but that he even feels antipathy toward me. Am I wrong or not?" Again and again he sought refuge in alcohol:

"I drank like a sailor. Could hardly hold the pen in my hand." But it was not only doubts of Bob's love for him that tormented him, but also difficulties with his moody young friend Vanya, of whom he once wrote: "Love with Vanya. Restraint. Virtue wins out," and another time he was angry with him. And there were also the school boys, Schilling and Radin, who seemed to have caused him some agitation. For on 9 April 1887 he wrote in his diary: "The boys continued to pursue me. I hid near the riverbank." His irresistible attraction for young boys often gave rise to similar situations even later, for instance during a boat cruise on the Volga in May 1887:

> My friendship with the unusually attractive and
> lovable Sasha is advancing toward a crescendo.

The exertions during his concert tour through Western Europe did not remain without consequences for Tchaikovsky's physical and mental state. During his stay in Prague, he wrote an observation of his own about this: "I am getting old; when I look into the mirror, I am startled." His homesickness for Russia and for rest in Maidanovo became stronger and stronger the longer he was away from home, and his despondency shortly before returning home peaked in the diary entry of 15 March 1888:

> Had supper near the Opera [of Vienna]....Getting
> ready for the return trip home. Probably with this
> entry I will end the diary forever. Extreme old age
> is knocking, perhaps even death is no longer far.

During the return trip back to the desired rest, he wrote to Mrs. von Meck:

> Is it not strange that after an exhausting three-month
> tour in foreign countries I am already thinking of
> new travels?

And in his diary he noted after arriving in his house: "Strange thing, I long for solitude, and when it is there I suffer." At first, however, he moved from Maidanovo to a new house in Frolovskoye, also near Klin, where he was soon occupied with plans for a new symphony and the fantasy overture *Hamlet*.

Whereas he had not succeeded in his Fourth Symphony in making the "fate motif" the real "core of the whole symphony," the theme of "Providence" in the Fifth Symphony runs through all the movements of the work, according to the programmatic background he wrote for this composition:

> Complete surrender to destiny or—which is basically the same thing—to unfathomable predestination by Providence.

Actually, this symphony gives the hearer the impression that every attempt to oppose the relentless forces of Providence must be condemned to failure. This feeling of being unable to escape "destiny" is expressed most clearly in the finale, to which Tovey applied the accurate comparison with a nightmare "of wanting to run faster and faster but not being able to move from the spot." Today everyone agrees that this work must be ranked among the most effective popular symphonies of the entire 19th century. But even at the apex of his artistic creativity, he was overcome by doubts, as he confided to Mrs. von Meck:

> Often doubts overcome me, and I ask myself: Isn't it about time to stop? Have I not overexerted my fantasy? Has the source perhaps not run dry?

Probably when he wrote these lines he was smarting from the harsh criticism by Cui, who called the Fifth Symphony "characterless and common," although it was received enthusiastically by the audience during the premiere in St. Petersburg.

At the end of 1888 Tchaikovsky went to his house in Frolovskoye, where he began his work on the ballet *Sleeping Beauty*. But soon he set out on another concert tour that took him, via Cologne, Frankfurt, Dresden, Berlin, and Hanover, finally to Paris. From Marseilles he went by ship via Constantinople to Batum, and finally arrived home exhausted once more. In a few months he finished *Sleeping Beauty* in Frolovskoye; it is without a doubt one of his best works and he intended to spend the winter of 1889/90 directing several concerts of the Music Society. How much of a strain on him this was can be seen from a letter to Mrs. von Meck of 4 December 1889:

There were moments when my strength was so drained that I feared for my life....I will only admit to you that from 1 to 19 November I suffered a martyrdom and now I am still astounded that I was able to bear it all.

On the one hand, he longed for relaxation; on the other hand, the unpleasant and insulting letters from his wife Antonina virtually drove him to flee far away. That is why at the beginning of 1890 he wrote to Nadezhda von Meck:

I have no strength left and have decided to forego all concerts at home or abroad and to travel to Italy for four months in order to rest up and to work on my future opera. As subject I have selected Pushkin's *Queen of Spades*....I spent last week in an extremely bad mood....To go away, only to go away as fast as possible! To see no one, to know nothing, only to work, work, work...that is what my soul longs for.

His brother Modest speaks of a "severe nervous disturbance and a certain absentmindedness," in which Tchaikovsky was that month, and a strange, revealing letter written by Peter Ilyich on 11 February 1890 to the great Russian composer, Alexander Glasunov, can be interpreted in this sense:

I find myself in a very puzzling stage on the way to the grave. Something strange and incomprehensible is going on in me. Something like surfeit with life has taken hold of me: at times insane sorrow, but not that kind of sorrow in which a new love of life is germinating, but rather something hopeless...perhaps my entire sickness consists in the fifty years of age that I will exceed in two months.

These words sound like those of a person who finds himself immersed in a mid-life crisis and plagued by depressive mood swings. Yet he was able to overcome this emotional low by working intensely. In feverish eagerness he succeeded in writing the opera *Queen of Spades* in Florence in the incredibly short time of only six weeks. The main reason for the overwhelming success of this work is surely the fact that he was inwardly most strongly engaged and during its composition totally absorbed by the world of this opera. He himself considered it, as he told his brother Modest, to be absolutely his most important work.

In early May he arrived in Frolovskoye again, and there he carried out the idea, conceived in Italy, of writing a string sextet. Pleased with the result of his last two compositions, in September 1890 he rode to visit his brother Anatoly in Tiflis, where he was deeply shaken by a totally unexpected occurrence. Mrs. von Meck wrote him a letter informing him that due to external circumstances she was at the edge of financial ruin and therefore could no longer send him his yearly pension in the future. The letter ended with the words:

> Farewell, my dear, unforgettable friend and don't
> forget the woman whose love for you will never
> end.

Since in recent years his income had increased significantly, the announced financial loss did not affect him too much. What deeply offended him, however, and shook his sense of self-worth to its foundations was Nadezhda's seemingly incomprehensible attitude toward their fourteen-year friendship that now with the termination of her financial subventions the friendship also was at an end. It gave him the appearance that she had bought his friendship merely by creating a financial dependence. But when he learned that Mrs. von Meck had not at all lost her whole fortune, he was completely beside himself with offended pride. The suspicion that he had all these years been only the plaything of a wealthy coldhearted lady, who now had tired of her plaything and dismissed it from her service like a superfluous lackey, was, according to Modest, "one of those insults that took Peter Ilyich to the grave." First he answered immediately on 4 October 1890 to her devastating letter; he tried to make it clear to her that he had the greatest sympathy with her concerns and that his financial situation, because of his considerable incomes, was in no way endangered by the necessary elimination of his yearly pension.

The Tchaikovsky brothers in 1890. From left to right: Anatoly, Nicolai, Hippolyt, Peter Ilyich, and Modest.

As Modest reports, the fact that Nadezhda answered neither this letter nor any further letters, was for him "the most mortal insult" and "neither the splendid success of *Queen of Spades* nor the deep grief over the death of his beloved sister (in April 1891), nor the triumphal procession through America could soothe this pain." He himself wrote a closing comment about this affair:

> Never did I feel so debased; never was my pride
> so humiliated.

What reasons really caused Mrs. von Meck to break off her relations with Tchaikovsky so abruptly can no longer be answered with certainty. Possibly, as some authors believe, it was a guilt complex toward her family for having concerned herself all these years almost exclusively with Tchaikovsky and neglected her own dependents. For meanwhile her oldest son Valdemar had degenerated into a mental and physical wreck; and her illegitimate daughter Ludmilla, who stemmed from the relationship with her husband's secretary and indirectly was to blame for Mr. von Meck's death, was entangled in a bribery scandal together with her husband, Prince Shirinsky. According to another version, Nadezhda's second daughter Alexandra, the black sheep in the Meck family, supposedly informed her mother about Tchaikovsky's homosexual orientation, thus causing her to make this momentous decision. Since Nadezhda shortly before her decisive letter to Tchaikovsky had the pension paid to him in Frolovskoye by a personal messenger, not as usual by means of a check, but in cash, and moreover a whole year's pension in advance, there can hardly have been an inner alienation. This would seem to be confirmed by the answer sent by Nadezhda's son-in-law and Tchaikovsky's former pupil, Pachulsky, through whom he tried in vain to reestablish contact with Mrs. von Meck. He informed him that her "external indifference [in leaving his letters unanswered] was the result of severe nervous ailments, but that in her innermost soul she was still fond of Peter Ilyich." By this "nervous ailment" Pachulsky apparently was alluding to the severe illness Nadezhda was already suffering from. Modest indeed reports that "since 1890 the life of Nadezhda von Meck was in fact a slow degeneration due to a terrible nervous ailment." The available documents show that Mrs. von Meck must have labored under a kidney disease, at a very advanced stage by then and possibly resulting in a stroke caused by high blood pressure with collateral kidney damage—a stroke which led "to the loss of the use of one hand." Since her son Vladimir too suffered several strokes, which finally led to his death, it would certainly be conceivable that both mother and son had become ill of high blood pressure, which sometimes runs in families. In Nadezhda it led to a shrunken kidney with all the clinical effects and finally to her death, either by kidney failure or by a stroke. She herself outlived Tchaikovsky by only a few months, but not without first becoming reconciled with him, as Galina von Meck, Nadezhda's granddaughter, assures us in her *Memoirs* published in 1973.

An Old Man at Fifty

The entire mental anguish unleashed in Tchaikovsky's soul by the sudden end of his legendary friendship by correspondence is reflected in the symphonic ballad *The Voyevoda*, with whose composition he began one week after receiving the fateful letter, namely, on 10 October 1890. The premiere of his opera *Queen of Spades* followed on 19 December 1890 in St. Petersburg and was received enthusiastically by the audience. In these weeks he often frequented a new circle of artists financed by a wealthy industrialist, a circle to which Rimsky-Korsakov also belonged and where a great deal of drinking went on until early morning. As Rimsky-Korsakov reports, Tchaikovsky was able to consume "great quantities of wine," and yet to keep under control "all his strength, physical and mental" in contrast with companions less able to hold their liquor. In addition, he began working on the *Nutcracker* ballet, commissioned with him by the theater direction in St. Petersburg.

In his letters at that time, he revealed nothing about what was really going on inside him, not even to his closest relatives, who worried about the extraordinary burst of activity which seemed to contradict his dismal and embittered mood. Modest, too, could not understand this unusual behavior of his brother's, for he wrote:

> I absolutely refuse to take on my shoulders the task, which exceeds my strength, of deciphering the last psychological development of Peter Ilyich's soul.

Modest may be right in his view that Nadezhda's definitive rejection changed him decisively in his nature and that "the wound never healed, pained him incessantly, and darkened the last years of his life." The restless and frenzied activity which now began gave his brother the impression "as if he had ceased belonging to himself; as if he had fallen into the power of a certain something that had robbed him of his will and cast him arbitrarily back and forth....This mysterious something is that unfathomable, dismal, restless, hopeless mood which he sought to calm in distractions of whatever kind."

Such a diversion was given to him by the tour through the United States begun in April 1891, where he attained roaring success as a conductor and his works found total recognition. In a detailed diary he kept during this stay, he noted about the performance of his First Piano Concerto in New York: "A storm of applause rose up, such as I have never experienced, not even in Russia." A shadow fell over this journey when the news reached him shortly after the ship's departure, that his beloved sister Sasha had died. Foremost in his mind was worry about how her son Bob, his adored nephew, would take this loss. Outwardly, to be sure, no one noticed anything of these events inside him, for he seemed extremely calm and in good spirits, as an article in the *New York Herald* of 24 April 1891 says: "Tchaikovsky is a tall, cool, well-built, interesting man, going on his sixties." He was thought to be this age surely because of his very grayed hair, for in truth he had just turned fifty-one years of age, almost to the day. He himself was rather amused by this error.

He arrived back in St. Petersburg on 1 June, somewhat exhausted, but more cheerful than before this journey. Yet the newspaper article published in America, estimating him to be ten years older than he really was, seemed to have put him in a rather pensive mood, for he noted under the date of 8 May in connection with his having confused the names of two pianists in a conversation:

> My absentmindedness is gradually becoming unbearable, and I consider it a sign of my advanced age....Everyone thought I was much older. Have I aged so much in recent years? Quite possibly.... Influenced by conversations about my aged appearance I had terrible dreams in the night.

Even after his return, slight weaknesses of concentration brought him back again and again to this topic. So he wrote on 7 July 1891:

> Again a proof I am getting old. I no longer see so well, my hair is falling out, my teeth are getting loose, my stride is more ponderous.

A weakening of his vision first became noticeable in November 1872; since that time he therefore liked to use a pince-nez while at work composing. The bad condition of his teeth which repeatedly caused him toothaches was referred to several times in his diaries.

During the summer he continued working on the *Nutcracker* ballet, but by December, without visible motivation, rather surrendering to a spontaneous urge, he went on another tour, traveling via Warsaw to Hamburg, where he was to experience a memorable German performance of his opera *Eugene Onegin*. On 19 January 1892 he wrote to his nephew Bob:

> The Kapellmeister here is not a mediocre nobody, but a many-talented genius....The singers, the orchestra...and the Kapellmeister (his name is Mahler) are completely in love with *Eugene Onegin*.

After this magnificent performance of his opera, he traveled on to Paris, where because of excessive homesickness he simply canceled his further concerts planned in the Netherlands and hastily began the return journey. On 17 May he moved into a new house at the edge of Klin; this was to become his last residence, where today the Tchaikovsky Museum is located. There he planned the design for a new symphony, but soon signs of overwork showed up in the form of irritability and repeated stomach ailments, and therefore a three-week treatment in Vichy was recommended to him, and he was accompanied by his nephew Bob. Back in Klin again, he corrected a few scores that were going to press, but soon he was again seized by a restless urge to travel. After a short trip to Vienna and Prague in September 1892, one week after the premiere of *Nutcracker*, which was performed on stage with moderate success on 18 December, he began another concert tour, which took him to Berlin, Paris, Brussels, and Basel, from where he took an excursion to Montbélliard to visit Fanny Dürbach, his former governess, who was now seventy years of age. He reported about this meeting to his brother Nicolai, who likewise remembered Fanny from his childhood:

> Although she meanwhile has turned seventy, she has changed only a little. I was very worried that there would be tears and a scene, but nothing of the sort occurred. She greeted me as if it were only a year ago that we had last seen one another,

"An old man
at fifty years"—
P. I. Tchaikovsky
in 1893.

with joy, exuberance, and without formalities....
Later she showed me our school notebooks...but,
most interesting of all, wonderful dear letters from
Mama....I believed I was breathing the aroma of
our house in Votkinsk and hearing the voices of
Mama and the others.

After ending his concert in Brussels he directed five concerts
in Odessa, where he was given a truly triumphal reception. Yet
melancholy moods and a lack of self-confidence still seemed to
torment him, as can be read in a letter to Modest:

I must regain my faith in myself, for it is very
shaken; it seems to me as if my role had been
played out.

During this stay in Odessa, incidentally, the famous portrait of Tchaikovsky was painted by Kusnetsov; Modest called it the most living likeness of his brother. In this picture he appears as a white-haired man with an intelligent countenance, who despite being only fifty-three years old would be estimated a good ten years older. From about the same time we have a sketch by Door, who was literally alarmed at sight of him:

> He had aged so much that I could recognize him only by his sky-blue eyes. An old man of fifty years! I tried hard not to let him notice it. His already delicate constitution had suffered under his strong productivity.

Probably what was most responsible for his premature aging process, besides his considerable alcohol consumption and his constant mental pressures, was in fact his almost feverish activity as a composer and conductor.

In early February 1893, he had returned from his most recent, highly successful tour and arrived back in Klin. But during the return trip severe stomachaches began. He described them as follows:

> In the railroad car I became so sick that to the horror of my fellow passengers I had fevered fantasies and had to get off at Charkov. After having taken the usual measures and getting plenty of sleep I woke up as a healthy man again. I think it was an acute stomach fever.

Probably this time, too, it was a nervous-conditioned functional disturbance in the area of the stomach or the large intestine that led to the "acute" pains and was triggered by the preceding exertions of the strenuous tour. Evidence of this would also be the fact that in early March because of violent and persistent headaches he was ordered by the doctor to strictly avoid all mental exertions until further notice. By 20 March, he reported to Modest with utmost satisfaction:

Just think, precisely on the 14th day after the headache began—I had already begun to think it would
last forever—suddenly it disappeared.

Meanwhile the plan for his Sixth Symphony was already beginning to take tangible form, as he told his nephew Bob in a
letter of 23 February 1893:

On my journeys I got an idea for my new symphony, this time a program-symphony, but with a
program that is to remain a mystery for everyone—
let them break their heads about it, the symphony
will be called only "A Program-Symphony" (no. 6).
The program is subjective down to its innermost
core....You will understand how much it fills me
with happiness to be convinced that my time is
not yet over, but that I can still work.

Work on this symphony was, to be sure, interrupted several times
by various journeys inside Russia and—as if to allow his ideas for
orchestrating the work to mature—by intervening composition of
smaller pieces, such as Eighteen Pieces op. 72 for piano. Although he himself called them rather "mediocre," a few of them
are really noteworthy, above all the *Valse à cinq temps*, for this
five-beat waltz has a parallel in the second movement of his Sixth
Symphony. Likewise of higher quality among the works composed at this time is Six Songs op. 73, of which the last one, *Alone
Again as Before*, is particularly outstanding. This song-style in
Tchaikovsky's later creation gives some idea of what we could
have expected of another opera from his pen.

After visiting London at the end of May, where he had a concert to direct and received an honorary doctorate in Cambridge,
he finally could think of orchestrating his new symphony. All the
more so, since the mental and physical ailments he had still complained of that month seem to have fled. Then he had written:

Yesterday my torments went so far that I lost sleep
and appetite, which is seldom for me. I suffer not
only from homesickness, which cannot be described with words (in my new symphony there is
a passage which, it seems to me, expresses it well),

TCHAIKOVSKY WITH HIS NEPHEW, VLADIMIR L. DAVIDOV [BOB], WITH WHOM
HE HAD AN EXTREMELY CLOSE RELATIONSHIP.

but also from xenophobia, by an indefinite feeling
of fear and the devil knows what else. Physically
this state is expressed in a painful feeling in the
lower abdomen and in a nagging pain and weakness in the legs.

Probably it was due to this antipathy and indifference to strangers
alluded to here that he accepted with surprising indifference the
series of sad occurrences that awaited him after his arrival in Klin
at the end of July. Modest described what happened then:

The breath of death prevailed on all sides. After first learning of the death of Konstantin Shilovsky [Vladimir Shilovsky's brother], the news arrived of the demise of his old friend, K. Albrecht, and only ten days later the Countess Shilovsky wrote him that her husband Vladimir [Volodya, whom Tchaikovsky had once fallen in love with] had died. Moreover, in St. Petersburg Apuchtin [writer and former classmate of Tchaikovsky, who played an active role in the development of his homosexual tendencies] lay dying....A few years earlier, a single one of such news items would have affected Peter Ilyich more strongly than all of them together now.

Modest ascribed this to Tchaikovsky's exultant mood while working on the Sixth Symphony; in fact he considered this very work to be the pinnacle of his composition creations and the "most honest" of all, as he remarked to Bob: "I love it as I have never before loved one of my musical products." He expressed himself similarly in a letter to his brother Anatoly, of August 1893: "I am very proud of this symphony and believe it is my very best composition." But the nonchalance with which he accepted the aforementioned sad events must also be related to the egoism he increasingly developed and which he also admitted in his diary:

> I often think that my entire bad temper and dissatisfaction is related to my being too self-complacent and egoistic and incapable of self-sacrifice for others, not even for those near and dear to me.

Such confessions are found only in his diaries, while in his letters, he almost never gave away his true self, except, as he admits in his diary, in letters he "wrote while in a state of mental confusion."

The premiere of the Sixth Symphony, in the future to be called the *Pathétique* at Modest's suggestion, was directed by Tchaikovsky on 28 October 1893 in St. Petersburg and won polite but not enthusiastic applause from the audience and the critics. Therefore Tchaikovsky wrote to his friend and publisher Jürgenson on 30 October:

The symphony was not rejected, but it provoked some disappointment. I am proud of this piece as I never have been of any other composition.

Actually this symphony offered peculiarities which must have been completely strange to the audience and to which he himself referred in a letter to his nephew Bob, to whom this work was dedicated:

In its form, this symphony has much that is new, among other things the finale will not be a noisy allegro, but on the contrary a very long-drawn-out adagio.

What a legacy he wanted to leave in this work to his beloved "Bobik," with whom he was bound by a more than platonic love, will probably remain hidden from us forever. Edward Garden pointed out in his analysis that even at the beginning of the first movement one gets the impression that Tchaikovsky with the first theme wanted to express the struggles "connected with the urge to live," and with the downward pointing ladder he was trying to suggest a kind of "leitmotif of death." The passionate outbursts are accompanied by a completely opposite moment that "presents itself quite openly as a delightful love theme" and is intensified all the way to ecstasy. This peace is suddenly interrupted by the renewed introduction of the "death motif," which finally leads over to the elaboration of the orthodox sadness theme, "*With the Saints.*" This extremely concentrated movement is followed by the above-mentioned waltz in 5/4 or quintuple meter, which brings a liberating release. In the third movement a powerful triumphal march is gradually developed in which it ultimately becomes clear that none other than death was meant to be victorious. But the absolute climax of the symphony is, without a doubt, the last movement, whose despairing first theme corresponds to the "Requiem aeternam" of the Mass for the Dead and finally culminates in a despair that is hardly bearable. How much this must have been intended by Tchaikovsky can be seen from a letter of September 1893 to the Grand Prince Konstantin, with whom he was in contact for many years and who requested a Requiem

from him for Apuchtin, the recently deceased friend of his youth.
It reads:

> I am confused a little by the circumstance that my
> last symphony, which was just finished, is perme-
> ated especially in the finale by a mood that comes
> close to that of a Requiem....I'm afraid of repeat-
> ing myself when I immediately begin composing
> a work that is similar in its character and its na-
> ture.

A week after the premiere of his Sixth Symphony, Tchaikovsky
was dead, and so it was very natural that this work's autobiographical content opened the gateway to Romantic interpretations, since efforts were made to prove it had been written under
a premonition of imminent death. Some biographers even claimed
to see in it his death wish and in this context they pointed to the
bloodcurdling screams found in the second execution of the first
movement. But, according to Modest's indications, there were
absolutely no recognizable signs that Tchaikovsky had any premonitions of death or even a death wish. On the contrary, he
spoke of new composition plans and his behavior was as usual.

> His frame of mind in the last days was neither
> exclusively joyful, nor particularly depressed. In
> the circle of his intimate friends he was cheerful
> and satisfied; in the company of strangers as usual
> nervous and excited, and later exhausted and limp.
> Nothing gave cause to think of approaching death.

People closer to him noticed only that for some time he had
become more abstemious, drinking wine only diluted with mineral water and doing without meat at the evening meal.

On the morning of 2 November, according to Modest's narrative, he complained of feeling unwell and of a stomachache; so
he was advised to ingest castor oil. The cause of this indisposi-
tion and stomachache was suspected to be that he might possibly
have infected himself with cholera by drinking contaminated water.
For when, on the day before, he was having lunch with Modest
and Bobik, he is said to have poured faucet water from a pitcher

into his glass and drunk a few swallows. Since the water was not boiled and cholera was once again rampaging in St. Petersburg, such a connection seemed very conceivable, and in his portrayal of the subsequent events Modest tried to make this version correspondingly credible. For this report states that Tchaikovsky, due to the soon ensuing diarrhea accompanied by vomiting, became so weakened within a few hours that he even had difficulty speaking and his abdominal pains were so intense that he screamed loudly again and again. His physician Dr. Vasily Bertenson and his brother Dr. Lev Bertenson, whom he consulted, stayed overnight with the patient and were relieved by their assistant, Dr. Mamonov, only in the morning hours of 3 November. Then at three o'clock in the afternoon, Dr. Mamonov transferred the patient to the medical care of Dr. Sanders, also an assistant of Dr. Bertenson's. In the daytime a certain improvement had set in; and so Tchaikovsky greeted Dr. Bertenson, who came to see him, with the words: "Thank you, Doctor, you snatched me out of the claws of death." But by the next day, 4 November, he again felt much worse, and supposedly said to Modest: "I believe, it is death." In similar despair, he said to Dr. Bertenson: "How much kindness and patience you are wasting for nothing. I cannot be healed." The diarrheas increased in intensity, and the cramping pains in the muscles became almost unbearable. Finally during 4 November, there began a decrease in urinary output, announcing an imminent kidney failure. The doctors therefore are said to have recommended a warm bath. The patient, remembering the outcome of this procedure for his mother's cholera illness, answered: "Gladly. The washing is welcome to me; however I will certainly die like my mother did, if you put me in the tub." Because of the patient's extreme weakness, the doctors then temporarily omitted the bath.

On 5 November, his condition worsened rapidly and he fell into a coma, in which allegedly he repeatedly was delirious and murmured the name Nadezhda Philaretovna to himself. Since by noon the kidneys threatened to go into complete failure, Dr. Lev Bertenson finally decided on a hot bath, after all. However, following a spell of sweating, this weakened the patient even more, while the desired improvement of the kidney function did not materialize. Within a few hours, his physical decline took on threatening forms. Dr. Sanders then requested that Dr. Lev Bertenson be notified immediately; but he too, as could be expected, was equally powerless to stop the baneful outcome. Tchaikovsky's brother Nicolai in all haste sent for a priest, who however is said to have denied the dying man the sacraments since he was no longer capable of confessing. On the morning of 6 November, at 3 A.M. the death struggle was over. Modest wrote:

> Suddenly Peter Ilyich opened his eyes. An indescribable expression of clear consciousness came over him. He let his glance rest successively on the three persons standing closest to him, then turned it up toward heaven. For a few moments something gleamed in his eyes and soon was extinguished together with his last breath.

Review of the Diagnosis of the Cause of Death

Based on Modest's impressive portrayal, biographers as well as doctors believed it certain that Tchaikovsky had died of the consequences of cholera, prevalent in St. Petersburg at that time. There was disagreement only about whether the infection with cholera resulted from carelessness or was intentional. Recently, indeed, the tendency was rather in favor of the second version, namely, suicide. But since Modest, in his voluminous biography of his brother, did not discuss this question, it seemed unanswerable for all time.

Meanwhile, however, the discovery of new documents and statements of contemporaries who themselves were eyewitnesses of the event has, surprisingly, made it possible not only to cast doubt on Modest's portrayal, given above, but even to refute it beyond any doubt. From the first, even some of Tchaikovsky's contemporaries had suspected that Modest's version did not fit the facts. A first contradiction can be seen in two press reports of a St. Petersburg newspaper. First, we have the St. Petersburg *News and Stock Exchange Gazette*, dated 24 October. (This date of the Julian Calendar, customary in Russia at that time, corresponds to 5 November of our Western Gregorian Calendar. To maintain continuity in the narrative and avoid confusion, any following dates will be given in both forms: 24 October/ 5 November). That newspaper reported:

> The whole music world has been disturbed by news of a severe illness of P.I. Tchaikovsky. Fortunately, according to the latest communiqué, a favorable outcome of his sickness (presumably typhus) is expected.

But on the very next day, the day on which the artist died, the same newspaper contains the notice:

> The virulent epidemic did not spare even our famous composer P.I. Tchaikovsky.   He fell ill on Thursday [21 October/2 November] during the day, and his illness immediately assumed dangerous character.

Two medical bulletins followed the article, and after them came the statement:

> At two-thirty in the morning the doctors left, absolutely convinced that the case was hopeless.   By 3 A.M., P.I. Tchaikovsky was no longer alive.

The contradiction in these two news reports is obvious. The first one spoke of a typhus illness that was already showing signs of improvement on 23 October/4 November, while the second article claimed that the disease had from the very first presented a dangerous character.   Although the disease here was not mentioned by name, clearly the term "epidemic" meant cholera. However, even then a cholera infection was doubted, as we can gather from a report in the *St. Petersburg Gazette* of 26 October/ 7 November:

> How could Tchaikovsky get cholera if he lived under the best conceivable hygienic conditions and moreover arrived in St. Petersburg only a few days before?

In fact, an infection in October 1893 was most improbable, since the most severe cholera epidemic that occurred in Russia, raged in the summer of 1892, while in the following year 1893 only a greatly weakened form was displayed. Moreover, the really rather mild epidemic of 1893 was—as is generally usual—steeply in decline by autumn, so that by the end of the year only isolated cases were observed.

No wonder rumors in the city refused to be silenced that Tchaikovsky had not died of cholera at all, but rather had committed suicide; and this suspicion was confirmed by the contradictory interviews of the doctors treating him. According to Dr. Vasily Bertenson, whom Tchaikovsky had particularly trusted for years, the composer had become ill on Thursday, 21 October/ 2 November, but had called on his medical help only on Friday evening. On the next day, Saturday, 23 October/4 November, a clear improvement then began, so that it was already believed that the patient was cured of cholera. Only the precipitant decline of his strength remained a cause for concern.

At the same time as this interview, a report was printed in the *News and Stock Exchange Gazette* by Dr. Nicolai Mamonov, who as a prominent clinician also took medical care of the Czar's family and together with Dr. Alexander Sanders alternatively kept watch at Tchaikovsky's sickbed. This Dr. Mamonov now stated that Tchaikovsky had no longer felt completely well by Wednesday 20 October/1 November, whereas Modest in his report insisted that his brother on the day before the onset of his fatal disease had presented not the slightest signs of discomfort and until late in the evening still enjoyed the best health.

Given such contradictory statements by eyewitnesses, the *New Time* of 27 October/8 November felt the need to inquire of Dr. Lev Bertenson, who had been directing the medical treatment of the deceased composer. However, his portrayal only widened the existing discrepancies even more. For in contrast with his brother, Vasily, Lev Bertenson stressed that from the very start of the illness the danger of kidney failure had existed and that on 23 October/4 November the patient not only had not improved, but already lay dying. Actually, death then followed in the first morning hours of the next day.

Such contradictions can only be explained by the fact that efforts were being made to conceal the truth and that in view of the imminent catastrophe the doctors in charge were incapable of keeping a cool head or at least agreeing on a unified medical portrayal of the occurrence. In addition, Dr. Lev Bertenson's report does not withstand scrutiny from a medical perspective. For the so-called "painful stage" of cholera, in which he allegedly already found the patient on his first visit, would correspond to the second stage of this disease and so cannot have been present at the beginning. The answer to this discrepancy can be found in Vasily Bertenson's retrospection, first published in 1980, in which he says apologetically: "I must admit that before this event I never had the occasion to witness a real case of cholera." In fact, the two brothers had under their medical care only the elite classes of St. Petersburg society, which hardly ever came in contact with cholera because of their excellent hygienic environmental conditions. Compelled knowingly to distort the real facts, the two brothers used terminology they still recalled from medical books with the intention of making cholera credible to the public as the cause of death—although, as we know today, they had exact knowledge of the true circumstances.

Modest, it can be assumed, in describing his brother's last days, relied essentially on a letter by Dr. Lev Bertenson, in which he tried to describe the whole process in medically credible form, corresponding to the textbook course of cholera. This letter was found in 1938 while sifting through Modest's archives and was preserved until before World War II in the Tchaikovsky Museum of Klin, where it can today, however, allegedly not be found. Only a second letter, written by Lev Bertenson immediately after Tchaikovsky's demise to the latter's brother is known to the public. It contains only the doctor's personal feelings, but no medical details:

> I would like to embrace you and tell you how upset I am at our common great misfortune, but I can hardly stand on my feet and cannot go out. The terrible disease that swept away your dear brother, had the effect that I feel as one with him,

with you, and with all to whom he was dear. I still
cannot at all recover from this terrible tragedy,
whose witness I was destined to be, and I cannot
describe to you all the torments I am now going
through. I can tell you only one thing! That I feel
like you. Your faithful and very devoted

Lev Bertenson.

The other letter of more factual content was, together with a
short letter of Modest's, placed at the disposal of the *St. Petersburg Gazette* of 1 November/13 November. It was printed above
the article "Tchaikovsky's Sickness" and is worded as follows:

To complement the short but very precise report
on the last day in my brother's life written by
L.B. Bertenson, I consider it necessary, in order to
put an end to the various contradictory rumors, to
put at your disposal as complete a report as possible about all I experienced as an eyewitness.

Apart from the fact that Dr. Bertenson in this article dates
Tchaikovsky's death as 24 October/5 November, Modest on the
contrary as 25 October/6 November, the portrayals of the two
men differ on other points from the medical bulletins published
in the press.

Especially noteworthy is Modest's statement that the patient
on the first day of his illness complained of the most violent pains
in the chest as well as of an unquenchable thirst—symptoms that
do not apply to cholera and probably for that reason are not
mentioned by Dr. Bertenson. But even other details that appear
in Modest's portrayal are difficult or impossible to bring into harmony with the assumption of a cholera infection in Tchaikovsky.
For example in Modest's apartment, where his brother was lodged,
not even the most elementary precautionary measures were taken
as strictly prescribed in case of a cholera illness by a government
regulation:

In case of a death due to cholera the corpse must
be removed from the house as quickly as possible,

namely, in a sealed, hermetically closed casket; moreover, it is recommended to do without a public burial ceremony or a subsequent wake.

In Tchaikovsky's case, all these regulations were disregarded. No less than fifteen persons, not counting the priest, surrounded the dying man's bed, and the corpse lay in state in the apartment— the first day on a sofa, and the second day in an open coffin which was not closed until 26 October/7 November. The *Moscow Gazette* of 27 October/8 November commented about this:

> Peter Ilyich lies there as if he were still alive, his face peaceful; only the awful pallor seems to express the suffering the deceased man had to endure during the last three days of his life.

Rimsky-Korsakov, too, in his *Chronicle of My Musical Life*, published in Moscow in 1955, expressed his astonishment at how little bother was taken to observe the hygienic measures otherwise prescribed for a person who died of cholera:

> It was strange that there was open admittance to the Mass for the Dead, although his death resulted from cholera. I remember seeing Verzhbilovich [a cellist friend] kiss the head and cheek of the corpse.

Finally on the evening of 25 October/6 November the sculptor Tselinsky was permitted to make a death mask, which again decisively militates against the version that Tchaikovsky died of cholera.

Two other discrepancies absolutely do not match the story of a cholera infection which Modest tried to hand down to posterity. First, the problem would have to be raised as to what role is attributable to the unboiled water Tchaikovsky drank on the evening of 20 October/1 November in a restaurant or, according to Modest's statement, in his apartment on 21 October/2 November and by which he is supposed to have become infected with cholera. For, in all instructions to fight the spread of cholera, it was for understandable reasons strictly forbidden not only to drink unboiled water, but even to use it for washing the body or even eating utensils. It is therefore absolutely inconceivable that water could be served in a restaurant or in a family circle in a time of a cholera epidemic. But even if Tchaikovsky had drunk such water on that day on which he lay severely ill by evening, the infection could not have been noticeable at that point in time, since the necessary incubation period would have been too short. The last discrepancy, finally, has to do with the ominous "warm bath" that tended to be prescribed at that time to stimulate kidney activity and in which, according to Dr. Lev Bertenson's account, Tchaikovsky was laid on Saturday, but according to Modest's, on Sunday. We know today that such a bath was not at all considered by the doctors, for in a diary of Alexei Suvorin, owner of the newspaper *New Time*, one finds the remarkable entry:

> Tchaikovsky was buried yesterday. I grieve terribly for him. The Bertenson brothers treated him and did not prescribe a bath.

This remark indicates that the doctors in reality did not at all think of a diagnosis of cholera.

The very fact that after the composer's death the press was so intensively preoccupied with the details of the symptoms of his disease and the treatment measures taken and that both the doctors in charge and his brother Modest saw the necessity of making public explanatory statements suggests that the rumors of a possible suicide continued to smolder. But not until the 1920s was surprising light cast on the disputed and mysterious affair of Tchaikovsky's death. One of the treating physicians, Dr. Vasily Bertenson, who also was a personal friend of the deceased, no longer wanted to hide the truth and he told the musicologist Georgy Orlov, who was a friend of his son Nicolai, that Tchaikovsky had not died of cholera, but had taken his own life. Almost at the same time Georgy Orlov received confirmation of this exciting information from another friend of his, the son of Dr. Sanders, the doctor who had watched at Tchaikovsky's sickbed together with Dr. Bertenson. When Georgy Orlov married his wife Alexandra, who in the 1940s was working at the Scientific Institute for Music and Dramaturgy in Moscow, he finally had this news confirmed

TCHAIKOVSKY'S DEATH MASK.

for a third time by the director of that institute, Professor Alexander Ossovsky.

Today it is certain, then, that Tchaikovsky actually did not die of cholera, as was previously assumed, but rather that he committed suicide. And he intentionally shaped the way he died so that his death looked like an event brought on by fate. Involuntarily, the comparison with his suicide attempt shortly after his tragic marriage with Antonina comes to mind here; for there too he aimed to simulate an act of fate by a pulmonary infection. Why Tchaikovsky made this decision just at that point in time when he was reaching the zenith of his artistic career and the peak of his fame, has been clarified by Mrs. Orlova, based on a report she received in 1966 from Alexander Voitov, the former curator of the numismatic division of the Russian Museum in Leningrad. Mr. Voitov was a student in the same law school as Tchaikovsky and he collected all attainable biographical material about many former pupils of that institution. And he came upon the name Nicolai Jacobi, who as it would turn out occupies a key position in clearing up the more detailed circumstances around Tchaikovsky's death. In summary, the following is what took place in that fateful October of 1893:

A certain Prince Stenbock-Fermor addressed a letter of complaint to Czar Alexander III, pointing out that "the composer was busying himself too much with his young nephew." This letter was officially handed over to the Procurator of the Appeals Court at that time, Mr. Nicolai Jacobi, a former fellow student with Tchaikovsky, to be transmitted to the Czar. Jacobi realized that this would have meant not only unavoidable shame and disgrace for Tchaikovsky himself, but also for the entire, highly respected law school and all its graduates. In order not to let the matter become public, Jacobi decided to hold a kind of "court of honor" in his house. Besides the accused, six former fellow students, then living in St. Petersburg, were called in. The "court" met on 19 October in Jacobi's apartment and, after a stormy discussion lasting more than five hours, came to the conclusion that the only way to prevent the complaint letter from being handed over to the Czar was for Tchaikovsky voluntarily to commit suicide—a demand which the unfortunate musician, in a state of extreme agitation, finally accepted. The accuracy of this report by Alexander Voitov was attested to by Vera Kusnetsova, a sister-in-law of Nicolai Tchaikovsky who died in 1955. The poison, it is suspected, was given to Tchaikovsky by his former fellow student, the attorney August Gerke, who—as Vasily Bessel announced in the *Russian Musical Journal*—was supposed to mediate an agreement between the composer and the Bessel press concerning the opera *The Oprichnik.*

In 1981, Galina von Meck, the daughter of Tchaikovsky's niece Anna, published his *Letters to His Family*, to which she added an epilogue. In it she states that three days after the letter of 18 October to the publisher Jürgenson, about his Sixth Symphony, the composer had come home very excited. He had allegedly spoken a few incomprehensible sentences to himself and then asked his brother for a glass of water. When his brother pointed out the necessity of boiling the water first, he went to the kitchen himself and got a glass and drank from it with the remark "Who cares about that!" On that same evening [21 October] he felt very ill. Possibly he took the poison with the water.

Thus today we can reconstruct very precisely why and how Tchaikovsky committed suicide and for what reason the doctors as well as his fully informed brothers, Modest and Nicolai, tried to conceal this kind of death. Understandably, in their state of utmost excitement, the attempt to make cholera credible as the cause of death caused justifiable doubts among contemporaries. The complete disregard of the prescribed epidemic regulations contributed to these doubts. From a present-day vantage point, of course, the reason for Tchaikovsky's terrible "sacrificial death" is incomprehensible and absurd, and it seems that even for those times it seems by no means to have been compulsory to demand such a step from a person with a homosexual disposition, as Jacobi and his former fellow students did in their "court of honor." There was indeed in the code of Russian law from the years 1868 and 1885 an article 995 which said that homosexuality was punishable by the removal of all civil rights and banishment to Siberia. In reality, however, the Czarist court seems to have closed its eyes to this offense since many of the Czar's relatives and highest court officials themselves were homosexuals. If it ever came to public scandals, then the persons in question were transferred to the most remote provinces, but not put on trial or banished to Siberia. Tchaikovsky, however, in his heroic decision, must have been thinking less of a possible punishment than of the loss of his honor and his reputation in the world.

If it was believed that the secret of this "court of honor" and the suicide it imposed was buried for all time with the dead man, still it turned out later that the archives contained documents about this incident. For Mrs. Orlova reports that in 1960, on the occasion of a lecture at the Forensic Medicine Institute of the University of Leningrad, the "Tchaikovsky case" was portrayed as the classical example of a coerced suicide—a proof that the mysterious events of October 1893 must have been recorded in the files after all.

As an expression of his admiration for Russia's greatest composer, Czar Alexander III had a magnificent funeral performed in the Kasan Cathedral—an honor given for the first time to an "ordinary" citizen. Delegations from various societies and academic institutions accompanied the dead man, together with several thousand mourners across Nevsky Prospect, which was blocked from all traffic for several hours, to the cemetery of the Alexander Nevsky Monastery, where he found his last resting place close to the graves of Glinka, Borodin, and Mussorgsky.

In a closing medical examination of the notable details recalled in Tchaikovsky's biography, our attention must focus primarily on his complicated psychic structure and the resulting
somatic effects.

In his earliest years of life, he was described as a hypersensitive, extremely delicate boy. His governess Fanny Dürbach therefore called him her "porcelain child." Probably this unusually
delicate emotional reactivity was inherited from his maternal grandfather, who was said to have been a strikingly nervous man, probably suffering from epilepsy. Because of his tender and very
empathetic nature, Fanny, soon after entering into service with
the family, became for the four-year-old Peter the most important
reference person besides his mother, and he latched onto her
passionately and, with feelings of jealousy toward his brother
Nicolai, he wanted to claim her, as well as his mother, for himself
alone. This jealousy and the fixation on certain objects are psychic phenomena of childhood age corresponding to a regular
development of sexual life until near the end of the fifth year and
are of considerable importance in early childhood. For the mother
and the equivalent mother-substitute person with whom the child
establishes the first intimate human relationship always represent
the child's first love and at the same time also the first object of
his erotic desires. But since the child cannot claim the love of the
reference person exclusively for himself, but must share her with
siblings or above all with the father, the child's passionate love
can never be fully satisfied. From this situation, in Peter too, a
secret jealousy of the older brother and certainly also of the father
must have developed, since the child intuitively experienced them
both as rivals.

One can imagine, then, what a catastrophe broke in on eight-
year-old Peter, when his beloved Fanny had to be dismissed because the family was moving to Moscow. Until that point in his
life, this young woman's protective wings had been spread over
him, but now the hypersensitive child was suddenly transported
into a completely different, strange, and cold world. These circumstances, extremely traumatic for the sensitive lad, also promptly
led to an abrupt change of his nature, characterized by a
lack of concentration, apathy toward the world around him,

and heightened irritability. Since Peter had at this time just gotten over the measles, the doctors even believed that the changes in the child's temperament were the result of an accompanying inflammation of the brain or a "spinal cord consumption," which of course was sheer nonsense.

The increasingly distraught and totally insecure boy began to capsule himself off more and more and egoistically to occupy himself mainly with his own self. His mother, whom he idolized, was completely bewildered by this development and reacted with over-concerned behavior, thereby further strengthening Peter's idealization of the feminine, whose embodiment he saw in Fanny and in his mother. This idealization of the feminine, which arose in his childhood and later also found expression in the heroic roles of his operas, was one of the reasons why Tchaikovsky all his life remained distant from women he loved and strictly avoided any intimate relation with them.

Recently the suspicion has been stated that his mother's exaggerated concern favored the early development of his homosexual tendencies, since more recent studies assign an important significance to the influence of mothers who are simultaneously clinging, sexually provocative, and tabooizing. Herbert Weinstock, however, holds the opinion that Tchaikovsky's homosexuality must rather have been inborn, since both his brother Modest and his nephew Vladimir had the same orientation. Although admittedly homosexuality actually can run in some families and more recent findings in research with twins make inherent hereditary factors probable, still the influence of environmental experiences in childhood development, for instance the result of upbringing in certain channels transmitted in family traditions, may play a greater role. Tchaikovsky's sexual development may have essentially been influenced by the above-mentioned idealization of the two women around him in his early childhood as well as by the identification with his mother. For in a psychoanalytical sense, homosexuality stems from an inverted, negative oedipal orientation, that is, an identification with the mother. That is why homosexuals usually take up intensive nonsexual relationships with older women—as was the case of Tchaikovsky with Mrs. von Meck.

At any rate, the causes of homosexual development are located to a considerable extent in early childhood at an age when
children do not yet know the sexual difference and the mother as
the first need-satisfying object is also the object of the child's
earliest identification. Whether in later years a transgression of
the sexual life of a normal adult follows depends on how far into
adult age the individual clings to one of the variegated and undifferentiated sexual activities of childhood. Since the child's imma-
ture and undifferentiated sexuality has an almost unlimited variety
of partial, incomplete possibilities of satisfaction, extending from
the stimulation of erogenous zones such as mouth and anus to
childhood masturbation of the genitals, there is also a broad pal-
ette of sexual deviations from the norm at an adult age.

Probably the most widespread deviation from the norm is
homosexuality, which today is regarded rather as an inversion,
that is, as a narcissistic turning of the libido to an object resembling one's own person, rather than as a perversion. In adolescence such a narcissism, that is, preoccupation with one's own
person as a love object, can to a certain extent be regarded as a
transitory normal phenomenon. The same applies to a transitional phase with homophile tendencies manifested in often enthusiastic friendships of boys and girls for their own gender. A
later accentuation of the normal transitional homosexual phase of
adolescence can make this developmental stage, however, the
most that is attainable by the individual. In such a case, sexual
feelings can be expressed only in a form of physical union with
emotional reference to a partner of the same sex. In Tchaikovsky's
case, probably his school friend, the later writer Alexander
Apuchtin, as well as Luigi Piccioli, who almost reminds one of a
transvestite, with whom Peter took singing lessons at the age of
fifteen, probably played a decisive role in this accentuation.

The discussion of these questions plays a not inconsiderable
role from a medical point of view, because they stand in close
connection with the origin of his neurosis. The fixation of adult
sexual activity upon an earlier stage of childish sexual development that prevents advancement beyond that stage and the resulting limitation of disposable sexual drive energy are the two
supporting pillars of Sigmund Freud's general theory of neurosis.

A neurosis is defined broadly as a defective psychic attitude in the sense of a wrong adaptation to an actual situation. And it is in the first six years of life that the roots of conflict between the drive demands and the traditionally inculcated social norms must generally be sought, and this conflict is often manifested in the form of inhibitions. As a rule, a neurosis is clinically detectable at the age of puberty or soon thereafter, when disturbances of the thought structure, the sphere of feeling, and the mode of behavior develop and become noticeable in the individual's life and increasingly constrict his capacity to lead a normal life.

Tchaikovsky's neurosis also expressed itself clinically in a series of psychic eccentricities, functional neurotic complaints, and psychosomatic organic ailments.

Hysterical reactions are among the frequent psychic symptoms of a neurosis. The first such reaction occurred when he was ten years old, on the occasion of parting from his mother in St. Petersburg, when he demonstratively braced himself against the spokes of her carriage wheel and finally aware of his powerlessness he broke out in loud screams, striking wildly around himself. In those childhood years, hearing music could so excite him that he began trembling in his whole body and experienced hallucinations at night. But even later we learn of hysterical reactions manifested in outbreaks of rage when disturbed by the noise of a passing carriage. Indeed, his irritability sometimes went so far that even the ticking of a clock could bother him. A particularly impressive hysterical attack that led to a fainting spell occurred in 1881, when his beloved Alyosha, after receiving a draft notice, said farewell to him, and Tchaikovsky reportedly gave bloodcurdling screams.

Tchaikovsky's neurosis was also displayed in typical reactions of fear and alarm. It is reported that he was notoriously afraid of storms, burglars, and ghosts, and felt an insurmountable fearful aversion to the sight of a corpse. At the burial of his friend Rubinstein in Paris, by his own admission this fear was stronger than his feeling of grief. In general he was particularly easy to frighten, which frequently led his colleagues at the conservatory to make him a butt of their jokes—and he complained about this in his letters several times.

His typical phobic symptoms directed against his fellow humans are also characteristic. As his brother Modest tells us, he felt aversion and distrust toward almost all strangers, but it also subsided rapidly:

> He considered every person unknown to him from the first to be an enemy....Therefore they were all punished with contempt, but only until the first kindly word or friendly look. Then he forgave them immediately and even found them to be likable.

From this behavior, the uncertainty so typical of neuroses can easily be recognized. These phobic symptoms appeared mainly toward masses of people, and they could be intensified to the point of hatred. For years, this marked fear of any larger crowd of people even gave him difficulties in conducting. Frequently he felt mocked or treated with hostility, which explains his unusual sensitivity to any criticism. Such almost paranoid ideas often led him to go traveling even after slight personal or professional disagreements or failures, and repeatedly he expressed the wish to flee to solitude in order to live undisturbed by the stares of people.

His depressive phases, in which often enough suicidal thoughts also resonated, deserve special mention. A depression made itself noticeable for the first time in 1865. It stemmed from a feeling of failure in life as the expression of a lowered sense of self-value, so typical for a neurosis, and heightened itself to suicidal dreams. After completing his First Symphony, his depressive despondency accompanied by premonitions of death was so bad that the doctor threatened to have him committed to an insane asylum. In a letter to his sister Sasha from 1868 he himself gave a classic description of the most important symptoms of a depression: indecision, lack of joy, weakened motivation (which he described as laziness and taciturnity), weariness with life, insomnia, lack of appetite, and "despondent moods without external reason," which, together with a general feebleness, were most pronounced in the morning. These and similar phases of depression and "melancholy," as he himself occasionally called them, were repeated several times in his life with varying intensity. Of course, in Tchaikovsky's case it was not a matter of a depression within the context of a manic-depressive cycle, which arises spontaneously and for which heredity plays an essential role, but rather of depression as a process of development in which reactions to the surrounding world or internal conflicts are the triggering cause. For both forms, however, a suicidal tendency is the most dangerous symptom. Tchaikovsky, indeed, did make a suicide attempt in 1877, considering it the only way out of an intolerable state of marriage.

The predominant factor in Tchaikovsky's neurosis consists of the sexual, libidinous components. These also occupy a primary role in the conflict model of Freud's neurosis doctrine, followed only later by separate aggressive impulses directed not only against the surrounding world but principally also against one's own person. Tchaikovsky's homosexually conditioned life in anonymity and isolation gave rise to guilt feelings aggravated by the need to keep his homosexual contacts secret and the fear of discovery or even punishment as a criminal for his abnormal sexual tendencies. These guilt feelings must have been a severe spiritual burden. Rumors about his private behavior, which came to his ears, made him even more distrustful of the people around him and fostered self-reproach that his friends must possibly often be ashamed of him. Moreover, aggressive tendencies against his own person further intensified his guilt feelings and led him to fight by all means at his disposal against his sexual perversions which seemed reprehensible in his own eyes. Yet, as can be seen in his diaries, it was not at all a question of homosexual partners—although jealousy and offended feelings often played a role—but frequently of the narcissistic preoccupation with his own person. Unfortunately the ever so serious resolve to repress the unrestrained satisfaction of his sexual desires—which he himself once called "excessive"—remained unsuccessful, so that on 23 April 1884 he noted resignedly in his diary: "What a monstrous person I am." The danger of discovery, which "hung over him like a Damocles-sword" and the awareness of his powerlessness to oppose his nature by his own strength, finally led him in his despair to make the insane decision to marry, though this had to end in catastrophe.

Music was again and again the most effective help in over-coming all these crises. It became a kind of escape valve through which he could channel his inner conflicts outward during the creative process, as he himself states after completing his First Symphony: "Without music I would have gone insane." The emotional part of human life being of decisive significance for art, it is not surprising that the neurotic elements in Tchaikovsky's character are inseparably bound up with his music.

Besides the healing effect of his compositional activity in his attempt to overcome his mental problems, various stimulations also played an ever more important role. In his youth, nicotine best served his wish for anesthetization, and that is why he praised smoking highly during his whole later life and felt it to be a virtu-ally necessary incitement for his artistic creativity. But soon alco-hol, with its calming effect assumed increasing importance, and before long he could no longer do without it. He admitted this quite openly to his brother Anatoly in a letter:

> I do not feel calm until I have drunk a little too much. I have become so accustomed to this secret drinking that at the mere sight of the bottle, which I always have nearby, I feel something like joy.

In later years he consumed much greater quantities of alcohol, so that even Mussorgsky, himself more than inclined toward alco-hol, praised him for his astonishing ability to hold his liquor. In Tchaikovsky's diaries one then finds countless references to alco-hol abuse, documenting his drunken state and its effects. On 11 July 1886 in his diary he presented a philosophical view of his alcoholism, which at the same time sounds like a justification:

> It is said that alcohol abuse is harmful, and I admit this. But a man tormented by his nerves can sim-ply not live without alcohol poison....I, for ex-ample, am drunk every evening and I cannot at all live otherwise. In the first stage of drunkenness I feel splendid and in this condition I grasp incom-parably more than when I abstain from the poison.

Nor have I noticed that my health suffers especially from it. Moreover: *Quod licet Jovi, non licet bovi* [What is permitted to Jove is not permitted to an ox].

Tchaikovsky is here thinking as originally and as naively as people in the Middle Ages. In those times, intoxication was still considered a matter-of-course state of consciousness, in accord with an attitude toward drunkenness which, unrestrained and unimpeded by inhibitions, still valued and sought intoxication for its own sake. In the 19th century, when self-mastery and control of the emotions by reason constituted a new orientation, this image changed. Now one drank to release the affects, and that is why European artists, especially men of letters, increasingly resorted to alcohol to give wings to their world of thought and their creativity, but also better to master their own personal problems. This is most particularly true of the writers of Romanticism and surrealism, such as Novalis in Germany, Keats in England, Baudelaire in France, and certainly also Tchaikovsky in Russia. But these literary men also increasingly used opiates as narcotics, whereas this is probably not true of Tchaikovsky. Only one single time in his diaries is there a remark, set off with three question marks, that alludes to a novella by Alphonse Daudet suggesting a desire for heroin. We do not know what he meant by this reference.

Aside from psychic symptoms of a neurosis, Tchaikovsky was also tormented more and more frequently by organic neuroses, that is, functional disturbances of various organs. These ailments represented the translation of mental conflicts into organic symptoms. In individual cases, a very specific psychosomatic choice of organ takes place with a preference for a few organs, such as heart, stomach, large intestine, lungs. It is understandable why these neurotic ailments of organs tend to occur predominantly in personal or professional stress situations; and in Tchaikovsky's diaries there is a striking coincidence between his ailments and premieres or concerts. Besides headaches or insomnia, he repeatedly lists stomachaches, nausea, and abdominal cramps. These symptoms would indicate an irritable bowel syndrome. The often-reported episodes of diarrhea would also fit within this context. Besides these stomach and intestinal complaints, he often experienced a pounding heart and an irregular heartbeat (extra systoles), as well as stabbing sensations in the area of the heart, sometimes accompanied by oppressive feelings of anxiety. Tchaikovsky noted in one passage of his diary that such "heart ailments" were occasionally associated with a choking feeling. This description probably matches the functional breathing disturbance, called Da Costa's syndrome or effort syndrome, which gives the patient the feeling of no longer being able to inhale sufficiently. All these ailments of Tchaikovsky's match the typical symptoms of an organ-neurosis and the doctors treating him therefore repeatedly assured him that no pathological organic damage could be discovered.

But the analysis of his diaries also shows, beyond this, that Tchaikovsky also was not spared organic diseases. Apart from his susceptibility to colds and infections of the upper airways, including the bronchia, connected with long-lasting coughing periods, it was mainly his stomach that gave him recurrent difficulties. Modest's biography says about this:

> The catarrhal condition of his stomach plagued him since the end of the sixties. Once in Nisy, Peter Ilyich…was introduced to the use of sodium bicarbonate….The sickness was not healed by this; on the contrary, it became worse and worse, so that Peter Ilyich in 1876 had to undergo treatment at a spa. Since that treatment his health improved. But the catarrh had not disappeared completely and it made itself felt now more strongly, now more weakly, but without reaching the intensity it did in 1876….Toward the end of the eighties, his stomach condition again became worse: besides the constant heartburn, upset stomachs recurred more and more often and frequently frightened him very much. At the time of *Queen of Spades*, when he was living in the Hotel Rossiya in

St. Petersburg, he sent for me one morning and told me the minute I entered that he thought he could not survive the night.

Modest, apparently agreeing with the doctors who treated Tchaikovsky, saw the cause of these complaints as a "catarrhal condition of his stomach" with a resulting excessive acidity of the gastric juices, which in turn caused the frequent heartburn and required constant use of sodium bicarbonate. But if the entries in Tchaikovsky's diaries are consulted, the diagnosis of an ulcer in the area of the stomach or the duodenum can be made almost with certainty. This ailment has long been considered one of the classic psychosomatic diseases. It displays a pronouncedly chronic recidivistic character with ever-recurring spells that typically coincide in time with very severe situations of mental stress. Occasionally during such an ulcerous spell, a particularly deep penetration of the ulcer can result, that is, a perforated ulcer in current terminology, with especially strong, almost unbearable stabbing pains that reach their greatest intensity in the night. Tchaikovsky's stomach pains during the rehearsals for his opera *Queen of Spades* could have involved such a condition. But not only the recidivist nature of his stomach ailment supports the diagnosis of an ulcerous occurrence, but also a few detailed data in the diary, for instance, his apparently surprised observation that his stomach pains vanished completely for a time by ingesting food. This symptom known as the "food-relief" sign is practically pathognomic for an ulcer ailment.

The strong hyperacidity of the gastric fluid, combined with considerable chronic consumption of alcohol, promoted the origin of a so-called reflux esophagitis, an inflammation of the mucus membrane in the lower section of the esophagus due to a backflow of the acidic stomach contents. Understandably, this condition worsens when the body is reclined horizontally and the acidic gastric juice can act on the esophageal mucus membrane for a longer time, as is the case during nocturnal rest. The pains triggered by this can be considerable and can radiate up to the throat or the heart area, but they subside quickly when the body is erect or the patient stands up. This very fact is described by Tchaikovsky in his diary when after a big meal with large amounts of alcohol he woke up at night from pains and was forced to spend several hours sitting out of bed, which then also gave him real relief. This establishes the diagnosis of reflux esophagitis, which apparently existed since the mid-1880s.

Immoderate consumption of alcohol, years of using lots of nicotine, uncontrolled sexual activity, his intensive mode of working as a composer, and exhausting tours as a conductor took their toll and made his physical appearance by the age of fifty seem like that of a man ten years older. Although he was fully aware of his premature aging upon looking in a mirror, he was nonetheless shocked when an American newspaper overestimated his real age by a whole decade, all the more so since the first signs of absentmindedness were beginning to show up. Under his mask, which he put on in the 1880s as a protective wall around his complicated inner world and behind which he maintained the appearance of self-certainty only with the greatest expenditure of energy, his doubts and self-reproach again became visible. This "mid-life" crisis, in which surfeit of life, despair, and depressive despondency spread, was greatly aggravated by the unexpected and offensive rejection by his soul-friend Mrs. von Meck, as well as by various difficulties in his homosexual relationships, characterized by jealousy and hurt feelings. The completion of his Sixth Symphony, in which he autobiographically elaborated in codified form the whole drama of his hurting soul seemed, however, to have greatly reduced the tension potential, since, according to Modest, in the circle of his closest friends he seemed cheerful and satisfied and gave no signs of despondency, not to mention any longing for death.

As has meanwhile been proven beyond any doubt, Tchaikovsky did not die of cholera, as was previously universally assumed. So the inconsistencies which became evident in the attempt to assign the described symptoms during his last days and hours to the classical disease profile of cholera need no longer be discussed. On the contrary, the suspicion expressed even shortly after Tchaikovsky's death, namely, that he voluntarily took his own life, is right. However, we know, since the discovery of new documents, that his suicide did not stem from an inner urge, but was proposed, or rather imposed on him by a "court of honor" as the only possible alternative in order to avoid a public scandal with unforeseeable consequences. Only in the sense that he accepted this horrendous proposal can it therefore be said that Tchaikovsky voluntarily parted from life. Furthermore, this suicide, planned down to the smallest details, was not supposed to be known as such to the public. Rather, the appearance was to be given that Tchaikovsky had died of a dangerous disease—so to speak, a natural death. Since cholera had not yet fully run its course in St. Petersburg in those days, apparently a form of suicide had been agreed upon that was as similar as possible to the picture of fatal cholera. The appropriate poison must have been delivered to Tchaikovsky by the attorney August Gerke, a former fellow student likewise present at the court of honor. This visit of Gerke's, for which negotiations with the publisher Bessel must have served as pretext, was not mentioned in Modest's biography, but it was expressly confirmed by Vasily Bessel personally in the *Russian Music Journal.*

The symptoms which arose within a few hours after emptying the glass (probably containing poison) clearly support the picture of an acute arsenic poisoning, which led within a few days to the composer's death under horrible pains. Among those symptoms were: watery profuse diarrhea, vomiting, rapidly increasing weakness, "horrid" abdominal colic, from which he cried out again and again, as well as pains in the chest, cramps in the calves of the legs which soon set in, renal failure, and deliriums which began after a severe circulatory collapse and finally faded into a coma. Since today this form of suicide is observed extremely rarely, the clinical picture of arsenic poisoning shall be described from a textbook in forensic medicine published in Vienna two years before Tchaikovsky's death at a time when arsenic poisonings were better known to doctors from direct experience:

> Although suicides by arsenic no longer occur as frequently as formerly was the case, they are by

no means seldom at present. The relative frequency of murders by arsenic poisoning can be explained, on the one hand, by the ease with which the poison can be obtained, since it is used in many businesses and for eliminating pests, and on the other hand because it is odorless and tasteless it can easily be administered secretly despite its difficult solubility. Even with large dosages, the symptoms of poisoning do not appear immediately, but as a rule only after an hour. Cases are more frequently observed in which three to ten hours have passed before the first symptoms of toxicity begin....The clinical picture of arsenic poisoning is by no means always the same. As a rule it is that of acute gastroenteritis. A burning or scratching feeling begins in the throat or in the esophagus; then severe pains in the stomach and a violent vomiting of mucus, rarely with bloody streaks, and profuse diarrheas, emptying watery excrements resembling rice water. At the same time, there is *tenesmus* [cramps in the rectum], an inextinguishable thirst, frequent headaches, and as a rule pain in the small of the back and cramplike pains in the extremities, but especially cramps in the calves. The skin is cool and covered with sweat; at first, pale, later cyanotic [with blue-black discoloration], as are also the hands and feet. Pulse weak and slight. Great feebleness, followed by death with a general collapse.

In other cases vomiting and the other acute symptoms cease, but others set in, among them the signs of nephritis. Further symptoms of increasing muscular weakness are: difficulty in breathing, weak heart activity, under which death can follow in three to ten days after the poisoning.

In yet other cases, both initially and subsequently, the prevailing course is less symptomatic of gastro-enteritis; rather, it takes on the appearance of a cerebrospinal infection [involving the brain and spinal cord]. The disease begins with dizziness and a headache, and a cramping pain in the limbs. Then coma and stupor set in, sometimes delirium, sometimes also convulsions, and finally general paralysis and death. Of course, there are many combinations of the above-mentioned forms of acute arsenic poisoning.

In this extensive description of acute arsenic poisoning leading to death are found nearly all the symptoms described by Modest and the doctors in attendance. From a medical perspective, beyond all doubt Tchaikovsky chose death by arsenic poisoning for his suicide. Apart from the terrible pains in the area of the esophagus, the stomach and the intestine, as well as the profuse vomiting, surprisingly a great many of the other symptoms display a remarkable similarity to those found in cholera: the massive watery, indeed, rice water-like diarrhea and the painful cramps in his calves, and muscle quivering provoked by the ensuing great loss of fluid and salt, the disturbance of kidney function leading to complete cessation of urinary output, and, at last, the states of confusion and the final coma as evidence of inadequate supply of blood to the brain due to circulatory collapse. The above-cited textbook from 1891 therefore expressly refers to the similarity of arsenic poisoning to cholera:

> The great losses of fluid in acute arsenic poisoning occur similarly in other profuse intestinal catarrhs, but especially in cholera, with which the picture of arsenic poisoning shows great similarity both during life and in the corpse, a fact frequently pointed out.

It seems unlikely that Tchaikovsky was aware of the tormenting death struggle he would endure from acute arsenic poisoning, and certainly after the end of the "court of honor" he was too excited to reflect on the meaning of such a sacrifice. This artist, who had struggled all his life with the demons in his breast and with the powers assailing him from the outside, was not spared by fate in his death struggle. If one tries to relate the secrets of his inner life to the decisive traits of his creativity, a gap ensues between the person and the artist that is hard to fathom. Both together created a work that kept his cares and his pains captive in his soul as well as in his music before the eyes of the world. That is why his music seldom could penetrate deeply, but achieved mainly surface effects. His works will delight people again and again in the coming centuries by their effervescent vitality, piquant rhythms, and captivating music, with occasional eruptions of brutal and unrestrained forms. But even with his great instrumental works, rightly ranked among the supreme achievements of European music, he never succeeded in developing his own unified style on a grand scale. In his music, West European influences of various kinds are found on all sides, mixed with Slavic elements but not classifiable as typical Russian compositions. For Tchaikovsky happened to be a musician interested in writing music in a pleasant and obliging style and not in undertaking revolutionary advances into new musical territory. From his psychograph it can be concluded that the loftiness of suffering always remained alien to him, while his own experience of suffering gave him rather a certain pleasure. This explains why Tchaikovsky could not express pity for other people, either verbally or musically, whereas he was able to describe self-pity, self-love, and accusatory feelings of guilt and atonement toward himself with a realism of appalling horror, the like of which can be found only in the poems of Baudelaire. Tchaikovsky's music displays neither extraordinary cleverness, nor humor, nor bitter sarcasm; nor does it want to veil or conceal anything. Rather, it engulfs the listener almost shamelessly in its sensuality and its glittering splendor. In light of this, it does not seem accidental that such music was thought up by a highly neurotic, rather shy, and mercilessly tormented artist.

Most revealing for us are the heartrending testimonies of his passionate nature in those few creations he himself regarded as the "musical confessions of his soul," letting his soul float out on a sea of music, free of reason's intellectual work. In these compositions, the inspiration of his genius led him to "heights just below the clouds" into spheres where a kind of illumination came over him. And, to close with Tchaikovsky's own words, only such music "can touch and move the heart as has been conceived in the unsettled depths of an artist's soul by the power of illumination."

Tchaikovsky's Doctors

Dr. J. B. H. Théophile d'Archambault (1806-1863)

Dr. d'Archambault was born in Tours; he graduated in Paris in 1829. Since 1840 he practiced at the Bicetre in the Department for Mental Diseases. In 1842 he became Director of the Mental Asylum in Mareville near Nancy, which he converted into a model institution in a few years. In 1850 he was called back to Paris to take over as Chief Doctor in the Men's Section of the Insane Asylum of Charenton near Paris.

D'Archambault made himself highly meritorious by effectively alleviating the horrible fate of the mentally ill, for instance, by strictly abolishing the "quarters for the unclean."

Dr. Balinsky

Popular psychiatrist in St. Petersburg.

Dr. Lev Bernardovich Bertenson (1850-1929)

Dr. Lev Bertenson was a famous physician in St. Petersburg, popular mainly with the aristocracy of the city. Because of his fame and outstanding reputation, he was appointed by the Czar to be his personal physician.

Dr. Vasily Bernardovich Bertenson (1853-1933)

A friend of Tchaikovsky's for many years, he was one of the doctors trusted by the composer. Dr. Bertenson attended mainly the upper class society of St. Petersburg. From the first days of

Tchaikovsky's fatal illness he was at his bedside, taking turns in tending him with his assistants, Dr. Nicolai Mamonov and Dr. Alexander Sanders. He also called for a consultation with his brother Lev.

Gustav Mahler

(1860–1911)

The contradictory reception of Gustav Mahler's works stands without compare in the whole history of music. Not even Richard Wagner's creations, indeed not even the "New Viennese School," unleashed such a sinister amount of hostile rejection and unreasonable resentment as did Mahler's middle, purely instrumental symphonies. Theodor W. Adorno saw this resentment against the new music not only as a "symptom of mere musical ignorance," but equally as a "sign of malaise toward artistic manifestations" that are felt to represent "deviations from the norm and rejections of society's approved modes of behavior." This ignorance and malaise concerning a musician like Mahler, who with his "self-chosen cosmic claim" dared to squeeze the whole "of our world and our world-feeling into a musical portrayal," found clear expression in various commentaries of his time. His music was said to be well instrumented, but without logic and taste, ungenuine and incomprehensible, often sugary and jubilant like an operetta, and eclectically compiled from third hand.

The doctrine in vogue, after Mahler's death at the latest, that his whole symphonic creation had to be understood as "absolute music," has caused serious difficulties for the right interpretation of his works. However, research into the literary, religious, and philosophical preconditions of his symphonic writing has shown that all Mahler's symphonies—even the purely instrumental ones— are based on a very definite program. Mahler himself claimed to be "able to put to music his entire world view, his philosophical conception of life, as well as any feeling, natural event, or landscape." If this is so, then of course his symphonic production can be understood only if one also knows the composer's intentions. If Mahler's symphonic creation is studied under this aspect, the surprised observer soon recognizes it clearly as highly programmatic, though not in the manner of the illustrative music of a Hector Berlioz, Franz Liszt, or Richard Strauss, but rather as a kind of "esoteric" program music. Besides works of world literature, Mahler's compositions often express personal experiences, confessions, visionary fantasies, or world-view ideas. That is why his symphonic creations could be epitomized either as autobiography or as metaphysics. He remained faithful to these principles of his program music all his life. When he announced in his Munich declaration of 1900 that in the future he would no longer reveal his extra-musical ideas, images, and views that were determinative for the confessional nature of his music, this was not a departure from the programmatic principles of his youth. His intention was, rather, to prevent the programmatic explanations of individual movements of his symphonies from provoking crude misunderstandings in the audience. He preferred "to be misunderstood at first rather than to be understood merely rationalistically or even in the sense of illustrative program music."

Although Mahler did not stand out as a writer to the same extent as Robert Schumann, Richard Wagner, or Arnold Schönberg, literarily he was himself one of the most well-read composers of late Romanticism with his comprehensive, virtually encyclopedic education. So it is not surprising that in his youth he saw himself as an author-composer and wrote his own texts for his songs and his fairy-tale operas. His philosophical horizon was astonishingly wide and extended from the intellectual world of antiquity to the German philosophers of the 19th century. "But it was Goethe who stood like the sun in the sky of his intellectual world, and he knew him with rare comprehensiveness and loved to quote him from his unlimited memory," as Bruno Walter stated quite poetically. Mahler's unconditional orientation on Goethe is manifested even in the diction of his statements, for instance, when he avowed that he never wrote a single note "that was not absolutely true"— a formulation Arnold Schönberg later expanded to the much-quoted sentence: "Music is not supposed to decorate, it is supposed to be true." As opposed to Schönberg, Mahler wrote no essays on music theory, but many statements in his letters and in sketches by his friends give us valuable clues to his view of art and his position on actual problems of music aesthetics, showing how much men of letters, poets, philosophers, and—not least of all—composers influenced Mahler's music-aesthetic thinking. Aside from Goethe, he received decisive intellectual impulses mainly from E.T.A. Hoffmann, Eichendorff, Schopenhauer, and Wagner. It seems remarkable that Mahler, for instance, in connection with his Third and, especially, his Eighth Symphony, speaks in similes related to the ancient doctrine of *"musica mundana."* His definition of the symphony as a likeness (*Abbild*) of the universe corresponds broadly with the doctrine of Boethius, the unfortunate chancellor of Theoderich the Great, who regarded *"musica instrumentalis"* as a faithful likeness of the inaudible music of the spheres, *"musica mundana."* Only when one knows Mahler's idea of the harmony of the spheres and his conviction that music is supposed to be an image of nature and realizes that all his symphonies have a philosophical-literary thought at their basis as an unexpressed program, does one also understand why he wanted his symphonies to be understood as the expression of an all-encompassing world view.

Mahler's disciples and admirers, in their striving to win support for this composer's work, at first remained caught in local or, at most, regional isolation. Due to their efforts, around 1920 he was still spoken of as the "composer of our time." But just a few years later, influenced by neoclassicism with its changed aesthetic and technical standards of composition, the reception of Mahler's works underwent a noticeable decline. By the end of the 1920s, a new understanding of Mahler was germinating in the United States and, under the auspices of the Bruckner Society of America, founded in 1931 by the most famous conductors of European origin, Mahler's symphonies appeared more and more frequently on the concert program. Meanwhile, in his own homeland this Austrian master's influence on society was restricted more and more by the hostile and destructive attitude of the adherents of the Great German Reich, which reached a venomous pitch of malice after the early 1930s. Finally, with National Socialism,

"Mahler's music was, as it were, frozen in the whole context of its problematic aesthetic reception." Polemical pamphlets, like those by K. Blessinger from 1944, were outraged at Mahler's "naked, undisguised sexuality...and natural sounds," and disgustedly lampooned the "lurid atmosphere of the dance floor" and the "disgusting howling and drawing-out of tones that is so typical of Jews." Blessinger believed he recognized typically Jewish traits in all Mahler's works, namely, aggressiveness, sugary sentimentality, empty loud pathos, and a "deep spiritual confusion."

Zionists, as well as anti-Semites, repeatedly tried to derive certain characteristics of Mahler's music from his Jewish origin. If both these groups were convinced of the "pronouncedly Jewish basic character" that is clearly audible in Mahler, others such as Gerhart Hauptmann saw "Gustav Mahler's genius as representative of the great traditions of German music." Theodor W. Adorno expressed himself perhaps in a most well-balanced way on this disputed question, when he said that the "attempt to deny the Jewish element in Mahler in order to reclaim him for a concept of German music infected with National Socialism is just as misguided as wanting to appropriate him as a national Jewish composer." In the discussion of the Jewish element in Mahler's music, however, it must not be overlooked that the Jew Mahler professed Christian doctrine with unusual devotion. As is clearly shown from his letters from his youth and confirmed by Alma Mahler in her memoirs, he seems to have virtually suffered from an "Ahasver complex," insofar as he identified with the fate of the Eternal Jew who is barred from reaching the God of the Christians. The religious-psychological aspect of this complex consisted in the fact that he proclaimed a strong inclination toward Catholicism at an early age and therefore converted to the Catholic faith out of deepest conviction, in which his Christian piety was genuine, as Alma assures us. She expressly stresses that his religious songs were as genuinely felt as his Second and Third Symphonies and all the chorales of his symphonic works and not brought in from the outside. His "Ahasver complex," however, also had a social-psychology aspect, connected with the 19th century assimilation of Jews, such as had already been significant for the Mendelssohn family. Although Alma testifies that "Mahler never denied his Jewish origin, rather he emphasized it," he nevertheless consistently strove all his life for integration into Christian society. After all this, it seems absolutely necessary to consider Mahler's world view also from this perspective, since it has its roots not only in Judaism but to an equal extent also in Christianity.

Whatever the case may be—opinions can survive for decades until they have to make room for new ways of seeing things. The role played by Richard Wagner's anti-Jewish music criticism with regard to Felix Mendelssohn-Bartholdy, was played for Mahler by National Socialist writers' "race-theoretical sum of immanent criticism of compositions"; their poisonous barbs continued to blur reception of Gustav Mahler's creations for years after the demise of the Third Reich. As late as 1958 one could still read:

> Mahler's works once passionately moved the musical world; today, almost five decades after his early death, his symphonies, except for the First and the Second, are rarely to be heard.

Actually up to that point in time, what even some few musicians in Mahler's lifetime had felt to be an epoch-making accomplishment was disparaged by arch-conservative music theorists "with the belated help of National Socialist cultural arguments" and finally committed to an apparent death.

At long last, celebrations in honor of Mahler's one hundredth birthday prepared the way for a decisive resurgence. Besides a first German broadcast of a complete Mahler cycle on the Austrian Radio Network, various publications appeared, highlighting the significance of this long-forgotten and ostracized composer's artistic legacy. Theodor W. Adorno's "Musical Physiognomy" of Mahler probably ranks highest. From then on, a worldwide Mahler renaissance began. By 1962 someone remarked with surprise that "Gustav Mahler, of whom excessive popularity would certainly not so easily be expected, seems to be advancing practically to the ranks of best-sellers." In fact, hardly another composer was ever snatched so unexpectedly from oblivion as Mahler. In the context of mastering the past, people felt practically obligated to make restitution "for the wrong done and the common guilt."

And efforts to make the work of this gigantic mind known in its entire greatness to the music-loving world even alerted critical voices who feared that after years of repression the danger now threatened of a commercial market exploitation.

Mahler's prophecy, "My time will eventually come," has long since been fulfilled. Today he is considered the perfecter of the symphonic tradition of the 19th century and at the same time the most important forerunner of the New Music, and his influence reaches from Arnold Schönberg, via Alban Berg, Anton Webern, Sergei Prokofiev, and Dmitri Shostakovich, to our contemporary composers.

Childhood, Youth, and the Beginning of His Musical Career

Gustav was born as the second son among a total of fourteen children on 7 July 1860 in the little village of Kalisht located on the border between Bohemia and Moravia. Seven of his siblings died in early childhood, while his brother Otto committed suicide in 1895. Although in the 19th century, in view of the child mortality rate of almost fifty percent, the death of a small child of the family was accepted with a matter-of-course resignation that may seem bewildering to us today, the sight of the little children's coffins must have left a deep and ineradicable impression on the surviving brothers and sisters. Gustav's memory of his sister Justine, who was eight years younger than he, gives impressive evidence of this:

> Yet a child, she stuck wax candles all around the edge of the bed. Then she lay down in bed, lit the candles, and now almost believed she was dead.

He was particularly hard-hit by the fate of his brother Ernst, just one year younger, whom he had closed into his heart with unusual love and who died after long suffering in the spring of 1874. This loss found its artistic outcome four years later in his youthful opera *Duke Ernst of Swabia*, which unfortunately has not been preserved. In it he tried to identify his brother with the hero of the opera, as we can learn from a letter of June 1879 to his friend Josef Steiner:

And in the off-key tones I hear the greeting of Ernst of Swabia, and he comes forth and extends his arms toward me, and, as I look, it is my poor brother.

This psychologically revealing passage from a letter points clearly to Gustav's tendency, also recognizable in other documents, to flee into a dream world, a tendency reaching back to his early childhood.

His mother, whom he describes as a "woman of suffering," had heart trouble and limped since birth—as did Johannes Brahms' mother. She was the daughter of a soapmaker, in whose house great value was placed on faultless behavior. His father therefore jokingly liked to call this "noble" family "the Dukes," and for Gustav, in turn, his grandparents on his mother's side were important because in the attic of this prosperous middle-class environment he discovered a piano from which as a four-year-old child he tried to entice tones to the greatest delight of the whole family. The memory of his mother, plagued by pains and bent from work, with her careworn, "suffering" facial features, however, caused an unusual bond between mother and son, which psychoanalytically must be regarded as a determining factor in Mahler's later psychic attitude toward his wife.

His father Bernhard came from a poor Jewish family, who lived from the scanty income of a peddler's existence in the eastern part of Bohemia. While his paternal grandmother had formerly peddled her wares from door to door on foot, the son Bernhard carried on his business with a horse-drawn wagon. His thirst for knowledge led him to spend the time on his travels reading various books, which earned him the nickname of "the wagon-seat scholar." Striving to improve his life circumstances, he also worked as a tutor and after several attempts he even succeeded in opening a little brandy factory and purchasing a modest little house in Kalisht. Gustav's father, described as domineering, ran a strict disciplinary system in his family. Mahler therefore later could never find "a word of love for his father" and in his memoirs he spoke of a "sad, unhappy childhood." On the other hand, his father did everything to provide Gustav with the best education possible and to promote his musical talent. Bernhard Mahler was a free thinker who rejected every religious custom of traditional Judaism and avoided whatever could remind him of Jewish segregation from the surrounding gentile world with its different belief. His striving to assimilate to the German-speaking culture, like so many Jews of this period, stemmed not least of all from the hope in this way of having better chances with the "October Diploma" of 1860, even as a member of the Jewish lower-middle class in Bohemia. So in December of that reform year, he moved from the Bohemian border settlement of Kalisht to Iglau, the center of the German-language enclave in Moravia, where he expected better sales opportunities for his products. Under such circumstances, it is not surprising that all signs of Gustav's education in the sense of the Jewish faith are lacking. Even as a child, the Catholic religious services seemed to appeal more to him, while, according to Alma Mahler's assurances, "he never got anything" out of Jewish ritual.

In his earliest childhood years, playing music gave Gustav the greatest joy, as he himself later reported:

> Since my fourth year of life I always made and composed music, before I could even play the scales.

At first it was on an accordion that he tried to play Czech songs for young dancers or to imitate the trumpet sounds of the nearby military camp. But soon his ambitious father, ready to do everything to promote his son's unusual musical talent, decided to fulfill young Gustav's dream by purchasing a piano. Although considered "unreliable" and "distracted" in elementary school, he made such rapid progress with his piano lessons that by October 1870 at a concert in the Iglau Theater he made his debut as a "child prodigy" or Wunderkind—an event reported by the local newspaper, which already identified "the nine-year-old son of a local Israelite businessman" as a future piano virtuoso.

His career as a middle-school pupil seems to have developed less successfully. His father therefore sent him to Prague in expectation of stricter school instruction. In order simultaneously also to continue developing his musical talent, Gustav was lodged with a family that was to provide piano lessons. For one of the two sons in this family was Alfred Grünfeld, then nine years old, who later would rise to be one of the most eminent pianists of the outgoing 19th century. Unfortunately they seem to have bothered precious little with Gustav, so that the dreamy boy was left to his own devices for the greater part of the day. Among the unpleasant memories of this time, one event remained in his memory all his life and in later years was not without significance for his relation to the female gender. This traumatic youthful experience consisted in the eleven-year-old boy's being the involuntary witness of a "brutal love scene between the housemaid and the son of the house," and it may be assumed that this shocking scene unconsciously strengthened his bond with his mother and led to his striving as an adult not to allow moral purity and tenderness to be endangered by crude passion.

Since Gustav at the end of the school year got the worst final grades in the class, his father fetched him back to Iglau, where he was to continue his education at the local high school. But here, too, he showed little inclination to be an industrious and attentive student. He much preferred to browse in his father's books, which constituted "almost a little library" and must have had greater significance for his further education. Mahler's later statement suggests as much: "Spent my youth in high school—learned nothing."

Little value as he set on school lessons, he eagerly engaged in playing the piano and making first efforts at composition. Among the many acquaintances in Iglau and the surrounding area who followed Gustav's progress with admiration and pride, one man was of special importance for Mahler's artistic development, namely, the administrator of the Morovan dairy farm, Gustav Schwarz. This music lover was so impressed by Mahler's pianistic talents that he formed the plan, with the help of his personal connections, to bring the "frail, awkward little boy" to Vienna because of his unusual musical talent. In order to realize this dream, the boy proved for the first time that he was not just an unrealistic dreamer, but rather that, when necessary, he could also be a clever and purposeful tactician. Since his father, though agreeing in principle with the proposal, still hesitated to give his final permission, the boy appealed directly to his protector, Schwarz, to whom he wrote on 28 August 1875:

> Father fears sometimes that I will neglect or inter-
> rupt my studies, sometimes that I could be spoiled
> by bad companions in Vienna....I therefore ask
> you...to do us the honor of a visit; for only thus
> can my father be completely persuaded.

And so it was. Just two weeks later his benefactor brought him to Vienna, where he entered the Conservatory of the Society of Music Friends and was taken under the wings of Julius Epstein, the famous pianist. When he returned to Iglau in 1876, he could show his father not only a good grade, but also his own piano quartet, with which he had won first prize in a composition contest. In the summer of 1877 he passed the closing examination at the high school in Iglau as a day-student, and a year later he again won first prize for a piano quintet which was performed publicly at the Conservatory's closing concert. Playing with him then was the violoncello student Eduard Rosé, brother of the later famous concertmaster of the Vienna Philharmonic, Arnold Rosé. Later, both of these musicians formed even closer ties with Gustav by marrying his sisters Justine and Emma.

Although Mahler later called himself a legitimate follower and student of Anton Bruckner and was even in his student days among the great symphony writer's most convinced and loyal adherents, he never took part in his instruction on harmony theory and counterpoint at the Conservatory. His harmony teacher was, rather, Robert Fuchs, and he studied counterpoint and composition with Franz Krenn. Since there was at that time still no school for conductors, Mahler, like the famous conductors, Felix Mottl, Arthur Nikisch, or Hans Richter, must be ranked among the "baton-autodidacts." The entry of Richard Wagner's music into Vienna became the shaping and dominating experience for all of them, although Mahler from the very first did not so much go along with the Wagner cult, but rather he was attached to the ideas and the musical work of the music-master of Bayreuth out of inner conviction. This also explains why in his young years he rarely visited opera performances and preferred to take in Wagner's music as "pure music," which was also true of the Wagner admirer, Anton Bruckner. On the other hand, young Mahler, who was inclined to asceticism and as a child had expressed the wish to become a "martyr," was deeply impressed by Richard Wagner's treatise *Religion and Art*, as can be seen from a letter to a friend in November 1880:

> I have been a complete vegetarian since a month ago. The moral effect of this way of life is immense as a result of this voluntary subjugation of my body and the resulting lack of needs. You can imagine how permeated I am with this, if I expect a regeneration of the human race thereby.

When he was nineteen, this attitude also began to take effect in another respect, namely, in building a field of tension between sexuality and asceticism. For an artist like Mahler, who was more than susceptible to all female charms, the subjugation of the body also corresponded to an enslavement of his own soul, which presupposed considerable power to overcome. As in Wagner's *Tristan* "highest pleasure" is equated with physical death, similarly in Mahler's heart "the highest fire of most joyful vital force" ruled alternatively with "the most consuming longing for death." This desperate struggle between sensuality and ethics had, moreover, at that time yet another, very real background, which Stefan Zweig portrays so impressively in his book *The World of Yesterday* and which cast a threatening shadow over the love life of young people then, namely, fear of infection with a venereal disease.

> Fear of infection was aggravated by the repulsive and demeaning forms of cures then existing and even after such a gruesome cure the affected person all his life could not be certain whether the tricky virus might not awaken any moment out of its encapsulation, from the spinal cord laming the limbs, behind the forehead softening the brain.

By this "virus" was meant *Spirochaeta pallida*, the pathogenic organism causing syphilis, which led to the death of Mahler's colleague Hugo Wolf, as well as of Bedrich Smetana, from a progressive paralysis. Nonetheless, Mahler's passionate nature and intense capacity for love overcame such appalling thoughts. By the age of nineteen he had for the first time "grasped this world very materially...and now the waves are rolling over my head." In the following years, he fell "from one stupidity to the other" and not until he was twenty-five did he seem to have become somewhat more prudent, as he admitted to a friend: "This time, however, I want to be more cautious, otherwise things will go bad for me again." For a few years he wore a beard, which was supposed to make him look more grown up, but gradually it was reduced to a mustache, and later given up completely. Although in his love life he probably never could free himself from his bonding with his mother—which later was transferred to his sister Justine—with increasing age, his erotic feelings were shaped by a balance between sensuality and ethics.

In order to eke out a livelihood in Vienna, he was forced to give lessons. At the same time he sought an influential theater agent who was supposed to help him obtain a position as Kapellmeister. He found this man in Gustav Lewy, who owned a music shop on Petersplatz, and he signed a five-year contract with him on 12 May 1880. His first assignment took him to Bad Hall in upper Austria, where he had to direct operettas in the little summer theater, but at the same time also to perform menial services. After returning to Vienna with few savings, he completed his fairy-tale play *Das klagende Lied (The Plaintive Song)* for chorus, solos and orchestra, op. 1, in which are recognizable essential stylistic elements of his later art of instrumentation— among others, the "far-away orchestra." In autumn 1881 he was finally assured the position of a theater Kapellmeister in Laibach, which soon let him forget memories of the servile job in Bad Hall. But after season's end, it was necessary to wait once more for a new assignment. This time it was Olmütz, whose theater activity was in a miserable state and where the young, impulsive, and myopic conductor with the tangled head of hair and prominent nose equipped with a pince-nez at first had a hard time reestablishing order. His energetic and expert style of wielding the baton, which no one dared resist, succeeded, however, in raising the level of this provincial theater to an astonishing height. When in spring 1883 no opening was found for Mahler, he returned to Vienna, and on 31 May he signed a contract with Kassel, Germany.

After just a few weeks, he realized that his position there could not at all be as dominant as was the case in Laibach and Olmütz, since he was in many regards responsible to the first Kapellmeister and the chorus personnel were subject to the main stage-manager. Mahler found all this to be humiliating; so he intended to take the first opportunity for a new change of position. On the other hand, the yearly salary of 2100 marks was nothing to be sneezed at, especially since he had to help his family out with financial subventions due to difficult times they were then undergoing. These expenditures are surely the explanation for Mahler's surprising money shortage in Kassel, which for a time resulted in compulsory tax requisitions from his salary. From letters to his friend Fritz Löhr in Vienna, we learn that an unhappy love for a young songstress caught him under its spell and he had a hard time freeing himself from this entanglement. From the text of his autobiographical work, *Songs of a Wayfarer*, composed at this time, we can deduce that his love must have been returned by the adored girl, but a union of the loving couple was foiled by external circumstances otherwise unknown. That this really is an autobiographical document can be seen from a remark in a letter: "I have written a cycle of songs all dedicated to her."

Before leaving Kassel, Mahler had already established solid contacts with Prague; and when Angelo Neumann, an enthusiastic Wagner fan, was named director of the German Landestheater in Prague, he engaged Mahler for his stage for a year. Audience and critics were enthusiastic about the new Kapellmeister, and indeed not only as opera director with works of Wagner and Mozart, but also as concert conductor. Mahler, who had been familiar with the specific nature of Czech music since earliest childhood, also tried to make Smetana's original and captivating music known to a greater circle of listeners, and he remained loyal to this great master of Slavic musical art even later.

Whereas he felt at home in Prague, the capital of his Bohemian homeland, the next position as second Kapellmeister in Leipzig meant a resettlement abroad. Rivalry with the First Kapellmeister, Arthur Nikisch, who was one of the greatest conductors of that epoch, made tensions to be expected from the first. But when Mahler had to temporarily take over the position of First Kapellmeister due to Nikisch's falling ill, he soon was able to "conquer a very strong position," which made him very confident for the future, for he wrote: "I believe that Nikisch will not be able to stand it long with me and sooner or later will go elsewhere." In his struggle for predominance, he had planned for the 1887/88 season, besides the presentation of a Wagner cycle, also one with works of Carl Maria von Weber, a plan that was to have unexpected consequences. For when he was searching for the fragments of Weber's posthumous opera *The Three Pintos* in the house of Weber's grandson, he met this grandson's wife and fell head over heels passionately in love with her, which she seems to have encouraged. This relation to Frau von Weber led to such turmoil in his soul that he thought the only way to release this erotic tension was by creatively transposing it into music. Similarly to how his unhappy love in Kassel had resulted in the composition of his *Songs of a Wayfarer*, now the decision to compose his First Symphony in D was unleashed by the ardor of his love for Frau von Weber. Mahler, however, pointed out "that the symphony starts beyond the love affair; it underlies it—or respectively it came first in the composer's emotional life. But the external experience became the occasion for and not the content of the work." This knowledge of the external circumstances and of Mahler's completely detached mood at the time this work originated is important for interpreting its musical content. But on the basis of more recent knowledge of sources, we know that he had probably begun to conceive this symphony four years earlier and merely elaborated and perfected it, as if in a creative exhilaration, under the spell of Frau von Weber's "musical, luminous nature, turned toward the highest ideal." Not only did this creative "transformation process" affect the transformation of his erotic feelings for this woman, but, by his breakthrough into the fascinating world of the great symphony, it also caused a visible change in Mahler toward his surrounding world. Immersed in the work of composition, he at times neglected his duties as theatrical Kapellmeister, became exaggeratedly sensitive to noise during his creative activity, and often surprised his conversation partner by his absentmindedness.

The difficulties with the theater management in Leipzig ensuing from this behavior were not to last long. In September 1888, Mahler signed a ten-year contract as "artistic director" of the Royal Hungarian Opera in Budapest. The yearly salary offer not only gave him an unfamiliar feeling of financial security, but also enabled him to alleviate his family's situation in Iglau, which had meanwhile become very miserable. As opera director, he turned with greatest zeal to the operas of Wagner and Mozart and also was assigned to manage a Hungarian National Institute. However, in building up an indigenous Hungarian national ensemble, he soon ran into criticism from the public, who preferred to hear beautiful international voices. Also, when Mahler on 20 November 1889 finally presented his First Symphony in its premiere performance, some critics expressed their displeasure, stating that the composition of this symphony was "just as unclear as Mahler's activity as opera director." When in January 1891 the intrigues against him mounted, he left Budapest for a settlement sum of 25,000 guilders, and on 1 April he went to the City Theater of Hamburg, which was managed by Bernhard Pohl—alias Pollini. Although the authority of this theater manager restricted him in his powers, compared with Budapest, it offered him a much wider field for artistic activity. Thus, as early as 1892, Pollini recommended him to the impresario of the London Covent Garden Opera as the most important conductor for a German operatic season and even put a part of the Hamburg orchestra at his disposal.

In Hamburg, Mahler immediately stood out for seeking to improve the strength and beauty of the voices by countless individual rehearsals with each singer, which Pollini called "exaggeration." But, in general, people were impressed with his work as conductor. When in January 1892 he conducted the German premiere of Tchaikovsky's *Eugene Onegin* instead of the composer, Tchaikovsky found the performance "simply magnificent" and wrote to his nephew Bob:

> The conductor here is absolutely not average but a man of genius who leaves his life to conduct the premiere.

Not only his success in London, but also several new rehearsals in Hamburg, plus his activity as concert conductor, visibly strengthened Mahler's position in the Hanseatic city. One of his admirers was no less than Hans von Bülow, who fully recognized Mahler's genius as a conductor and after the concert even gave him a laurel wreath with the inscription: "To the Pygmalion of the Hamburg Opera." But much as he revered Kapellmeister Mahler, so little did he esteem the composer Mahler and his music. So, not surprisingly, Mahler's attitude toward Bülow remained ambivalent. But a psychoanalytical study on this topic published in February 1894 after Mahler's death seems to go too far when it states:

> Mahler had in his deepest soul wished for the death of the man who refused to give him recognition as a composer.

Bülow represented for Mahler, as we know, a fatherly model whom he wanted to emulate. Only thus can it be understood what creative forces were released by the experience of Bülow's funeral for the Second Symphony in C Minor, work on which had came to a halt. Mahler himself reported on the effect of this event upon the final formation of his Second Symphony as follows:

> I had then for a long time been thinking of bringing in the chorus for the last movement, and only concern that this might be felt to be an external imitation of Beethoven caused me to delay it again and again! The mood in which I sat remembering the deceased man was very much in the spirit of the work I was then carrying about in my mind. Then the chorus of the organ intoned the Klopstock

chorale "Rise again!" This struck me like a lightning bolt, and everything stood clear and distinct
before my soul.

Meanwhile, some things had changed in Mahler's closer family circle. His father, his mother, and his sister Leopoldine had
died in the year of grief 1889, and since then Gustav alone bore
the responsibility for his two sisters Justine and Emma, as well as
his brother Otto, whose musical talent he was very convinced of
and wanted to promote with all his might. The love he had felt
for his mother was now transferred exclusively to his sister Justine,
with whom he had all his life been tied by a particularly close
bond. He established a household for his siblings in Vienna,
which now spiritually was his homeland and where friends of his
lived, of whom he was especially fond. A rather dominant member of this circle of friends was Siegfried Lipiner, who is mostly
unknown today as a poet and thinker, and is at most mentioned
as the translator into German of works by the great Polish poet,
Adam Mickiewicz. In his lifetime, however, Lipiner was a highly
regarded artist, whom Nietzsche considered a "veritable genius"
and whose *Prometheus Unchained* was considered to be "the
most important German poem since Goethe's *Faust.*" This man,
born in Galicia in 1856 as a son of Jewish parents, must have
radiated a fascinating aura to also draw so strong a personality as
Mahler under its spell. As new analyses have shown, Lipiner
played quite a key role in Mahler's spiritual life. For Lipiner helped
give a decisive stamp not only to Mahler's world view but also to
his creativity, which is particularly true of the Second and Third,
as well as the unfinished Tenth Symphony. Since Lipiner's works
circle mainly around the problem of Christianity, as a Jew he is
one of the few German writers and philosophers of the outgoing
19th century whose core problem was Christian metaphysics, and
among musicians Gustav Mahler is really the only one who can
be placed at his side.

In 1892 Mahler published the *Songs and Chants from Childhood (Lieder und Gesänge aus der Jugendzeit)*, all harking back
to the *Wunderhorn* collection, an anthology of old German songs
collected in the years 1806 to 1808 by Achim von Arnim and

Clemens Brentano under the title *Des Knaben Wunderhorn* (*The Boy's Magic Horn*). Setting texts from this anthology to music occupied Mahler even in later times and they are significant not only for his songwriting, but also as seeds for the development of his symphonic structures. More than a few of these songs entered into the shaping of the Second and the Third Symphony. In his Third Symphony, however, he used not only texts from *Des Knaben Wunderhorn,* but also some from *Thus Spoke Zarathustra* by Friedrich Nietzsche, whose ideas his mentor Lipiner had acquainted him with even before the 1890s. In contrast with Richard Strauss, in this musical composition man also occupies the center, not in the sense of the superman, but rather as a human being imbedded in nature. He stressed expressly that this symphony was completely new both in content and in form, since it was supposed to reflect the whole world and had something "cosmic about it," according to his maxim that a symphony, as the highest and most elevated genre of music, must be a likeness of the whole world. With this confessional work of the Third Symphony, he at the same time made a first critique of Nietzsche, and with the finale, which people like to compare with the slow closing movement of Tchaikovsky's "*Pathétique,*" he created a closing for a symphonic composition until then unexcelled in boldness. Mahler composed the huge score of this monumental work in the summer holidays of 1895 and 1896 in Steinbach on Lake Atter, where he had taken lodgings in an inn together with his sister Justine. As Natalie Bauer-Lechner reports, he had a "composing cottage" built on a meadow between the inn and the lake in order to be able to work completely undisturbed and shielded from the noise of the world. Natalie was a woman who lived for many years in the immediate vicinity of her revered idol and to whom, as to no other person, Mahler confided the deepest secrets of his thinking and his compositional creations, but whose love he did not return. In one of their conversations, they also discussed his feelings during the development process of a composition, in which he believed he noticed analogies between physical and mental birth:

Mahler's "composition cottage" in Steinbach on Lake Atter, to which Gustav Mahler withdrew in the summer months of 1893 to 1897 for hours of uninterrupted composition work.

What indiscretion and lack of delicacy that violates any inner shame there is in exposing to others' ears the yet undeveloped being which is still in the process of originating! It seems to be like wanting to show the child in its mother's womb to the world.

When he suspected that someone wanted to observe him or was even trying to get near him as he composed, he was unable to continue working. This absolute shielding off needed by him for his work was, however, by no means only external in nature. Just as his creative activity was incompatible with conducting—for which reason he always had to relegate the work on his symphonies to the summer holidays—so, in order to be able to compose,

he frequently had to shut himself off from his closest environment and from people he loved and was close to.

During the work on his Third Symphony, this also applied to
Anna von Mildenburg, with whom he was already engaged. This
extraordinarily gifted young singer was a student of Rosa Papier,
a teacher at the Vienna Conservatory, who herself had been a
grandiose Wagner-singer at the Viennese Court Opera and recommended her student to Hamburg in 1895. At her first rehearsal
with the strict Kapellmeister Gustav Mahler, whom her colleagues
had described to her as a real tyrant, she felt "a redeeming trust
that freed her of all doubts and fears and an infinite sense of
being sheltered." Later, when she became a celebrated, great
Wagner-singer, she owed this primarily to him, whom she soon
looked up to with great reverence and who more and more also
conquered her heart. Mahler, too, loved this woman, whom he
also felt to be a valuable spiritual partner, so that nothing stood in
the way of an engagement of the two compatible beings. But
during Mahler's work on the Third Symphony, at the latest, she
learned what renunciation he expected of a woman who "is supposed to live with him." Whereas he had previously written a
letter to her almost every day, during the summer months at Lake
Atter, the correspondence declined noticeably—which his twenty-
year-old fiancée could not understand. The explanation for his
behavior casts revealing light on his mental state during the birth
of a symphony:

> Don't you understand that this requires the whole
> person and that one is so often so deeply immersed
> in it as if dead to the outside world....I have ex-
> plained this to you so often and you must accept
> it if you really understand me. See, everyone who
> is supposed to live with me must accept this. In
> such moments I no longer belong to myself....The
> creator of such a work suffers terrible birth pangs;
> and a great deal of preoccupation, concentration,
> and mortification from the outside world is needed
> before all this is ordered, constructed, and con-
> jured up in his head.

Possibly his work intensity also helped him to overcome the loss of his brother Otto, on whom he had set such great hopes as a composer. Otto took his own life at the age of twenty with a pistol shot because—as he wrote in a few farewell words on a sheet of paper—he no longer enjoyed life and for that reason was giving his entry ticket back to life.

"The God of Southern Zones"

As early as 1895, Mahler began to look into the possibilities of an assignment in Vienna, in order to finally bring his long-cherished dream of a "call to the God of southern zones" closer to reality. Mounting tensions between himself and the Hamburg Director Pollini strengthened him in this resolve, although he fully realized the almost insurmountable difficulties connected with this plan. One impediment especially preoccupied him:

> The way things now stand in the world, my Juda-
> ism debars me from access to the Court Theater.
> Neither Vienna, nor Berlin, nor Dresden, nor
> Munich stands open to me. The same wind blows
> everywhere.

Under these circumstances, the performance of his Second Symphony on 13 December 1895 in Berlin was very important. For, according to Bruno Walter, who experienced this event, the "impression of the greatness and originality of the work, of the power of Mahler's nature, was so deep that his rise as a composer can be dated from that day on." Incidentally, Bruno Walter was similarly impressed by Mahler's Third Symphony when the composer played the just completed work on the piano:

> The power and newness of its musical language
> absolutely stunned me....Only now and only
> through this music did I believe I knew him. His
> whole being seemed to me to breathe a mysteri-
> ous solidarity with nature. How deep, how
> elementary it was, I had always been able only to

intimate, but now I experienced it directly from the musical language of his symphonic dream of worlds.

This had created the basis for Mahler's recognition as a symphonist. Now he used all his influence and personal connections to achieve his dream of a "call to the God of southern zones." In this struggle, Anna von Mildenburg and her former teacher Rosa Papier, mother of the later famous Mozart interpreter and Mozart scholar Bernhard Paumgartner, were valuable helpers. Since the resignation of Wilhelm Jahn, the prior Kapellmeister at the Vienna Court Opera, for health reasons had already been decided upon, Mahler wrote to the manager of the Court Theater, Joseph von Beseczny, on 21 December 1896 applying for the newly opened position. Two days later, in order to remove—as he thought—a decisive obstacle, he sent a second letter, probably to the Chancellery Director Wlassik, in which he made the supplementary remark:

> Given the current circumstances in Vienna I do not consider it superfluous to inform you that a long time ago, in accord with an old desire, I converted to Catholicism.

His Catholic baptism took place on 23 February 1897 in the little Michaelis-Church in Hamburg, and the contract engaging him as Kapellmeister at the Vienna Court Theater was signed on 15 April 1897, initially for one year starting on 1 June. Mahler's indication that he had converted to the Catholic faith "a long time ago" takes on an opportunistic tinge under these circumstances. Although Alma Mahler in her biography denies an opportunistic motive, asserting that Mahler "believed in Christ and by no means had himself baptized only out of opportunism in order to obtain the position as director of the Court Theater in Vienna," it must be concluded from various references in his letters that the timing of his conversion was chosen in view of the sought-after call to Vienna. That this step must not at all have been easy for him to take can be concluded from a report of his biographer, Ludwig Karpath. He reports Mahler as saying:

> What really offends and annoys me is that I had to be baptized to obtain a position; I cannot get over it....Undeniably, it cost me a great deal of self-overcoming—it can well be said—to have to do from a sense of self-preservation an action one was internally not averse to doing anyway.

This last hint underscores the presumption that Mahler's inner turn to Christianity must surely have occurred long before. Information given by Natalie Bauer-Lechner points in the same direction, for christological questions fascinated him long before his conversion, and it can also be proved definitively from other sources that Christian dogma, mysticism, and eschatology occupied a privileged and prominent place in his faith-world. How strongly Mahler was permeated with Catholicism is also evidenced by his later wife Alma Schindler in her memoirs when she tells of a conversation from 1901 with her fiancé who "believed in Christ," whom she also called a "Jewish Christian":

> Although raised a Catholic, later influenced by Schopenhauer and Nietzsche I became very much a free thinker. Mahler heatedly opposed this mentality, and the strange paradox ensued that a Jew was arguing zealously for Christ with a Christian woman.

Mahler's Christian faith must, after all this evidence, surely have been genuine and have taken form years before his actual conversion. Otherwise, it would be hard to understand the convincing setting to music of Klopstock's text for the Resurrection chorale of his Second Symphony, the so-called "Resurrection Symphony," completed in 1894.

After his debut as conductor of the Vienna Opera House with the performance of *Lohengrin* on 11 May 1897, he reported to Anna von Mildenburg in Hamburg: "All Vienna greeted me enthusiastically....It can hardly be doubted any more that I will in the foreseeable future become director," a prophecy fulfilled by 12 October. Why from that moment on the personal ties between the two engaged persons began unraveling, we do not know.

The only thing certain is that a gradual separation occurred without destroying the ties of friendship and artistic understanding between them. Even on the occasion of Mahler's dismissal from the Court Opera in December 1907, he assured Frau von Mildenburg, who became the wife of Hermann Bahr in 1909, that for her "even from afar he remained a friend she could count on."

Today everyone agrees that the Mahler era marked a "golden age" of the Vienna Opera. His supreme maxim was to preserve the integrity of the work of art created for the opera, and he subjected everything else unconditionally to that principle. This applied even to the auditorium, whose entire staff had to be committed to discipline and unconditional dedication to the work. When Hans Richter resigned from the directorship of the Philharmonic concerts, Mahler was entrusted with that function. His authoritarian rule, whereby he tried to impose his will completely on the musicians, as well as his fanatic rehearsal work, soon brought him into disfavor with the musicians of the Philharmonic. Mahler's revisions of the instrumentation of important works of world literature contributed further to this loss of favor, since they placed an additional burden on the orchestra. On the other hand, his merits were recognized and valued positively by the members of the orchestra.

After a successful concert journey to Paris in June 1900, Mahler retreated to the beneficial silence and solitude of his Kärnten refuge in Maiernigg, where in that same summer he finished writing his Fourth Symphony. It is one of his symphonies that most quickly won a broader public and today is felt to be a thoroughly "friendly work"—quite in contrast with the rather unfriendly reception it got at its premiere in Munich in the fall of 1901. But soon even his opponents at the time, such as William Ritter, born in French Switzerland, realized that Mahler by his musical innovations was in the process of shaping the music of the early 20th century, and, alluding to a comparison with the Vienna Secession, he wrote a few years later:

> Play this music in the architectural space of Otto
> Wagner, with staging and costumes by Klimt and
> Kolo Moser, and it will symbolize modern Vienna.

In fact, Mahler was closely associated with the artists of the Vienna Secession, and he participated as a musical editor, for instance by revising a section of Beethoven's Ninth Symphony for a Max Klinger Exposition in the Secession; and he even hired one of the members of the Association of Artists, Alfred Roller, as director of staging and costumes at the Court Opera, thus beginning the most brilliant period of his activity as an opera director.

In April 1901, Mahler announced to the musicians of the Vienna Philharmonic that due to his weakened health he "no longer felt capable of directing the Philharmonic concerts." One thing that led to this decision was an ailment that gave him considerable trouble early in 1901. Internal hemorrhoids, his "subterranean ailment," as he expressed it, had already been causing him some pains for quite some time, but also repeated bleedings. The worst incident of this kind occurred in the evening of 24 February 1901 during the presentation of the *Magic Flute*. Only with effort was he able to conceal from the people around him how miserable he felt, for a real hemorrhage followed. According to an eyewitness report he looked "like Lucifer: his face white, his eyes burning coals. I empathized deeply with him and told the people around me, 'This man will not be able to endure that.'" This statement came from none other than Alma, who at that time did not yet know Mahler personally. When the Emperor learned that his Chief Director had that night been practically swimming in his own blood, he gave orders for the then famous surgeon, von Hochenegg, to personally take charge of the illustrious patient. After an operation had immediately been performed, the third of this kind, Mahler, considerably weakened by loss of blood, had to go on a recuperation leave in Abbazia. For several months, he reportedly was able to walk only with two canes, and his awareness of having escaped death by a hair seems to have shaken him more than the physical pain. But with the start of summer his old activity returned. Only his unusually long stays on the toilet, which he sometimes alluded to jokingly, pointed to the traces of the operation that had been performed. Yet during the summer vacation in Maiernigg, besides a few songs, he was composing his Fifth Symphony and was able to finish the first two movements.

During his stay in Paris in June 1900, he had made an acquaintanceship that was decisive for the rest of his life, namely, with Berta Zuckerkandl, sister-in-law of George Clemenceau, and wife of the respected anatomist Emil Zuckerkandl. This extremely cultured, musically schooled lady, devoted to the Vienna Secessionists, ran a kind of salon in Vienna, where the most renowned artists of the city met and where Mahler likewise was invited. And there he met the woman of his life, the young Alma Maria Schindler, daughter of the famous landscape painter, Emil Jacob Schindler. The twenty-two-year-old girl seems to have radiated an unusual fascination on others, for not only Gustav Klimt, but also Max Burckhard, who had resigned from the office of director of the Burgtheater, fell in love with her; and the same thing happened to Mahler. From the first moment he was seized by a passionate affection, and she too was deeply impressed by his personality: "I must admit that he pleased me tremendously. Of course, he is terribly nervous. He sprang about the room like a wild animal. The man is pure oxygen; you burn up if you get too close to him," she wrote in her diary. So it is not surprising that a few weeks after their first meeting, namely, on 28 December 1901, the official engagement of the two was announced. But while he was absolutely sure of his cause, Alma was not so sure about her feelings for him, whose music she strongly disliked. Her uncertainty can be seen from a diary entry: "I don't know whether I love him or not, whether I love the opera director, the famous conductor, or the man." There was also the circumstance that Mahler no doubt must have been a far better conductor than lover, for in her diary we read of their first intimate relations: "His male strength lets him down...he lies there and sobs with shame...a failure, speechless." And a few weeks later, she was unsettled by an event that no doubt was connected with his hemorrhoidal ailments, but which she in her inexperience associated with other causes:

> My poor Gustav had to undergo a medical treatment. Inflammation, swelling, ice-bag, sitting baths, etc. Is my resistance possibly to blame?

Finally, there was a further point that touched her unpleasantly and even led to a painful argument shortly before their engagement, namely, his categorical "prohibition" for her to continue composing. To understand the effect of this measure in her mind, it must be known that Alma had already produced quite significant compositions. Indeed, a few of her songs, according to a recent study, deserve not to be forgotten. If she nonetheless was willing tearfully to accede to his wishes, this did not mean that she had given up composing definitively from an artistic point of view. For in her diary she wrote: "From now on I must struggle by all means to claim the place that is mine. I mean from an artistic perspective. He has a low opinion of my art and a very high one of his, and I have a low opinion of his art, but a very high one of mine," and in fact all her life she was not willing to accept Mahler's greatness as a composer. Her own sketches reveal that she was probably influenced by Burckhard's theory that a Jew could never become a genuine productive artist. On 9 March 1902 the wedding ceremony was celebrated in the Karls-Church in Vienna. In St. Petersburg, where Mahler conducted several concerts and where the young couple at the same time spent their honeymoon, during a supper at the Duke of Mecklenburg's, Mahler got one of his terrible migraine headaches that plagued him from time to time. Otherwise this stay in Russia went successfully, and Alma's pregnancy, "a source of great torments," was no longer accompanied by the illnesses that had earlier assailed her.

The couple spent the summer in Maiernigg on Lake Wörth, where likewise a little "composing cottage" had been constructed, in which Mahler immediately began working on his Fifth Symphony. In the afternoon Mahler used to go swimming in the lake, for he was an excellent swimmer and not deterred even by ice-cold water. Long rides on a bicycle also gave him great pleasure. His eating habits were relatively Spartan. Everything had to be boiled soft, and he tolerated only light, nearly unspiced foods, which Alma could not understand. But she suffered most from the solitude to which she was condemned for hours on end while he was working on a symphony. She complained about this in her diary: "I have lost all my friends and found instead one who does not understand me." The loving dedication of his completed Fifth Symphony was no help: "To my dearest Almie, my brave and loyal companion."

On 3 November, a girl was born, and baptized with the name Maria Anna. The birth was extremely difficult, because the child was in a breech position. When the doctor told this to Mahler after the successful delivery, Mahler answered with relief: "That is exactly my child, she shows the world what it deserves: her backside!" In June 1903 the next child was born and received the name Anna Justine. Again the summer months in Maiernigg were used by Mahler for composing, while Alma spent the time with the two children. In view of the happy and satisfied mood, attributable to quite an extent to the blessing of children, Alma found it strange, indeed unsettling, that her husband precisely at this point in time wished to compose *Kindertotenlieder (Songs on the Death of Children)* and would not let her dissuade him from this plan.

It is hardly imaginable for us today how Mahler in the years from 1901 to 1905, his most successful period as an opera director and concert conductor, could still muster the energy to create those three symphonies, V, VI, and VII, which "initiated the symphonic history of our century." As Alma Mahler stressed, his Sixth was "his most personal work, and moreover a prophetic one." Presumably the artist, forced with strong inner tensions during the process of creating such tremendous works, literally thirsted for a counterbalancing practical activity, and he found it in his work as conductor. Nor did he feel all these burdens to be an overexertion at all, and when friends occasionally warned him of his exhausted appearance, he explained this condition as a "very ordinary physical tiredness" and no more. Romain Rolland in 1905 wrote a very laudatory essay on Mahler and believed him to be at the height of his powers; nonetheless, he thought "that Mahler was suffering severely from the hypnosis of power which drove him to almost feverish activity."

There is sharp contrast between his mighty symphonies, which tended to revolutionize everything previous both in form and instrumentation, and his *Songs on the Death of Children*, also written in the glorious year 1905, although some had been written four years earlier and he was now publishing their second cycle. The text was written by Friedrich Rückert after the death of two of his children and published only posthumously. Why Mahler wanted to put precisely these heartrending poems to music has given posterity a few psychological riddles, and some writers, among them Mahler's wife Alma, saw it as virtually a challenge to fate. Indeed, Alma even saw the fate that was fulfilled two years later with the death of Mahler's older little daughter as a punishment for such a sacrilege. But it is part of Mahler's profile and it must therefore be underscored here that he finished composing these *Songs on the Death of Children* at a time when the possibility of himself being afflicted by a similar misfortune could never have entered his head. If any motive played a role in his choice of Rückert's texts, from a psychological perspective it would have to be sought in his childhood—for instance in the painful remembrance of the death of his beloved brother Ernst, whom he had seen dying as a child, or the loss of his brother Otto, with so many musical talents, whose life had ended so tragically by suicide. These memories, engraved deeply into his soul, show why Mahler was so moved by Rückert's heartrending death plaints that he felt the urge to set those lyrical texts to music. He selected the five songs with a particularly moving, deep mood, and by linking them into a unity he created a deeply stirring new work. The purity and the simple fervor of the music literally "ennobled" the words "and lifted them to the height of a salvation."

At this point it seems appropriate to take a brief look at Mahler's faith in the doctrine of predestination and of art as the anticipation of destiny. According to statements by Richard Specht, who knew Mahler in his Hamburg period, the composer believed firmly in a "meaningful rule by a predestinating world being," and he therefore condemned suicide and denied man any right "to interfere over-hastily and prematurely to impede the higher plan in which the individual is interwoven from the primeval beginning." Given such a conviction, the suicide of his brother Otto must have struck him especially hard. But beyond this, Mahler knew how to relate his faith to the artistic experience. As a complete determinist, he was convinced "that in hours of inspiration the creative power anticipates in his production the experience that everyday life must later bring." Specht reports that it often happened to Mahler "that he wrote in tones what happened only later." And Alma, too, in her memoirs reports twice of Mahler's conviction that with the *Songs on the Death of Children* and with his Sixth Symphony he "musically anticipated" his life. Paul Stefan's statement in his biography agrees with these reports: "Mahler used to say that his works were anticipated events."

The year 1906 was dedicated to the 150th anniversary of Mozart's birth. For Mahler this meant the new staging of no less than five Mozart productions in the Vienna Court Opera and, on the Emperor's instructions, a festive performance of *Figaro* in the city of Mozart's birth. This performance was later described by Bernhard Paumgartner as "the most important ensemble-achievement of the Salzburg Music Festival, perhaps of recent operatic history in general." For this festive event, Mahler had to interrupt briefly his summer vacation in Maiernigg, which was not very convenient for him. For he was in the process of completing a new symphony, truly gigantic in scale, requiring almost a thousand musicians for its performance. By August, radiant with joy, he was able to write to his Dutch friend, Wilhelm Mengelberg, giving him the news:

> I have just completed my Eighth Symphony—it is
> the greatest thing I have ever done. And so unique
> in content and form that it is impossible to write
> about it. Just imagine that the universe begins to
> ring and resound. It is no longer human voices
> but planets and suns circling in their orbits.

This joy at the completion of this gigantic work was followed by successes he reaped by the performance of various of his symphonies in Berlin, Breslau, and Munich, so that he was able to greet the New Year full of confidence.

The Fateful Year 1907

The year 1907 was to be a fateful year for Gustav Mahler. A press campaign against him began early in the year, criticizing his way of running his business as director of the Opera. At the same time the Chief Forester Prince Montenuovo deplored the quality of the offerings and the decline in income of the Court Opera caused by the many leaves the conductor took to perform concerts abroad. Of course, such attacks worried him, as did rumors that arose about his imminent resignation, although outwardly he gave the appearance of inner calm. Alfred Roller, his stage decorator, wrote on 29 April 1907 to his wife:

> I admire Mahler for not letting himself be thrown off balance, but going his way step by step. It seems that now all forces are to be united to bring him to a fall. If people only knew how glad he is to leave!

In fact, once the possibility of his resigning became known, several attractive offers came fluttering to Mahler's door, and he found the one from New York most attractive. After brief negotiations, a contract with Heinrich Conried, manager of the Metropolitan Opera, was agreed upon, stipulating that Mahler, starting in November 1907, was to work at the Metropolitan for four years, three months per year. In May 1907, when he definitely handed in his resignation, Alma was not exactly happy, but she was visibly relieved because at least his future income would exceed many times over what he had been paid as director of the Vienna Court Opera.

Mahler decided to spend the remaining time until November together with his family in Maiernigg resting from the excessive exertions of the past year. Instead, in Maiernigg the tragedy of his life occurred. In a letter of 4 July 1907, he informed his friend, the physicist Arnold Berliner of signing the contract with New York, and he added the so significant words:

> We are having terrible bad luck! I'll tell you more in person. Now my oldest daughter has scarlet fever—diphtheria!

In fact, his four-year-old daughter Maria Anna, whom he tenderly called "Putzi" and with whom he was attached with special love, had fallen ill with diphtheria. Since a vaccine or a diphtheria antitoxin was not available then, this disease meant death for many children. Putzi struggled for fourteen days, until one evening choking spells ensued and the quickly summoned doctor tried to stop them by an immediate tracheotomy. But twenty-four hours later the child was dead. Mahler, shaken by a paroxysm of tears, ran confusedly through the house; for him the death of this child was a terrible tragedy. Putzi, with her independent character and her musical talent, took completely after her father and so his relation to her was especially close, as Alma described it:

> She was his child. Marvelously beautiful and obstinate, at the same time unapproachable, she promised to become dangerous. Black curls, big blue eyes! Though it was not granted to her to live a long life, she was chosen to have been his joy for a few years, and that in itself has eternal value.

When the little child's coffin was taken away two days later, Alma fell unconscious and Dr. Blumenthal had to be called in. Before leaving, he gave Mahler a physical examination. The result was as surprising as it was alarming, for this doctor, apparently not overendowed with psychological talents, said only: "Well, you don't need to be proud of this heart!" Worried by this vague pronouncement, Mahler went to Vienna without delay, to get a more precise diagnosis from Dr. Kovacs. It was:

> Compensated heart valve defect with narrowing of the mitral valve opening; hence all bodily exertion must be avoided starting immediately.

For Mahler this revelation was a heavy blow. He was an enthusiastic hiker, bicyclist, and swimmer, and he was also able to row on Lake Wörth so strongly and rapidly that as a rule only a few people could keep up with him. Accordingly, with a height of only 5 feet, 4 inches, he had an athletically trained body that surprised many a bathing guest by its muscular build. And now

ALMA MAHLER WITH THEIR
TWO DAUGHTERS MARIA ANNA
AND ANNA JUSTINA. MARIA
ANNA'S DEATH IN 1907
PLUNGED GUSTAV MAHLER
INTO A DEEP CRISIS.

he was supposed to avoid any physical activity, something he could hardly imagine. A further problem from now on was the constant fear of any movement—mentally a tremendous additional burden.

On 24 November an extraordinary concert of the Society of Music Friends was given, at which Mahler said farewell to his Viennese friends by a performance of his Second Symphony. According to a press report, the conductor was moved to tears by the wild, seemingly unending applause and the cheers of the audience, the orchestra, and the singing club. He wrote a farewell letter to the members of the Court Opera, showing that he left the city without rancor:

> The hour has come that puts a limit to our common activity. I am leaving from a place of work that has become dear to me, and I hereby tell you farewell. Instead of something whole and rounded, as I dreamed, I am leaving behind incomplete

piecework, as is man's fate....Under pressure of the struggle, in the heat of the moment neither you nor I were spared wounds and confusion. But when a work succeeded or a task was resolved, we forgot all hardship and effort and we felt richly rewarded—even without external signs of success....I give my heartfelt thanks to all of you who have supported me in my difficult, often thankless task; you have helped and struggled together with me.

He found it harder to say farewell to his closest friends, especially the Zuckerkandl family, whom he visited last and to whom he spoke words that were intended to console himself:

I am taking my homeland with me. My Alma, my child. And only now that the heavy work-load is removed from me, do I know what my most beautiful task from now on will be. Alma has sacrificed ten years of her youth for me. No one knows, nor can ever know, with what absolute unselfishness she subordinated her life to me and to my work. With a light heart I go my way with her.

After selling their home in Maiernigg, which would have only reminded them of the tragedy they had suffered, nothing stood in the way of their departure. Once again, Mahler was deeply moved. For about two hundred people gathered to say farewell and shake his hand one last time—among them Alban Berg, Arnold Schönberg, Gustav Klimt, and Anton von Webern, who had organized this surprise. When he boarded ship in Cherbourg together with his family, a farewell telegram was waiting for him there, worded as follows:

Dear Friend. With all my heart, good luck with your journey on the beautiful ship, on which I made the return trip from America years ago. Come back happily to beloved Europe, which needs men like you as its daily bread.

Your Gerhart Hauptmann.

And actually, despite all exhilarating successes in America, Austria and its capital remained his real homeland, although formerly he often used to say to Alma:

> I am triply without a homeland: as a Bohemian among the Austrians, as an Austrian among the Germans, and as a Jew in the whole world. Everywhere, one is an intruder; and wanted nowhere.

On 1 January 1908, Mahler took up his activity as conductor at the Metropolitan Opera in New York with the performance of *Tristan and Isolde*. The family lived luxuriously in an apartment of the elegant Hotel Majestic, where they had complete privacy. Gustav fearfully avoided any physical strain and in general had changed greatly since the death of his beloved child. He had become more sociable, although he still drummed on the table and "scraped his feet like a wild boar." This habit was noticed many years before by Natalie Bauer-Lechner, when he came along with his peculiarly agitated stride: "He lifts a leg and stomps on the floor like a horse. He never takes more than two steps in the same rhythm." This often disturbing twitching and stomping of the right leg was already mentioned with regret in the sketches of the Kassel Theater. And these uncontrolled movements were noticed in Vienna, too. Leo Slezak spoke of a "syncopated" running stride, and Alfred Roller, too, described this "twitch foot" in his portrayal of Gustav Mahler's external appearance. But no one was able to give a real interpretation of this strange stride. It seems certain, in retrospect, that it was probably not of organic origin, since he was able, without difficulty, to stop this twitching by conscious application of his will. But as soon as his concentration on this process declined due to an external distraction, the twitching of his right foot returned. To explain this nervous phenomenon, someone made the hypothesis that it was connected with the memory of his dearly loved mother, who definitely limped.

When in spring the previous manager of the Metropolitan Opera, Heinrich Conried, resigned and was replaced by the Director of the Milan Scala, who brought along Arturo Toscanini as his conductor, Mahler felt so insecure that he was thinking of terminating his contract. But before he returned to Europe in spring, he had abandoned this idea. After his arrival in Hamburg in April 1908 he conducted his First Symphony in Wiesbaden, then he withdrew to Tolbach in South Tirol, where he had found a spacious house for his summer holidays. In the garden house, which again became his "work room," he composed the draft to his *Song of the Earth* for two singing voices and orchestra in which the strength of the orchestra stands between that of the songs and the symphonies. Mahler was so delighted with an anthology of old and new Chinese lyrics assembled in verse translation by Hans Bethke, that he selected the seven most beautiful poems from this book and translated them into his own language. With the last song, "The Farewell," the heartrending complaint dies without finding the peace of a redeeming final chord. In this connection, Paul Bekker speaks of Mahler's "old-age style," full of intimations of the future and speaking his own judgment as if subconsciously. How very much the work matches his state of mind, matured by the experience of death, can be intimated from a remark of Bruno Walter's in his autobiography:

> It was the first time he did not play a new work for me himself—probably he feared the excitement. I studied it and experienced a time of the most terrible emotion from this uniquely passionate, bitter, resigned, and blessing sound of farewell and fading away.

Alma Mahler, too, wrote about this summer in Toblach:

> This summer, full of grief over the lost child, full of concern for Mahler's health, was the hardest and saddest we had experienced and were to experience together.

What it looked like in his heart during those months was depicted by Mahler in a letter to Bruno Walter:

> I want to tell you that at a single stroke I have simply lost all clarity and calmness I had ever acquired, and I stood facing nothingness (*vis-à-vis de rien*) and now at the end of my life I have to learn to walk and stand again.

This was almost literally true of his physical condition, for according to his doctor's senseless instructions he had to "accustom himself to walking with watch in hand," stopping again and again at intervals to count his pulse.

After returning to New York, some difficulties arose, as could be expected, from the new situation of having to work side by side with Toscanini. But a circumstance came his way and held up hope of fulfilling a lifelong desire, namely, the management of a concert orchestra. On the initiative of a few wealthy ladies who had admired his abilities as a conductor in the previous season, it was accomplished that the unrestricted command over the New York Philharmonic Orchestra was transferred to him, and he celebrated his debut on 31 March 1909 at Carnegie Hall. After obtaining this position as the fulfillment of his desires, he returned to Europe to spend the summer composing his Ninth Symphony, which, like the *Song of the Earth*, was made known only after his death and was completed in final form during his third stay in New York. Mahler, who went through a severe grippe shortly before departure, spent the summer in Toblach again, while his wife, whose state of health likewise was damaged due to a second miscarriage, was sent, together with her daughter, to a spa in Levico, not far from Trient. In the joyous feeling of having escaped the grueling operatic activity, he felt like "another man," for whom the "habit of existence" was sweeter than ever. The only drop of bitterness was that his heart ailment manifested itself in accelerated pulse and states of anxiety: "An ordinary modest march gives me such an accelerated pulse and anxiety that I do not achieve its purpose of forgetting one's body," he wrote to Bruno Walter. And in a letter to his wife he said:

> I now shudder at the thought of my various composing cottages; although I spent the most beautiful hours of my life there, probably I have had to pay for it with my health.

The insecure feeling of fear that speaks from these lines finds a parallel in the thoughts that moved him while composing his Ninth Symphony. For Mahler feared that by this work he was probably challenging fate, since death had carried away Beethoven,

Schubert, Bruckner, and Dvořák after they had reached this number of their symphonies! He also wrote something similar in a
letter to Arnold Schönberg:

> The Ninth Symphony seems to be a boundary.
> Whoever goes beyond it must die. It seems as if
> the Tenth could tell us something we are not sup-
> posed to know, for which we are not mature
> enough. Those who have written a Ninth stood
> close to the Beyond.

Marital Crisis and Outbreak of Disease

In the autumn of 1909, Mahler came to New York for the third
time, but this time to open a concert season. To all appearances
the winter passed without troubling incidents and the successes
of his tours through the United States apparently put Mahler in a
happy mood. For he wrote to Vienna: "I look healthy, have
normal weight, and am tolerating the great deal of work outstandingly." When he returned to Europe in this mood, after
giving some concerts in Paris, Rome, and Munich, he concentrated his whole energy on the "Symphony of a Thousand," which
had been finished some years before, that is, his Eighth, which
was to be performed for the first time in September. Before beginning his summer vacation in Toblach, on the doctors' advice
he sent his young wife for treatment at the popular Tobel spa
without suspecting what consequences would follow from this
decision. For there Alma found a soothing and healing of her
ailments not in the thermal springs, but in the form of the young,
blond architect, Walter Gropius—later famous as founder of the
Bauhaus, one of the most famous art academies in the world.

While Alma lay in Gropius' arms at night, Mahler was worry-
ing about the "tormenting ailments" she had to bear, and when
her "short, sad letters" became shorter and shorter, he wrote
worriedly: "Are you hiding something from me? For I believe I
am always reading something between the lines." After Alma had
finished her treatment period in Tobel spa and returned to her

husband in Toblach, she regularly received letters general delivery from Gropius assuring her that he could no longer live without her and pleading with her to leave everything and come to him. And now something happened for which Gropius even later could not give a satisfactory explanation. He wrote his lover a passionate letter urging her especially fervently to leave Mahler and come to him—and he sent this letter to Mr. Director Gustav Mahler! It cannot be assumed that this was an accidental oversight in the sense of mere "absentmindedness," but rather an action by which Gropius hoped best to obtain a decision in his favor. Mahler was aware that all this was the result of years of repression of all mental impulses and feelings of his wife, whom he had treated almost as a bodiless being and whose individuality he thus had quite erased. We know that this gradually brought Alma to such desperation that she finally summarized her situation with the words: "I am married with an abstraction, not with a human being." All of a sudden it now became clear to Mahler that he had actually in all those years been blind to everything that existed outside his art, and accordingly he reacted to Alma's admission after opening the fateful letter "neither annoyed nor embittered." What was going on within him resembled rather an inner process of dissolution, always with the fearful thoughts on his mind of losing his beautiful young wife. He did what accorded with his clean and forthright character as a man by taking the first step and seeking a direct conversation with Gropius. When Alma, after initial hesitation, sought him out in his room, to which he had withdrawn, he received her very calmly with the words: "Whatever you do will be done rightly. You decide." What things really looked like inside him can be learned from Alma's diary:

> He was in a state of utmost internal turmoil. At that time he wrote all those exclamations and words to me into the rough draft of the score of the Tenth Symphony.

These sentences scribbled fleetingly on the rough score give us a moving impression of Mahler's frame of mind:

> Oh God, oh God, why have you abandoned me!...
> You alone know what that means!...Ah! Ah! Ah!
> Farewell, my music!...To live for you, to die for
> you, Almie!

From now on, the relationship in his marriage turned completely around. Whereas formerly he exclusively made decisions, now he subjected himself unconditionally to her rule to the point of self-denial. He even took out Alma's compositions, and his enthusiasm for her songs, which he had previously totally ignored, now knew no bounds, as he himself avowed:

> My dear songs, the delightful heralds of a divine
> Being, should be my guiding stars until the sun of
> my life appears in my firmament.

And he could hardly expect this sun every day:

> How I long to see you and hold you in my arms.
> You dear, deeply loved one....She loves me! This
> statement is the quintessence of my life! When I
> may no longer say that, I am dead!

In this desperate situation, his infinite love for Alma became conscious. And from fear of losing her he began to humiliate himself to the point of masochistic self-surrender, so he decided to seek out Sigmund Freud, who at this time was on vacation in Holland. He postponed the appointment twice—perhaps also because of his damaged general health due to an angina he had survived once again—until finally he boarded the train for Leyden. There exist three different reports on this memorable meeting between the two great men, Freud and Mahler, namely, the sketches of the Freud biographer Ernest Jones, the report of Freud's pupil Marie Bonaparte, and a letter of Freud's to the ardent Mahler admirer and psychoanalyst Theodor Reik. Jones writes:

> During the summer of 1910, Gustav Mahler was
> greatly distressed about his relationship with his
> wife, and Dr. Nepallek, a Viennese psychoanalyst
> who was a relative of Mahler's wife, advised him
> to consult Freud. He telegraphed from the Tyrol
> to Freud, who was vacationing that year on the

THE MANUSCRIPT OF THE TENTH SYMPHONY SHOWS GUSTAV MAHLER'S DESPAIRING
STRUGGLE FOR HIS WIFE ALMA'S LOVE.

Baltic coast, asking for an appointment. Freud
was always loathe to interrupt his holidays for any
professional work, but he could not refuse a man
of Mahler's worth. His telegram making an appointment, however, was followed by another one
from Mahler countermanding it. Soon there came
another request, with the same result. Mahler suffered from the *folie de doute* of his obsessional
neurosis and repeated his performance three times.
Finally Freud had to tell him that his last chance of
seeing him was before the end of August, since he
was planning to leave then for Sicily. So they met
in a hotel in Leyden and then spent four hours
strolling through the town and conducting a sort
of psychoanalysis. Although Mahler had had no
previous contact with psychoanalysis, Freud said

he had never met anyone who seemed to understand it so swiftly. Mahler was greatly impressed by a remark of Freud's: "I take it your mother was called Marie. I should surmise it from various hints in your conversation. How comes it that you married someone with another name, Alma, since your mother evidently played a dominating part in your life?" Mahler then told him his wife's name was Alma Maria, but that he called her Marie! She was the daughter of the famous painter Schindler, whose statue stands in the Vienna City Park, so a name probably played a part in her life too. This analytic talk evidently produced an effect, since Mahler recovered his potency and the marriage was a happy one until his death, which unfortunately took place only a year later.

After hours of conversation, Freud actually succeeded in calming Mahler. This concerned especially the great difference in age, which caused Mahler worries, but in Freud's view precisely that was what made him so attractive to a young, cultured, and beautiful woman. So it came that Alma, who loved her father, could bind herself only to a man who offered her a fatherly substitute; while Mahler in turn was seeking his wife completely in the likeness of his suffering and embittered mother. When Alma Mahler reported this finding of Sigmund Freud's psychoanalysis, she wrote in her diary:

> And how right Freud was in both these cases! When he met me he wanted to have me "more long-suffering"—these were his words. I, in turn, really was always seeking a little man with wisdom and with intellectual superiority, such as I had known and loved in my father.

Freud's statement to his student, Marie Bonaparte, dealt with another chapter in Mahler's life, namely, music—an area that interested psychoanalysis only peripherally and perhaps for that reason it misled him to a highly dubious conclusion:

In the course of the talk Mahler suddenly said that now he understood why his music had always prevented him from achieving the highest rank through the noblest passages, those inspired by the most profound emotions, being spoiled by the intrusion of some commonplace melody. His father, apparently a brutal person, treated his wife very badly, and when Mahler was a young boy there was a specially painful scene between them. It became quite unbearable to the boy, who rushed away from the house. At that moment, however, a hurdy-gurdy in the street was grinding out the popular Viennese air "*Ach, Du lieber Augustin.*" In Mahler's opinion the conjunction of high tragedy and light amusement was from then on inextricably fixed in his mind, and the one mood inevitably brought the other with it.

Problematic as this interpretation of Mahler may be in this report of Sigmund Freud's, the statement made to Theodor Reik a few years later proved that the analytical conversation in Leyden had some effect on Mahler:

I analyzed Mahler for an afternoon in the year 1912 (or 1913) [it was 1910] in Leyden. If I may believe reports, I achieved much with him at that time. The visit appeared necessary for him, because his wife at that time rebelled against the fact that he withdrew his libido from her. In highly interesting expeditions through his life history, we discovered his personal conditions for love, especially his Holy Mary complex (mother fixation). I had plenty of opportunity to admire the capability for psychological understanding of this man of genius. No light fell at that time on the symptomatic façade of his obsessional neurosis. It was as if you would dig a single shaft through a mysterious building.

Much as Mahler's meeting with Freud brought relief and enabled him to live a normal life again, Alma was confused by the change in her husband, who now literally showered her with proofs of his love. She described this to her lover as follows:

> I am, for my part, experiencing something I would not have considered possible. Namely, that love is so boundless, that my remaining—despite all that has happened—will be life for him; and my leaving, his death.

And this certainty that she would be killing Mahler if she left him was surely the reason she finally dropped any such idea and remained by his side as a lovingly caring spouse and married Gropius only many years later.

Toward the end of the summer holidays in Toblach, Mahler immersed himself in work as if possessed. How much he had to struggle internally with self-reproach and despair is indicated by other handwritten comments in the draft of the Tenth Symphony: "The devil dances it with me! Madness seizes me, damned as I am; annihilate me, so I will forget I exist." This is written above the second scherzo. These statements give the impression that he was starting to lose control over himself and was in danger of sliding into a psychosis through the imminent disintegration of his ego. That he nonetheless found his way back to reality and avoided the last step in his longing for death, was ascribable to his now rapidly deteriorating health. For sickness and distress often trigger the development of a regression, and so Mahler, too, was able to overcome his crisis by a drastic step forward. On his arrival in Munich, where the memorable premiere of his Eighth Symphony was to be presented on the stage on 12 September 1910, his friends noticed signs of physical weakness as well as a sickly, yellow complexion, which gave him a pallid and decrepit look. In addition there was a new relapse of *angina tonsillaris* that put the whole gigantic musical project in question until the last moment. In a letter from early September, he wrote:

> Imagine, when I arrived at the hotel [in Munich], my feverish feeling became so much more intense yesterday (even as I was writing to you) that I had

to lie in bed with alarm right away and send for the doctor (all because of the coming week). On examining me, he discovered a white coating of pus on the right side with strong redness of the entire throat. This gave me an insane fear and he ordered me wrapped up for sweating immediately. He did not want to apply any ointment, but he gave me a wonderful antiseptic, with instructions to take half a tablet every half hour; this preparation [aspirin] is being used in Germany since a year ago. I first had to make the whole house rebellious to obtain the necessary woolen blankets. I lay for three hours without moving, sweating profusely....In the evening the doctor came back and discovered a slight improvement. The night passed quietly—today I awakened without fever and ate with good appetite. The doctor came, found great improvement and allowed me to do the rehearsal.

Thus the concert could still take place on the planned date. The success was so great that it had to be repeated the following day, and Alma noted proudly: "Mahler, this divine daimon, was controlling tremendous masses," and without a doubt he had with this event reached the absolute zenith of his fame. When he traveled to Vienna after the concerts, he had himself reexamined for his repeated inflammation of the tonsils. Unfortunately the tonsils were then merely cauterized and not removed by an operation—allegedly because Mahler rejected such an intrusive treatment because of his sensitivity to pain.

In November 1910 the Mahlers boarded ship for the fourth and very last time in Cherbourg, to travel to the United States. Arriving in New York, he was swamped with the task awaiting him at the Metropolitan Opera and the Philharmonic Orchestra. Mahler no longer seemed equal to these enormous demands to the same extent as formerly was the case and he seemed rather unsure of himself. Then in December a mild relapse of angina tonsillaris occurred, further weakening him physically. On

20 February 1911, fever set in again, accompanied by severe throat pains, and since the attending physician, Dr. Joseph Fraenkel, found coatings of pus on the tonsils, he warned Mahler against conducting under these circumstances. Mahler, however, said he had often conducted with fever and, probably also in consideration for the premiere of Feruccio Busoni's work *Berceuse élégiaque (Cradle Song at the Grave of My Mother)*, he did not allow himself to be dissuaded from conducting this concert in Carnegie Hall. Although the following morning his strength temporarily left him during rehearsal, that evening the concert took place under his baton. It was also the last concert Gustav Mahler ever conducted.

The prescribed aspirin removed the inflammation of the throat within a few days and his condition seemed to improve. But the fever rose again after a few days, and during the following intermittent spells of fever, blood circulation problems now assailed the bedridden patient. Due to various disagreements he had had recently with the management of the orchestra, leading to considerable subordination of the embittered conductor, many believed the sudden illness to be simulated as a pretext. In reality, a dangerous disease had developed, allowing Mahler only three more months to live. The blood test ordered by Dr. Fraenkel showed the presence of a streptococcus infection leading to an endocarditis, that is, an inflammation of the lining of the heart. Following the idea of an unspecific antipathogenic therapy, enemas were administered to the patient and he was soon so weakened that he had to be fed. In the following weeks, Alma was torn between hope of recovery, whenever the temperatures sank, and the worst fears, when the fever rose again. As in the case of the life-threatening hemorrhage in the spring of 1901, now, too, according to Bruno Walter, Mahler intensely pondered the problem of death, which had always exercised a weird fascination over his thinking. After the recovery in 1901, the experience of illness had led to such a change of his sense of life that a deeply serious calm "had permeated his being." Mahler himself supposedly said about this: "Yes, I learned something then, but it belongs to things one cannot talk about." The diagnosis of a heart valve defect in 1907 had an essentially different effect on his frame of mind. As he himself stated in a letter of 18 July 1908, he was seized by "panic terror" that made him very insecure:

> You don't know what went on and what is going on in me; but by no means was it that hypochondriac fear of death, as you suspect. I already knew before that I must die. But without trying to explain or describe to you something for which there are perhaps no words at all, I want to tell you that all of a sudden I have lost all the clarity and assurance I had ever acquired.

And now he was directly confronted with the problem of death, for "death, to whose mystery his thoughts and feelings had often taken flight, had suddenly come into view." Repression mechanisms began to work, and on days when he felt somewhat better they caused him again to be absolutely convinced of his recovery and even inclined to joke. Thus he once said to Alma:

> When I kick the bucket, you will be a good match, you're young, you're beautiful, so whom will we marry?—But it's really better for me to stay with you.

Then he again fell into a deep despair, tormented by fears of death, for an inner voice told him that he was going to die. The days passed, and Mahler was already so weakened by the "ruinous consuming fever" that he dragged himself from the bed to the sofa, and finally he could not get up at all. Alma, although she continued to correspond with Gropius even at this time, hardly left the sickroom any more and unselfishly cared for her mortally ill husband. Since Mahler tolerated no nurse or caretaker, Alma called on her mother to help, and she quickly arrived from Vienna and relieved her daughter at his bedside during the day. But Alma insisted on doing the night watch herself.

After a consultation convoked by Dr. Fraenkel, the doctors agreed to entrust Mahler's further care to a famous European colleague. Dr. Fraenkel apparently wanted to restore some hope to the patient by this proposal, and he seems to have succeeded. The departure was soon prepared. Accompanied by his wife, his mother-in-law, and his child, Mahler was brought to the ship's cabin personally with great effort by Dr. Fraenkel, who then said farewell to his prominent patient forever. During the crossing, despite his constant peaks of fever, alternating with excessively low valleys, Mahler insisted on being brought to the sun deck almost every day. A young man traveling on the same ship offered his help—it was Stefan Zweig. Later he described the heart-moving impression that the terminally ill composer made on him:

> He lay there, pale like a dying man, unmoving,
> with closed eyelids....I saw him, this fiery man,
> weak for the first time. But this silhouette of his—
> unforgettable, incomparable—was outlined against
> an infinity of sky and sea. Boundless sadness was
> in his look, but also something transfigured with
> greatness, something that faded away into sublim-
> ity like music.

From Cherbourg, they went directly to Paris, where Mahler was examined by Dr. André Chantemesse, a bacteriologist at the Pasteur Institute; then he was taken to the sanitarium of Dr. Duprès on the Rue Dupont. A serum therapy was initiated right away, but it remained without success. Cold shivers, threatening a failure of the blood circulation, recurred again and again, and so the patient was given camphor injections. The hours in which he still had any hope became more seldom and soon gave way to a despairing resignation and depressive despondency, in which he wept and began speaking of his burial. Since his arrival in Paris, his condition was described in detail each day in the Viennese *Neue Freie Presse*. And in the 28 April 1911 issue of the *Illustrierte Wiener Extrablatt*, a photograph of Gustav Mahler in the sanitarium was even printed on the front page. Meanwhile his sister Justine had also arrived in Paris, and Bruno Walter also could not forego hurrying to his revered friend's bedside.

Since Mahler's condition, after a temporary slight improvement, again rapidly worsened in early May, Professor Franz Chvostek was in all haste telegraphed to please come from Trieste. He, too, could only confirm to Alma that her husband could no longer be moved. But he tried to reassure the patient that to save

Illuſtrirtes Wiener

Extrablatt.

Nr. 116.   Wien, Freitag 28. April 1911.   40. Jahrgang.

Guſtav Mahler im Pariſer Sanatorium.

(Der Text zu dieſem Bilde befindet ſich im Innern des Blattes.)

Die heutige Nummer iſt 18 Seiten ſtark und enthält mehrere Bilder.

THE MEDIA AND THE PUBLIC WERE ALSO PREOCCUPIED WITH MAHLER'S SEVERE ILLNESS.

him he would have to take him to Vienna and that he himself wanted to supervise the transport. Once again Mahler drew some slight hope. The railroad trip to Vienna was extremely worrisome since his pulse several times was so weak that his demise was feared. The room prepared in the Viennese sanitarium was his last stop: "Before me lay his ravaged head with fever spots and the poor emaciated body," Alma described her husband as worn down to a skeleton. The increasing weakness of his heart was causing him ever more tormenting breathing difficulties, which they tried to alleviate by administering oxygen, and his legs began swelling. They tried to remedy this swelling by administering radium pads. The daily medical reports issued since his arrival in Vienna on 12 May, showed that his condition was rapidly getting worse. His consciousness was becoming more and more clouded; he grew delirious, calling Mozart's name several times and making conducting motions with his hands. And finally after an injection of morphine, the death agony began. Shortly before midnight on 18 May 1911, an unusually stormy night, his sufferings were over.

His Tenth Symphony remained an incomplete fragment, as he had predicted and feared. Not completely without conscience, Alma later wrote:

> His truthful struggle for eternal values, his death,
> the grandeur of his face, which became more and
> more beautiful near death—I neither want to nor
> will ever forget. At least all moments not experi-
> enced completely in love lie as guilt on the heart.

After his death, Alma displayed no signs of recognizable pain or visible grief. Her husband's death struggle, lasting almost three months, had so exhausted her that the doctors thought it necessary to forbid her from attending the funeral ceremonies. Thus her stepfather Carl Moll attended the wake, and he was also willing to make the death mask. It was Mahler's expressed wish that his heart be pierced after his death and that he be laid to rest next to his beloved little daughter Putzi in the Grinzing cemetery. Only his name was to be marked on the grave stone, for he said while dying: "Those who seek me will know who I was, and the others need not know."

Final Medical Appraisal

More recent knowledge makes it seem doubtful whether Gustav Mahler really was the neurotic some biographers and psychoanalysts of our time like to portray—an obsessed hypochondriac, egocentric, and difficult person, torn apart internally by dreams of his youth, doubts, guilt feelings, and anxieties. This kind of criticism began with his tormenting, almost insatiable perfectionism as a conductor and a composer. For instance, in the fourth movement of his Ninth Symphony he inserted no less than eighty-four explanatory markings and instructions in a passage of only five measures. This could be interpreted as a kind of compulsive neurosis. But it could just as easily be the expression of a

GUSTAV MAHLER'S DEATH MASK, MADE BY CARL MOLL, THE STEPFATHER OF ALMA MAHLER.

masterful craftsmanship, striving for the highest achievement in the realm of music. Other signs of an allegedly severe neurosis can also, under a critical medical examination, be given a different interpretation, for instance, his uncoordinated stride and "twitch foot," with which he used to carry on peculiar shuffling movements. The explanation for this phenomenon, known since his childhood and accompanying his entire life, could just as well have been caused by Sydenham's chorea suffered in his early childhood. It has till now obviously been overlooked that as a child Mahler fell ill of such a form of chorea, also called "St. Vitus' dance," apparently subsequent to a rheumatism of the joints, already mentioned by Dieter Kerner. This involves a late manifestation of rheumatic fever, which always appears only a long time after a rheumatic illness of the joints and is triggered by a disturbance in the central nervous system, more precisely in the basal ganglia of the brain. St. Vitus' dance is characterized by sudden, directionless, irregular movements, which can be of a twitching nature. These twitching, cramplike movements can appear in the face, the trunk, or the extremities. The patients, generally young people, seem especially fidgety and suddenly begin making grimaces, dropping things, or having difficulty in writing. If the symptoms are more severely pronounced, a muscular feebleness can follow and be so great that the patient no longer can walk or speak and one even thinks of a paralysis. In this context, a report seems noteworthy, namely, that as a child Gustav had been able to stay in one place for hours without moving. This behavior would be readily explainable in the context of Sydenham's chorea; at any rate, more easily than by the attempted psychoanalytical interpretation that "a child who cannot move is in a conflict situation forbidding him any action as guilty, destructive, and punishable, and the only way out of this predicament is anticipatory deathlike rigidity." Although the interpretation is somewhat far-fetched and fanciful, the psychoanalyst, too, incidentally, is not surprised when "rigidity is accompanied by a complementary wriggling; both things are evidence of unfreedom and alienation from the body."

These twitching, involuntary movements in St. Vitus' dance, however, as a rule disappear completely later on. But there is also the rare, chronic, even perennial form of Sydenham's chorea, which starts in earliest childhood and can last for years or even accompany the patient through his whole life. Otherwise, we also know of a special form of chorea that begins sporadically without any previous rheumatic disease in childhood and also can persist throughout one's life. Thus, the fact that Mahler in childhood demonstrably suffered from involuntary, twitching movements of the extremities and a strange "tic in his right leg" and that his excited foot-stomping persisted later in life, this probably indicates a specific form of chorea and not, as inventive psychoanalysts suspect, a tic "as a sign of an unconscious identification with his limping mother."

It should not, however, for that reason be denied that for Mahler—as for every person—his relation to his parents played a significant role. According to his own words, they were as compatible "as fire and water," for "my father was headstrong, my mother gentleness personified." The frequent quarrels between his parents and the father's brutality certainly brought on tormenting infantile fantasies, resulting in an unconscious wish for punishment as well as in his inclination for composing, which began so early in life, including a recognizable "secrecy compulsion." One gets the impression that young Mahler's composing was inseparably linked with his parents' unhappy relationship and that he was thereby trying to project his inner conflicts outward in order to master them. But his relation to his parents must not be imagined as if he loved his mother to the same extent as he rejected his father. Rather, his attitude toward both his parents was very ambivalent.

No doubt he felt some hatred for his father due to his uncontrolled and violent ways. But as soon as Gustav had left his oedipal phase behind, the hatred of the paternal inimical rival necessarily gave way to identification with the masculine model. In fact his father, with his great initiative, purposefulness, and enormous dynamism, was for the son an impressive figure whom he tried to emulate.

But he had very ambivalent feelings toward his mother, too. On the one hand, he felt unlimited love for his mother who suffered under his father's moods; indeed, he virtually tried to identify with this suffering beloved creature. On the other hand, he was deeply disappointed by his mother from repeatedly having to experience how she could not deal with her problems and was forced deeper and deeper into a depressive state. This lacking aura of security was a maternal quality which brought insecurity to the child; and both things, the childish fixation on the "suffering" mother and the constant fear of disappointment, must have shaped Mahler's relationship to women in a negative sense. Sigmund Freud even spoke of a "Holy Mary complex," when Mahler consulted him because of his marital crisis in 1901:

> Since in your childhood you experienced a constantly sad mother, it is your unconscious intention, following the neurotic tendency to repetition, also to sadden women who later played a role in your life, because for you love and depression of the loved woman were inseparably linked in your childhood.

In fact, the relationship between Mahler and his wife was from the first—incidentally, on both sides—a mixture of idolization and domination claims over the other, and from Alma's memoirs and letters one learns how unhappy she often was under her husband's despotic rule.

Mahler's identification with his "suffering" mother, however, certainly also strengthened the guilt feelings in his childhood flowing from aggressions against his parents. An indication that even in young years self-punishment tendencies typical of this were present in little Gustav's answer to the question of what he wanted to be someday: "A martyr." He played this role full of conviction as conductor when humility toward the great musical masterpieces made him willing to take on all the troubles and gripes of an opposing orchestra in order to achieve an optimal rendition. But since a self-imagined "martyr" moves, so to speak, in the "sadomasochistic circle," Mahler did not always assume a submissive position but occasionally also the attitude of a tyrant. His at times nearly sadistic methods of treating orchestra members, which later took on almost paranoid traits, often made productive cooperation extremely difficult. Only his unconditional devotion to the work and the economic delectation of narcissistic wishes toward the public prevented the seeds, also present in his siblings, from developing in a psychotic direction, as Alma Mahler once accurately suggested:

> All the episodes described here, such as his sister's death fantasy, his brother Alois' foolish ambition to conquer the city and court of Vienna in romantic disguise, the dismal suicide of the Ahasveric Otto—all these traits can be called Gustav-Mahleresque. They are the sheet lightning that precedes the lightning bolts; the formlessness that announces the form.

A condition that dominated Mahler's thinking since earliest childhood was the problem of death. In fact, death was present in his life from the beginning. By his fourteenth year he had witnessed the death of no less than six newborn siblings. The death of his beloved brother Ernst, only one year younger than himself, in whose memory he wrote the lost opera of his youth *Duke Ernst of Swabia*, struck him especially hard. But even much earlier, at the age of seven, he was inspired by death to compose a polka with a dirge as accompaniment, and even his first work included in the list of compositions, *The Plaintive Song*, sings the theme of the murdering brother. But the sad farewell experiences of his childhood are especially recreated in the *Songs on the Death of Children*, of which he later once said:

> I feel sorry for the world that will have to hear these songs someday; their content is so sad.

But the constant presence of death also pervades the program of his symphonies; indeed, the last one literally tries to represent death in music and surely is supposed to mean a farewell to life.

A longing for death repeatedly resounds in his written statements, too. For instance:

> My much-loved earth, when, oh when will you receive the abandoned one into your bosom....Oh, receive the lonesome one, the restless one, all-eternal mother.

This longing for eternal rest showed up in Mahler especially pen-
etratingly whenever he found himself in a state of greatest internal unrest, until finally the longing for death overflowed in 1907
into a pathological "death-drive" due to three decisive, terrible
blows of fate: the "voluntary" resignation as director of the
Vienna Court Opera, which was in reality forced by intolerable
intrigues and anti-Semitic machinations; the terrible death of his
most beloved little daughter Maria Anna; and finally, his doctor's
informing him, like a bolt out of the blue, that he was suffering
from a heart valve defect. Mahler tried to resolve the ensuing
tremendous tensions by a "flight into work," without reflecting
that such a pathological life-style of producing maximal achievements at any price can mean self-destruction. This whole process
reached its absolute peak in 1910 when, after the architect Walter
Gropius' "mistake," he suddenly realized that he was in the process of losing his wife Alma forever—not least of all through his
own fault. Although he now tried to make up for his culpable
neglect and tyrannical patronizing of Alma by an exaggerated
devotion and almost masochistic submission to her ruling scepter
in the sense of overcompensation, this could not remove his deeply
anchored insecurity and his tormenting sense of guilt. Not even
Sigmund Freud's attempt to counter this crisis in his life led to a
decisive success, although it manifestly did help, as Mahler recognized. The sketches of the Tenth Symphony show only too clearly
that the admissions of guilt and the cries for help were not only
scattered words scribbled in the margins of the manuscript, but
rather that they luxuriate into the melodic fabric and block the
further development of the symphonic structure. Mahler's previous works—for instance, the Second Symphony or the funeral
marches in the First and Fifth Symphonies—gave the impression
that the preferred themes of eternity and resurrection were rooted
in constant preoccupation with the thought of death and the beyond, and that he was thereby trying to repress his own fear of
death, so to speak by a direct confrontation. Now, in view of his
imminent death, in the Ninth and the Tenth Symphony, as well as
in the *Song of the Earth*, a major change seems recognizable in
the tone-coloration and style of his music.

In the posthumous writings of the well-known psychoanalyst, Theodor Reik, is found a manuscript with the title "Mahler Before the End," which was translated into English by Reik's son and first made known to the public in 1970 by Nicholas Christy in a lecture before a New York circle of doctors. Theodor Reik describes Mahler before the end of his life, as follows:

> The last Mahler is the real one, is he himself....No more flirtation with German folk songs, no theatrical, operatic arrangements, no thoughts about effects nor about impressions. He no longer looks toward the balcony or the orchestra. The vision is straight ahead to see what is coming, what is so near, what is nearly here already, the end, the terror of the end which he has always thought about and yet which is absolutely unthinkable, death.... Thoughts about death had occupied him often, he had looked at it, sometimes seriously, sometimes playfully....Now it is no longer an *idée fixe* with doubts and speculations, now there is safety, now that death stands at the threshold....Death is no longer the riddle that it has always been before.... Now no philosophy, no meditation, no metaphysics could help....Now it became not a matter of "the ultimate questions" but a matter of one's own final dissolution. Now it was no longer important to have some conceptual grasp of general humanity but to understand one's own humanity, its most human part, before one stopped being a human being, before one became a thing....One can trace through his letters, through certain things he said, but most of all through his music how his reaction to the near end was changing, how he himself changed, how he discarded everything that was alien to him....When he confronts perdition naked, there is no more sentimentality, no false emotionality, no false tones....Here a man rises highest at the moment he is crushed, when he realizes...

how small he is. Here, where fate crushes him, he becomes master of himself. While blessing the earth and while wondering whether to curse his own artisanship, he becomes artistically the greatest. There, where others are lost, he finds himself. There, where others sink, he soars to an unsurpassable height.

Physically, Mahler was plagued by two ailments all his life; namely, his hemorrhoids, which required an operation at least three times and in 1901 led to a life-threatening hemorrhage, and his migraine headaches, which sometimes assailed him strongly. Medical textbooks classically list the character traits of migraine patients also manifested by Mahler: anxious, orderly, self-disciplined and strict, unusually ambitious, perfectionist. Added to this the enormous professional burdens and the unimaginable composition work and more than enough triggering factors are found for his migraine spells. Apart from this, until he was forty-seven years old, Mahler was a remarkably healthy man, an enthusiastically active athlete, whether it was hiking, mountain-climbing, bicycling, or swimming, who by no means had the "weak constitution" repeatedly ascribed to him by many biographers.

He was all the more dismayed when during a chance examination in the summer of 1907 the general practitioner, Dr. Blumenthal gave him the surprising information—moreover, from a lack of psychological talent, in an incredibly brutal way— that he was suffering from a "chronic bilateral heart valve defect." This diagnosis was confirmed in Vienna, where Mahler went without delay for a more precise heart examination, although the findings were interpreted very differently by two different examining physicians. As Mahler wrote to his wife in a letter on 30 September 1907, Dr. Hamperl found "a slight heart valve defect, which is fully compensated. He does not make a big deal of the whole matter and told me that I can surely continue doing my work like before and otherwise lead a normal life, apart from avoiding over-exertion." In contrast with this, Alma reports in her biography about the result of the examination by Dr. Friedrich Kovacs:

> He confirmed the diagnosis...and forbade him to
> walk on uphill paths, to ride a bicycle or to swim;
> he was even so injudicious as to give him precise
> information on how to perform walking exercises:
> first, for only five minutes, then for ten, and so
> forth, until he would be trained enough—and this
> to a man who was accustomed to strong physical
> exertion! And Mahler did everything he told him
> to do. He had to accustom himself to walking
> with watch in hand.

Her report also says that "Mahler was so shaken by the doctor's
judgment on his heart that in that winter he spent the greatest
part of the day in bed and only got up for rehearsals or for performances he had to conduct at the Opera." Actually Dr. Kovacs'
unfortunate advice seems to have led to Mahler's obsessive concentration on his sick heart at this time.

> Since we knew that he had a heart valve defect,
> we feared everything. During a walk he stopped
> every few moments to feel his pulse...and often
> he asked me...to listen to his heart and determine
> whether the heart activity was clear, fast, or slow....
> He had a pedometer in his pocket. His step and
> his pulse-beats were counted, and his life became
> a torment.

This dramatic picture of the sick Mahler drawn by Alma Mahler
does not, however, agree completely with his strenuous activities
as conductor and composer, which he was able to carry out in the
years 1908 to 1911. Besides finishing the Ninth Symphony and
the *Song of the Earth*, the sketches for the five movements of the
Tenth Symphony and the revisions of his Fourth and Fifth Symphonies, he conducted in America in this period alone no less
than twenty-four concerts. Such demands no doubt were an enormous burden on him and it is told in New York that after some
rehearsals and performances he had to be brought back to the
hotel "like an invalid." His facial features also showed clear signs
of excessive exertions, as can be seen from the last photographs

from those years. This earned him at that time the epithet "ugly Mahler."

There are no direct medical data on the precise nature of his heart valve defect. The diagnosis spoke of a "bilateral, congenital, but compensated valve defect" with a "hissing sound, which the colleague identified 'on the second beat.'" From these vague indications, one can probably assume this was a so-called combined valve defect, involving both the mitral valve and the aortic valve, a problem that can go without symptoms for a strikingly long time. Since Mahler could perform considerable long-range achievements in his athletic activities, the clinical probability is that it was mainly a defect of the aortic valve, that is, of the heart valve located at the opening of the aorta in the left ventricle of the heart. The long-lasting existence of such a valve defect can, due to the increased enlargement of the overburdened left ventricle, also lead to damage to the mitral valve, that is, the valve located between the left atrium and the left ventricle of the heart, so that a combined heart valve defect then is present. But this situation can also happen through the simultaneous illness of the aortic and mitral valves.

Mahler's medical history shows that even as a child he often suffered from throat infections and in his youth he once had an inflammation of the joints, as well as Sydenham's chorea, that is, St. Vitus' dance. All these sicknesses are manifestations of rheumatic fever, an inflammatory disease occurring as a late effect of throat infections by bacteria classified as Group A streptococci. Besides the involvement of the joints in the form of polyarthritis or of the central nervous system, for instance in St. Vitus' dance, the characteristic effect on the heart has the greatest consequences for the patients, who are generally juveniles between five and fifteen years of age. Although all layers of the heart can be affected, the most severe and, above all, lasting damages to the valve systems result from endocarditis, that is, inflammation of the lining of the heart. The inflammatory lesions cause a narrowing or inability of the valves to close and affect mainly the mitral and aortic valves. The damage to the aortic valve can remain clinically without symptoms for decades, and all indications are that, in Mahler's case, the problem was such a post-endocarditic aortic valve disease, eventually also involving the mitral valve.

Mahler's fatal illness began in February 1911 with fever, at first associated by the doctor with tonsillitis. But when the fever, accompanied by nighttime sweating, continued in irregular spells and the patient's condition gradually worsened, the New York physician, Dr. Fraenkel, in view of the preexisting heart valve defect, suspected the presence of infectious endocarditis and transferred Mahler to Dr. Emanuel Libman, student of the famous Professor Sir William Osler of Johns Hopkins Hospital and at that time the foremost expert in this field. Libman first clinically confirmed the diagnosis of a rheumatic heart valve defect and, based on the irregular spells of fever, an enlarged palpable spleen, and the typical little red lesions of the conjunctiva and the skin, he suspected the rightness of the diagnosis of his transferring colleague, Dr. Fraenkel. All that was needed now was confirmation by a blood sample; and therefore, with some difficulties the required amount of blood was drawn by the surgeon, Dr. George Baehr. This Dr. Baehr, who in 1911 was a fellow in Libman's laboratory at the Institute of Pathology and Bacteriology of Mount Sinai Hospital in New York, told of this event as reported by Nicholas P. Christy, et al., in "Gustav Mahler and His Illnesses," *Transactions of the American Clinical and Climatological Association*:

> Sometime in February 1911 Dr. Emanuel Libman was called in consultation by Mahler's personal physician, Dr. Fraenkel, to see the famous composer and director. Apparently Dr. Fraenkel had suspected that Mahler's prolonged fever and physical debility might be due to subacute bacterial endocarditis and therefore called Libman, Chief of the First Medical Service and Associate Director of Laboratories at the Mt. Sinai Hospital, in consultation. Libman was at that time the outstanding authority on the disease. At the time of the consultation, the Mahlers were occupying a suite of rooms at the old Savoy Plaza Hotel (or it may have been the Plaza) at Fifth Avenue and 59th Street

overlooking Central Park. Libman confirmed the diagnosis clinically by finding a loud systolic-presystolic murmur over the precordium characteristic of chronic rheumatic mitral disease, a history of prolonged low grade fever, a palpable spleen, characteristic petechiae on the conjunctivae and skin, and slight clubbing of fingers. To confirm the diagnosis bacteriologically, Libman telephoned me to join him at the hotel and bring the paraphernalia and culture media required for a blood culture.

On arrival I withdrew 20 c.cm. of blood from an arm vein with syringe and needle, squirted part of it into several bouillon flasks and mixed the remainder with melted agar media which I then poured into sterile Petri dishes. After 4 or 5 days of incubation in the hospital laboratory, the Petri plates revealed numerous bacteriological colonies and all the bouillon flasks were found to show a pure culture of the same organism which was subsequently identified as *streptococcus viridans*.

As this was long before the days of antibiotics, the bacterial findings sealed Mahler's doom. He insisted on being told the truth and then expressed a wish to die in Vienna. Accordingly, he and his wife left shortly thereafter for Paris, where the diagnosis and prognosis were reconfirmed, and then proceeded to Vienna.

A blood sample was also taken in Paris by the well-known bacteriologist at the Pasteur Institute, André Chantemesse, and it confirmed Libman's diagnosis completely. However, the way this French doctor notified Alma Mahler of the results of this test was a prime example of tactless and heartless behavior of a medical professional, who should perhaps call himself a scientist but not a doctor: "Well, Madame Mahler, come and see for yourself. Even I have never before seen streptococci in such a fabulous state of

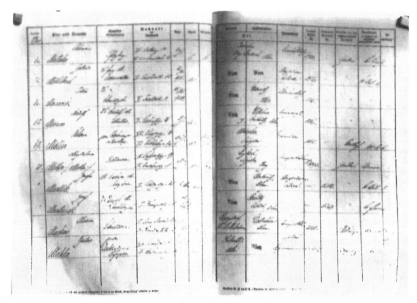

THE ENTRY IN THE CORONER'S REPORT ON GUSTAV MAHLER'S DEMISE. THE CAUSE OF DEATH IS LISTED AS: "SEPTIC INFLAMMATION OF THE LINING OF THE HEART."

development. Look at those threads, they look like seaweeds." Alma was "speechless with horror" at this scientific demonstration.

The diagnosis "*endocarditis lenta*," also called subacute infectious endocarditis, designates an extremely dangerous disease even in the age of antibiotics, but today more than seventy percent of such patients can be cured. In Mahler's time, however, when only symptomatic treatments were available to alleviate the complaints and the doctors' equipment was limited to the administration of circulation-strengthening medications, blood transfusions, and at best the attempt at an anti-streptococci vaccination, the disease was always fatal. The discoloring streptococci responsible for the symptoms of the disease probably are located on already damaged heart valves and there, together with infectious changes of the tissue, they form deposits, so-called "vegetation" that can lead to destruction of the heart valves. If this process of destruction has advanced, the functioning of the affected heart valves is largely impaired. The effect can be a collection of fluid in the lungs, pulmonary edema, bringing death to the patient. Parts of the deposited "vegetation" can also be torn away by the bloodstream and then cause emboli in certain blood vessels, such as in the capillaries, in arterioles of the fingers and toes, and in the blood vessels of the kidneys and the brain. Drumstick fingers, or the dying off of the end segments of the extremities, kidney failure, or brain seizures with paralysis then follow.

Mahler's fatal illness lasted barely four months. He spent the last days of his life, emaciated down to a skeleton and delirious, in Loew Sanitarium in Vienna, where he was under Professor Chvostek's care. On 18 May he breathed his last, after having lain in a deep coma for several hours. In her memoirs Alma recalls this last sector of his life:

> He lay groaning there. A large swelling formed on his knees, then also on his legs. Radium was applied and the swelling immediately vanished. In the evening he was washed and his bed put in order. Two attendants lifted his naked emaciated body. It was like removal from the cross. That thought came to all our minds. He had great difficulty in breathing and was given oxygen. Then came uremia—and the end. Chvostek was called. Mahler lay there with a confused look; a finger was conducting on the blanket. He had a smile on his lips and twice he said: "Mozart!" His eyes were very large. I asked Chvostek to give him a dose of morphine, so that he would not feel anything more. He answered in a loud voice. I seized his hands: "Speak softly, he could hear you." "He doesn't hear anything any more." How terrible the indifference of the doctors in such moments. And how could he know that he heard nothing? Perhaps he could merely not move? The death-agony began. I was sent to the next room. The death-rattle lasted several hours.

Suddenly at midnight of 18 May, during a horrible hurricane-like storm, those grizzly sounds stopped. With that last breath, his beloved and wonderful soul fled, and the silence was more deadly than anything else. As long as he was still breathing, he was here. But now everything was over.

From this description it can be assumed that terminally a pulmonary edema developed, probably associated with an inflammation of the lungs, as well as kidney failure and coma, followed by death. The swelling of the knee joints, occurring pre-terminally, could have corresponded to arthritis, since otherwise the rapid reduction of the edema by the use of radium would be inexplicable. Severe anemia was certainly a partial cause of his weakness and decrepitude of the last weeks. On the death certificate, endocarditis was named as the cause of death. No autopsy was requested.

Mahler was conscious of death all his life, and since his thoughts recurrently circled on the themes of death and the Beyond, he worked out all stages of this problem intellectually as a thinker and a composer—from premonitions of death to fear of death, to the certainty of death. Death, however, did not mean the end of man, for despite all belief in Christ he was completely permeated with the doctrine of eternal return. That is also the reason why in his last time he was preoccupied not only with ongoing life in the Beyond, but more and more also with life in our world. In close dependence on Goethe's views of life and immortality in his world of belief, the doctrine of return always occupied a privileged position, as when he said:

We all return, all life makes sense only through this certainty, and it is completely indifferent whether in a later stage of return we remember an earlier one. For what matters is not the individual and his remembering and comfort, but only the great call to perfection—to the purification that progresses in every incarnation. Therefore I must live ethically in order even now to spare my ego a

part of the road, when it comes again, and make
its existence easier. My ethical duty points in that
direction.

This certainty of his earthly posthumous future and the conviction that his music, already in this life, was "the anticipation of the future," makes it more understandable why Mahler sometimes reacted with astonishing nonchalance to critics who misunderstood or rejected him. He gave the following reason: "My time will yet come—I have time on my side, living or dead, that is indifferent, I can wait."

In his Ninth and in the unfinished Tenth Symphony, as well as in his *Song of the Earth*, Mahler tried to work out his past which had not been spared disappointments and blows of fate. He thereby performed a kind of "work of grieving," by which he must have succeeded in gradually letting go of what had been and allowing it to become a part of himself as something irretrievable. In this farewell-taking work of grieving, he once more achieved an inimitable beauty of his own, namely, the closing part of the *Song of the Earth*, where painfully looking back on his life he was able to express the moment of farewell in such simple and moving music with his intonation of the words: "Oh you, my friend, fortune was not kind to me in this world."

Mahler's Doctors

Dr. George Baehr

Dr. Baehr was head of the Department of Internal Medicine at Mount Sinai Hospital in New York. Starting in 1911, he was a fellow in Emanuel Libman's Laboratory for Pathology and Bacteriology.

Dr. André Chantemesse

Dr. Chantemesse was a bacteriologist at the Pasteur Institute in Paris. He tended Mahler during his short stay in Paris and confirmed Libman's diagnosis with the microscopic proof of viridical streptococci in the patient's blood.

Dr. Franz Chvostek, Jr. (1864-1944)

Dr. Chvostek was born in Vienna, graduated in 1888 and qualified as a lecturer for the specialty of Internal Medicine in 1895. In 1897 he became Associate Professor, and in 1912 Professor, and was assigned as Director of the Fourth Medical Clinic. He was interested mainly in questions of internal secretion, and more especially the thyroid gland. This was expressed in his monograph *Morbus Basedow and the Hyperthyreoses*. But his first scientific works came from the field of neural psychiatry, and it was really the influence of his teacher Kahler, and above all, Neusser, that finally directed him to internal medicine. He had an outstanding reputation as a teacher and a diagnostician, who again and again could convince and enthuse others by his perfect art of doing the case histories and physical examinations without technical aids. One of his more significant works was his study of the pathogens of cirrhosis of the liver.

Dr. Sigmund Freud (1856-1939)

Freud was born in Freiburg in Moravia. He studied in Vienna from 1873 to 1881, where he was more active as a researcher than as a student. From 1882 to 1885 he worked as a secondary doctor in the General Hospital in Vienna and there he was concerned mainly with neuropathological questions. Later he devoted himself to philosophical and zoological studies; and he finally ended in the physiological laboratory of Brücke, his "teacher honored above all others." He himself summed up his almost six-year period with Professor Brücke as follows:

> It is Brücke's physiology, solidly grounded on
> physical ideas with their ideal of the measurability
> of all processes, that stood at the starting point of
> the formation of psychoanalytical theory.

One year after his graduation in 1881, he decided on a practical career. In this time he wrote his works on the anatomy of the brain and neurology, as well as the "cocaine episode" with the discovery of the anesthetic effect of cocaine. After qualifying as a lecturer in 1885, he received a grant for the Salpetrière Clinic of the University of Paris, where Charcot became his decisive scientific experience. Soon after his return to Vienna in 1886 he began to turn from neurology to psychology and psychopathology, and by 1895 his *Study on Hysteria*, written in conjunction with Joseph Breuer, was published. Inspired by Charcot, who had made academically acceptable the disease profile of hysteria, previously neglected by school medicine, and who achieved quite astonishing phenomena with hypnosis, Freud, too, now used hypnosis instead of electrotherapy. Breuer too had already been using it intensively since 1880. The academic faculty's passive resistance to hypnosis, which Meynert called a "favorite field of undoctorlike charlatans," forced Freud to give up his academic career. Here Breuer and Freud soon parted ways, since Breuer could not follow Freud's ideas on the sexual cause of all neuroses.

Subsequently, in the years 1895 to 1898 Freud reshaped the cathartic technique to the core technique of psychoanalysis, so that he now was able to penetrate to deeper strata of the subconscious. In this period, he published several works on neuroses, for instance, *Sexuality in the Etiology of Neuroses*, which were of particular significance for the development of his psychopathology. His most original publication was, however, *The Interpretation of Dreams*, published in 1900. All these conceptions unleashed arguments reaching to our time, and Freud literature appearing since then has reached boundless proportions.

Dr. Friedrich Kovacs (1861-1931)

Dr. Kovacs was born in Vienna. After graduating in 1885, he received his further training at the Vienna University Clinics for Internal Medicine under Nothnagel, Kahler, and Bamberg. In 1893 he qualified as a university lecturer for internal medicine. Then in 1900, he was appointed chief surgeon of the Fourth Department of Internal Medicine at the General Hospital in Vienna, and in 1908 he received the rank of Associate Professor.

His numerous scientific works are mainly in the field of diseases of the heart and the circulatory system. Both as a teacher and as a diagnostician he enjoyed an outstanding reputation in the city.

Dr. Julius von Hochenegg (1859-1940)

Julius Hochenegg was born in Vienna and had to finish his high school studies in Bolzano, Tyrol, due to tuberculosis. As son of a Viennese lawyer, he too was supposed to study law, but he soon switched to medicine. His activity with Alberti and Billroth soon aroused his enthusiasm for the field of surgery. So just a few months after graduation in 1884, he enrolled at the First Surgical University Clinic in Vienna under the directorship of Professor Alberti, where he stayed until 1891. That year he was named head of the Surgery Department of the Vienna Polyclinic, after having qualified in that field in 1889. He was appointed Associate Professor of Surgery in 1894, and in 1904, after Gussenbauer's retirement, he was made head of the Second Surgical University Clinic in Vienna.

Together with the head of the First Surgical University Clinic, Professor Eiselsberg, he established a separate accident station. His student Lorenz Böhler, who later established a special accident hospital in Vienna, came from that first accident station.

He passed on to his students not only his eminent operation techniques, but also the ethical mission of always dealing with their patients with concern, sympathy, and consideration. His achievements of note are the total removal of the larynx with simultaneous reconstruction of the esophagus, as well as the first successful liver resection on man due to cancer of the gallbladder. His main field of work was surgical therapy of cancer of the rectum, with a technique of operation in which a part of the sacrum had to be removed. The results of this procedure inaugurated by him attracted a great deal of attention. Some of his students who later became famous were Hans Lorenz, the "father of orthopedics," the goiter surgeon Fritz Kaspar, Felix Mandl, and the gastrointestinal surgeon with world repute Hans Finsterer.

Dr. Emanuel Libman (1872-1946)

Born in New York, Emanuel Libman studied at the College of Physicians of Columbia University, where he graduated in 1894. His advanced studies were then done at the Universities of Berlin and Vienna, as well as at Johns Hopkins University.

At first he was employed at Mount Sinai Hospital as House Physician, Associate Pathologist, and Consulting Physician. He taught Clinical Medicine at Columbia University. His scientific works deal with the internal fields of diseases of the heart and blood vessels, as well as skin infections. Later his work was mainly bacteriological and pathological-anatomical at Mount Sinai Hospital, where he functioned as head of the First Medical Clinic and Associate Director of Laboratories. He was considered the prime authority in the field of bacterial endocarditis. Together with Sacks, Libman has the merit in 1923 of having studied in detail the particular kind of heart involvement in the sense of a visceral form of manifestation of lupus erythematosus. This atypical abacterial endocarditis has gone down in medical history as Libman-endocarditis, or the Libman-Sacks syndrome.

Bibliography

FRÉDÉRIC CHOPIN

Audley A.: Frédéric Chopin, sa vie et ses Œuvres. Paris 1880.

Barry K.: Chopin und seine 14 Ärzte. In: Chopin Almanach. Potsdam 1949.

Blume F.: Die Musik in Geschichte und Gegenwart. Bd. 2, Kassel 1952.

Böhme H.: Medizinische Portraits berühmter Komponisten. New York-Stuttgart 1979.

Bord B.: La complexion amoureuse de George Sand et de Chopin exposée par George Sand. Aesculape 25 u. 26, 1935/36.

Bordes M.: La maladie et l'œuvre de Chopin. Lyon 1932.

Bourniquel C.: Frédéric Chopin. Hamburg 1977.

Braun A.: Krankheit und Tod im Schicksal bedeutender Menschen. Stuttgart 1934.

Bräutigam W.: Beitrag zur Psychosomatik der Lungentuberkulösen. Fortschr. Tuberk. Forsch. 7, 184, 1956.

Burger E.: Frédéric Chopin: Eine Lebenschronik in Bildern und Dokumenten. München 1990.

Bury R.: La vie de Frédéric Chopin. Genf 1951.

Cabanès A.: La maladie de Chopin. La Chronique Médicale, 673, 1899.

Carrère C.: George Sand, Liebende und Geliebte. Bergisch-Gladbach 1979.

Cherbuliez A.E.: Frédéric Chopin, Leben und Werk. Zürich 1948.

Chominski J.M.: Fryderyk Chopin. Leipzig 1980.

Cortot A.: Chopin. Wesen und Gestalt. Zürich 1960.

Dahms W.: Chopin. München 1924.

Delacroix E.: Lettres 1815—1863. Paris 1978.

Egert P.: Friedrich Chopin. Potsdam 1936.

Eichhorst H.: Lehrbuch der praktischen Medicin. Wien 1899.

Eigeldinger J.J.: Chopin vu par ses élèves. Neuchatel 1970.

Enault L.: Chopin. Paris 1856.

Ernest G.: Friedrich Chopin. Genie und Krankheit. Med. Welt 4, 723, 1930.

Franken F.H.: Krankheit und Tod großer Komponisten. Baden-Baden-Köln-New York 1979.

Gal H.: In Dur und Moll. Briefe großer Komponisten. Frankfurt a. M. 1966.

Ganche E.: Souffrance de Frédéric Chopin. Paris 1935.

Gavoty B.: Chopin. Aus dem Französischen von Susi Piroué. Tübingen 1977.

Gide A.: Notizen über Chopin. Frankfurt/Main 1962.

Guttry A.: Chopins gesammelte Briefe. München 1928.

Hadden J.C.: Chopin. London 1903.

Hedley A.: Chopin. London 1947.

Heine H.: Sämtliche Werke. Hrsg. Vortriede W. und Schweikert U., München 1972.

Hoesick F.: Chopin. His Life and Works. Warschau 1927.

Hübschmann H.: Psyche und Tuberkulose. Stuttgart 1952.

Huneker J.: Chopin. Der Mensch, der Künstler. München 1917.

Iwaszkiewicz J.: Chopin. Leipzig 1964.

Jaspers K.: Allgemeine Psychopathologie. Berlin 1973.

Junker E.: Die Entwicklung der Tuberkulose in Mitteleuropa. Münch. Med. Wschr. 112, 985, 1970.

Karasowski M.: Friedrich Chopin. Sein Leben und seine Briefe. Berlin 1914.

Karenberg A.: Frédéric Chopin als Mensch, Patient und Künstler. Bergisch-Gladbach-Köln (Reihe: Medizinische Forschung, Band 2) 1986.

Kaupert W.: Chopin ais Lehrer. Musik im Unterricht, 42, 1951.

Kerner D.: Krankheiten großer Musiker. 4. Aufl. Stuttgart-New York 1968.

Kobylanska K.: Chopin in der Heimat. Urkunden und Andenken. Krakau 1955.

Koszalski R.: Frédéric Chopin: Beobachtungen, Skizzen, Analysen. Köln 1936.

Kümmel W.F.: Musik und Medizin. Freiburg 1977.

Ladaique G.: Die väterlichen Vorfahren von Frédéric François Chopin. Z. Internatl. Chopin-Ges. in Wien, 1, 1989.

Lami G.: Patografia di Chopin. Rif. med. 52, 163, 1953.

Lange-Eichbaum W., Kurth W.: Genie, Irrsinn und Ruhm. München 1967.

Leichtentritt H.: Friedrich Chopin. In: Berühmte Musiker, 2. Aufl. Bd. 16. Berlin 1920.

Leitner H.: Krankheit und Schicksal: Frédéric Chopin. Der niedergelassene Arzt 8, 82, 1981.

Liszt E.: Chopins Persönlichkeit, 1852. In: Neue Musikzeitschrift 3, 257, 1949.

Long E.R.: The case of Frédéric Chopin. Univ. of Kansas Press 1956.

Martinez Duran C.: La tuberculosis de Frédérico Chopin. Médico (Mex.) 58, 1958.

Meneses Hoyos J.: Federico Chopin fue un Ftisico o un Cardiasco? Médico (Mex.) 14/3, 37, 1964.

Metzger H.K. und Riehn R.: Musik-Konzepte 45: Fryderyk Chopin. München 1985.

Mullan F.: The sickness of Frederic Chopin. A study of disease and society. Rocky Mtn. Med. J. 70, 29, 1973.

Niecks F.: Friedrich Chopin als Mensch und Musiker. Leipzig 1890.

O'Shea J.: Music and Medicine. London 1990.

Onuf O.: Frederick Chopins mental makeup. Dementia praecox studies (Chicago) 3, 199, 1920/21.

Petzold R.: Fryderyk Chopin. Sein Leben in Bildern. Leipzig 1960.

Pourtales G. de: Der blaue Klang. Chopins Leben. Freiburg 1935.

Redenbacher E.: Chopin. Leipzig 1923.

Rehberg W. und P.: Chopin, sein Leben und seine Werke. Zürich 1949.

Reich W.: Frédéric Chopin. Briefe und Dokumente. Zürich 1959.

Rocchietta S.: Omaggio a Chopin nel 150 anniversario della nascita. Minerva med. 51, 1284, 1960.

Rocchietta S.: Contributo della psicanalisi alla musicologia: Chopin. Minerva medica 42, 706, 1951.

Rosenheim Th.: Krankheiten des Darms. Wien u. Leipzig 1893.

Sand G.: Histoire de ma vie. Paris 1865.

Sand G.: Un hiver à Majorque. Paris 1843.

Sand G.: Lucrezia Floriani. Leipzig 1863.

Scharlitt B.: Chopin. Leipzig 1919.

Schweisheimer W.: Der kranke Chopin. Ärztl. Praxis 12, 694, 1960.

Severi L.: Frederico Chopin e il suo male. Ref. Zbl. ges. Neurol. 107, 460, 1949.

Stegemann M.: Immanenz und Transzendenz: Chopin und die pianistische Ornamentik. In: Musikkonzepte 45, Hrsg. Metzger und Riehn, München 1985.

Sterpellone L.: Pazienti illustrissimi. Roma 1985.

Sydow B.E.: Correspondance de Frédéric Chopin. Bd. I-III, Paris 1953-1960.

Szpilczynski S.: War Frédéric Chopin Allergiker? Ciba Symp. 9/6, 283, 1961.

Tarasti E.: Zu einer Narratologic Chopins. Int. Review of the Aesthetics and Sociology of Music IRASM, Zagreb 1, 53, 1984.

Tenand S.: Portraits de Chopin. Paris 1950.

Tutenberg F: Chopin und die Frauen. Neue Musikzeitschrift 3, 262, 1949.

Venzmer G.: Macht und Ohnmacht der Großen. München 1970.

Vuillermoz E.: La vie amoureuse de Chopin. Paris 1927.

Weinstock H.: Chopin. Mensch und Werk. München 1950.

Weissmann A.: Chopin. Berlin 1912.

Wierzynski C.: The Life and Death of Chopin. New York 1949.

Willms J.: Chopin und die Ärzte. Med. Welt 8, 1140, 1175, 1934.

Zagiba F.: Chopin und Wien. Wien 1951.

Zuber B.: Syndrom des Salons und Autonomie. In: Musik-Konzepte 45, Hrsg. Metzger und Riehn, München 1985.

BEDRICH SMETANA

Bankl H.: Viele Wege führten in die Ewigkeit. Wien 1990.

Balthasar V: Bedrich Smetana. Prag 1924.

Bartos F.: Smetana in Briefen und Erinnerungen. Prag 1954.

Bistron J.: Friedrich Smetana. Wien 1924.

Böhme G.: Medizinische Portraits berühmter Komponisten. Stuttgart-New York 1987.

Büchner F.: Spezielle Pathologie. München-Berlin 1965.

Eichhorst H.: Lehrbuch der praktischen Medicin Innerer Krankheiten. Berlin-Wien 1899.

Feldmann H.: Die Krankheit Friedrich Smetanas in otologischer Sicht auf Grund neuer Quellenstudien. Monatsschrift f. Ohrenheilkunde 98, 209, 1964.

Goerke H.: Arzt und Heilkunde. München 1984.

Haskovec L.: Die Krankheit Smetanas. Referiert in: Zentralblatt der gesamten Neurologie 42, 593, 1926.

Helfert V.: Die schöpferische Entwicklung Smetanas. Leipzig 1956.

Heveroch A.: Über die Krankheit Smetanas. Referiert in: Zentralblatt der gesamten Neurologie 41, 332, 1925.

Honolka K.: Bedrich Smetana in Selbstzeugnissen und Bilddokumenten. Reinbek bei Hamburg 1978.

Honolka K.: Dalibor - eine monothematische Oper. In: Musica. Kassel 1970.

Kerner D.: Krankheiten großer Musiker. Stuttgart-New York 1986.

Krejci F.V.: Friedrich Smetana. Berlin 1906.

Lange-Eichbaum W. und Kurth W.: Genie, Irrsinn und Ruhm. Basel 1985.

Lhotsky J.: Psychiatrisches zur Krankheit und Todesursache Friedrich Smetanas. In: Münchner Medizinische Wochenschrift 101, 91, 1959.

Lhotsky J.: Friedrich Smetana, der Streit über seine Krankheit. In: Münchner Medizinische Wochenschrift 102, 654, 1960.

Rychnovsky E.: Smetana. Stuttgart-Berlin 1924.

Sequardtova H.: Bedrich Smetana. Leipzig 1985.

Sournia, Poult und Martiny: Illustrierte Geschichte der Medizin. Paris 1978.

Springer B.: Die genialen Syphilitiker. Berlin 1926.

Vnejedly Z.: Dvorák und Smetana. Prag 1934.

Weller B.: Friedrich Smetana. Prag 1895.

Wessely E.A.: Klinik der Hals-, Nasen- und Ohrenerkrankungen. Berlin-Wien 1942.

Zweig H.: Die Krankheit Friedrich Smetanas. In: Deutsche Medizinische Wochenschrift 60, 722, 1934.

Peter Ilyich Tchaikovsky

Abraham G.: Tschaikowsky. London 1944.

Abraham G.: Tschaikowsky. A Symposium. London 1945.

Berberova N.: Tschaikowsky. Düsseldorf 1989.

Böhme G.: Medizinische Portraits berühmter Koniponisten. Bd. 1. Stuttgart 1981.

Bowen C.D. und von Meck B.: Geliebte Freundin. Tschaikowskys Leben und sein Briefwechsel mit Nadeshda von Meck. Leipzig 1938.

Brown D.: Tschaikowsky. A biographical and critical study. London 1978.

Cherbuliez A.: Tschaikowsky und die russische Musik. Zürich 1948.

Garden E.: Tschaikowsky. Leben und Werk. Stuttgart 1986.

Helm E.: Tschaikowsky. Reinbek/Hamburg 1979.

Hofmann E.: Lehrbuch der gerichtlichen Medizin. Wien 1891.

Kerner D.: Krankheiten großer Musiker. 4. Aufl. Stuttgart-New York 1986.

Knorr I.: Peter Tschaikowsky. Berlin 1900.

Lakond W.: Die Tagebücher von Tschaikowsky. New York 1945.

Orlova A.: Tschaikowsky A self-portrait. Oxford-New York 1990.

Orlova J.M.: Tschaikowsky. Leipzig 1978.

Pahlen K.: Tschaikowsky. Ein Lebensbild. Stuttgart 1959.

Pals N.v.d.: Peter Tschaikowsky. Potsdam 1940.

Petzold R.: Peter Tschaikowsky. Leipzig 1953.

Pribegina G.A.: Pjotr Iljitsch Tschaikowsky. Berlin 1988.

Rachmanowa A.: Tschaikowsky Schicksal und Schaffen. Wien 1972.

Rimsky-Korsakow N.: Chronik meines musikalischen Lebens. Leipzig 1968.

Stafford-Clark D.: Was Freud wirklich sagte. Wien 1967.

Stein R.: Tschaikowsky. Stuttgart 1927.

Tovey D.: Essays in Musical Analysis. London 1935-39.

Tschaikowsky M.: Leben des Peter lljitsch Tschaikowsky. Dt. Ausg. Leipzig-Moskau 1900-02.

Tschaikowsky P.: Letters to his family. Übersetzt von Galina von Meck. London 1981.

Tschaikowsky P.: Erinnerungen und Musikkritiken. Leipzig 1961.

Vigh J.: Wenn Tschaikowsky ein Tagebuch geführt hätte. Budapest 1957.

Weinstock H.: Tschaikowsky. München 1948.

Wolfurt K. von: Peter I. Tschaikowsky Bildnis des Menschen und Musikers. Zürich 1952.

Zagiba F.: Tschaikowskij. Wien 1953.

GUSTAV MAHLER

Adler G.: Gustav Mahler. Wien 1916.

Adorno Th.W.: Mahler. Frankfurt am Main 1960.

Bahr-Mildenburg A.: Erinnerungen. Wien-Berlin 1921.

Bauer-Lechner N.: Erinnerungen an Gustav Mahler. Leipzig 1923.

Bekker P.: Gustav Mahlers Sinfonien. Berlin 1921.

Berl H.: Das Judentum in der Musik. Berlin 1926.

Bernstein L.: Gustav Mahler - Seine Zeit ist gekommen. Neue Zeitschrift f. Musik 1967, 450.

Blaukopf K.: Gustav Mahler oder der Zeitgenosse der Zukunft. Kassel 1989.

Blessinger K.: Judentum und Musik. Ein Beitrag zur Kultur- und Rassenpolitik. Berlin 1944.

Braungart R.: Gustav Mahler und die Programmusik. In: Musikalische Rundschau, München 1905.

Brod M.: Gustav Mahler. Beispiel einer deutsch-jüdischen Symbiose. Fraükfurt am Main 1961.

Cardus N.: Gustav Mahler: His Mind and his Music. London 1965.

Christy N.P., Christy B., and Wood, B.G.: Gustav Mahler and his Illnesses. Transactions of the Amer. Clin. and Climatolog. Association 1970, 200-217.

De la Grange H.L.: Mahler I. New York 1973.

Engel G.: Gustav Mahler: Song-Symphonist. New York 1970.

Fechner G.Th.: Das Büchlein vom Leben nach dem Tode. Hamburg und Leipzig 1903.

Floros C.: Gustav Mahler. Die geistige Welt Gustav Mahlers in systematischer Darstellung. Wiesbaden 1987.

Giroud F.: Alma Mahler oder die Kunst geliebt zu werden. Wien-Darmstadt 1990.

Hauptmann G.: Gustav Mahler. Ein Bild seiner Persönlichkeit in Widmungen. München 1910.

Jones E.: Das Leben und Werk von Sigmund Freud. Band II. Jahre der Reife 1901-1919. Bern 1962.

Karpath L.: Begegnung mit dem Genius. Wien 1934.

Kerner D.: Krankheiten großer Musiker. Stuttgart-New York 1986.

Klemperer O.: Meine Erinnerungen an Gustav Mahler und andere autobiographische Skizzen. Freiburg i. Br.-Zürich 1960.

Loeser N.: Gustav Mahler. Haarlem-Antwerpen 1950.

Mahler A.M.: Gustav Mahler Briefe. Berlin-Wien-Leipzig 1924.

Mahler-Werfel A.: Mein Leben. Frankfurt am Main 1963.

Mahler-Werfel A.: Erinnerungen und Briefe. Amsterdam 1949.

Mahler-Werfel A.: Gustav Mahler: Erinnerungen an Gustav Mahler/Briefe an Alma Mahler, Wien 1971.

Mengelberg R.: Gustav Mahler. Leipzig 1923.

Metzger H.K. und Riehn R.: Gustav Mahler: Musik-Konzepte, Sonderband. München 1989.

Meysels L.: In meinem Salon ist Österreich. Berta Zuckerkandl und ihre Zeit. Wien 1987.

Monson K.: Alma Mahler-Werfel. Die unbezähmbare Muse. München 1985.

Neißer A.: Gustav Mahler. Leipzig 1918.

O'Shea J.: Music and Medicine. London 1990.

Redlich H.F.: Bruckner und Mahler. London 1963.

Reich W.: Gustav Mahler. Im eigenen Wort - Im Wort der Freunde. Zürich 1958.

Reik Th.: Dreißig Jahre mit Sigmund Freud. München 1976.

Ringel E.: Die österreichische Seele. Wien-Köln-Graz 1986.

Roller A.: Die Bildnisse von Gustav Mahler. Leipzig-Wien-Zürich 1922.

Schiedermair L.: Gustav Mahler. Eine biographisch-kritische Würdigung. Leipzig 1900.

Scholem G.: Die jüdische Musik in ihren Hauptströmungen. Frankfurt am Main 1967.

Schreiber W.: Gustav Mahler. Reinbek/Hamburg 1971.

Schumann K.: Das kleine Gustav Mahler-Buch. Salzburg 1972.

Specht R.: Gustav Mahler. Berlin-Leipzig 1922.

Stefan P.: Gustav Mahler. München 1912.

Stephan R.: Mahler-Interpretation. Mainz 1985.

Wagner R.: Das Judentum in der Musik. In: Die Kunst und die Revolution, Hrsg. T. Kneif, München 1975.

Walter B.: Gustav Mahler. Frankfurt am Main 1957.

Wessling B.W.: Gustav Mahler. Ein prohetisches Leben. Hamburg 1974.

Worbs Ch.: Gustav Mahler. Berlin 1960.

Sources of Illustrations

Dust jacket: Nielson M. Carlin, Kennett Square, Pennsylvania

Chopin: with kind permission of Ernst Burger; Bibliotèque Nationale, Paris; Photo Archives of the Austrian National Library

Smetana: B. Smetana Museum, Prague

Tchaikovsky: Verlag für Musik, Liepzig

Mahler: Photo Archives of the Austrian National Library; Historical Museum of the City of Vienna

Index of Musical Compositions

Explanation of Abbreviations:
—BWV: Bach Werke Verzeichnis (catalog of Bach's works)
—D: Catalog numbers of Schubert's works according to Otto Erich Deutch
—KV: Köchel Verzeichnis (Köchel's catalog of Mozart's works)
—T: Teige (Teige catalogue of Smetana's works)

Index of Names